IMPERIAL CAULDRON

Book 3
BITTER LEGACY

Elizabeth Legge

Imperial Cauldron
Book 3 – Bitter Legacy

Elizabeth Legge

Copyright © 2023

ISBN: 978-1-7391621-6-0

Published by ESME Publishing in conjunction with Writersworld. This book is produced entirely in the UK, is available to order from most book shops in the United Kingdom and is globally available via UK-based Internet book retailers and www.amazon.com.

Copy Edited by Ian Large

Cover Design by Jag Lall (www.jaglallart.com)

Cover Image by Alexander Gresbek from Pixabay

Border Image by Gordon Johnson from Pixabay

Spine Photo Credit: © Bwag

www.writersworld.co.uk

WRITERSWORLD

2 Bear Close Flats, Bear Close, Woodstock,
Oxfordshire, OX20 1JX, United Kingdom

☎ 01993 812500
☎ +44 1993 812500

The text pages of this book are produced via an independent certification process that ensures the trees from which the paper is produced come from well managed sources that exclude the risk of using illegally logged timber while leaving options to use post-consumer recycled paper as well.

Book 1
GATHERING SHADOWS

Book 2
THE FADING OF THE LIGHT

Book 3
BITTER LEGACY

Chapter 79

Marie-Luise was never subjected to any official questioning about her part in the tragedy of Mayerling – she was simply barred from court. The gates of the Hofburg would henceforth be closed to her. She never saw Elisabeth again.

In her books she relates that she received a visit from Dr. Widerhofer, who had once been her own doctor. This was the moment when Dr. Widerhofer is supposed to have told Marie-Luise in such detail exactly how he found Mary. It is impossible to believe that Dr. Widerhofer would have discussed with Marie-Luise what he had seen at Mayerling. He had given his word to the Emperor that he would not speak of anything he knew about what had happened at Mayerling – and he never did.

Dr. Widerhofer had come to find out what Marie-Luise knew and to report back to Elisabeth, so she wrote. Marie-Luise refused to talk, insisting that she would tell all to Elisabeth face to face. In tears she begged him to speak with Elisabeth and ask her to receive her. But Elisabeth refused to see her. A letter to Ida Ferenczy requesting an audience with the Empress also failed. She never got the chance to explain to anyone what – as she saw it – had really happened.

From the moment that Rudolf's death became known Marie-Luise had no further position in Austrian society; she was treated like a leper. Massive assumptions, some true, some not, were made about her and her role in it all and she was never able to refute any of them. She was ostracised wherever she went. The trickle of malicious gossip grew apace and turned into a flood of vilification. She was reviled wherever she went. And those who stood by her were equally cold-shouldered.

Her life as an Austrian Princess died at that moment. She had never really been one. She had always been rather like a child knocking on the door crying, "Don't shut me out!" Helen's door was locked to her, too. And history has tended to shut the door on Marie-Luise at this point and push her out of sight – with great distaste. If Rudolf's affair with Mary dear had ended in a brief scandal and soon forgotten, would Marie-Luise have been judged in the way that she was?

On 4th February Marie-Luise and Georg travelled to Vienna for Rudolf's funeral. Later, Marie-Luise would write:

> "As we entered the entrance hall of the Grand Hotel I was shocked at how people stared at me and whispered surreptitious comments behind their hands as I went by. I did not know then that a thousand cruel lies about me had begun to spread throughout Vienna."

Whether anyone spoke directly to Georg and Marie-Luise indicating that their presence at Rudolf's funeral would not be welcome or whether it simply became clear to them from the treatment they got is not clear, but they decided to make their departure from Vienna before the funeral.

This should not have been quite as much of a shock as Marie-Luise says it was. Thanks to the story that Taaffe had put about that Mary had travelled with Marie-Luise to Pardubitz instead to going to Mayerling, a number of people had called upon Marie-Luise in those early days immediately after Rudolf's death. They pretended to come to offer her their sympathies but in reality it was more to pump her for information.

However, while she was at the Grand Hotel on Sunday, 4th February, Marie-Luise received a visit from Count Georg Stockau, Mary's uncle. He had come to beg her to come clean about all she knew. He told her what Agnes had now revealed and he must have told her how he and Alexander Baltazzi had been required to smuggle Mary's body out of the hunting lodge and get it over to the monastery at Heiligenkreuz. Even if Count Stockau had chosen to present things in as dry a manner as he could Marie-Luise would have picked up the repressed anger in his voice and noticed how tense his jaw was. But Marie-Luise was too upset herself to find much sympathy for Mary's family.

Another visiter Marie-Luise received before she left Vienna was her own father. Baron Krauß noted in his reports that Duke Ludwig (Louis) had been to see his daughter, that Marie-Luise had fainted and that Dr. Widerhofer had to be called. Whatever passed between father and daughter is not known but Marie-Luise was in such a state by then that even something small might have been enough to bring about a fainting fit. The issue may well have been that Louis, too, had been told not to attend Rudolf's funeral and this would have been enough to make him very angry. Rudolf was his nephew!

In actual fact, one of the people whose opinion of Marie-Luise was rather more thoughtful and balanced was her own husband, Georg Larisch. Various people, including Georg, took the view that:

> "Had her Majesty, the Empress, all that time ago in Gödöllő suspected that Marie-Luise's marriage to Georg Larisch would be the first nail in her son's coffin, she would have taken a riding whip to her niece rather than let her walk up the aisle.

> "Their marriage was cursed from the beginning and had to end in scandal and misery – their marriage was the beginning of Mayerling."

Nor did Georg place all the blame for Mayerling upon Marie-Luise:

> "If he [Rudolf] had not used Marie-Luise, there were a thousand others only too willing to have taken her place."

Nevertheless, Georg wanted nothing more to do with Marie-Luise. Within months of Rudolf's death Georg Larisch had separated from his wife. Eventually, seven years later Georg wanted to be completely free of Marie-Luise. They were divorced on 4th December 1896.

But in all the histories written about Mayerling possible alternative go-betweens are never mentioned, so that, in consequence, the impression comes across that Marie-Luise was the only person who might have aided Mary to meet up with Rudolf in the way that she did. But, in fact, it is hard to think of anyone else who could have done what Marie-Luise did. Just as Mary Vetsera was the perfect victim, so Marie-Luise was the perfect go-between. Rudolf could control and manipulate each of them to achieve his own aims.

Towards the end of May 1889 Marie-Luise was back in Vienna on her own. One day while she was out walking she saw someone coming towards her, someone very well known to her and her husband, whom she had always considered a close friend. But on this occasion this person made moves to ignore Marie-Luise and walk round her. Marie-Luise, however, greeted her friend and asked, "What are you doing in Vienna?"

"I was about to ask that same question of you, Madame Countess," was the reply in a tone heavy with disapproval, followed by a hurried 'good-bye'. A moment later Marie-Luise found herself standing alone, smarting at the rebuff, as she watched her friend scurrying away.

Spring rolled into summer. Marie-Luise stayed on in Vienna for several weeks more until she found she could not endure being cold-shouldered any more.

Marie-Luise moved back to Munich, with her two youngest children, five-year-old Marie-Henriette (whom Marie-Luise always called 'Mary') and three-year-old Georg. She went to seek refuge with her parents in Bavaria.

Here in Bavaria opinions about Marie-Luise varied considerably but by and large their judgement was nothing like as harsh as the stories going round Vienna. One person who boldly came right out in Marie-Luise's defence was her aunt, the ex-Queen of Naples, Marie-Sophie. Some time later, when Marie-Luise was in Paris at the same time that Marie-Sophie was living there, Marie-Sophie expressed her very critical view of Rudolf. Marie-Luise fell into her arms and suddenly burst out sobbing against Marie-Sophie's shoulder. Just to find somebody who was not holding her at arm's length and tearing her apart in criticism was a relief for Marie-Luise.

In Bavaria Marie-Luise found her mother slowly dying of cancer and two years later on 12th November 1891 Henriette breathed her last breath. Franz Joseph sent a wreath to her funeral and wrote to Kathi Schratt speaking warmly of Henriette's kindness. In spite of the fact that both the Imperial Family in Vienna and the Wittelsbach family in Bavaria had largely pretended Henriette wasn't there, a large number of people from both families came to Henriette's funeral. Three months after Henriette had been laid to rest Ludovika followed her to the grave. And in the following year the family gathered to mourn Mapperl's death.

Marie-Luise from now on was living in Munich, with her two youngest children. Little had changed in her father's house since Marie-Luise left to marry Georg. Her father still occupied himself with horses and theatre. The house was still full of producers, actors and playwrights. Louis was also interested in productions at the Opera House. And as a result a young baritone singer on the cusp of his finest work – Otto Brucks – was spending a good deal of time there. He had sung the lead role in *Lohengrin* on 13th June 1883 in Dresden, from which moment his star took flight.

The story goes that in the sorrowful days following so many deaths within so short a time – Nené, too, had died in Regensburg and the life of ex-King Francesco II of Naples, Marie-Sophie's husband, also came to an end (he was diabetic) – one evening Otto Brucks came round to the house to comfort the grieving family with some music. He, too, had his own losses to bear. His young wife, Eda, for whom he had recently bought a house on the Tegernsee, died before she could move into her new home.

Louis, Marie-Luise's father, was bitterly against her ever thinking of marrying again. She should henceforth play a self-effacing, unobtrusive role in life and at all times remain in the shadows. Her family could only be a support to her if she did nothing that might bring shame upon them.

This was important to Louis because he himself wished to marry again. Within a year of Henriette's death he remarried. His new wife was a ballet dancer, Antonie Barth, twenty-one years old. Having remarried, it suited Louis if Marie-Luise stopped living under the same roof. So Marie-Luise moved out.

High society in Munich found this a wonderfully romantic story, particularly since the rumours going around spoke of there being a number of hopeful countesses or baronesses, not quite in the first flush of youth, now having to come to terms with their disappointed feelings. Henriette's death had sparked many a hope, now dashed. The newspapers played on the image of the sweet rose-like bride, flushed with shy blushes, on the arm of her fascinating husband whose satanic looks could only subjugate every maiden's heart.

Behind the scenes there had been family rows and outrage and most of them were not present at the wedding. Nor was Marie-Luise. But it was not long afterwards that she went to visit her father and met her new stepmother. She decided that Antonie was charming and nice and feared for her, suspecting that Antonie would meet a lot of opposition and ill-feeling. Marie-Luise decided the solution was to take Antonie to the opera and face down all their critics together.

That may have helped but it was never going to be enough. One major problem was Antonie's own mother. Louis, when he first met her, took offence and lost his temper in the most dramatic way. The marriage also was not a success. Antonie could never have stepped into Henriette's shoes. However, Marie-Luise was very much on Antonie's side and that led to rows with her father. Louis became more and more jealous and embittered.

All along Louis had made it only too clear that he disliked the gossip about Marie-Luise that never stopped. There was talk about a certain Karl Ernst von Otto-Kreckwitz. And in 1894 Marie-Luise gave birth to a son, Karl. Georg Larisch could not have been his father and for most people the name, Karl, was giveaway enough to establish who his father was. Furthermore, Marie-Luise's financial problems had not gone away and in the early years of the new century she decided to earn her way out of her difficulties by writing a book about her life as a member of the Imperial Family. Her co-author was Karl Ernst von Otto-Kreckwitz.

There was talk, too, about a certain opera singer, again with good reason. Marie-Luise was taking singing lessons with Otto Brucks which gave them the opportunity to get to know each other. Louis was enraged. It was not appropriate for Marie-Luise who lacked "suitable male protection" to be enjoying the company of a music teacher!

Marie-Luise married Otto Brucks on 15th May 1897, losing her titles in the process, and she became plain Frau Brucks. All her life Marie-Luise had suffered from the scorn of the Austrian aristocracy, she who was the niece of the Empress herself! She had felt batted about by other people's criticism and judgement. There had never been any real support and always, always money had been a problem. She no longer felt that she owed the Imperial Family anything. So if her knowledge of life within the Imperial Family could earn her an income she would use it. The Imperial Family may have thought they were free of Marie-Luise now that she was a mere Frau Brucks but they were wrong.

Franz Joseph was appalled and set about buying up all the rights to her work and preventing it ever becoming public. Both Marie-Luise and Karl Ernst von Otto-Kreckwitz were to be silenced with substantial annual payments. Marie-Luise was now able to offer to have a fine house built for Otto Brucks. Castle Wotansquell it was called and it had an elegant park with lakes and fountains, a place to retreat to and live down the cruel and snide comments that had always haunted Marie-Luise's life. And on 10th

March 1899 the happy couple were blessed with a son, Friedrich Josef Otto.

But these huge outlays of money brought the Emperor no more than a reprieve. Marie-Luise had learned that she had the power to 'kiss and tell'. Franz Joseph had bought up all the rights to any book based upon her memories, but what about a book based upon the love affairs of the Empress Elisabeth?

But even if their financial situation was improved, the continuing gossip soon began to affect Otto Brucks' career and earning capacity. Invitations to appear in leading roles at the Opera House in Vienna dried up. There were those who said that Otto was drinking increasingly heavily and it was this that was affecting his voice and singing opportunities.

But Otto himself always believed that he became sacrificed to the ill-feeling there was towards his wife. Otto Brucks' fame no longer lay in his brilliant career as an opera singer but in his relationships with a rejected member of the Imperial Family. Their relationship began to turn sour.

Otto's prospects picked up when he was offered the position of Director of the State Theatre in Metz, and on 23rd September 1906 all-Metz turned out to enjoy his production of *Lohengrin*. To begin with he enjoyed huge success. But ill-health made this difficult to maintain. Otto Brucks was suffering from cirrhosis of the liver, high blood pressure and heart disease. His marriage, already very shaky, was to suffer a new blow when Marie-Luise's younger daughter, Mary-Henriette, died of smallpox in Metz on 25th March 1907. Again the gossips had a field-day picking Marie-Luise's life and relationships apart – and all with malicious intent.

Otto Brucks' health had not been strong when he moved to Metz and went steadily downhill until he died just before the outbreak of war.

By the outbreak of the First World War, Louis had divorced his second wife. He lived through the First World War and died at the age of 89 in November 1920. He died as he had lived, prickly and demanding right up until the end. It was his wish to be buried as unobtrusively as possible and that nobody from his family should be present when his coffin was put into the ground. In fact, that was ignored. Around his grave stood a small bunch including Gisela, Sophie (the oldest surviving daughter of his younger brother, Gackel) and his eldest grandson, Franz-Joseph Larisch. But his own daughter was not there.

Marie-Luise's eldest daughter, Marie Valerie, died on 31st October 1915. She had been a nurse in a mission hospital in Africa where she had contracted an uncurable infection. She returned to Lausanne where her mother found her and nursed her through her last months. Marie-Luise watched her daughter slip away from her and then decided to focus upon the needs of the sick and war-wounded. She signed up with the Red Cross and threw herself into her new work.

But when the end of the war came she found herself alone with nothing, no home, no work and no income. Castle Wotansquell had been claimed by her creditors and sold in 1916 to pay off her debts. Marie-Luise ended up working as a domestic servant in Berlin.

Marie-Luise also turned to her writing as the only way to put bread on her table. And then she got a letter out of the blue from a certain William Henry Meyers. The letter had come from America.

Meyers claimed to be a wealthy farmer in Florida who had put his wealth into establishing a luxurious sanatorium for the rich. He was of Belgian origin and he had read Marie-Luise's book, *My Past*. It would be fascinating to know what picture of Marie-Luise he had formed in his mind, but she had impressed him enough for him to have decided to send her a cheque and a ticket for luxury cabin on the *Bremen* which was sailing from Hamburg to New York. Meyers' wish was to place Marie-Luise in charge of the sisters who cared for the patients in his sanatorium.

In 1924 Marie-Luise was sixty-six years old when she sailed to the New World to build a new life for herself with a man she had never met and knew nothing about. Within a few weeks of arriving in Florida Marie-Luise and William Henry Meyers were married.

Why? Nothing was what she had been led to expect. The farm was a deserted piece of land barely capable of sustaining life let alone producing the wealth of produce that might have underpinned a luxurious sanatorium for the rich. The building that was supposed to house the sanatorium was a run-down shack. And Meyers was no wealthy capitalist devoting himself to the needs of the sick. Her shock and bewilderment and disappointment could not have been greater.

Meyers was equally disappointed. Marie-Luise was at least twenty years older than he had envisaged and she had grown stout. The person who stood before him had no appeal at all. He had looked for a slender, elegant, aristocratic woman and he was angry with Marie-Luise for not being that woman. He could not contain his anger. He soon fell into a pattern of playing petty, cruel tricks upon her. Her meals consisted of milk along with corn-on-the cob. Meyers hid her clothes to prevent her escaping from him. He often imprisoned her in her room and turned the key upon her, leaving her to listen, frightened, to the sound of rats running around in the floorboards and the rafters.

Did she ever during those days think back to Georg Larisch and his petty cruelties? Her father had intimidated her mother, her first husband had frightened her, her second husband had withdrawn in resentment blaming her in part for the way the Viennese turned against him, and now she had a third husband whose cruelty equalled all that had gone before and more. Had anyone ever genuinely liked her for herself and treated her with sincere warmth?

Marie-Luise became sick. She had got malaria and slowly became weaker and weaker and more and more feverish. It is not clear how events panned out but it seems likely that Meyers finally wanted rid of her. Local officials began to take an interest in what was happening and this gave Marie-Luise the chance to plead for help.

She got some help which enabled her to get to New York where she found shelter in a home for the destitute. She set about earning her keep by cleaning and cooking and washing.

"I am completely beaten down by starvation and fevers," she wrote. "I have escaped to this poor house. There is no door to the space where I lie down at night and all the warmth I have comes from an old threadbare blanket. There are cracks in the floor which I stuff with paper to keep the rats out. I have nothing, only a stump of a candle and a large knife for self-protection."

But once again the fact that she had once been a member of the imperial Habsburg family and the favourite of the Empress Elisabeth was to bring her to the attention of people who could do something for her. The wife of one particular multi-millionaire started inviting Marie-Luise to her salon on Park Avenue. Here she met Paul Maerker Branden. He was an American of German origins and the publisher of a journal, *American Monthly*. Thanks to him Marie-Luise found a way to earn a rather easier life through her writing.

Her book *Her Majesty Elizabeth of Austria-Hungary, the Beautiful Tragic Empress of Europe's Most Brilliant Court*, written in collaboration with Paul Maerker and Elsa Branden, was published in 1934 in New York and further editions appeared later in Paris and London. This was followed by *Kaiserin Elisabeth und ich* and then *Die Heldin von Gaeta*.[1] Marie-Luise's earnings from her writing were never great. These books attracted an interested readership but it was her publishers who took the lion's share of her earnings.

She died on 4th July 1940. She had succeeded in returning to Europe and the last months of her life were spent in a home for the poor, St. Servatiusstift, in Augsburg. She died alone and destitute. Of all her six children only her son, Otto Brucks, outlived her.

---

[1] It was in this work that she claimed to have been the daughter of her aunt, Marie, Queen of Naples and the Two Sicilies and her father was a 'Count Armand de Lavaÿss', mention of whom cannot be found anywhere else.

Chapter 80

The R.I.O.U. box that Rudolf handed over to Marie-Luise on the morning of 27th January 1889 remains a puzzle. By and large, many historians are convinced it never existed, one more example of Marie-Luise's imagination working overtime. To them it was a story which turns up in Marie-Luise's *My Past* many years after the shockwaves of Mayerling had subsided.

If that were the case, what did Marie-Luise stand to gain from the story? It does not show her in a particularly good light; it focusses attention upon her activities on behalf of her imperial relatives as a spy, a go-between or as an agent useful in covering up whatever was going on. If she still had the box when she came to write her book she would have attracted attention and interest. That she craved but not this sort of attention. But by then she no longer had the box. According to her, just as Rudolf had intended, she duly received the message within a few days of Rudolf's death. This was 4th Frebruary, the day before Rudolf's funeral.

Monday, 4th February must have been a very busy day for Marie-Luise. Early on the morning of 4th February Marie-Luise's maid, Jenny, received a letter that was clearly intended for Marie-Luise. "Someone known to her" was to walk up and down between the Schwarzenbergplatz and the Heugasse at half past ten that evening and when Marie-Luise approached this person she would know it was the right person because they would pronounce those mysterious four letters. The secret code reassured Marie-Luise and she went to her rendez-vous.

Later, much later, Marie-Luise would write in her book *Kaiserin Elisabeth und Ich* that she never knew what the letters stood for or meant, that she honoured Rudolf's wishes and never opened the box or found out what it contained, and that by the time she got the message on 4th February all she wanted was to be rid of it, innocent of any complicity in anything that Rudolf might have been brewing up.

It is hard to imagine that this was so. She was clearly in a real mess in those days after Mayerling. She was already upset, worried, frightened and deeply hurt. She had begun to get a taste of what her future life was likely to be. And the picture that was emerging was one to frighten her all the more.

Georg had turned against her. It must have hit Georg that all his hopes that he and his family would be drawn into the close inner circle of the Imperial Family were now blown away on the wind. They had put their money on Marie-Luise and now it must have become clear that they had backed the wrong horse.

Georg was full of reproaches against her. With Georg being the man he was, there may have been more than reproaches. If he had hit her before he would have hit her now. Even if he did not Georg was capable of frightening Marie-Luise.

It was a very heavy box, so heavy it might have been solid metal. Marie-Luise would later drop hints that the box contained dangerous plans for the overthrow of the existing political system and the crowning of Rudolf as King of Hungary. And Gianni, Rudolf's cousin was to rule over the Austrian half of the Empire. Given their very chequered relationship, a relationship which was growing ever more sour each year that passed, nothing seems more improbable than the idea of these two plotting to divide the Empire, with the one ruling in Hungary and the other in Austria. Yet, it is often hinted that the papers contained in the R.I.O.U. box would, if they had ever been found, have exposed just such a plot. If these two had ever got involved in such a plot, when did they do the plotting? Gianni was already falling out of favour with the Imperial Family and there is no indication that suggests he ever brewed up ideas of ruling in Vienna.

In some accounts it is claimed that the documents were all in code and it seems most unlikely that Marie-Luise knew the key to the code. Rudolf would have trusted her with some things but not that far.

But did she ever peak inside it? Just lift the lid? If she had lifted the lid, would it have been obvious what the papers were about or how incriminating they would have been if they fell into the wrong hands, especially if they were in code? On the other hand if some of the documents had either not been coded or had official stamps on them, then the fact that other documents were coded would have given rise to the suspicion that it was all about something both dangerous and political.

According to Marie-Luise's account, right up until her dark rendez-vous in the Schwarzenbergplatz, Marie-Luise had no idea who she would end up giving the box to. Would she be handing it over into the right hands? Whose, in her opinion, were the right hands? And if she blindly handed it over to the person who whispered those fateful letters R.I.O.U. could she know that it was the person Rudolf had intended it for? There are no answers to any of these questions. But surely, some such thoughts and doubts and uncertainties must have gone through Marie-Luise's mind.

She may well have felt quite jittery as she set off, heavily-veiled and struggling to conceal the box beneath her cloak. Her shivers would not all have been because of the cold. It is not known how long she had to hang around in the dark, getting increasingly nervous. The box was heavy and difficult to carry unobtrusively. She may have wondered whether anyone was watching her.

Finally, according to Marie-Luise's account, a figure emerged from the dark and came up to her. She recognised the Archduke Johann Salvator

(Gianni) which would have been reassuring – at least he was not a stranger to her and it would not have seemed unreasonable to Marie-Luise's mind that Rudolf might want to get something surreptitiously to Gianni without anyone knowing.

Marie-Luise would have handed over the box hurriedly, glad to be relieved of its weight and even more glad to be relieved of the responsibility. She might even have been glad that she was giving it to Gianni – far more than most of her other relatives, he was robust and straightforward. He would know how to deal with it. But then again, if Marie-Luise had known much about Gianni's difficulties with the Emperor and with Archduke Albrecht, and something of the ups and downs in Gianni's relationship with Rudolf, she might have wondered whether Gianni was the worst sort of person to give something so incriminating to. But even if thoughts along those lines had gone through her mind, she would have been so glad to get rid of the box that she would not have let anything prevent her handing it over.

They surely would not have hung around for long in the dark street. Marie-Luise would have wanted to be shot of the box as quickly as possible. As Marie-Luise turned to go back to her hotel, it may have crossed her mind that never again would she be involved as a slightly nefarious go-between on behalf of her half-crazy Wittelsbach relatives. And that, too, would have been a relief – but also a loss.

But there is so much that just does not stand up to closer scrutiny; there is no evidence at any time during those first few weeks after Rudolf's death that Gianni left Italy to travel to Vienna. There is no evidence that Gianni had been in on any plot with Rudolf in the months before. Could Rudolf have imagined that if things went very badly wrong then Gianni was going to take over his role? Nothing about Gianni suggests that he wanted to do such a thing or that he might have had any support whatsoever for such a scheme.

Yet surely only politically dangerous papers would have justified all the manoeuvres Rudolf must have gone to in order to ensure that the box did not fall into the wrong hands? When did Rudolf and Gianni agree upon those significant letters? Presumably when they did agree to those letters they were looking ahead to a possible moment when it might be imperative for Rudolf to get rid of the box but would not be able to hand it over himself. It also seems likely that when plans were made to ensure the safe disposal of the box, Rudolf told Gianni that it would be Marie-Luise who would hand it over to him.

Just collecting the box might have been a dangerous thing to do. Most members of the Imperial Family were spied upon to a greater or lesser extent. Yet – according to Marie-Luise – Gianni turned up in the Schwarzenbergplatz to collect the R.I.O.U. box from Marie-Luise. Then, as Gianni was taking his leave of Marie-Luise, he is supposed to have told her, "Rudolf has betrayed me – Rudolf was a weakling..."

He went on, "Don't feel sorry for Rudolf – if the Emperor had found these papers, things would have been far worse for him. The Crown Prince is now dead by his own hand; but if the Emperor had known everything he would have had to arraign his own son before a military tribunal and there he would have been found guilty of high treason and been shot!"

"My God!" cried Marie-Luise, "What has he done... Was he thinking of the crown of Hungary?" And the Archduke nodded in agreement.

He is then supposed to have added, *„Ich werde sterben, ohne tot zu sein, denn ich bin der Nichtigkeiten des Lebens müde und gedenke, eine neue Laufbahn zu beginnen..."* ("I shall die without being dead. I am tired of the pointlessness of life and am seeking out a new path...")

All this sounds far more like Marie-Luise than Gianni. It would not have been in his character to speak of things that it would be better she didn't know anything about. And it is hard to imagine them hanging around on a dark street corner exchanging fatalistic remarks about the pointlessness of life.

But Marie-Luise was not the only person to make mention of the R.I.O.U. box. Ten years later Marie Zwirner (Milli Stubel's sister) put down on paper her memories of Gianni and these were published in a Viennese newspaper. Here Marie claimed that Gianni had been handed a steel box by the Countess Larisch, a steel box which contained a number of letters in cipher, and Gianni had given the box to Marie's sister, Milli, with strict instructions to keep it safe. Gianni was in a terrible state when he handed the box over to Milli.

Marie remembered the occasion: "He came in, white as a sheet, and sank into the yellow sofa. He was breathing heavily as though he was suppressing desperate sobs. It is terrible when men cry. I asked him, 'Gianni, what is it?'"

Marie Zwirner worded her piece with extreme care. She referred to it as the often-mentioned steel box. She described it as medium-sized, long and narrow in shape and nondescript and went on to say that she did not know whether the generally accepted assumption that the box contained treasonable papers was true or not. What she did know was that the steel box did appear to have existed and that it had been in Gianni's possession. If so, why did he keep it? What benefit might he have imagined it provided him with that justified hanging on to it? Surely possession of that box presented dangerous ramifications that could have backfired upon him?

Marie also said that her sister, Milli, had known what the box contained and the significance of what it contained. Apparently, Milli, more than once, had sobbed in terror, "That box! That box!"

What is odd here is that Marie said the box 'appeared' to have existed. Maybe Marie had not actually seen it and her only source of information must have been Milli.[2] And it is likely that Marie might have given free rein to dramatic exaggeration. The Stubel women were every bit as likely to have let imagination run wild as Marie-Luise.

Milli Stubel was Gianni's mistress.

---

[2]   It is not impossible but unlikely that Marie-Luise and Milli Stubel ever met. But both refer to the same box and the same letters. This leaves the question: could one or other of them have picked up the story from the other?

Chapter 81

Rudolf and Gianni were not always at loggerheads with each other. There were occasions when they clearly enjoyed the other's company. Once, early in Rudolf's marriage when he and Stéphanie were living in Prague, Rudolf and Gianni enjoyed a prank which involved filling a chamber pot with scent and hanging it out of the window of the Hradschin Palace. They then set fire to the liquid which resulted in a very loud bang. The elderly and rather nervous German Empress Augusta was staying at Hradschin Palace and the explosion just outside her window sent her into a nervous fit. No doubt, Rudolf and Gianni could barely stifle their giggles.

They also collaborated in debunking the spiritualist medium Bastian who was enjoying huge popularity with European aristocracy. Spiritualism was very much in vogue at the time. Elisabeth had gone overboard over it and refused to consider that there might be any reason for even mild scepticism. Rudolf inevitably loathed spiritualism and spoke of "dark apostles of a still darker teaching".

Rudolf persuaded Gianni to hold a few séances in a room with a heavy curtain hanging in front of a pair of folding doors that were left open. Gianni had attached a device to these doors so that when a string was pulled they slammed shut. Gianni did nothing until the third séance. On this occasion there was the haunting sound of something twanging in the remote distance and in the darkness an ethereal white form could be perceived. Gianni pulled the string. Rudolf grabbed the white form which was desperately trying to push open the doors, and there was Bastian in his socks draped in white muslin, caught in huge embarrassment before the assembled company.

However, Rudolf regarded so many of Gianni's activities as highly dubious. He did not find Gianni very easy to get on with, either. Yet it has frequently been stated that the two men were close friends and often acted together.

How little this was so can be seen from the matter of Rudolf's great literary work *Die Österreichisch-Ungarische Monarchie in Wort und Bild* ('Austria-Hungary in words and pictures'). The idea sprang from Gianni. He envisaged a large ten-volume book, comprehensively covering all the nationalities within the Empire. As always with Gianni, he poured his enthusiasm into it, so that when he went to Rudolf with the suggestion that they collaborate on it his words would have spilled out eagerly and he couldn't sit still, so caught up was he in it. He fired Rudolf's interest.

In March 1884 Rudolf went to his father to obtain his support for the project. He had made a few changes to Gianni's ideas and then forgot to tell Franz Joseph that the idea originally came from Gianni. Franz Joseph approved and Rudolf went ahead finding collaborators to contribute to the work and proceeded to invite Gianni (in his letter to his mother Gianni used the word 'command') to a meeting.

Gianni's nose was badly put out of joint by the way things were turning out. He withdrew from the whole project. Rudolf wrote to him, "I fully understand that you would wish to lead the project but that your duties in Linz stand in the way." And he went on to speak of Gianni's knowledge and talents and how much Rudolf wanted Gianni's participation. Some weeks later Rudolf wrote again. He told Gianni that the work was missing out upon an important contributor and then Rudolf's prissy side came out: "I only mean the best. You don't like hearing the truth and that has upset me... I just want us to work well together." To Rudolf's mind Gianni was being unreasonable. Gianni stuck to his guns.

Rudolf set to work on the compilation and publication of the work. It was an impressive achievement. He could be proud of it. The first volume appeared in December 1885 and Franz Joseph was impressed. Franz Joseph's pride in his son was very evident: "Did my son really write that article himself?" He glowed.

But this incident had left a bitter taste in the mouths of both Rudolf and Gianni. On various occasions Rudolf was heard complaining of Gianni's underhand behaviour.

Gianni in the meantime had turned his attention to other things. He had new fish to fry; he was now caught up in helping Prince Ferdinand in his negotiations with the Bulgarian delegates[3] over the throne of Bulgaria that Sandro had vacated. Ferdinand at the time was serving in the Austrian Army in Linz and Gianni was his commanding officer. It was Gianni who approached the Bulgarians on behalf of Ferdinand but the Bulgarians then immediately offered the throne to the Archduke who firmly turned it down (Gianni was not eligible because of the Treaty of Berlin).

All this rubbed Rudolf up the wrong way and he wrote to Gianni, "I find your Bulgarian affair odious. I would rather see you as an Admiral and head of the Austrian-Hungarian Navy than as a 'Balkanese'."

It is likely that what Rudolf disliked so much had more to do with the person that Prince Ferdinand was than with the political situation in Bulgaria. There was something slippery about Prince Ferdinand. He acquired the name 'Foxy Ferdinand' and nothing could have been more appropriate. Foxy Ferdinand was always conspicuous and stood out from the crowd in ways that were often uncomfortable.

Even from the age of about fourteen Foxy Ferdinand was already strikingly tall. His pale face was dominated by a very large Bourbon nose and he had a nervous tic and a furtive air. The personality that was to ruffle so many feathers in later years (especially Franz Joseph's feathers) was clearly emerging.

---

3   Note 1 in the Notes Section.

What came across so strongly was his air of condescension and sarcasm – this was not a man who suffered fools gladly or even at all. There was something about Foxy Ferdinand that made many men feel slightly uncomfortable. Nor did the fact that he had an almost hysterical fear of horses. He was an appalling rider even though he was an officer in the cavalry. (When the motor car became a feasible reality Foxy Ferdinand would have a gleaming fleet of them and no doubt he waved good-bye to the horse with a large sigh of relief.)

He was not popular with women either. Queen Victoria's lips would curl at the mention of him and she found him far too effeminate. He liked wearing jewellery and rich furs and he was once described as '*une vieille cocotte*'. Walpurga Paget wrote of him, "His affectations are innumerable. He wears bracelets and powders his face. He sleeps in pink surah nightgowns, trimmed with Valenciennes lace. His constitution is so delicate and his nerves so finely strung that he only consults ladies' doctors."

Years later Louise would insist that he dabbled in black magic and that she assisted in some of his séances.

But with Foxy Ferdinand the condescension and sarcasm were defensive. He was well aware of the effect he had upon others. He was particularly self-conscious of his large nose and his large ears. Before others could start sniggering at his appearance he himself would draw attention to the fact that he resembled an elephant – a very thin one. He was also intelligent enough to sense that he disliked in other people the very faults he possessed himself. He was precisely the kind of man who would have made Rudolf feel uncomfortable.

Inevitably Rudolf never got on with Foxy Ferdinand and Gianni's interest in what was happening in Bulgaria irritated him.

Yet, in spite of that, as the months went by these high feelings began to simmer down and once again the two young men tried to find some sort of conciliation with the other, with Gianni offering Rudolf an olive branch. It seems that Gianni's attitude had done a complete U-turn and he now had only good words for Rudolf – no one was more admirable, conciliatory or more generous than Rudolf.

Gianni was the youngest son of the expelled Tuscan branch of the Habsburg family and within the Imperial Family a very junior and insignificant figure, albeit a very irritating and maddening one. It had been a big problem for Franz Joseph and Archduke Albrecht to accommodate and integrate the whole Tuscan branch of the family when they all arrived in Austria in 1859. A number of the younger members one way or another would go off the rails. Gianni wasn't unique in that.

But Gianni was the *enfant terrible* of the family. He seems to have been seen very much as a loose cannon, causing mayhem in his refusal to accept that his duties to the Imperial Family included buttoning his lips and not speaking out of turn. So many of the clashes Gianni had with Archduke Albrecht can largely be summarised thus: he could see what was going wrong, he could not refrain from speaking out and often he published his criticisms, supposedly anonymously, but few were deceived and this was the kind of provocation that Albrecht could not ignore. Albrecht felt responsible because, after the death of Leopold, Gianni's father, in 1870, he had been made guardian of the boy who was not yet of age.

Albrecht's character comes through in the letter he sent Gianni two years later when he did come of age. The letter starts off full of praise for young Gianni, his sharp intelligence, his drive and determination to achieve what was demanded of him. "Those above you," wrote Albrecht, "are very satisfied... But in your character there is an apparent resistance to authority." Gianni had sometimes made uncalled-for comments, not just light remarks but out of strong conviction – and Albrecht wanted to warn him.

Albrecht had a number of warnings: to take religious observance more seriously; not to meddle in politics; to show politeness and courtesy particularly to the ladies; and above all to rein in his more rebellious side and submit himself to his duties and obligations. He signed off the letter "your loving uncle and friend, Albrecht". He certainly meant well but he was blowing in the wind.

All too often Gianni was a good deal brighter and far more on the ball than his various military tutors. Gianni once wrote to his mother that he had been made to study the Franco-Prussian war, not an easy matter – to Gianni's mind – given that the tutor suffered from holes in the brain.

But hidden behind all Gianni's obstinacy was a very real wish to do well, to fit in and to win the approval of his seniors. He was, in fact, dutiful. But he was the one who was churned up inside over this issue or that far more than they. He could not see how they could be so stupid. Gianni, without ever intending it, was sliding down a path that would lead to his being the person on whom people would want to pin blame, and not just with old fogeys like Albrecht, but far more so with people like Rudolf.

Gianni would so often end up getting a serious dressing down and then he would be transferred to some army outpost, some drab, spiritless place offering nothing but relentless army exercises from five in the morning until eight at night with nothing to interest him in what little free time he had. Lemberg was an ugly place, a place of burning heat in summer and raked by cold, biting wind and rain in winter. When Gianni did not pull his socks up to the satisfaction of Count Neipperg, he was transferred to somewhere even less attractive. Gianni now found himself far from Vienna in Galizia. Gianni was even more unhappy in Temesvár, but for very different reasons. And the reason for Gianni's unhappiness was not something that those in authority over him would ever have grasped.

Gianni had a strong sense of justice. The way the place was run must have enraged him. The officers barely did their jobs while the men endured seriously substandard conditions even for those times. The regiment's commander was doing what he could to improve conditions for the men, both on the ground and fighting the authorities back in Vienna. He was, however, fighting a losing battle. Gianni threw himself into the fight with all his energy and drive.

But somehow Gianni overstepped the mark. Suddenly the regimental commander was against him. Gianni found himself on the way back to Vienna to face Archduke Albrecht, enraged by all that was wrong in Temesvár. Interestingly, Albrecht was willing to listen to the young man. He gave him a fair hearing but in the end Gianni had to return to Temesvár.

That September he performed well in manoeuvres and before the end of the year this led to his promotion. By the autumn of 1883 he had been promoted to Lieutenant-General. This promotion brought him back to Vienna, a mixed blessing because, while Vienna was a great deal more agreeable than some of the outposts he had been pushed off to, it also meant he was obliged to attend a number of court functions which Gianni hated. One of the things Gianni hated was dancing. He really did not enjoy inviting some prim-faced young woman on to the dance floor in order to push her around in a mechanical, desultory manner. Being in Vienna meant that something of a spotlight was now turned on him. All too obvious to everyone and anyone were Gianni's critical attitudes.

He considered that many of the aristocratic officers in the army did not take their profession seriously so he would seek out those of humbler origins whose competence he appreciated. He himself was outstanding which made it difficult for his detractors to undermine him.

Gianni caused shockwaves and his actions surprised everybody, but they should not have done so. If those around him had thought back to Baron Piers they might have seen what was coming. Baron Piers was one of Gianni's various tutors during the time he was being educated in the Hofburg. Baron Piers taught him arithmetic and German and these were Gianni's weakest subjects. Most little boys dislike the subjects they are not good at and Gianni was no exception. However, Alexander von Piers was a good teacher and he was supportive of the young boy. He was broadminded and he had a wide spread of interests which would have drawn Gianni to him. It was commented upon how well he could explain his ideas and pass on his knowledge in a way that others could quickly grasp. Gianni had been taken from his parents' home and planted in the Hofburg at the age of twelve and Piers must quickly have become his guide and his mentor.

In 1868 Piers received an anonymous letter. The writer warned him that there were intrigues against Piers afoot because news had got back to Gianni's father and mother that Gianni was not being brought up with a strong Christian belief. They wanted Piers removed from his position.

Gianni spilled his protests out in a long letter to his mother. He ended up threatening to refuse to work at his studies if Piers went. Finally he begged his mother not to believe all the gossip she might hear about his religious beliefs. "Sometimes jokingly you let slip a remark," he wrote. It had to be these that his critics were picking up – "but you know me. And at my age one might say more than one knows."

Gianni won the day and Piers kept his position. He also kept the affection of his charge long after he had retired and they exchanged some lively letters over the years, right up until Piers died in 1889. It is even possible that the death of Piers was just one more factor behind Gianni's seemingly erratic and unreasonable actions that year, actions which would lead to Gianni's own death in July 1890.

Then there was the case of Major Menrad Laaba von Rosenfeld.

The roots of the Laaba affair were to be found back in 1875. Gianni had – back then – written a number of articles including one which drew attention to various injustices within the system. Laaba wrote a stinging criticism of the Archduke's article. Gianni's article might have been considered as insubordinate; Laaba's surely had to be viewed as reflecting his loyalty to his Emperor, his country and the army.

But it was Laaba who was court-martialled.[4] He was found guilty of a gross breach of discipline. He lost his rank, was cashiered out of the army without a pension in spite of the fact that, after thirty years' service, Laaba was entitled to a pension. In the eyes of all, Laaba was guilty of attacking a member of the Imperial Family. Against that his support for the official line of the army did not count.

No one was more angered by this than Gianni. He wrote, "This man who, after all, only tried to defend the army against my youthful attack, has suffered a fate far too harsh, not to mention an unjust one."

Pictures of Gianni show a rather stolid-looking, thick-set young man with plenty of facial hair bristling all over the place. He comes across as more of a bruiser than as a romantic. But deep in his heart he was a romantic. His

---

4   A description of the events leading up to Laaba's court-martial is to be found in *Clash of the Generations* by Lavender Cassels, published in 1973. In *Ein Aussteiger aus dem Kaiserhaus: Johann Orth* by Friedrich Weissensteiner, 1985, there is no mention of Laaba's court-martial or of Gianni's role in it.

feelings towards women were romantic, unlike Rudolf's. His desire for justice and integrity was romantic and often it was this that led so many to despise him. That it should be Gianni who stood up for Laaba of all people would have seemed at the time to be incomprehensible. But Gianni did not just speak out for Laaba, he maintained a constant battle to get his critic re-instated in the army.

He remained in touch with Laaba. He was active in trying to find him alternative work and from time to time took him into his own employment. In 1877 Gianni succeeded in persuading Franz Joseph to show Laaba "an act of clemency" – the pension Laaba was entitled to was restored to him.

In 1880 a Court of Enquiry was set up to review Laaba's case and recommended that his rank should be restored to him. This recommendation was sent to Franz Joseph for confirmation together with a comment that the original sentence had been necessary at the time in order to make an example. Franz Joseph passed this along to Archduke Albrecht whose view was that, whatever the rights or wrongs of the matter, changing the sentence set a dangerous precedent.

The Court of Enquiry added a note that the Emperor himself should not be associated with the move to reinstate Laaba and here Franz Joseph had written in the margin "absolutely right". This would have indicated to Albrecht that it was up to him to take the final decision, and Albrecht's greatest concern was always that nothing should tarnish the reputation of the Imperial Family.

Albrecht's refusal to reinstate Laaba enraged Gianni and, being enraged, Gianni felt provoked into taking risks.

Little is known about Laaba. He was a minor aristocrat who depended upon his army career. If he had been of high standing and wealthy Gianni would not have fought so relentlessly on his behalf.

When Laaba defended army traditions, was he kowtowing to those above him in the belief that the move would win him favours? Had anyone surreptitiously put him up to it,[5] hinting obliquely that any unpleasant consequences would be fended off behind the scenes? Was there an element of antagonism towards Gianni himself? Did Laaba feel that he had been totally wrong-footed when he found himself standing before a court martial? Any one of these possibilities could have been the case. Laaba may have been stunned by the way things had turned out.

Gianni respected Laaba as an army officer. When he was able to take

---

5   Note 2 in the Notes Section.

Laaba into his own employment it was as a confidential secretary which again suggests that he trusted Laaba.

Laaba may have started out motivated by some feelings of antagonism towards that privileged young Archduke but surely over time his thoughts and feelings must have changed. His thoughts and feelings about the army must have been turned upside down, too.

Gianni raised the stakes. On 3rd November 1883 he appeared at the Association for Military Studies at the Officers' Club and gave a lecture which he called 'Drill or Education'. Underpinning Gianni's ideas was the defeat of the Battle of Königgrätz. The Prussians had been successful because, as von Moltke put it, "Superiority can no longer be found in the weapon but in the hand carrying it."

Gianni argued that men needed to understand their orders, not just be drilled into automatons. "No lunatic is cured by being put into a strait jacket, nor can the mind be disciplined through the body." Gianni ended up asking how it was the leaders could go on repeating something that experience in war had shown led to failure. Was it conviction or opportunism? and he hinted that the desire to dominate played a part.

A few days later he gave a press conference insisting that he did not wish to place the blame on anyone but rather the system. Then a delighted Gianni wrote to his mother and told her with glee that the Emperor had given permission for the lecture to be printed. Franz Joseph then suspended that permission because he had heard from Albrecht. However, the papers had already seen the lecture and Franz Joseph then felt that these false versions should be corrected and it would be better to publish the true lecture. He would only forbid publication if Albrecht could not agree. Gianni told his mother that Franz Joseph had said that the lecture was very well written and most patriotic and loyal.

Albrecht was now unable to prevent publication but he was very, very angry. The publication attracted a lot of interest and there was much praise for the ideas in it in both Berlin and Paris. But Albrecht's nose had been put so far out of joint that he required that action should be taken against Gianni. This had to be tempered so as not to cause a bad impression abroad. Once again Gianni was posted to the provinces – this time to Linz.

Gianni came to love Linz. Linz came to love Gianni and that, too, would cause trouble.

Chapter 82

Frau Stubel, together with her daughters, could throw a temperamental fit that would send anyone in the vicinity fleeing for the hills in terror. Her histrionics were legendary. Her husband, Andreas, a tall, large man, had learned over the years to let the waves of exploding female emotion float over his head. He was an authoritative and organised man who could competently run a large estate and make it look easy. He may have thought running a large estate was child's play compared to weaving his way around first one crisis organised by his wife and then the next. Quite reasonably he was frequently absent from the family home. Here reigned what an outside observer might have thought was a tribe of over-emotional, hormone-charged viragos. The outside observer might have thought, also, that the tribe was three and four times larger than it actually was. He might have thought they were permanently at loggerheads. But they weren't.

The tribe was made up of Frau Stubel and her four daughters. There was a son, Ernst, who did not get a look in; Ernst sided with his father. The daughters took after their mother. They were beautiful, passionate, emotional and actresses through and through. Their names were Lori, Marie, Milli (short for Ludmilla) and Jenny, named after Jenny Lind, the Swedish nightingale.

Frau Stubel was aware that none of her daughters were likely to go down in history as great actresses, but fame on the stage was not the only door that the theatre might open for her children. Milli, like her sisters, began her theatrical career by attending a ballet school from a very young age. Eventually she finished up in the ballet corps at the Hofoper. She was not particularly talented but she was pretty, with thick blonde hair and light blue eyes and a delicate childish face. She had a kittenish manner; moods that switched like lightning from a sunny childish sweetness to utter misery and floods of tears. She was the sort of girl that men fall for. In the world of the theatre girls like Milli attracted young Archdukes and aristocrats like wasps to a jam pot. Usually such flirts had no hope of lasting.

Milli's older sister, Marie (Marie Zwirner), a bit more level-headed than the rest, turned her theatrical training to good use as a model in a high-class ladies' clothes shop. Here she once had an opportunity to see Mary Vetsera who had come to order some dresses. Marie was struck by Mary's good looks and said, "One was lucky just to set eyes on her!"

Milli's relationship with Gianni has been turned into the perfect operetta story with the irresistible maiden whose love the Archduke found more powerful than himself. However, neither Milli herself nor the power of her love were what cemented their relationship. On the contrary, it was not long before Gianni wanted to back off. He had received a nudge and a wink on behalf of the Emperor that this affair was far too public and far too undignified for a member of the Imperial Family. Had it remained discreet and well hushed-up it would have been another matter. All the young Archdukes courted the pretty little ballet dancers at the Hofoper.

But that wasn't Gianni's way. There was nothing secretive about Gianni. He had been round to the Stubel household and was often their guest, much to the delight of all the Stubel women. They all responded to him and loved him and Gianni warmed to them. Gianni was a romantic – short, stocky Gianni with his bulldog head who looked anything but romantic.

Nor was his interest simply getting Milli into bed. He enjoyed her company. It soon became noticeable that Milli was becoming a great deal more polished than before. Apparently she came to speak fluent Italian and French,[6] found a passion for playing the piano and had even succeeded in some small musical compositions,[7] all of which she had Gianni to thank for.

So he wrote her a letter in which he openly explained that it pained him to do this but that pressure was being put upon him. He went on to say that he thought their continuing to see each other could only harm her. He ended up telling her that he wished to help in any way he could and that he had opened an account with the Rothschild Bank and put in twenty thousand gulden. And that should have been the end of his 'Miltschi'.

Milli's father had died in 1867 and the Stubel household was finding life something of a struggle. Gianni's letter must have been a bombshell. The Stubels were not going to let Gianni go just like that, not without a fight. A man like Gianni was worth his weight in gold to the Stubel family. There was a reproachful letter from Milli's sister, Marie: he had been so good to the family, they were stunned by this; Milli was almost near death so great was her grief – oh, and they would like a letter to take to the Rothschild Bank.

Gianni was fortunate that he wasn't present to witness Frau Stubel's explosion of anguish, anger and desperation. Nothing in the letter he got from her was reasonable or measured; it was an incoherent mixture of accusations – did Gianni think her daughter was a streetwalker? – and vague, incomprehensible threats, most of which could hardly be unpicked, let alone put into action. The letter ended with a mass of conditions the family intended to impose upon the errant Archduke. Most of these were of a financial nature and they included a demand for a hundred gulden for Frau Stubel herself. Any other Archduke would have tossed Frau Stubel's letters (there were more than one) at the head of his household to deal with and, with that, be done with the whole matter.

---

[6]   It is doubtful that she learned these languages fluently, given that her German was fairly mangled and very ungrammatical.

[7]   These achievements, too, sound rather improbable.

Gianni felt sorry for his Miltschi. Once again for having annoyed those in authority over him he was posted somewhere a long way away from Vienna – this time to Krakow. Then Gianni in his madness took Milli with him to Krakow.

While eyes popped from their sockets in the senior ranks of the Archhouse and the military, Gianni wrote a glowing, happy letter to Rudolf full of how Milli's presence charmed all and gave the whole atmosphere of the place new gaiety. Soon after he wrote again, "I cannot understand why everybody has got it in for Milli. If their anger was directed at me... but what has she done wrong but follow her heart?" Further on, he went on, "She was fifteen[8] when I first knew her. In everything about her glowed the charm of youth. She was like a rosebud glistening with dew in springtime..."

And he really didn't understand. He had got used to people attacking him – that never seemed to stop – but to get at him by hurting another... "I can forgive those who go for me but I will hate them for the rest of time for going for Milli." And the thing that hurt Gianni the most was the fact that his beloved mother wanted to know nothing about Milli.

There were long periods when Gianni and Milli were separated. She now had no income and was dependent upon Gianni to support her. She also had nothing to fill her days with. At these times life for Milli was miserable and she moaned and whined. Gianni complained that she did not write to him often enough but when she did her letters were a mass of misery. She was spending all her time back at home with her mother and sister. She was also turning into a hypochondriac.

In 1877 she wrote to tell him that she had seen the doctor and that he had recommended that all her aches and pains and suffering would go if she had a child. That was the last thing Gianni wanted. She wrote to him another rather confused letter[9] which suggests that Gianni had asked her to take measures to ensure that she never had a child. He may not have asked this of her but by now Gianni's interest in her was fading. His eye had been caught by Milli's older sister, Lori. Lori's warmth and brightness must have been a welcome change to Milli's moaning.

Lori made the mistake of asking for money. This was too much for Gianni. Lori wrote him a letter accepting that their affair was over but begging him for a little something – "You are so rich; you could help me..." – and she would not tell Milli. However, Milli did know and was jealous and went on being jealous, for Lori never entirely gave up pestering Gianni – often with threats that she would tell Milli.

---

8   In fact, she wasn't fifteen, she was nineteen. Milli was born in September 1852; Gianni in November 1852. Milli had a number of pet-names for Gianni, one of which was 'Old Man'.

9   Virtually none of Gianni's letters to Milli have survived. Mostly, historians have needed to guess at what Gianni wrote to Milli from her replies to him.

But by the spring of 1882 Gianni's thoughts had turned to marriage. His mother and his older sister, Luise, had both been pressing him for some time to get married and find happiness. Gianni had been ill during the winter of 1879 and while on his sickbed he exchanged a number of letters with his sister discussing the whole idea of marriage. Gianni protested to her that she seemed to consider marriage and happiness as one and the same thing. She wrote back and told him that his heart yearned for love but only in marriage would he find the happiness of love; he would also find happiness in heaven in the next life.

Gianni was of the opinion that the girl who possessed all the qualities he sought did not exist. She had to be virtuous, someone who would never bring scandal upon his head. He didn't want a blue-stocking but she did need to have plenty of interests and to be interesting.

Countess Carla[10] Attems certainly wasn't a blue-stocking. It was she who picked Gianni out and she seems to have thrown herself at him. She did not hold herself back. She had one big card up her sleeve: Gianni's mother was quite willing to accept her as her daughter-in-law. And it was not long before Gianni believed himself to be in love. Carla was head over heels in love with him and writing him letter after letter full of purple prose and ecstatic expressions of passion.

However, before they could get married Gianni had to get the permission of the Emperor. He sought a meeting with Franz Joseph. Gianni spoke of the Countess Attems' virtue and how serious were his feelings for her and he explained that he had given it serious consideration before coming to seek permission to marry her. Gianni described what happened in detail in his letter to his mother of 8th April 1883.

"Oho, so that's what you have in mind," said Franz Joseph when he had got over his surprise. The Emperor went on to tell Gianni that he hoped the matter was not serious because it was his wish that Gianni give up all idea of marrying the Countess.

Gianni replied with courtesy, "Your Majesty, if I were not serious I would not have come to you seeking permission to marry."

"There are already enough such marriages in the family and I wish you to give up the idea."

For Franz Joseph that was all that needed to be said. But Gianni was shocked and he spoke of respecting the duty he owed the Emperor, of the honour the Emperor's agreement would mean to him, and that the Emperor's refusing was a harsh blow.

---

[10] Her real name was Caroline and she was a lady-in-waiting to the Archduchess Maria Immaculata.

Franz Joseph replied calmly, "On the contrary, dear Johann, I thank you for your loyalty in coming to me and I thank you to respect my wishes."

Gianni protested that perhaps he had not made it clear how much this meant to him.

Franz Joseph's reply was, "Nobody will hear of this conversation." And with that the audience was at an end. Franz Joseph extended his hand to Gianni with the air of someone who had done no more than say no to a particular hat at some function. His refusal, Gianni wrote to his mother, was not against Gianni, it was just that the idea did not fit in with the Emperor's principles. Carla Attems was not of royal blood and if Franz Joseph had agreed to their marrying it would have had to be a morganatic marriage. Gianni had failed to mention during the interview that he understood and accepted that that would have to be the case. But when Franz Joseph said that there were already too many such marriages in the family he must have meant morganatic marriages.

Maria Antonia (Gianni's mother) went to Franz Joseph to beg him to reconsider but she was brushed aside in the same way that he was.

Carla went on hoping. In the meantime Milli had found out and there was a huge scene from which Milli flounced off in rage and tears. She wrote to Gianni accusing him of doing all this in order to get rid of her – "and now you have your freedom, enjoy it and I wish you all the best for the future!!!" Her next letter suggests that he has begged her to return (which he may not have done but Milli would have wanted to believe he had) and she went on about how much her heart pressed her to return to him but that after everything she needed to give it some thought. She also wanted to impose some conditions: she would be free to go where she wanted, to see whom she wanted and to earn her own bread. She had done nothing wrong. Her greatest fault had been to love him too much.

Gianni did not reply.

Nine days later Milli wrote again and told him that his silence was torture to her. There were other letters on and off and most of them told him what pain the thought of him caused her but that it was all over now.

Quite at what point the two of them got back together is not known. But from 1887 onwards Milli was accompanying Gianni on various cruises and when he went out sailing she would come too. Baron Hamilkar de Fin, the head of Gianni's household, was shocked at how Gianni made no attempt to hide the fact that there was a lady on board his yacht when he came into harbour in Venice in May 1888.

Gianni had changed. "Why can't the human soul be tuned as a piano is for just five gulden?" – but he could find no answer to that question.

Perhaps he would return from an energetic day on the seas, tired, he would run his hands through his bristly hair and go over in his mind how far his life was going wrong. Perhaps his mind would go back to those days in Florence. Perhaps into his head would come some old Italian song that he had once heard women in the street singing. Maybe he took that old melody and found himself expanding and adapting it into a waltz or musical fantasy. It would have crossed his mind that Johann Strauß was free to spend his life immersed in music. Johann Strauß knew nothing about army tactics and nobody held it against him; he built his career where his talents lay. Johann Strauß did not find himself batted back and forth between one remote army garrison and another like a ping-pong ball. At that moment he may have tasted salt from the sea on his lips and into his mind swept a whole picture of surging waves with the wheeling gulls above crying out their mournful calls.

Gianni had begun to see the sea as freedom. It would not be long before he saw the sea as escape. He was being dragged down and the craving for escape was growing ever more intense.

Chapter 83

The storm clouds began to gather over Gianni's head sometime during the summer of 1887. Gianni's moods were growing darker; his escape from them was the sea. During the summer of 1887 he was staying in Ostende on the Belgian coast and sailing every day.

He returned to Linz for the army's summer manoeuvres and appeared to be as good-humoured as ever and as committed to playing his part in the army as he always had been.

In September Gianni was out of the army altogether, apparently at his own request. On 14th September he left unexpectedly for England and nearly two weeks later there was an announcement in the *Military Gazette* that he had been relieved of his command of the 3rd Infantry Division.

There have been some who have argued that Gianni's renunciation of his position and privileges amounted to proof that he was involved in some conspiracy with Rudolf. Many have since wondered whether it was all in some way connected with that mysterious R.I.O.U. box.

Rudolf would have been watching the course of events with interest. All the indications are that Rudolf was still looking forward hopefully to the future; he had not yet reached the point where he had given up. So if Rudolf had been secretly chewing over thoughts of forcing some kind of change in the ruling of the country, would what was happening have made Gianni a more interesting potential collaborator in such political scheming? Or would Rudolf have seen Gianni as far too much of a loose cannon? Would Rudolf have even trusted Gianni? These two had snarled at each other so often over first one issue and then the next. It is hard to believe that these two could have formed a team and really worked together.

Where did Rudolf fit into it all? Plotting secret schemes was very much in Rudolf's character, but far less so in Gianni's character. Surely the one thing Rudolf did know was that here he was dealing with a man who was not afraid to speak out, and almost certainly would have done so if there was any aspect that he did not accept or agree with.

There have been suggestions that it was the Emperor who forced Gianni to resign his command in the army. And it is usually assumed that the reason for this had to do with Gianni's involvement with Prince Ferdinand taking the throne of Bulgaria. However, in spite of the fact that both Franz Joseph and Rudolf had initially been bitterly opposed to Foxy Ferdinand becoming

Emperor of Bulgaria, and that both had blamed Gianni for his part in it, nevertheless both had largely come round to the view that Ferdinand might end up being useful to Austria and promoting Austrian interests in the Balkans.

It seems also that Gianni's enemies were insinuating to the Emperor that his ultimate aim was to seize the throne of Bulgaria for himself. Far more likely is that Gianni was waiting for Ferdinand to call him to Sofia and appoint him head of the new Bulgarian Army which would have removed what he considered as the layers of irritating fools to whom he had to kowtow. He wrote to Laaba who was in Sofia begging him to find out what was happening there. However, Laaba appears to have decided that his best course forward from then on was to throw in his allegiance with Prince Ferdinand and to distance himself from Gianni. Laaba did not reply.

It has been suggested that Gianni's insubordination had been particularly flagrant that summer. It was an understood thing that in army manoeuvres Rudolf and his side had to win. Gianni had come round to the view that if the men knew who was going to win then they would not really try. He had long resented the fact that Rudolf could get away with murder. That summer he made his point of view a little bit too clear.

By 1887 Rudolf's health and state of mind were beginning to affect his military abilities. His men were finding that under Rudolf – with his slack timekeeping, his sudden rages, his inability to concentrate – it was becoming increasingly difficult for them to perform well. The side that Rudolf led was visibly falling behind. When in August 1887 Rudolf was travelling through Linz, Gianni put it to him that if he saw a hole in the ranks of Rudolf's men he would feel it his duty to take over the command of those men. Rudolf responded by writing to Gianni with the 'shattering news' that the Emperor no longer trusted him. Was the news really so surprising to Gianni? Did Gianni entirely believe Rudolf? Clearly all trust between Gianni and Franz Joseph had broken down.

Gianni did not want to leave the army. For a long time he nursed hopes that Franz Joseph would speak out on his behalf and the whole issue would be put aside. Instead Franz Joseph signed everything off. In September 1887 Gianni had written, resigning from the army and Franz Joseph took it entirely literally. Had Gianni's arm been twisted? Did Franz Joseph know of it, if it were so? Gianni's reaction was bitter and a huge cloud of depression smothered him.

Having left the army and gone to England, he wrote to all those who had served under him with his regrets at what had come about and his personal appreciation of how well they had served him. "I do not need to tell you how hard, how painful for me, is leaving you... All my life I will think of you as my comrades" and it went on in the same vein. This was a letter from someone who had not chosen to go and who did not wish to go.

He also wrote to the Mayor of Linz. It was unusual for the army to show any concern for the people who lived and worked in the towns where troops were stationed. Gianni was the exception. He had wanted good relations between the army and the people of Linz and he also supported a number of charitable activities out of his own purse. When the Mayor received Gianni's letter full of thanks for the Mayor's unfailing help and support, he must have been deeply sorrowed that it had come to this. And then he would have thought, Linz could not let Gianni go just like that without some gesture from them. The city council voted unanimously that Gianni be awarded the freedom of Linz. Never before had any city in Austria accorded such an honour on any Archduke.

Gianni was delighted. He immediately accepted with much enthusiasm and very real gratitude. Franz Joseph was enraged. Once more here was a member of the Imperial Family stepping out of line. You suspect, also, that for Franz Joseph Gianni's popularity wherever he went was becoming vaguely threatening. Franz Joseph would never have admitted as much to himself. He could not understand why Gianni always had people on his side; Gianni was obstinate, he could be hot-tempered, he was certainly outspoken and he wasn't afraid to speak his mind to anyone's face – how come he was so popular?

Part of the problem was that outside Austria there were many who unashamedly admired and supported Gianni. They were watching what was happening making it difficult for Franz Joseph to keep it all as low-key and inconspicuous as possible. The British Military Attaché wrote back to London:

> "It is reported that the Archduke Johann is returning to Austria and
> will take up his residence at Gmunden under an assumed title. It is
> to be hoped that in the event of war his services may be utilised."

Franz Joseph wrote to Count Taaffe with instructions to get Linz to withdraw the honour. Taaffe came back with the answer that it was not in their power to force Linz to withdraw the honour. But Franz Joseph could and did write requesting Linz to withdraw the honour, and then he wrote to Gianni requesting him to refuse the honour. The following January Gianni bent to Franz Joseph's will and informed the Mayor of Linz that he could not accept the award.

From the moment Gianni left the army Austrian bureaucracy cranked into action with a steady sequence of petty restrictions or spiteful prohibitions. Far from being freer out of the army Gianni found life a frustrating succession of tripwires. True, Gianni sought to conciliate Rudolf, possibly hoping for some support from him at a difficult time. But they saw little of each other during the course of 1888 since Gianni had set his heart upon getting qualifications that would allow him to captain a ship.

Before 1887 was out Gianni had bought himself a yacht in England called *Bessie* which he described as a small palace, and he set sail from Southampton to cruise down to Gibraltar and into the Mediterranean. He was not alone; Milli accompanied him on his voyages which offended Baron de Fin so much that he requested the Emperor that he be relieved of his position as head of Gianni's household.

By this time moves were being made to prevent him setting foot on Austrian soil again. He had to get permission to visit his mother at Arco near Lake Garda. She found Gianni struggling to regain some few grains of optimism and he was still hoping that he might return to the army. But he was beginning to fear that all that anyone in Austria wanted was his 'effacement'. "My life – I no longer have a life – my existence is like a mist-shrouded, dimlit and miserable autumn day," he wrote to his mother.

The beginning of 1889 found him in Fiume. Here he sold *Bessie* and concentrated upon getting his captain's certificate. He was studying navigation and seamanship with a certain Antonio Budinich. "I am continuing my study of navigation and I am devoting as much time to them as the professor has time to give me. I hope to be able to master all the material during the next two months." He wrote to his mother. Some weeks later he wrote again to tell her that he was now learning about running a ship and engineering, as well as mathematics. Gianni brought his full concentration to bear. He had set his heart on taking the exams before the end of September 1889. And he succeeded.

In October 1889, two years after he left the army, Gianni ceased to be an Archduke completely. He renounced rank and position. He could no longer continue "the unworthy existence of an idle prince"; he was "too young to sit still forever, too proud to be paid for doing nothing". He took the name Johann Orth and set about building an independent life. He did, however, stress his loyalty and devotion to Franz Joseph and he asked one thing: if there should ever be a war he might be permitted to return and to offer his life in the service of Austria, if only as an ordinary soldier.

He wrote this letter in Zurich. There in Switzerland all around him were voices speaking German but sounding so different from the voices he might have heard in Vienna. He was experiencing twinges of apprehension about what was happening to him. Did he think back to when his family had fled Italy and wonder whether he had been born to be restless and rootless, only truly at home on the high seas, like the tides – growling one moment, smiling serenely soon after? He was leaving behind his family, his home, property he owned in Austria which he loved, and a huge chunk of his own personal identity. He was even giving up his nationality – Franz Joseph soon intimated that Johann Orth would only be considered Austrian for six months and after that he would be stateless. Franz Joseph wished him to take Swiss nationality.

Nobody back in Austria gave much thought to whatever anguish over his future Gianni might be experiencing. They were shocked at his actions. Nobody had ever done this before. They regarded his comments about princes doing nothing, which was true of a lot of them, as highly insulting. Franz Joseph felt Gianni's step as a form of desertion for which he could not forgive him. He became the Habsburg who had "renounced his family, his position and his duties and fled from them like a thief", as Nando expressed it in a letter to their mother.

And there was one aspect that rankled almost more than any other: Gianni's actions attracted the curiosity and interest of eminent people in other countries and put Austria in a light that the Imperial Family found offensive. In France and England he was admired. He had been described as the hope of the Imperial Army and he was seen as one of Austria's most popular and distinguished generals.

The Times newspaper called him 'a Prince of remarkable ability and character' and went on to explain to its readers that the Archduke feared that the spirit in which the organisation of the army worked was injurious to the efficiency of the service. Comments like these did not reflect well on Austria. It became clear that England looked forward to Gianni making his future home there and intended to welcome him with open arms. What made all this worse was that the authorities in Austria were trying to keep everything under wraps, trying to ease Gianni out of the picture as unobtrusively as possible in the vague hope that perhaps very few people would notice that he was no longer there.

Quite what was really happening throughout this period has never been made clear. Everything about Gianni's own words and actions suggests that he was being forced to do what he did very much against his will. Nowhere in any of Gianni's own words is there anything other than loyalty and integrity. He saw himself as a devoted servant of the family he was a member of and the country he belonged to.

Gianni did not find any of it easy and one of the things that upset him the most was the distress it was causing his mother – "I implore your blessing from the depths of my deeply disturbed soul at this grave moment of my life." She would give him her blessing even though she could not understand why he had done it and she did not approve at all. He was her favourite son, always had been, and when, less than a year later, they came to her with news that Gianni had died at sea, she refused to believe it. She went to her grave believing that he had to be still alive somewhere.

There was to be a new shock for Gianni. He learned that once he ceased to be an Austrian citizen at the end of March 1890 then his master's certificate which qualified him to captain a ship anywhere in the world would no longer be valid. He had worked so hard for that certificate – it was his passport to earning his living now that all his allowances from the Habsburg purse had been cut off. In desperation Gianni found himself once again struggling to deal with Austrian bureaucracy – could the Emperor perhaps allow him to remain an Austrian citizen, or if not, then allow him to captain a ship sailing under an Austrian flag?

Franz Joseph did not want to know anything more about him and none of his officials wanted to ruffle his feathers by taking an unpopular decision, nor indeed by taking any decision at all. None of them dared approach the Emperor. Meanwhile Gianni wanted a printed statement that he had been compelled to change his nationality and only done so in obedience to the Emperor. Gianni was growing increasingly frantic and, largely out of fear that his aim to earn a living from the sea might at the last moment be frustrated, he travelled in desperation to Sofia to seek an audience with Foxy Ferdinand. On 2nd March 1890 Moritz von Schenk arrived in the Bulgarian capital – this was Gianni's incognito. That same evening he saw Foxy Ferdinand.

Foxy Ferdinand did not want to have anything to do with him. At that point Gianni was reduced to begging for a position in the Bulgarian Army, any position.

Gianni was in a highly emotional state. According to the report the Austrian Ambassador sent back to Vienna, he was at the point of nervous collapse and he completely threw himself at the feet of Foxy Ferdinand, begging for a position in the Bulgarian Army. He ended up saying that if he could not serve Bulgaria then he would be forced to look to Turkey for a military position. The meeting went on until one o'clock in the morning, all to no avail. Ferdinand ordered him to leave Sofia.

The Austrian Ambassador then sent a telegramme to Constantinople to ensure that Gianni would get no more joy from the Ottoman Empire than he had from Bulgaria. Franz Joseph wrote to the Ambassador to praise his actions. In Franz Joseph's view Prince Ferdinand had acted admirably in rebuffing the 'intriguer' Herr Orth. Gianni in their eyes had become a non-person.

Gianni now had no intention of waiting for Franz Joseph's response to his request that he might remain an Austrian citizen. He went to the Austro-Hungarian Consul General in London to inform him that he had bought a ship, the *Saint Margaret*, had obtained a cargo and he intended to sail for South America under the Austrian sail while he still possessed Austrian nationality and his captain's certificate was still valid.

The Consul General reported that this conformed with the law and he then forwarded an application for the registration of the *Saint Margaret* to the maritime authorities in Fiume. Back in Vienna senior officials were wriggling frantically to evade taking a decision. Nobody wanted ever to be seen as the person who had actually rubber-stamped permission for Gianni to do this. And it all took a long time and Gianni was getting worried that time would run out before he set sail. Furthermore, acquiring the *Saint Margaret* with its crew and cargo had left him penniless and in debt.

If Franz Joseph had wanted to prevent him sailing, he certainly could have done so but perhaps in the end he merely wanted Gianni as far away as possible. On March 26th 1890 the *Saint Margaret* sailed for South America. Gianni did not captain the ship himself because he did not feel confident enough of his abilities and he then found it difficult to accept a more junior position on the ship. He did not enjoy the voyage which had been rough and grindingly difficult and he arrived feeling utterly crushed. Milli had travelled by passenger ship to Buenos Aires and joined him there in July. She was not happy either and wrote to her mother, "God knows if I will survive..."

Gianni now wanted only one thing: to sail the *Saint Margaret* himself with a new crew round Cape Horn to Valparaiso.

He had reached the point of shutting out from his mind all doubts. He himself was not yet experienced enough for so dangerous a voyage? – then he would gain the experience in doing it. It was the worst season of the year for rounding the Horn? – there would never be a better time for testing what one was made of. All reason argued against his doing this? – had he ever flinched in the face of difficulties or danger? No, and he wouldn't now. His mind was made up; he refused to admit to himself any doubt. Milli was miserable. She wanted only that this wretched voyage would come to an end. She may even have turned on him and snapped that she never wanted to go to sea with him again.

He set sail from La Plata on 12th July. On 31st July as the *Saint Margaret* was rounding the Horn there was a raging hurricane and five degrees of frost. Nothing in Gianni's sailing experience had prepared him for such conditions.

The *Saint Margaret* was never seen again and nobody who sailed in her was ever seen again, not Gianni, not Milli, nor any of the crew. In 1911 he was presumed dead. His mother never gave up believing that her son was alive somewhere.

For Franz Joseph a long-standing thorn in his side was gone. What he privately thought of the final outcome nobody knows. Relief, no doubt.

Sorrow that it had to come to this. Regret, probably. But Gianni had left behind a legacy that Franz Joseph would never have understood. Gianni had chipped away at that huge monolith that was the Habsburg Arch-house and he had left cracks in the concrete. He had paid a very high price for his refusal to become a Habsburg clone and few would have wanted to step into his shoes. But he had shown it could be done[11] and he had shown that their powers of reprisal were not unlimited.

And might it not be the case that Franz Ferdinand was emboldened by these fore-runners in his determination to marry Sophie Chotek? It certainly would have been brought home to Franz Ferdinand that, were he to have renounced his right to the throne in order to marry Sophe Chotek, he, too, would have been forced into exile and possibly largely prevented from seeing his own family ever again. A little of his determination may have stemmed from the fact that he could not bear the thought of living anywhere else but within the Empire where his family would have continued to live.

The Austro-Hungarian Empire has often been compared to a pressure cooker with the lid clamped on so tightly that all the tensions within it were sooner or later going to bring about an explosion. The same could be said of the Habsburg Arch-house. And after Rudolf's death the lid was clamped down even more tightly. Senior members of the family wanted to put the past behind them and present to the world a harmonious front. Might the turn that Gianni's life took not have occurred if this had not been the case? Gianni never wanted to leave the army, let alone Austria, nor did he ever wish to be in any way disloyal to Franz Joseph.

---

[11]   Would Leopold Ferdinand, the son of Gianni's eldest brother, Ferdinand (Nando), have also left the Arch-house to become Leopold Wölfling if Gianni had not led the way?

Chapter 84

There was some kind of psychological acid eating away in the mind of Queen Marie-Henriette. Neither Stéphanie nor Clémentine could understand it. What they saw was that the smallest rebuff led to an explosion of rage in Marie-Henriette and it was invariably Clémentine who got it in the neck.

Marie-Henriette now controlled every moment of Clémentine's life. As the years went by she had intensified her efforts to prevent Stéphanie from visiting Belgium. It has been suggested that the Belgian royal couple feared the outcome if Clémentine saw too much of her sister. What they feared was that Stéphanie might in her confidences reveal things that went on in Vienna that Marie-Henriette regarded as shocking. They did not want Clémentine to discover that Louise had a lover, even worse that Stéphanie was quite willing to receive her sister on a regular basis even though she knew that Louise had a lover. But most of all they did not want Clémentine to discover before her wedding night that there was an intimate and physical side to marriage.

In convoluted ways this was hinted at in the Belgian newspapers and Clémentine without knowing exactly what was going on here wrote to Stéphanie to advise that if she wanted to come to Brussels she needed to be prudent and careful. She begged Stéphanie to show restraint because it was becoming ever clearer that their mother opposed the longed-for visit. As her state of mind became more unstable Marie-Henriette fought more furiously than before to kill any pleasure either of the two girls might find together.

Marie-Henriette slowly grew more and more angry at everything and anything – usually without any cause. Her anger and her aggression were incomprehensible to those around her. We might wonder today whether Marie-Henriette was suffering from some form of dementia which was changing her whole personality. If she was becoming increasingly forgetful, few around her would have paid it very much attention. A Queen like Marie-Henriette was permanently surrounded by an entourage of ladies-in-waiting whose job it was to remember things for her. She did not have to remember things, but inside her own mind she may have been panicked by the increasing holes in her memories. Further indications that suggest dementia: as Marie-Henriette aged she became interested only in her dogs and seemed less and less aware of her daughters to the point where she gave the impression that she was not sure who they were. Towards the end of her life when Stéphanie went to visit, Marie-Henriette pushed Stéphanie away brusquely and barely spoke to her. And Marie-Henriette clung to photographs of herself and her family.

On 1st January 1890 a fire broke out at Laeken and it was not long before the left wing of the palace was ablaze. The whole wing was badly destroyed, the dome over the grand staircase crumbled to the ground and Napoleon's library on the first floor was burnt out completely. Marie-Henriette with her husband were attending New Year celebrations in Brussels and when they returned the only thing that seems to have concerned Marie-Henriette was the fact that a large number of her precious photographs had been burnt. One of these photographs was the only picture the royal family possessed of their only son who had died in 1869.

Marie-Henriette seemed indifferent to the fact that Clémentine – alone that night playing the piano rather mournfully in a semi-darkened room – was there in the left wing of the palace and might so easily have been burned or killed. Nor did she grasp the fact that Clémentine's governess, Mlle Drancourt, had, in fact, died in the flames. Marie-Henriette gave the impression that she had no idea who Mlle Drancourt could possibly be. A year later memories of the governess had come back to her and Marie-Henriette turned upon Clémentine reproaching her for failing to rescue Mlle Drancourt.

But Clémentine was distraught at the death of her governess who had also been her friend. Her mother couldn't see this.

For Clémentine it started when she was startled by screams of «*Au feu! Au feu!*» She rushed out onto the landing to be hit by choking black smoke. She could hear Toni Schariry crying desperately «*Sauvez-vous!*» At the same time Toni held out a coat to her young mistress and pushed Clémentine down the stairs. When Clémentine realised that she could not see Mlle Drancourt she turned back to find her. It needed one of the officers, who were now trying to guide the frightened bunch of people out of the building, to hold Clémentine back and prevent her from rushing back upstairs to Mlle Drancourt's room. It was here that Mlle Drancourt had shut herself in. Captain Dupré tried to obey Clémentine's pleading with him to go back for Mlle Drancourt but by now the smoke and flames made all attempts to reach her impossible.

Fire engines had reached the buildings and the fire engineers were doing all they could to put out the blaze. It took nearly two hours to get the fire under some sort of control. Clémentine attempted to help the firemen, getting in their way more than anything, until she found herself pushed back on to the lawn, in a state of shock, shaking and shivering in the biting cold. She realised that she herself owed her life to Toni and Captain Dupré.

In the immediate aftermath of the fire Clémentine found herself almost without any clothes. Stéphanie rushed to send her a mass of gifts but Marie-

Henriette, burning with resentment and bad temper, immediately confiscated the clothes sent from Vienna. It went so far that if Leo had not intervened Clémentine would not have been allowed to do anything to replace her lost wardrobe. And in the years that followed Clémentine became effectively Marie-Henriette's prisoner, trapped within the arbitrary control of an unreasonable and irrational being whose own life was falling apart.

Clémentine struggled with it. Each and every day she was faced with hours on her own, alone with little to distract herself with; she could read, she could play the piano, she could pray or go for a walk within the palace grounds. For company she was dependent upon her new lady-in-waiting, the Baroness d'Oldenneel. In spite of these restrictions she showed an optimistic face in her letters to Stéphanie.

It is just possible, during their time together at Miramare in 1889 when the two of them found a moment alone with each other, that Stéphanie picked up clues that led her to prise from Clémentine her great secret – she was in love. The young man Clémentine had fallen for was her first cousin, Prince Baudouin. He was the eldest son of the Count of Flanders. Clémentine had known Prince Baudouin all her life; they had played together as children and then slowly childhood affection had flowered into deeper feelings.

There are no hints as to how Stéphanie reacted to Clem's revelation. She must have had mixed feelings. On one level Stéphanie's first thoughts may have been that love is painful and can only bring sorrow.

Clémentine was aware that over the years her father had come to regard Baudouin with much of the affection he might have given his own son if he had lived. Consequently Leo had long insisted that Baudouin should be welcomed at Laeken and special attention given him as the future King. From when Baudouin was around twelve years old, Leo established a regular weekly lunch at the palace every Sunday for his younger brother, sister-in-law and, most importantly, Baudouin. Leo was under no illusion that these invitations were welcome, so he did his best to make it almost impossible to get out of them. The Count of Flanders, Philippe, in a letter to his wife, Marie, wrote, "There is nothing natural about the family of the King." Marie also deplored the total lack of human warmth, affection or interest in each other that they found at Laeken every time they went there.

They did their best to keep their children away from it all but in the case of Baudouin this was particularly difficult to do. With time Baudouin became adept either of getting out of these visits or of cutting them short. On one occasion in 1885 Stéphanie and Rudolf were staying in Brussels and

Baudouin was pressed into joining them at Laeken. The meal began at seven o'clock but Baudouin made good his escape as soon as he could and he was back in his own home by nine.

Of course, Baudouin did not enjoy going to Laeken, though he knew perfectly well why he, particularly, was so often invited there. With heavy irony, he once wrote sarcastically to his sister, Henriette, "Family dinners at Laeken are so gay!" In short, they were an endurance test. He added that he could not stand the constant yapping of the four griffon dogs, Gileppe, When II, Mouche and Spa, nor could he endure the terrible smells that emanated from them. (Perhaps sensitive noses ran in the family; like Stéphanie, Baudouin seems to have been very aware of smells.)

So the dogs yapped and Marie-Henriette maintained a stiff silence, tense and mute. And Leo's very obvious attentions towards him made Baudouin feel uncomfortable so that he feared that all too soon Leo would start putting more and more pressure upon him to marry Clémentine. A match between Baudouin and Clémentine appealed greatly to Leo.

But Baudouin's own parents were very much against it, mostly because of the fact that Baudouin and Clémentine were first cousins. Yet both Philippe and Marie felt a good deal of anguish and pity for Clémentine. Philippe thought of her as Cinderella and sometimes they invited her to spend time with them just to get her away from the terrible atmosphere at Laeken. Even so Clémentine did not find favour with her aunt, no matter how much Marie pitied her. Baudouin's mother, Marie, considered Clémentine too tall and too affected. She was certainly tall for a young woman. Perhaps the affectedness was part of the controlled mask that all Leo's three daughters learned to wear at all times to protect themselves from their father's control over them.

Frequent visits to Laeken must have begun to teach Baudouin to wear a similar mask himself. So Baudouin largely kept his thoughts and his feelings to himself. He was only twenty-one and not ready for marriage. From his point of view, one of the biggest difficulties facing him if he were to consider Clémentine as a possible wife was that it would draw him into Leo's control in a way that he would find difficult to evade. Furthermore, when Baudouin was ten years old on 23rd March 1879, he was taken to the chateau of Tervuren. For ten years Charlotte, the widow of Maximilian, and the younger sister of both King Leopold and of the Count of Flanders, had been effectively imprisoned here. The belief was that Charlotte had gone mad with grief after her return to Europe from Mexico, and nobody spoke about her. It was as if she never had existed and no longer did so. Baudouin did not even know that he had an aunt shut away out of sight.

That day they went to see the chateau Charlotte was not there. There had been a massive fire that had destroyed a large part of the building. What struck Baudouin was the grounds, which he found beautiful, fascinating and perhaps a bit unreal. He described what he saw at great length in an essay he was called upon to write for his homework. Baudouin was a sensitive boy and it seems likely that memories of that day stuck in his mind. What we can never know is whether in amongst those memories lingered a sense of disquiet about how those close to the throne ended up being treated. Particularly if they didn't do what the King required. Possibly such thoughts too would have made Baudouin wary of linking himself too closely into the royal family.

So it would have needed someone a lot more beautiful, a lot brighter and more interesting and charming than Clémentine to counter-balance the disquiet Baudouin may have felt about being drawn into Leo's clutches. And perhaps, in spite of all the years he and Clémentine had known each other and played with each other, he may well have sensed that he hardly really knew her. Too often the times that they had spent in each other's company had been at Laeken where Clémentine's behaviour would have been constrained because of the presence of her parents.

Yet he liked her and enjoyed her company. He found her interesting, intelligent, amusing and a delightful tease. She wasn't a great beauty but she had a certain attractiveness that sprang from her ease of manner and her wit.

Baudouin himself was rather uptight and withdrawn. Few got behind his defences. This was never more true than when he was at some ball or grand dinner where he treated the ladies with great courtesy but very rarely indeed did he invite anyone to dance with him. "He only dances out of duty and throughout the dance he barely speaks to his partner," his mother said.

His family saw in him an idealist and feared that he was a poet who lacked ambition and did not appreciate military matters. Privately, his mother thought he was "not quite masculine". She thought Baudouin was too soft and that he lacked energy or any kind of get-up-and-go. When Baudouin was ten years old, his mother wrote to one of her closest friends, the Countess Cerrini, "My son causes me much anxiety – he is so soft. He is a handsome and honest boy, but thus far he completely lacks energy and drive."

When Baudouin was fourteen years old, Marie's anxieties had not abated at all: "He is the best young man in the world, terribly kind and gentle. For me personally he is too gentle... but he has talent and he is generous and open, loyalty itself." Again and again Baudouin was described in these terms: he was kind and considerate, perceptive and understanding, a young man who treated all with perfect courtesy regardless of rank or status. But he always seemed to have a softness that ran through him. He seemed to lack drive or energy. And the opinion of his German grandmother in 1884 at the end of the regular autumn visit of the Count and Countess of Flanders to Castle Sigmaringen in southern Germany, "Baudouin has won many hearts here, having inherited from his father his friendliness."

Clémentine confided in Stéphanie, "Every time I see him I love him even more – he is so good-looking!" In all likelihood, it wasn't so much his good looks that sparked such longing for him but rather his friendliness. Clémentine's life had always been so empty of friendliness from anyone. But Baudouin was not ready to tie himself down into a relationship and the more obvious it became that Clémentine was very taken with him, the more he hung back. These feelings between them were very one-sided. Initially she must have been buoyed up by her hopes that Baudouin might one day recognise that he was in love with her.

Once struck by Cupid's arrow Clémentine's longing for the next time she might see him filled her heart and mind. In church she prayed to the Virgin Mary to protect this great romantic feeling. In May 1890 Clémentine attended an important horse show in Brussels where she was able to spend several hours at her cousin's side. In delight she wrote and told Stéphanie how proud and happy she had been to be able to talk and laugh with him in front of the whole world. Not long after, the whole city celebrated Baudouin's birthday with extravagant festivities. Here, too, just how much Clémentine clung to the side of Baudouin was noted. The result of that was that the next day all the newspapers were speculating as to when their engagement would be announced. Clémentine glowed with joy. "Dear God, let it be," she prayed.

The Countess of Flanders, her aunt and Baudouin's mother, was less impressed: "These stupid reports in the news of an engagement are boring us all, myself particularly… Baudouin does not wish to get married. He is too young; he is in fact younger than his age."

Come July Clémentine's heart beat faster. She accompanied her parents on a summer visit to Ostende. A pressing invitation from the King had brought Baudouin to the coast to join them there. Warm summer days and the young people were free to go for long walks along the sand. Again and again the perfect moment for a declaration of love presented itself. Again and again Clémentine trembled in an anguish of waiting.

Yet the visit came to an end and nothing had been said. Clémentine was obliged to accompany her mother to Spa for the month of September. Marie-Henriette insisted that she had always disliked the North Sea and its coast and now was finding she disliked it more and more, whereas the peaceful, green, wooded countryside around Liège…

For Clémentine the first chill in the air, the fall of leaves as autumn advanced with its grey skies, the drawing in of the nights, all reflected her mood. It was as if her great love had followed the seasons, bright and warm at the height of summer and now fading away into the cold of winter. She had never liked winter except when snow had fallen and the world turned white. Then her spirits lifted and she escaped into a winter wonderworld of skating on the frozen lake at Laeken or whooshing through the forests in a horse-drawn sleigh until her cheeks glowed and her eyes were bright. But

Belgium is too close to the sea to promise snow every winter and mostly she dreaded the days shortening.

That November was particularly cold and rain and wind drove her indoors. Of an evening she would stare brooding into the embers of the fire. "I am afraid that what I dreamed of will never come about. But I must find courage – I am ready to accept this terrible sacrifice. I didn't think I had the strength but God will help me." Was Stéphanie's reply to this of any comfort to her?

What intensified Clémentine's pain all the more were rumours swirling around Brussels that Baudouin was going to propose to Hélène d'Orléans, the younger daughter of Philippe VII, Comte de Paris. Here busybody matchmakers were doing all they could to manoeuvre the young man into marriage, but Baudouin was no more drawn to Hélène d'Orléans than he ever was to Clémentine. Baudouin wrote to his mother, "This whole story is so ridiculous it made me laugh!" In fact, Baudouin barely knew Hélène. She had accompanied her mother on a brief visit to Amerois, the country retreat in the Ardennes of the Count of Flanders. Baudouin decided that she had been good company for his two sisters.

But what all these machinations achieved was to push Baudouin into backing off and refusing to consider marriage yet – he was still too young to settle down. It may have crossed his mind that at around about the same age Rudolf had been pushed into seeking a bride – and look where that had ended.

Over Christmas Clémentine kept to her room suffering from a feverish flu. As New Year's Day approached Marie-Henriette turned upon her daughter full of embittered recriminations – she had taken it into her head that Mlle Drancourt's death in the fire a year ago was Clémentine's fault; she should have done more to rescue her governess from the flames. Clémentine did not know how to defend herself. She sunk in despondency. She had neither the will nor the energy to go out or take part in any of the festivities.

The final blow came on 23rd January 1891. At five o'clock in the morning Marie-Henriette burst into Clémentine's room with the terrible news that Baudouin was dead. It seems that Marie-Henriette found that Clémentine's tears irritated her.

Through that month of flus and chills all the children of the Count of Flanders went down one by one with some kind of flu. The first had been Baudouin's eldest sister, Henriette, whose attack of flu had soon turned to pneumonia. Marie, on 5th January, noted that the season of flu epidemics had begun – "Albert is under 'hausarrest' and Baudouin and Henriette have been affected by it." On the 10th, a Saturday, there was to be a New Year's Ball which should have been the occasion for Joséphine to show herself in public for the first time. However, Marie feared that neither she nor

Henriette would be well enough to go to it. Nor did they. Henriette was seriously ill; during the night of 12th January the last rites were administered to her. However, before the week was out Henriette had managed to pull through. But she had passed the infection on to her brother. He, too, kept to his bed with fever and pneumonia and four days later he suffered a renal haemorrhage. He, too, received the last rites. He, too, then showed every indication that, like his sister, he might yet pull through.

He died in the night.

Clémentine was not allowed to attend Baudouin's funeral, nor follow the cortège to the crypt below the Notre Dame church. From her room she could hear the funeral music, the mournful rolling bells over the roofs of the city. By day she was required to support and sustain the strength of her mother but alone she crumbled. She wrote to Stéphanie describing how hard she found it to contain her own pain in order not to exacerbate her mother's. Nevertheless, Clémentine could not help suspecting that her mother felt little real grief.

Clémentine's grief was all too real: «*Penser que je ne le verrai plus jamais, celui que j'ai tant aimé, qu'il est mort, je ne peux le croire encore quand il y a quelque jours à peine je le taquinais encore et riais avec lui!*» ("To think that I shall never see him again, that he is dead, he whom I loved so much and only a few days ago I was teasing him and laughing with him!") She noted the similarities in their situations – "We have both suffered in a similar way. I understand now just how much you felt your loss." And she mentioned how much she leant upon Toni Schariry and clung to Toni's kindness.

On the anniversary of Baudouin's death the royal family appeared in public and Leo spoke of their loss. He spoke of how Baudouin would have been a model King, how much he had loved his country and desired the happiness of all, but "God judged otherwise. He has called this angel up to Him. In the silence of death we must give ourselves to its mystery!" With Baudouin's going it might have been expected that Leo would turn his attention to the younger son, Albert, but he never did show much interest in Albert.

Marie-Henriette could not hold back her tears but when Clémentine burst into heavy sobbing Marie-Henriette was outraged and she painfully kicked Clémentine's ankle with her foot.

As far as the outside world was concerned the royal family had done all they could to play down how seriously ill Henriette and Baudouin had been. The people of Brussels had been unaware that Baudouin was even ill when the headlines that he was dead hit the papers.

As a result there was a reaction similar to that which followed upon the death of Rudolf. There was a mass of speculation full of highly improbable aspersions. On every side there were reports insinuating that perhaps Baudouin's death had not been a natural one. The correspondent of the French newspaper *L'Intransigeant* sent a report back to Paris claiming that Baudouin had committed suicide out of a desperate love for his cousin, the Princess Clémentine, because the King had forbidden the young couple to marry. Another story which flew around was that Baudouin had gone to a rendez-vous with the wife of the Prince de Ligne. As Baudouin left her boudoir he came face to face with her husband who, so enraged that he could not make out who it was, shot Baudouin at point blank range. An alternative version involved a duel between the Prince de Ligne and Baudouin triggered by old jealousies that had long festered between them.

Most of this was pure speculation, often on a grotesque scale. Slightly more credible was the story about Baudouin and the American singer, Sibyl Sanderson. Sibyl had been engaged to sing in a number of operas in Brussels at the Théâtre de la Monnaie. She arrived from America at the end of August 1890. Baudouin's stay in Ostende with the King and Queen and Clémentine had come to an end and he had been able to return to Brussels, heaving a massive sigh of relief at his escape, while Clémentine had been dragged off with her mother to Spa for the month of September. So maybe the timing was right for Baudouin.

The season opened on 6th September with Sibyl singing the leading role in Massenet's opera *Esclarmonde* and for the first time Baudouin was smitten. According to some reports the King was concerned that this would lead to a scandal and he ordered Baudouin to leave Brussels to take up military duties in Antwerp. Baudouin refused but he travelled to Antwerp to explain his actions to the governor of the city and then, having courteously paid his respects, he hurried back to the Hôtel de Suede where Sibyl awaited him. The story goes on that a few moments later the duc de Ligne burst in upon the couple and fired a bullet at Baudouin as the Prince was scurrying away. Baudouin tripped at the top of the stairs and fell down them to his death.

On 3rd February 1891 the *San Francisco Chronicle* printed an article confirming that a bundle of very compromising letters from a number of admirers were found in Baudouin's rooms after his death. Amongst these was one from Sibyl Sanderson which could not have been more correct and innocent.

Baudouin had once written, "Unfortunately in Brussels in certain *milieux* the most ordinary things come to be seen in a fantastic and sensational light." If he had been able to see the stories spread about his own death he might well have been amused. But what wasn't funny was how these stories became laden with heavy undertones presenting Baudouin as cruel or criminal.

All the emphasis was upon the comparison with Mayerling. After all, Mayerling, too, had occurred in January and only two years earlier. Right across Europe sensationalism had free rein. Were the royal houses of Europe accursed?

Chapter 85

In December 1909 King Leopold II died, having outlived Queen Marie-Henriette by seven years. In the years after Marie-Henriette's death he spent more and more time with his last mistress, Blanche Zélia Joséphine Delacroix (sometimes known as Caroline Delacroix – this was the name she herself preferred to go by). She gave him two sons, Lucien and Philippe, who sparked far more pride and satisfaction in Leo than his legitimate daughters ever could. It was a re-run of his father's preference for his mistress and her sons over his legitimate family. Like his father, Leo preferred plump, even voluptuous women.

Leo seethed with anger against Louise and Stéphanie, Louise because she had run off with Count Géza von Mattačić-Kéglévić and brought scandal and shame upon her whole family, and Stéphanie because she had married an insignificant Hungarian Count and given up all her royal standing in the world. Infuriated, Leo spent the last years of his life seeking out any means he could find to punish his daughters. In this process Clémentine got caught up, too, though she little deserved it.

When Stéphanie married Elemér Leo stopped all payments to her even though he was breaking the marriage contract he had signed on her behalf when she married Rudolf, according to which he was required to pay her an allowance for the rest of her life. Money was something Leo worshipped and money was, for him, the weapon of choice for punishing his daughters, so his one aim became to prevent them from inheriting anything from either their mother or from himself.

One way of doing this was to smother his young mistress with properties, jewels, and wealth. He gave her a title: Baroness de Vaughan. When Leo died he left Caroline Delacroix a multimillionaire.

He had succeeded in making Caroline pretty much the most hated person in Belgium. Mention her name and people spat fire and brimstone upon it. Caroline did not care. She was wealthy enough to face down all who snubbed her, wealthy enough to get her own way for the rest of her years, wealthy enough to live a life of utmost luxury.

Her parentage was French but she was born in Bucharest. She started out life as a barmaid, then found her way to Paris where she became the mistress of a young former officer in the French Army, Antoine-Emmanuel Durrieux. When these two hit financial difficulties, largely thanks to Durrieux's betting on horses, Caroline's lover became her pimp and she turned to prostitution. She was sixteen when she caught the eye of Leo (he was sixty-five). Leo had had many, many mistresses throughout his lifetime but he had never flaunted them in the way he flaunted Caroline, nor had he devoted as much time to any of them as he devoted to Caroline. People hated Caroline because it was all so public and so offensive. She went with Leo to all the fashionable spas in Europe causing massive outrage. Leo did not mind who he offended by showing her off so blatantly. He was besotted with her.

At the beginning of December 1909 Leo returned to Laeken after one of his long stays with Caroline. His appearance shocked people by how ill he looked, how drawn, pale and obviously in pain he was. A few days later he was doubled up in agony. His doctor, the Professor Jules Thiriar, diagnosed an obstruction of the intestine and insisted that all he could do was to operate as soon as possible. He estimated that the King had a one in ten chance of pulling through.

Caroline hurried to his side and the next day on 14th December Leo married Caroline. This was a religious ceremony which was subsequently recognised by the Pope but there was no civil ceremony so the Belgian people refused to consider it valid. Had Belgium had to accept Leo's second marriage then Caroline's eldest son might have become King. Perhaps that was Leo's intention – he was, by the end of his life, a resentful man who seemed to care only to snub those he felt had not accorded him the respect and admiration he craved.

On 15th December the operation was carried out and declared a success. He came round and seemed set for his convalescence and recovery. He told Caroline, "I have done enough for Belgium. We will settle at Balincourt and I shall take over the education of my sons!" But that same night a blood clot settled on his lungs and Leo was dead before morning. After Leo's death Caroline returned to Antoine-Emmanuel Durrieux, eventually marrying him. However, there is reason to think he had always been in her life but very much in the background. On one occasion Leo discovered Caroline with Durrieux and she hurriedly passed him off as her 'brother'.

When it became clear that Caroline had been given such a huge share of Leo's enormous wealth both Louise and Stéphanie turned to the courts to try to claw back some of that wealth. Neither was particularly successful and Clémentine chose not to bother at all. Clémentine, as she began to get over the shock of losing her father, had too many other things on her mind – her sister, first and foremost, and then marriage – to Victor Napoleon.

Clémentine was forced to wait until both her parents were dead before she was free to visit her sister in her own home in Oroszvár. 1910 was the year when Stéphanie and Clémentine could be reunited in a new way boosted by the hope that nothing in future could again come between them. Perhaps that was how Clémentine saw things.

Clémentine comes across almost as the perfect Victorian woman. She was submissive and docile and she put up no resistance to all the arbitrary constraints and strictures imposed upon her by her parents – so very different from Louise. She accepted that her father and mother had a total right to rule her life and to demand of her unquestioning obedience. Again and again in her letters to Stéphanie she expressed anguished regret when she was not allowed to see Stéphanie or write to her, but she never seems to have resented it or rebelled against it. Could she really have been so submissive without ever feeling a twinge of opposition?

For all the closeness between the two sisters there had been long gaps with little or no contact between them. To Clémentine these gaps could be washed aside as though they had never been. In Clémentine's mind she could pick up the threads each and every time where she had left off.

On 29th December 1909 Clémentine wrote to Stéphanie one of her effusive letters. In it she wrote, "A silence has separated us through the long years but my feelings have never wavered, just as sincere, faithful and profound as you have always found them. Sometimes we have been united in suffering. But now we are alone and a bond brings us together. It wipes out the pain of the past, making the present smile with the promise of joys to come..." But even as Clémentine glows with the joy of being closer to her sister, she does not yet dare speak to Stéphanie about her hopes of announcing her engagement. Approval must first be obtained from the new King of Belgium, her cousin Albert. Stéphanie would have to wait to learn all Clémentine's intimate secret revelations.

Stéphanie had long known about Victor Napoleon and she knew that their father had stepped in and forbidden Clémentine from seeing him. Stéphanie might have expected Clem to have opened up her heart to her. But Clem hadn't. Instead, she stopped writing to her sister and a long silence ensued when Stéphanie could only guess at Clémentine's thoughts and feelings.

Perhaps the reason for this was that, in spite of Leo's refusal to even consider the marriage, Clémentine had not given up hope and she remained secretly in contact with her new love. Meeting, even secretly, was pretty much impossible – too close a watch was kept on Clémentine – but letters could from time to time be exchanged and they were. For six years the two nursed their hopes and waited.

Leo's objection to Victor Napoleon was purely political.

Since 1870 France had been a republic and in 1886 the door was finally closed to any possibility of France again being ruled by either a royal or imperial dynasty.[12] Nevertheless there were two claimants to the throne and hopes that one or other might succeed simmered on.

The royal line based its claim through its connection with the last kings of France. The descendants of Napoleon Bonaparte upheld an alternative claim to the throne. Neither claim had the strength of being a direct descent. And within the Bonaparte family there was some dissension between two claimants. Napoleon III's only son had died in Africa fighting with the British Army in 1879 so the claim had passed to Napoleon III's uncle, Jérome Bonaparte, and then to his eldest son, Victor Napoleon. Between Victor Napoleon and his father there was a good deal of dissension. This family dispute was over whether it should be the father or the son who should be regarded as the true claimant to the French throne and it was complicated enough to cause plenty of high feelings and bad blood. In the end it was all wasted effort since France remained a republic.

Had there been any chance of Victor Napoleon gaining the throne of France Leo almost certainly would have welcomed him as his son-in-law but in the end Leo drew back and insisted that he did not wish to fall out with the government in Paris and he did not wish his daughter to marry someone who might cause difficulties between the two countries. Leo's words to Victor Napoleon were «*La France républicaine estimerait regrettable votre mariage avec ma fille!*» ("Your marriage with my daughter would be considered regrettable in France."). This was 1904. From that moment up until his death Leo would not change his mind.

On one occasion Clémentine screwed up her courage to go and beg her father to reconsider. She was thirty-one and she must have viewed this as her last chance of finding a husband.

She had known Victor for many years. In a letter to Stéphanie in 1888 she mentions in passing that Victor had been there and that he was nice. Back then Baudouin was still alive and all her thoughts were focussed upon him. But Victor made a good impression. Sixteen years on from 1888 she could press the point that neither he nor she was foolish and immature, their tastes and expectations were similar and their feelings for each other had strong roots.

Leo's reply was cutting.

Clémentine maintained her composure and insisted that she was now old enough to take such decisions for herself. There was a violent edge to Leo's voice as he brushed away her words. Clémentine, perhaps for the first time in her life, opposed her father. She did not need his consent, she said, and furthermore, alluding to Caroline Delacroix, her father's house had become an unpleasant place for her to be. Leo exploded in all the force of his fury.

---

[12]   Note 3 in the Notes Section.

Clémentine did not give way before him.

Yet she did give way, submitting herself in the end to her father's will and enduring many more years of waiting. It is not entirely clear why she crumbled before her father's opposition. But she had lived the whole of her life crushed beneath the harsh rule of her parents and perhaps standing up to a man like Leo was just too overwhelming for her. It would be understandable if that were the reason.

She also faced opposition from her aunt, Baudouin's mother, although Marie does not seem to have had any really good reasons for disliking Clémentine's marrying Victor. And it would not have been too surprising if Victor, himself, had not proposed judicious caution. He did not want an open clash with Leo.

Yet for all her submissiveness there was nothing simpering or self-effacing in her manner. Belgian high society saw in Clémentine a woman of determination, courage and intelligence with a sharp wit and ready repartee. She was ever bright and engaging.

Victor did not become a serious figure in Clémentine's life until around 1902-1903, a couple of years after Baudouin's death. He was ten years older than Clémentine. The early years of his life had been spent in Paris, but when Napoleon III and the Empress Eugénie left France in 1870 to go into exile in England, Jérome Bonaparte and his family also left France. They moved to Switzerland. Victor was eight years old. As a young man he returned to France only to be exiled again in 1886 and he never returned to the country of his birth for the rest of his life. This time he took up residence in Brussels. Leo had no objection to his living in Brussels but he had every objection to his organising an opposition to the legitimate government in Paris.

There was little danger of that. Victor was a man who pondered long and deeply every possible course of action and ended up choosing the prudent path which would not upset anyone. One of his aunts considered him intelligent but so irresolute and undecided that he needed years to come to a decision. All his writings emphasise his attachment to honour, integrity, legitimacy, especially legitimacy. Everything about him was considered and cautious. His manner was grave and rather withdrawn. This was not a man who would face down Leo.

If Clémentine had wanted to face up to her father she would have needed to be sure of Victor's backing all the way. And she could not be sure of that. So in the end things just drifted on. Life became more uncomfortable for Clémentine. In the last years of Marie-Henriette's life and after her death Clémentine had increasingly taken on the role of Queen. This had given her a role in life and provided for social occasions when she could go to balls, dinners, soirées, theatres and concerts; she could enjoy society and be a part of it.

But Leo was never going to forgive her for standing up to him. He now considered himself entirely justified in hating all three of his daughters and entirely justified in spending more and more time with Caroline Delacroix, mostly in France, either on the Riviera or in Paris. Clémentine found that she was leading a life of empty luxury alone in a palace, shut out from the world.

And it was exactly at this time that she no longer felt able to pour out her thoughts and feelings in long letters to Stéphanie. Stéphanie hurried to Brussels when she learned that her father was dying, but even then when the two sisters were able to have time together, Clémentine did not fully open up about all that had happened since she had last seen Stéphanie. Clémentine had no reason to doubt that the new King would readily agree to her marrying Victor Napoleon. The announcement would be made as soon as the official period of mourning was lifted. This might have been a good moment for Clémentine to have confided in Stéphanie – but she did not.

Immediately Stéphanie had departed from Brussels Clémentine's letters full of her eagerness to visit Oroszvár started to flow again, but her trip to Hungary proved difficult to organise. The reason for this was that Clémentine wanted to make a detour to visit her future mother-in-law in Lucerne.

In all Clémentine's correspondence she never criticised anyone, not even in the smallest way. Everyone she knew or met was charming, considerate and without fault. Everywhere she went she was received with the warmest welcome and the most perfect consideration for her comfort. In those weeks as Clémentine travelled around meeting various members of Victor's family, she was delighted to be welcomed with such affection and warmth. Her future mother-in-law was an angel of sweetness and kindness. Finally Stéphanie received an excited letter bubbling over with how wonderful Clémentine's time in Lucerne had been.

At last she told Stéphanie that she was now engaged (but not yet officially, of course), adding, "You'll understand that I could not confide in you earlier but it was not possible because my aunt [Countess of Flanders] and the King did not wish it."

Towards the end of April 1910 Clémentine at last arrived in Hungary to spend more than a month with her sister there. She was exhausted, both physically and emotionally, and Stéphanie set about cossetting her in every way she could. Stéphanie mothered her and smiled at Clémentine's torrent of anecdotes describing all the ups and downs that had finally brought her to this moment. They had both suffered so much but now the future looked rosy. In Clémentine's mind her life and Stéphanie's had followed almost parallel paths of pains and disappointments but now both could look forward optimistically to a happier future. Clémentine felt that there were similarities in how Stéphanie had built a new future for herself with Elemér and how she herself would now build her own future with Victor.

At such a moment, into Stéphanie's mind would crowd a mass of painful memories and she would find herself reliving so many difficult moments. She may have felt that Clémentine had not yet experienced those moments when into your mind leaps the thought 'If only I had done this... or that... or not done the other,' moments when you brood painfully over regrets and twinges of shame or guilt, along with the anguished wish that things might have been so different. Stéphanie had many of those moments, they haunted her, but she couldn't talk to her sister about them.

It was no great secret that the Countess of Flanders did not consider her niece to be very intelligent, nor did she approve of Victor. Marie believed that neither Victor nor Clémentine had any real affection for the other, let alone any passionate feelings. In her eyes, why shouldn't the marriage be a success, given that neither party felt any real attachment to the other?

In her correspondence with her own daughter, Henriette, Marie was open about her somewhat biting opinion of Clémentine and her marriage, but elsewhere she was tactful enough to keep her thoughts to herself. She also provided Clémentine with all the support a mother might have given her. So when Clémentine returned from Hungary it was to her aunt's house she went to stay. And the Countess of Flanders arranged a grand fête to celebrate the official announcement of the engagement.

In September 1910 Clémentine accompanied Victor to England to meet Napoleon III's widow, the Empress Eugénie. After the death of Napoleon III the Empress Eugénie had chosen to move from Chislehurst where she and her husband had lived out their exile in England. Eugénie moved to Farnborough Hill, chiefly because she wanted to build a mausoleum in honour of Napoleon III and had been prevented from doing so in Chislehurst. So it was to Farnborough Hill that Clémentine and Victor travelled. Although she had no idea at the time, Clémentine had visited for the first time the house where she would live through the whole of the First World War.

All this travelling was having an effect upon Clémentine's health and as her wedding day approached various decisions were taken to turn their big day into a much more low-key affair with a minimum number of guests. This tiny list would have consisted entirely of Victor's family if the choice had been entirely his mother's. Victor's mother wanted to exclude Clémentine's family. Clémentine begged that Stéphanie should be invited.

The invitation was for Stéphanie only and Elemér was not included in it. If Elemér was not invited then Stéphanie would not be there. Clémentine herself was almost certainly not to blame for this snub, but Stéphanie was hurt. Clémentine wrote to Stéphanie expressing her confidence that Stéphanie's generous heart would understand and forgive her.

Clémentine's wedding day was arranged for 14th November 1910. After the wedding Clémentine wrote one of her ecstatic letters to Stéphanie about how wonderful she found her new relationship with Victor: "My dear husband is good, kind, adorable, loving, intelligent and a connoisseur of things and people. He is so handsome, so very much the Prince in his gestures and actions, such an interesting conversationalist!" What thoughts went through Stéphanie's mind as she read those words? It had all been so very different for her.

Chapter 86

Louise's personality was a strange mixture. She could be so arrogant and high-handed. She could also be so childish and sweet. She was effusive and delightful. She was frivolous and light-hearted. She seems to have gone through life feeling hard-done-by. Other people had been mean towards her; other people had treated her badly; other people weren't fair – and Louise felt she was owed special attention. Why weren't people nice to her? What had she ever done to deserve it all? Louise seems to have had a picture of herself as the misunderstood and mistreated embodiment of all sweetness and kindness. She, too, like her sister, wrote and published her side of the story. Her style of writing reflects her personality. It is bespattered with exclamations of indignation. It is full of pronouncements from on high. But what it does not offer you is a straight account of events.

She had very little to occupy her or give her any kind of focus or challenge in life. She had nothing to do but amuse herself. She did what she liked, spent money without a thought, appeared at all the grand events and flirted immoderately. And all the time she never realised that her foolishness was tolerated because Philipp von Coburg tolerated it. She never gave a thought to her debts – she did not have to, Philipp paid them. People winced at her flirting and bad behaviour but put up with them because Philipp turned a blind eye to them. Philipp's name protected her. She believed she was a member of the Imperial Family[13] and could get away with much that would have seen lesser mortals shunned by society. But within the imperial court she was not liked.

Louise's view of Philipp was that he was little short of a cruel brute. He may very well have not been either the most perceptive of men nor the most sensitive, but he was certainly no cruel brute. He was educated and cultured with a great liking for books and music, as well as being, like almost all men of his class and time, a very fine huntsman. He was a close friend of Rudolf, although there was a thirteen-year age gap between them. Philipp and Rudolf spent a great deal of time together, most of it spent hunting. Philipp was a frequent and very welcome guest at Rudolf's various hunting lodges.[14] Rudolf used to call Philipp "fat boy" mockingly. Philipp just accepted it.

---

[13] In fact, she was not a member of the Imperial Family. Note 4 in the Notes Section.

[14] Rudolf first found and bought the hunting lodge at Görgény Szent Imre, in Transylvania, where he liked to go shooting bears; some years later he bought the lodge at Mayerling which was much nearer Vienna and made brief escapes from the city possible.

More to the point, Philipp was deeply fond of Louise. He was surprisingly tolerant; many another man would not have allowed Louise nearly as much rope as Philipp allowed her. But she was to push him to the point where he could no longer go on turning a blind eye to her behaviour. Yet if Louise had been discreet Philipp almost certainly would have gone on looking the other way.

Louise's affair with Baron Daniel d'Ablaing began in 1883. The Baron came from an aristocratic Dutch family. He quickly became very close to Philipp; he was certainly far more than just an aide-de-camp, he was also a friend and a hunting companion and upon occasion he accompanied Louise alone out riding. Everything about Daniel suggests that he was one of those cheery characters whose warm, open-hearted manner made everyone who met him open up to him in return. And on those long, pleasant rides side-by-side Louise opened up to him and Daniel responded.

Philipp may well have been aware of what was going on but for as long as it was not public knowledge he preferred not to stir up trouble. As it was, all around were those who watched fascinated, wondering when Louise would go too far and bring down Philipp's wrath upon her head.

It is possible that the year 1883 when Louise's affair with Daniel began was a significant one psychologically for Louise. Two years earlier Louise had 'lost' Rudolf when he got married. Not that she had ever had him, but in her mind there was an understanding, an unspoken emotional tie that bonded them. Then in 1883 Stéphanie had finally become pregnant and in September she gave birth to her only child. Rudolf seems to have been galvanised by the fact that he was about to become a father and he showed Stéphanie a whole lot more than usual affection and consideration. Louise felt pushed aside.

On 8th August 1883 Queen Marie-Henriette travelled to Austria to be with Stéphanie at her confinement and she stayed until just before Christmas that year. During those months Marie-Henriette was shocked by her elder daughter's behaviour and very clearly found time to give her a good talking to.

Marie-Henriette wrote to Louise upon her return to Belgium, "I left Austria deeply worried. Since then I have been waiting for a letter from you, reassuring me that you have taken my advice to heart." Marie-Henriette did not mince her words but insisted that Louise's way of life was frivolous and purposeless – above all, it transgressed the laws of the church and that was unforgiveable. She hoped to hear that Louise had taken her words to heart and set about changing her ways. She went on, "You are bad – the word is harsh but true. No, God protect me from believing this of you, you are only frivolous and rash."

This would have rubbed Louise up the wrong way. She was beginning to feel pushed out. Louise was the sort of person who would have sought angrily to fill the gap. If no one else paid her any attention at least Daniel did!

But Louise can hardly have wished for the way in which the gap was filled. In the spring of 1884 Louise felt seriously unwell. She had felt very unwell with each of her previous pregnancies[15] and she now believed that she was again pregnant but she was not sure. "How could Louise not know, yes or no, whether she is expecting a child!" Marie-Henriette burst out in exasperation. And for six months that remained the state of affairs.

Reading between the lines of one of Louise's letters it would seem that during those months she had experienced some bleeding but extremely little and very irregular and all the while she felt ill and mostly had to remain in bed. She had also grown very large. Finally Marie-Henriette could stand it no longer and ordered a doctor from Vienna to examine Louise. His report was blunt. The Princess was not pregnant but she had grown fat and her health had deteriorated because of it.

And Louise felt unattractive and craved attention even more.

To Louise's great shock Daniel died suddenly on 6th June 1888 at the age of forty-one and Philipp then took on a new aide from Hungary, Baron Miklós Döry de Jobaháza,[16] who came to be known within the household as Nicky. Almost at once Louise fell into his arms. This affair, too, involved long rides where Louise was alone with Nicky Döry. Nicky was a very different character to Daniel. He was flawlessly smooth and gracious but, at the same time there was something dark and vaguely threatening about him. Reading between the lines you get the feeling that, although Louise's affair with Nicky did not last long, this was the affair she never completely got over.

In July 1889 Philipp and Louise were staying at St. Antàl and Stéphanie came to visit them there. Here Stéphanie met Nicky and like Louise she was very much taken with him. They called him 'Monsieur Cognac' between themselves. The two girls enjoyed quiet little gossips about him and no doubt giggled together over little things he said and did that appealed to them.

Louise was a lot less inclined to be discreet about Nicky than she had been about Daniel, and out in the open enjoying the warm sunshine Louise's flirting showed little restraint. Yet Stéphanie still wanted to believe that Louise had not taken a step too far, that it was all innocent flirting. However, Stéphanie was shaken one evening when she witnessed Philipp fly off the handle. Louise had been out riding with Nicky and the pair did not return until very late. This was more than Philipp could take and he exploded. But what confounded Stéphanie all the more was how Louise sulked and resented Philipp's reaction.

---

[15] Leopold Clement was born in 1878 and Dora in 1881.

[16] In German texts Miklós became Nicholas.

Louise's attitude was 'you would have thought he would allow me some little fun in life – anyway we had a good laugh!' And Stéphanie did not know how to react. She was Stiéna, the close and tender sister who cared only for Ulyse's happiness, who wanted only what might bring happiness into Ulyse's life. But she couldn't approve of what was happening. Stéphanie was ever the one in the middle; much as she loved Louise, she also liked and respected Philipp and felt some concern for his feelings, too.

Just as Stéphanie desperately needed someone to talk to about 'Hamlet' and the only person she could have talked to had been Louise, Louise also needed someone to confide in about Nicky and the only person she could confide in was Stéphanie.

Her feelings were far from straightforward. There was a dark side to it as well. Louise once confessed that people told her she looked like a rose but if they could have seen into her heart they would have found the worm gnawing away at the heart of the rose. Did the violence of her feelings for Nicky frighten her? Was Nicky not just charming and delightful but also someone who provoked feelings of anguish within her? Was there possibly something of Rudolf about him?

Could it be that Louise could afford to have heart-stopping feelings for Rudolf or Nicky because it would never be reciprocated? Had she ever been able to loosen up with Philipp he would have more than reciprocated her feelings. But perhaps Louise dared not open up. The lid upon her feelings had to be kept firmly battened down at all times. The repressed little girl from Brussels dared not lift that lid.

Nearly a year later in April 1890 Philipp had to leave Louise at home in Vienna while he travelled to Hungary to look over his estates there. One Sunday he returned from church and wrote to Louise, "This morning at mass I re-read the words you once wrote in my prayer book – 'I love you with all my heart' – I would write those words again today. My feelings for you are the same as they were sixteen years ago – if anything, stronger! It is astounding but the more I advance in years the more my love for you grows, the more I am in love with you, the more I think of you – especially when I am far from you, like now." When Philipp wrote this he had to have been aware that things were deteriorating between him and Louise. His words have a desperate ring.

Once Marie-Henriette found out about Baron Miklós Döry de Jobaháza, she immediately sought a meeting with him. Döry agreed to visit her in Ostende. Ostende was chosen because it was considered far enough away from Brussels so that the whole matter could be hushed up and kept from Leo. 'Monsieur Cognac' was at his most smooth and elegant. Here the Baron promised that he would end the affair. Marie-Henriette was even moved by his polite behaviour and his courteous manners. Unfortunately, as soon as he returned to Philipp's household the affair was rekindled.

Marie-Henriette undoubtedly suspected that the driving force behind the affair was Louise. Louise had never stopped to think how others viewed her way of living and it was that that worried Marie-Henriette so much. Louise might think she was just enjoying herself, Marie-Henriette saw it in a completely different light. What of her daughter's good name? So she wrote and stressed that a woman's reputation was her most important possession. The world, she warned Louise, was not forgiving; society was always eager to sniff out scandal...

The thought of a scandal put Marie-Henriette in a panic. If Leo found out what steps might he take against Louise? Worse, what steps might he take against Marie-Henriette? He might forbid Marie-Henriette from ever seeing Louise again – and quite possibly, from ever seeing Stéphanie again as well. And if he once did that he would not ever back down thereafter.

Yet what more could she have done? For some ten years she had been struggling to get Louise to accept the restrictions society imposed upon a wife. Her struggles had intensified over that time. The tone of her letters was growing ever harsher. She had reached the point of believing her daughter was mad and should be locked up for her own safety and for the good name of the family.

By this point she was astounded that Philipp had so far done so little. "What a fine and wonderful man," she once wrote to Louise, "you owe him so much! Few husbands would have acted as he has!" and perhaps in her mind she pictured how Leo would have acted with vastly less provocation. By now she had turned her attention more and more towards Philipp and when in February 1891 Philipp and Louise came to Brussels for the funeral of Prince Baudouin, Marie-Henriette seized her opportunity to speak to him face-to-face and get things out in the open. She needed Philipp to do something. What she wanted was for Philipp to remove Döry from his household, quietly, discreetly and in an amicable fashion.

Philipp agreed. He was tired. He was being attacked on all sides. Everyone seemed to be getting at him. He would have said anything without really being committed to what he had just said he would do. Clémentine backed up her mother. She turned on him insisting that Döry had to go at once and that Philipp had to demand from him his oath never to see Louise again. It is possible that Clémentine was suddenly and unexpectedly hysterical in her outburst. The shock and surprise of the death of the man she loved (they were there attending Baudouin's funeral) had made her unstable and emotional.

Philipp wavered. Then almost before he managed to catch his breath a new attack came, this time from his younger brother, Foxy Ferdinand, who had long carried a torch for Louise. Ferdinand turned to his mother, the Princess Clémentine, and demanded that she do something, too.

Yet the end result of all of this was that Döry remained in the Coburg household. It was only in October 1891 that Döry took up a new position away from Vienna. Louise henceforth totally turned her back on Philipp, refused to speak to him or acknowledge his presence if he was in the same room as her. She wanted nothing to do with him.

A few months later in January 1892 Philipp and Louise were expected to attend the funeral of the Duke of Clarence in London but only Philipp went. Louise now found that she was left out of everything, no one would speak to her, and the letters from her mother had come to a complete halt – Marie-Henriette was expecting a letter of contrition from Louise begging her forgiveness and admitting how much she, Louise, was at fault, but that was a letter Louise was never going to write.

Finally, a year later in July 1893, Louise's great friend, Princess Amélie, lost her husband, Elisabeth's youngest brother, Mapperl.[17] Mapperl died very young at the age of forty-three. Amélie was one of the few women outside her own immediate family Louise was deeply attached to. This death stunned Louise who genuinely felt for her friend. Amélie herself did not survive the year but died a few months later. And then on 5th October 1893 she learned that Döry had married Daisy Jane Kann, a young girl fifteen years younger than Louise.

Inevitably, in time the world got its scandal. Louise fell in love with Count Géza von Mattačić-Kéglévić and ran away with him. It was to cost Louise everything – her good name, her marriage, both her children, her mother's love, her father's recognition that she was his daughter, her inheritance and her wealth. She would end up exiled from both Austria and Belgium.

Louise was no pretty young thing when she lost her heart to her Géza. She had been married for twenty years and was the mother of a son, Leopold Clément, and a daughter, Dorothea, usually known as Dora. When Leopold Clément was born Louise found motherhood fulfilling and she spent all the time she could in the nursery playing with her new baby. In due course, however, Philipp set about ensuring that Leopold Clément was brought up in a 'masculine' way. Louise's feminine influence had to be controlled and limited. A tutor, one Dr. Kocht who was Belgian (this choice was probably a gesture to assuage Louise's hurt), took charge of Leopold Clément's

---

[17] It was Amélie's first fiancé, Prince Leopold of Bavaria, whom Elisabeth lured away to become a husband for Gisela.

education. This was followed by the Army Academy and finally Leopold Clément would have a commission in a crack regiment.

The boy came to scorn his mother. Louise's reaction seems to have been to flounce off as if she did not care. To her, her own son had become arrogant and insolent, a young man who did not need her, since, after all, he was adored and spoilt by both his father and his grandfather, both of whom had done all they could to twist the boy's affections away from his mother. It was not her fault that her son had ceased to love her. When the scandal of Louise's relationship with Géza Mattačić became public knowledge and notorious, no one was more critical of Louise than Leopold Clément.

Leopold Clément never saw or spoke to his mother again after she ran away with Géza. Leopold Clément seems to have grown into a heavy, humourless man, full of his own self-importance. He once said of his mother, "This woman is a shame upon upon our House; there ought to be a power to have her killed!" Leopold Clément von Coburg was one of those people who proclaim loudly their beliefs and principles and consider themselves entitled to judge others until they find themselves faced with a similar situation. The irony for Leopold Clément was that he, just like his mother, would run away with the love of his life.

Camilla Rybiczka was the daughter of an official at the Austrian court, far below Leopold Clément in rank. She was a beauty with dark hair and green eyes. Camilla and her two sisters were actresses in Berlin where Camilla had adopted the stage name of Lotte Gregowicz.

Leopold Clément and Lotte met at a charity fete in 1912, not in Berlin but in Marienbad, where she was helping out by selling stuffed animals. Looking round the fairground her eye fell upon a good-looking young man, oh-so-handsome in his elegant Austrian Army uniform and the very fact that he came from her homeland would have caught her attention. She walked provocatively and seductively up to Leopold, hoping to persuade him to buy a stuffed cat. Those green eyes glanced up at him obliquely from under their dark lashes and flashed upon him a look of invitation. She clearly succeeded in seducing him. From that moment on he was besotted with her.

He made her his mistress and lived openly with her for three years. They travelled around and eventually went to Paris. Lotte soon began to crave marriage and Leopold Clément, on 1st July 1914, wrote her a letter promising her marriage and promising also to make her his sole heir. Once, a maiden of the people would have never considered there might be any possibility of an officer marrying her. But somebody like Lotte had probably heard stories about how Milli Stubel had actually married an Archduke – stories which, through constant repetition, had become distorted, magnified and exaggerated – and so to her mind what once had been an impossibility now perhaps was not... Lotte set her heart on marrying.

Leopold Clément had to return hurriedly to Vienna for the funeral of

Franz Ferdinand, leaving Lotte behind in Paris. When war was declared a few weeks later Lotte in Paris became an undesirable alien and she needed considerable help to get back to Vienna. There she stepped up the pressure on Leopold Clément to marry her before departing to the front. Leopold Clément now was on the horns of a dilemma. He knew that if he married a commoner he would have to resign his officer's commission. Furthermore, his father was bitterly opposed to their marrying and Philipp would have disinherited his son if he had married Lotte. But Leopold Clément was truly smitten and he believed he could bring his father round. With hindsight, it seems most unlikely that Philipp could have been persuaded. In the twenty years that had passed since the scandal with his own wife, his heart had hardened and Philipp would have been most unlikely to see things in terms of romance and true-love-ever-after.

Lotte finally exploded when she realised that he was never going to marry her. Instead he wanted to pay her off. On Tuesday, 14th October 1915 (some say it was Sunday, 17th October) Leopold Clément intended to visit her for the last time to say goodbye and give her half a million gulden. Lotte was expecting him and she had given her servants leave to go out, instructing them not to return until eight o'clock in the evening. Around five he arrived in his motor car and told his chauffeur to return at a quarter to seven.

Shortly before six a soldier passing the house was brought up short by the sound of gun shots. Startled, the soldier rushed in, calling the porter to follow him up to the apartment. With the porter's help the soldier broke the door down. Lotte's body was lying on the ground and nearby lay Leopold Clément, wounded, in agony, but still alive.

Keyed-up to near snapping-point, Lotte had been waiting for her lover's arrival with a gun to hand. She also had sulphuric acid to hand. She knew that this was goodbye but she had no intention of letting him just go. Later, upon investigation, the police ended up believing the rather incredible story that Lotte had shot several bullets at close range and then smashed a bottle of sulphuric acid into Leopold Clément's face. She had then shot him once more before turning the gun upon herself and killing herself. She left a note, saying that Leopold Clément had promised to marry her.

The acid blinded Leopold Clément and seriously disfigured him, burning away half his face; one bullet had also penetrated his lungs.

Leopold Clément did not die until 27th April 1916, six months later. During that time a number of operations were carried out, in an effort to restore his sight. His heart gave out during the last of these operations while he was under the anaesthetic.

In Viennese society everybody knew of the intimate relations between the Prince and Mlle. Rybiczka, and they also knew that the Prince had loved the girl very deeply and sincerely. After the tragedy the romantic Viennese wallowed in sentimental pity. They loved the romance of it all and conveniently forgot that if Leopold Clément had married Lotte their disapproval would have been as great as their pity was now.

After the tragedy the story that spread through Viennese society like wildfire was that Prince Philipp was to blame, preferring to see his son blind or even dead rather than happy with the girl he loved. Shockwaves were felt at court both in Vienna and in Berlin. There were many who believed that the whole affair was reminiscent of the tragedy at Mayerling and no doubt the whispers spread far and wide. For some it would have reminded them of Louise's fate. By then Louise had been divorced from Philipp for ten years and was living with her last lover in obscurity in Paris.

Louise does not seem to have ever felt a great deal of affection for Dora either. But in her book Louise gushes about how close she and Dora were. As was often the way in aristocratic families, Louise saw very little of her children while they were growing up. In 1895, when Louise first got to know Géza, Dora was fourteen years old and very childish for her age. Somehow Dora's childishness just rubbed Louise up the wrong way. But later on, when so many around her were turning their backs on Louise, she had a change of heart and began to smother Dora with affection in a way rather similar to the way Elisabeth treated Marie-Valérie.

Louise only ever had the two children. This may be because the relationship between her and Philipp was so bad that they ended up living totally separate lives under one roof. It is also possible that Philipp infected Louise and she could not have more children. It would not be surprising if Philipp had rendered Louise infertile – he was a known libertine. He and Rudolf were close companions and it would not be surprising, either, if they had not gone out on the town together upon many an occasion. Philipp would have known a good deal about Rudolf's tastes in women and about his sexual prowess or lack of it. Being the cynic he was, it would have amused him to watch his own wife swooning over Rudolf, thinking her secret hidden, and knowing what he knew about Rudolf. Louise always believed her husband's influence over Rudolf was very harmful.

By the time Louise reached her late thirties there must have been a great deal of bitterness and resentment seething away inside her. To the outside world she was spoilt and privileged. Inside her there was nothing but a hollow. She craved something but had no idea what. "The future seems so black and empty. If someone has to suffer it is preferable that it should be me, so that he may be happy!" she wrote. She was thinking of Nicky. He had almost certainly already forgotten her.

Chapter 87

It was a horse that brought Géza into her life. The first time she saw Géza was in the spring of 1895 out riding in the Prater.

In the eighteen months since Baron Miklós Döry de Jobahaza had got married, Louise had been very despondent. She missed him. This was not the painful regret over the inevitable that she might have expected. It burned deeper than that. She wasn't even sure whether the intensity of her feelings for 'Monsieur Cognac' was not greater than the feelings she had nursed for so long for Rudolf. Nicky's dark spirit haunted her.

By now the first of Döry's six children was born and, although during those months Louise had occasionally had brief opportunities to see him, she was well aware that her hold on him was over. Everything suggests that Döry was the love of Louise's life. It is likely that she never wholly got over Nicky, and the wound of his departure and then later his marriage to Daisy Jane never wholly healed. So the arrival of Géza on the scene did much to assuage her wretched feelings. It is likely that she never loved Géza the way she had loved Nicky. But the story of Louise's affair with Géza was such a sensational one and it is the story that has come to define Louise ever since.

Louise had chosen to go for a drive in the Prater in Vienna. Géza was out riding a new and very high-spirited young horse, and he appeared to have great difficulty in controlling the animal. The horse kept backing off, twisting and turning, bucking and rearing up, its front hooves punching the air. Froth had built up around the colt's mouth and nostrils, bespattering anyone who got too near. A crowd had gathered to watch the scene. Géza, a skilled horseman, was enjoying every moment.

It was at this moment that the Princess's carriage drove up with Louise and her friend, Countess Marie Függer, accompanied by Louise's lady-in-waiting, the Countess Sermage. Géza spurred his horse forward, which shied again and then suddenly bolted straight at the pedestrians. The crowd panicked and scattered.

There it was: the bright, warm sunny day, young green on the trees, and everyone out enjoying the spring air. The young lieutenant is showing off his fractious, spirited new horse, a beautiful, powerful beast bursting with tempestuous energy. He is showing off at the same time his fine riding skills. And here in the carriage rolling towards him are two of the finest and most elegant ladies from the highest levels of the aristocracy. He catches the admiration in their eyes, or at least in the eyes of the prettier, younger one, and holds himself even more proudly. The Countess Függer lets slip a small cry of alarm, but Louise cannot hide her glow of amusement. There is just something about the scene before her that stirs something exciting within her. The coachman steers the carriage deftly around the young man and when they have passed Louise turns to look back. The lieutenant has now brought his mount to a standstill although the animal is still snorting and pawing the ground with its hoof. But he is gazing in her direction and their glances meet. Louise saw on his face a suppressed smile – of triumph? of admiration? of longing?

Many, many years later, Géza von Mattačić wrote to the *New York Times* in defence of Princess Louise and he described that exchange of looks out in the Prater. He wrote that he did not know who the Princess was at the time but that he "knew she would henceforth mould and govern my life!" He spoke of his soul experiencing 'a strange exaltation' when she smiled and ordered her carriage to pass on.

In the days that followed Louise went driving in the Prater every day and, somehow, every day she passed the lieutenant out on his horse. She started looking out for him and noticed that after several days he no longer flashed a surreptitious, sidelong glance in her direction but now boldly bowed and saluted her as he rode by. It became a ritual.

During the autumn she seemed to have disappeared and he was in despair. At length he found out that she had been ill. "Had she succumbed I firmly believe that I should have died!" he wrote afterwards.

Then one evening after Louise had recovered from her illness, she attended the opera. We can imagine the scene: Philipp has reserved a box for a performance of Bellini's *Norma* with Dame Nellie Melba making a guest appearance. For an occasion like this Franz Joseph would grace the royal box and everybody who is anybody is there. The whole opera auditorium is jostling with finery, jewels and elegance. And in all that crowd, there is the young lieutenant staring intently at Princess Louise.

He was quite simply stalking her. Louise became increasingly aware of it. She was flattered, delighted, thrilled by it. But Géza had so far never had a chance to speak to her. All that they have had were stolen, secretive smiles across crowded places. This had made it all so much more romantic.

Had Géza been stalking Louise for longer than he would ever admit? Could it have been that Géza was well aware that Louise went out for a drive in the Prater frequently? He might have begun to look out for her and when the opportunity presented itself it would have been an easy matter for an experienced horseman like Géza to put on the whole dangerous, exciting act of the uncontrollable horse attracting every eye to him. Such an act would have been well out of line, but Géza was not the sort of man to hold back. He was a man who loved risks and drama.

How much was he genuinely in love with Louise? If he was in love with her in the beginning it seems unlikely that he remained in love with her. What was it that he wanted from it all?

It was not until early in the following year that they finally came face to face and spoke to each other. Stéphanie was staying in the seaside town of Abbazia, and she had invited Louise to bring Dora and come and stay with her. Louise did not hesitate. She did not really expect to enjoy staying in Abbazia in February, but anything was better than staying in the gloomy Coburg Palace with Philipp.

Louise frequently found Stéphanie irritating and found it hard to sympathise with her sister. Louise disliked it that none understood how she grieved for Rudolf; what little sympathy there was went to Stéphanie. Also, in Louise's mind Rudolf's death seemed to have accelerated her being eclipsed at court. Louise's ability to queen it at the big society functions and grand balls had begun to diminish, the young men no longer flirted with her so readily and she was no longer a young girl. Her fortieth birthday loomed and she did not want to face it.

Géza, of course, as soon as he learned that Princess Louise had gone to Abbazia, found a way of following her there. What did Louise think when she noticed that her lieutenant was also in Abbazia? Did she feel a sudden thrill of excitement? But it wasn't Louise who sought out the meeting. Stéphanie, when she was in Vienna, was always so stiff and correct. But away from Vienna, Stéphanie was so much more relaxed and informal in her social comings and goings and it was not long before Géza had been presented to her. That could not have happened in Vienna but here Stéphanie welcomed it. It was Stéphanie who invited him to an informal dance at her villa.

The informal dance was to be a fancy dress party. From hating the idea of dressing up in some silly costume – Louise's usual reaction to fancy dress parties – once she realised that Géza would be there in person and she would get an opportunity to speak to him for the first time, then Louise's mood swung round completely. She soon decided how she should appear. In one of the books brought along for Dora by her governess there was a picture of Diana, the moon goddess, the goddess of the hunt, and that picture had caught Louise's eye.

From that moment on, she was bullying and chivvying the hotel manager to rustle up seamstresses to make a copy of Diana's costume in time for the dance. Down in the basement of the hotel some ten local women were stitching their fingers raw. Not just that – Louise had to have a bow and a quiver full of golden arrows and special sandals, golden sandals with thongs that laced around her legs right up to the knee. Away from Philipp and his caustic disapproval, she felt free.

Thus, Count Géza von Mattačić was presented to the Princess he had already begun to idolise. There she was before him with bare legs and golden sandals on her feet and dressed in a far more skimpy dress than she ever would have dared wear in Vienna. She felt emboldened to be Diana the huntress in all her glory.

If Stéphanie had had any idea of what was simmering beneath the surface, would she have invited him? No, not Stéphanie. But Louise had learned to be devious and Stéphanie failed to pick up the clues as to what might be going on. Stéphanie welcomed Géza to soirées, card parties, dances and small dinners and Louise and Géza had frequent opportunities to speak to each other and for each to get to know the other. They also contrived to get away and go out riding together.

It was so much easier to do this in Abbazia than it would have been in Vienna. Under Stéphanie's nose and apparently without Stéphanie's guessing what was going on, Louise and Géza's affair kicked off. There in the small, quiet town of Abbazia in the cold weeks of February with a sharp wind blowing in off the sea, it was fairly easy to get away with it. It would not be so easy in Vienna. But the riding gave them the clue as to how they might continue their affair safely in Vienna, too.

There was one day with a hint of spring in the air and they had spent it cantering lazily out in the countryside behind Abbazia. And as they pulled their horses up to a walk and started to make their way back to the town, Louise turned to Géza and asked him what he thought of her as a horsewoman. He told her quite candidly that he thought she appeared ill at ease on horseback. That reply, given their relative ranks, was remarkably forward and it suggests that he, as a skilled rider, had acquired a slight authority over her. And she simply agreed with him that she was not as good a horsewoman as she would like to be. Géza's next remark was even more forward. She should, he told her, get herself a proper stable of horses and work at improving her horsemanship.

Upon their return to Vienna, Géza was put in charge of setting up her stable, acquiring some fifteen quality horses and he became her equerry. They would meet at a chosen riding school where she gradually became mistress of the equestrian art. Up until that point Géza had never had enough money and was constantly borrowing from one to pay back another and juggling a growing weight of debts. From then on, for the next three years, he had no further debt problems.

It might almost have been the storyline of a Viennese operetta – an impossible love affair that ultimately led to a duel and the two lovers living out the rest of their lives for each other – except that the way things turned out was anything but light-hearted and amusing, even though it did become an impossible love affair that ultimately led to a duel and the two lovers living out the rest of their lives for each other.

The Viennese loved their frivolous, naughty stories on the stage and, in fact, they loved them when they happened in life. With their strong sense of the romantic the Viennese loved following this affair or that. The whispers and gossip were the spice of their social events. The speculation about how things might turn out fed an on-going soap opera of exciting entertainment. So long as everyone could pretend that they didn't know anything about it.

Inevitably, this affair did not remain a secret. It soon came to be flaunted across Europe, so much so that the duel was almost inevitable. Nevertheless, the duel was still two years down the road.

The next scene in the story came in November 1896 with its cold long dark evenings. Louise had talked Géza into dining with her in one of the *chambres separées* for which Sacher's was famous. Sacher's was noted for its elegance and decadence, its discretion and the unmentionable goings-on that took place in those private rooms. Louise craved the excitement, the naughtiness and the risk of it all. She longed to be served by impeccably discreet, elegant waiters in an atmosphere of coquetry and naughtiness.

They would have champagne and caviar and they would laugh and glow with love. They would raise their champagne glasses to each other and their eyes would twinkle and tease across the tiny, fizzing champagne bubbles. The whole idea worried Géza but Louise was on a high and would not be deterred. Nobody would see them. They would enter through a side door and slip along the corridor to their room. Louise would be heavily veiled and she would turn up the collar of her fur coat. It would be impossible to distinguish her from any of the other adventurous ladies who frequented Sacher's.

And they might have got away with it. But in true melodramatic style, the very person who could do them most harm, and who would have no compunction about doing them all the harm he could, was the one person who saw two figures in that corridor and whose curiosity was aroused. He was also the one person who would be capable of recognising them in spite of the cover-up and camouflage. He was Franz Joseph's youngest brother, Archduke Ludwig Viktor,[18] the man the younger Archdukes called 'Luzi Wuzi' behind his back.

Ludwig Viktor was an inveterate gossip. With all his naughty stories of things that should not have happened, and his slightly waspish take on everything that appeared on the surface to be elegant and correct, Ludwig Viktor could be an amusing companion. With him people would open up

---

[18] Ludwig Viktor's biographer, Katrin Unterreiner, points out that it is not completely certain that it was Ludwig Viktor who revealed what was happening to Franz Joseph. In Louise's own memoirs it was Ludwig Viktor but there is no other corroboration.

far more than they ever intended, only to find later to their horror that he had passed on their indiscretions.

Ludwig Viktor also loved female company and flirting with the ladies. He was undoubtedly one of the many who had flirted with Louise. He had sent her presents and flowers. But he didn't appeal to her and she had brushed him aside without a thought; she had made fun of him and it had hurt.

He knew her well and he would have recognised her from her walk and her movements. He would have known her scent. He was the sort of person who already had his suspicions about Louise and her new equerry. If he had not recognised Louise he would have recognised Géza. Géza had never met Ludwig Viktor and it would not have crossed his mind to turn away and hide his face. Oblivious, the two of them continued down the corridor.

A few days later Louise was summoned by Franz Joseph. The audience took place in Stéphanie's apartment at the Hofburg and it was short. Franz Joseph did not wish to discuss the matter or to listen to Louise. "Indiscretions have been committed which it is not possible to overlook," was Franz Joseph's view and for that she would henceforth no longer be permitted to appear at court or at any court ball. And with that, Franz Joseph left.

In her memoirs Louise wrote, "I was in such a state of anger!" Louise considered her anger justified: she could never in the whole of her life control herself when faced with injustice or what she considered to be unfair accusations. "I thanked his Majesty for this audience and then, taking a stern grip upon myself, I said he ought to take my side and that I was the victim of the unfair attacks of a miserable cabal!" She put it to Franz Joseph that it was for him to put an end to these slanders. She expected justice from him.

"Madame, that is of no concern of mine. You have a husband – it is his affair. I believe that for the present you would do well to go travelling and you should not appear at the next Court Ball."

"But Sire, I am the victim. You are treating me as though I were the guilty one."

"Madame, I have listened to what Viktor has told me..."

In Louise's account she is a woman of pride and dignity and at this moment it was all she could do to pronounce with disdain: "The future, Sire, will show which of us is lying, the Archduke or me!"

Left alone in Stéphanie's rooms, it was Stéphanie who seemed to be the more upset. Louise was for brazening things out, but it had not yet completely dawned upon her just how serious this was, or how impossible her position would be in Viennese society once it got out that she was barred from the court. Louise looked at her sister, snivelling into her tiny lace handkerchief, with a stab of dislike.

But she could not just brazen it all out. She could not just turn up at court functions the way she had always done in the past. And if Philipp turned up on his own the whole city would enjoy the scandal to the hilt.

The next thing she had to face was Philipp's anger. Louise was no stranger to Philipp's outbursts of rage, but on this occasion he was icily cold and sarcastically scathing. This was all it needed to provoke Louise into insisting that Philipp had to challenge Ludwig Viktor to a duel and avenge her honour.

The story goes that Philipp just laughed. Why should he challenge the Emperor's younger brother to a duel? Because he had said the dinner at Sacher's had taken place on a Monday, when, in fact, it took place on the Sunday? Or because he had slept with Louise? If he had to challenge to a duel everyone Louise had flirted indiscreetly with, he would have to fight half of Vienna. Louise felt a wave of self-pity: that he could flaunt his debauchery and feel he had a right to accuse her!

As soon as she could Louise poured out her feelings to Stéphanie in an incoherent letter full of indignant outrage. She called upon Stéphanie to show her support by refusing to attend the next court ball herself.

Deep down, Louise had to have known that she just did not have a leg to stand on. It was that knowledge that stung her on to the offensive. Louise was not prepared to give way or apologise. She would make things a thousand times worse rather than concede the smallest point. Philipp knew these moods of hers. And he knew how to provoke her into arrogant defiance. He found it a real turn-on and had upon occasion forced himself upon her at such moments. Was this what he had in mind here? Suddenly, she felt sick.

A couple of days later she got a note from Stéphanie, saying that Erzsi had a terrible cold and so Stéphanie had decided to take her somewhere warm to get over it. Louise's lip probably curled when she read that. She had always thought Stéphanie was far too much the court stooge, far too ready to bow to what protocol demanded or what others insisted upon. In those words, she saw the manoeuvrings of some court flunkey who wished to protect the Crown Princess Widow from the taint of scandal by getting the Crown Princess Widow and her daughter away from Vienna for a while.

So Philipp took Louise travelling, first to the French Riviera and then to Paris. Louise took a huge entourage of some thirty-two servants and attendants with her. These included her companion, the Countess Marie Függer. Dora also came on this trip and her governess, Mlle. Rouvigard, accompanied her. When they got to the Riviera Louise pointedly went out on long drives with Dora and Mlle. Rouvigard, leaving Philipp behind.

During this time there was a heated exchange of letters between Marie-Henriette and Stéphanie with Stéphanie defending Louise and placing the blame for what had happened on to Ludwig Viktor and Marie-Henriette insisting that Ludwig Viktor had only done what he had to do.

Philipp travelled with Louise to Paris but then, leaving her there, he went on to oversee affairs on his estates in Hungary. It is quite possible that Philipp never again saw Louise alive on this earth.

It was while Philipp was in Hungary that Géza arrived in Paris.

Géza had left Austria without permission from his regimental officers and would now be considered officially a deserter. He could no longer count upon returning to his regiment to pick up the threads of his ordinary military duties. He risked facing a military tribunal and he must have known it. His position within the Austro-Hungarian Empire was compromised. There was a risk of his property within the Empire being confiscated and he must have been aware of that, too.

Géza had put all his eggs in one basket and placed his whole future at risk. Surely, he had to have known that. And the risks he was taking were pretty overwhelming. If everything had gone wrong for him, what would he have had left? It is very romantic to think he took those risks for the love of this particular Princess. But if he did there was madness in it.

From all we know about Géza's character and subsequent actions madness seems to be the wrong word. He was to prove himself a skilled organiser, an adroit manager of the opportunities that presented themselves to him. He was a careful planner and at every turn he succeeded in winning the support of many people of hugely varied skills and personalities. He could count upon the loyalty and commitment of his team, and even their co-operation with each other in spite of there being, at times, quite strong antipathy amongst them. Yet he was never in a position to promise any of them anything in return.

(However, nobody was more important to Géza than Maria Stöger, the first of Géza's adoring women. Without Maria Géza would never have succeeded in the way he did. Maria Stöger must have believed in Géza's attachment to her. It is hard to believe that she would have gone to the lengths she did to support Géza's plans if she had not believed that he cared for her deeply. She, too, took considerable risks because of Géza. Did Géza care for Maria? Indeed, did he care for Louise?)

When he arrived in Paris Louise welcomed him with open arms and made him her chamberlain and put him in charge of her household affairs. Suddenly the whole situation was very public. Both Louise and Géza had now taken the definitive step from which there could be no going back. Up until this moment, in spite of the mass of gossip, all the loud whispering on every side, and tongues clicking in disapproval, things could still have been patched up. It would have needed a considerable amount of conciliation on all sides but it could have been done. But now wherever Louise turned up doors were shut in her face; she was no longer welcome. Hither and thither across Europe Louise and Géza roamed restlessly.

Paris, Karlsbad, Nice...

Meantime, the most urgent thing for Philipp now was to get Dora away from her mother and this would require some subterfuge. For some time Dora had been unofficially engaged to be married to Ernst-Günther von Schleswig-Holstein whose sister was married to Kaiser Wilhelm of Prussia. Philipp now persuaded Günther to travel to Nice and to bring Dora away using the pretext of taking her for a short visit to Dresden to meet her future mother-in-law. However, this was to be no 'short visit'. Dora, together with her governess, Mlle Rouvigard, left Nice with Günther, never to see her mother again.

On the morning of her departure Louise was struck by a feeling of panic, a premonition...

Chapter 88

Almost two years to the day since Louise and Géza first met in Abbazia, Philipp challenged Géza to a duel. He sent Baron Féjérváry and Field Marshal Count Hugo von Würmbrand, to Nice to present his challenge to Géza.

It must have been galling for Philipp to do this – he had always looked down his nose upon that 'little Croatian lieutenant'. He could not understand how a man nine years younger than his wife could be so in love with her – or was it her money and the lifestyle that went with it? With his usual sarcasm, he had chosen 18th February 1898 for the duel – his wife's fortieth birthday. He had also chosen the Spanish Riding Academy for the place where the duel was to take place – the riding school where Géza had given Louise her riding lessons.

But why the duel at all?

There must have been so many in Vienna who would have taken the view that duelling was a thing of the past. This was no longer the seventeenth century, it was the nineteenth century – no, almost the twentieth century – a pragmatic world and such romantic, grandiose affairs as duels belonged only in operettas. Franz Joseph was known to disapprove most strongly of duels. Yet, it had been Franz Joseph who had brought things to this pass.

Officers in the army had become increasingly incensed at the unsatisfactory way things stood, and Philipp was being seen as a victim. Philipp must have thought long and hard before agreeing to a duel. There was a twenty-two year age gap between him and Géza. Géza was a fine shot and he was younger and fitter. Philipp was also known to be a good shot; he had been a constant companion of Rudolf's on hunting trips. However, Philipp was short-sighted.[19] There is something slightly puzzling here – how could he hope to succeed in that duel and come away alive? There comes a point when your eyesight is not as good as it was, nor your hand as steady...

Each man fired two shots at the other. Géza initially aimed at the groin but then chose to fire wide. Philipp's first shot missed him. Perhaps he was too angry. Again Géza chose to fire wide and again Philipp missed. At this point the seconds suggested that honour had been satisfied but Philipp refused. The duel then continued with sabres. It was brought to a close when Géza's sabre stabbed Philipp's hand between the thumb and the palm. There was a great deal of blood and Philipp's hand had to be bound up and his arm

---

[19] Philipp's eyesight had never been very good; he wore a lorgnon because he was short-sighted.

put in a sling. The doctor called an end to the duel.

Everything about the duel was humiliating for Philipp.

From the moment of the duel Philipp wanted nothing more to do with Louise. He ceased to pay her an allowance and he ceased to pay off her debts. Louise had some money that came to her from Belgium but her income henceforth was nothing like enough for her to continue living in the way she was used to. And Louise had no idea how to economise, she had never had to. She had never even handled money; when needed, that would be discreetly taken care of by a lady-in-waiting at her side. Words like 'bill' or 'credit' were meaningless to her. And like an awkward child, she refused to give it even passing consideration.

Nor did she realise until it was too late how different would be her position in society now that she was no longer effectively Philipp's wife. No longer did anyone need to hide from her their scorn or dislike. She was no longer welcome and no longer accepted in society. She could be treated abruptly, discourteously; she could be cold-shouldered and ignored; she could be flouted. And there was nothing she could do about it.

Pictures of Louise show an imperious woman. She was beautiful, far more beautiful than Stéphanie, and very elegant. This was the face of a woman who had never since her marriage been treated with anything less than obsequiousness. The change must have been shocking. But Louise was not going to change her ways. She saw absolutely no reason why she should. She was a Princess of the blood royal. A certain standard of living was due to her because of who she was. It was for others to see to it that she had that standard of living. How it was seen to or who saw to it was no concern of hers. Her husband was a very rich man and her father was, in all probability, the richest man in the world at that time – so no problem.

But both Philipp and King Leopold II were set on punishing Louise. They were both angry men. Leo was enraged by his daughter's behaviour. Leo had never seen any of his daughters as people in their own right, but rather as pawns who might serve to enhance his own standing and prestige. They existed to make royal marriages that would aggrandise the King of Belgium – himself. Leo had never greatly liked seeing Louise marry Philipp whose only claims to brilliance were his family's name and his great wealth.

To Leo, Louise's behaviour was beyond the pale. From then on Leo set about cutting Louise off and he went to great lengths to ensure that she should never inherit from either him or from her mother. True to character, Leo was vindictive; he meant to bring Louise to heel. She had humiliated him.

But Philipp, one suspects, would have taken Louise back if she had agreed to come back. Philipp's feelings seem to have been ambivalent. What he could not take was seeing Louise gallivanting around Europe with Géza Mattaćić. Nor was he willing to pay off debts that he believed were effectively Géza's debts. In the end many of Louise's creditors did get some money out of Philipp – quietly, because he did not want those who had lent to Louise in good faith to suffer losses.

Philipp was in an invidious position. He may sometimes have thought to himself how much he wished that it did not all have to be so public...

The banks started refusing Louise further credit. Before they would lend her money, they wanted someone else, someone creditworthy, to stand guarantor. Géza throughout was racking his brains as to whom she could approach. Would she find a sympathetic ear in the German Kaiser? The Russian Czar? Queen Victoria? And finally, perhaps her own sister, Stéphanie? But deep down Louise was upset and unhappy and she hated the idea of approaching anyone and begging them for help. Perhaps we can picture her twisting her shoulders uncomfortably, her irritation growing, as Géza kept pressing home the point. And Géza was imperceptibly treating her increasingly like a naughty child. It was Géza who was making the decisions; Géza who was in charge.

Louise had not seen Stéphanie since that day when the Emperor barred her from court. In her head she could still hear the whine in Stéphanie's voice as she bemoaned what had happened – as though it had happened to her and not to Louise! Louise's relationship with Stéphanie had always been coloured by Stéphanie's dependence upon Louise for support. Louise could never have accepted that the tables might ever be turned. Approaching Stéphanie was in some ways the easiest course of action, but in some ways the most difficult. And Louise could not do it. Instead she forged Stéphanie's signature on a credit note.

Never did it really come home to Louise just how serious this was. Stéphanie would have lent her a hat, and she would not even have had to ask whether she might borrow it. What was the difference?

Stéphanie at the time was seriously ill. Stéphanie was rarely ill, or if she was she made little of it. Only once back in 1886 had Stéphanie previously been very ill. So when Franz Joseph first heard that she had taken to her bed he brushed it aside and assumed that it was little more than a light fever. When Franz Joseph returned to Vienna (he had been in Hungary that winter) he found the doctors were seriously worried.

On 30th March 1898 Franz Joseph wrote to Elisabeth with news of Stéphanie's illness - an inflammation of the lungs. It is highly improbable that Elisabeth cared one way or the other about Stéphanie, but Franz Joseph's mention of how ill Stéphanie had been, and all about what was happening to Louise, as well as how Stéphanie was taking it, bears witness to his personal concern for his widowed daughter-in-law.

That March he found she looked very sick, was agonisingly thin and was still coughing to a worrying degree. Stéphanie was so ill that there were real fears for her life. She was running a high fever and there was very little the doctors could do for her. Finally the day came when Stéphanie's priest was called and she was given absolution.

Yet a few days later the crisis had passed and she was on the mend. Throughout her illness Stéphanie had been very distressed but Franz Joseph was pleased to see that when he visited her she was much calmer than she had been. On 3rd April he visited her again and was relieved to see that she now looked a lot better. Stéphanie was composed, he told Elisabeth. And she had taken all the commotion over her sister far better than he had feared she would.

It was at this time that Louise decided to forge Stéphanie's signature. Forging the signature amounted to expecting Stéphanie to pay the debt, since Louise did not have the money and would not have the money when the debt became due. But suspicions about the signature had arisen well before Louise's creditors came knocking at Stéphanie's door. As a result, the signature was discovered to be a forgery while Stéphanie was still ill and it was court officials who took the matter in hand. In the end, the one time when Louise needed Stéphanie's help Stéphanie was unable to give it. It will never be known whether Stéphanie would have paid off the debt. But if she had it would have resulted in Louise forging her signature again and again and again.

Once Stéphanie was on the mend Franz Joseph was content to allow Stéphanie and Erzsi to travel south to the town of Gries, near Bozen,[20] to recuperate. Franz Joseph may have been quite glad for Stéphanie and Erzsi to be out of the way, somewhere where Louise was not likely to get to them or seek their assistance. Stéphanie travelled south only partially knowing how serious was the situation Louise now found herself in. And there is no record of how she felt when she did find out all. Nor is there any record of Stéphanie's trying to get in touch with Louise. But if she had tried, she would not have succeeded. By then Louise was on the run.

It is not even known whether Stéphanie knew where Louise was that year of 1899. Stéphanie had other matters on her mind. She was increasingly preoccupied by the fact that she had met the man who was to become her second husband and she knew that when the news came out into the open she would be faced by nothing but intense opposition on all sides. Stéphanie had serious worries of her own.

---

[20] The city of Bozen was still part of the Austrian-Hungarian Empire, the region the Sud-Tirol. Today the region is in Italy.

Chapter 89

For Louise and Géza, once Philipp von Coburg had washed his hands of them, the financial situation grew ever more desperate. Louise and Géza were forced to flee from the south of France, and they fled to Croatia. They planned to take refuge in Castle Lobor where Géza's mother was living. They succeeded in boarding a train in secret and travelled for nearly forty-eight hours until they reached the Adriatic coast. Then they took a boat heading for Croatia. In Agram (Zagreb) Géza had to keep out of sight of his comrades from his old regiment who were posted in the garrison at Varaždìn. Every effort was made to keep their whereabouts secret. From Agram they headed first to Géza's relatives at Brežice. The whole journey must have been a shock for Louise; she had always travelled in the height of luxury, never on ordinary trains and boats. But she seems to have found the novelty of it all rather exciting and romantic. The need to avoid attention heightened the romance of it all.

Another thing that may well have heightened the romance of it all would have been their concentrating only upon what was happening there and then. They would not have wanted to look too far into the future because then it might have hit home to them just how bleak their prospects were. Where would they live? How would they live? What kind of life could they look forward to? These would have been questions that they studiously avoided because they did not know the answers to them. All of which made them experience each moment far more intensely than would normally be the case.

At Brežice a mass of relatives, neighbours and townsfolk turned up out of curiosity and there were evenings with gypsy violinists throbbing out their strange, melancholy tunes late into the night, while jugs of rough wine were passed round a rough wooden table laden with peasant food. And in the flickering candlelight Géza and Louise would catch each other's eye and experience an intensity of romantic love such as they would never find again.

And later village girls, giggling yet almost paralysed with awe at being in the same room as a real Princess, would desperately try to play the lady's maid, and, all fingers and thumbs, try to undress the Princess. And then Louise would climb into a bed alongside her long-suffering lady-in-waiting and pull up a voluminous feather quilt. And she would wake to hear the wind moaning and rattling at ill-fitting windows.

It was all unreal.

Géza chose to ride over to prepare his mother for Louise's arrival. He found his mother angry, spitting out her disapproval of a woman leaving her husband. And when the two of them did arrive at Castle Lobor they found that Géza's mother, rather than welcome an adulteress, had chosen to disappear. They were never more alone than at that moment.

Géza had described his parents' home as a chateau; Louise thought it was little more than a sprawling manor house that had been abandoned to them. There were a few servants around; she could not speak their language, nor they hers.

But it was summer time and warm and sunny. They had escaped from all the pestering, and all the people pressing in on them and importuning them and insisting that they do this or that or the other. The outside world could be shut out of their minds and they could enjoy their freedom and their love. And they were so in love.

Louise needed to be so very much in love. There could be no doubt that this was love in all its magnificence. She could not have faced the possibility that her actions smacked of childish recalcitrance. Nor could she allow into her mind the smallest twinge of doubt. From the very beginning her actions had been a gesture of protest directed at Philipp, a defiant snub to show him that she really was spiritually a Queen, if not in reality. Philipp had been assigned a role in this drama and it would never have crossed Louise's mind that he might not play the role allotted him. Louise did not recognise that with each flounce in her drama she was burning the bridges behind her.

Did she ever ask herself what her fate would be if Géza had disappeared? Louise by this time needed Géza. On her own she could not cope. If Géza had left her she would have been forced to crawl back to Philipp, tail between her legs, to beg for his forgiveness and his support. And what sort of reception would he have given her? Nothing could have been more painful for Louise. These were shadows she could never have looked into. So she didn't. She lived for the moment and in the moment and found the experience more intense and more vivid than anything she had ever known.

In later years Louise was to remember this as the happiest period in her life. It was the last carefree and happy period she ever had.

Chapter 90

Nothing lasts forever. Even the happiest days come to an end.

8th May 1898 – this was the day when Princess Louise of Belgium was forcibly taken to the clinic of Dr. Obersteiner in Döbling. Dr. Obersteiner specialised in the care of the mentally ill and many of his patients were so deranged that they needed restraint. Years later Louise would remember that she found herself in a room that resembled a prison cell with a grille in the door through which her gaolers could watch her. Over the window there were iron bars. Below was a sandy courtyard where the walls were covered with mattresses to prevent anyone there from hurting themselves. Looking out that first day, Louise saw a madman throwing himself about the yard and endlessly screaming in terrifying tones.

Géza himself was also in prison. Their wild escapade across Europe had cost both of them their independence and their freedom.

In 1898 Louise was still legally the wife of Philipp von Saxe-Coburg. It was Philipp, largely driven by the demands of Franz Joseph, who had had her brought to Dr. Obersteiner's clinic, to a place where Géza could no longer reach her and where she could no longer embarrass him. Embarrassment wasn't the only issue. Franz Joseph had terrible doubts over how all this would end and his great fear was that Géza Mattaćić might kill Louise and then himself rather than allow them to be taken back, as it were, into control. Franz Joseph feared another Mayerling with all that would follow if such a thing happened. The pair had to be separated for political reasons.

The man who undertook to make the appropriate arrangements was Adolf Bachrach, a government councillor and Philipp's lawyer. Bachrach spent about a week in Agram working out the lay of the land. Then he went over to Lobor and sought a meeting with Géza. Bachrach offered to arrange for the whole affair of the forged signatures to be quietly dealt with. He may have hinted that the matter of Géza's situation with the army could possibly also be sorted out satisfactorily. He then wished to know whether it was Louise's desire to seek a divorce from her husband. This he needed confirmed by Louise herself. And Bachrach rode away.

Louise and Géza must have been over the moon. At a stroke all their current problems would be removed. They could look forward to freedom and a new life together. They must have fizzed with excitement. They would have made plan after plan for their future together. Where would they go?

Belgium? Louise would have liked that. Géza may have preferred England where surely Louise could be confident of the protection of Queen Victoria. There would be greater safety the further they were from the Austro-Hungarian Empire. And on and on...

A few days later Bachrach was back; this time he was accompanied by a notary from Zlatar. For everything to be arranged there were papers to be signed. Géza had to agree to certain conditions but amongst these conditions was a commitment that he would separate from Louise and never see her again. Géza refused to sign.

Perhaps Géza was not too surprised when a couple of days later an officer from his regiment arrived at Lobor with an official order for him to present himself to his superior officer. There is no doubt that Géza was far from confident that he would come away from this with his freedom but on the evening of 8th May he and Louise, accompanied by Countess Függer, set off for Agram where they stayed at the Hotel Prukner. Géza's big concern was that he was technically a deserter. He had not presented himself to his commanding officer when the period of absence that he had been accorded came to an end. He had left the country without permission. He probably had no idea what he could do or should do in the situation.

The following morning the door to their room was broken down and two military figures burst into the room. Géza was arrested and dragged off to the local military prison where he remained imprisoned for the next eight months.

Back at the Hotel Prukner Bachrach had arrived for Louise. He had brought with him an officer from the Viennese police and Dr. Hinterstoisser from the Obersteiner Clinic.

Louise was still in bed when they entered her room. They refused to leave her alone to get dressed but remained in the room while the Countess Marie Függer helped her dress. Bachrach placed a document before Louise. He was offering her the choice of returning to her husband in Vienna or going to a clinic for her health. It never crossed Louise's mind what sort of clinic this would be; she assumed that it would be the kind of clinic she had often been to before for various health reasons.

From that moment on Louise was a prisoner, too. The staff in the clinic had orders to keep her permanently under surveillance and to treat her at all times as though she were at risk of harming herself. Dr. Obersteiner, who had had no part in the arrangements for Louise, set about assessing her mental condition and her health and after six weeks he made out a report stating that Louise's mental faculties were completely normal. Certainly, she was nervous and upset by her situation and during those weeks she had been sunk in a state of apathy and dejection, even refusing to concern herself over normal hygiene or personal care, but Dr. Obersteiner did not consider this abnormal.

However, Dr. Obersteiner's orders came from the authorities in Vienna.

On 16th June 1898 Louise was interviewed about the forged signature on the credit note. Louise never ever admitted that she forged her sister's signature. She could not deny her own signature on the document: "Of course, my signature was on the bill," she said, "But my sister's signature was forged at a later date – who forged it and why??" In her book this reads like a rhetorical question. Louise goes on with an extremely confused account, the gist of which was that Philipp, helped by a whole bunch of cronies and bureaucrats, wanted out of spite to befoul her name and crush her entirely.

During these interviews Louise was supported by her own lawyer, Dr. Neuda. It had been Géza who found Neuda for Louise but the lawyer chose to follow the line that Philipp was proposing. Philipp's great concern was that the minimum of blame should be placed upon Louise and in order to achieve this he wanted to deflect the blame on to Géza.

The matter of the forged signature has never been fully cleared up. In their separate interviews both Géza and Louise gave a variety of versions of how it came about, each trying to deflect culpability from the other. Each changed their story as they perceived which way the wind was blowing. Louise was growing ever more apprehensive about Géza's fate and she turned to Dr. Neuda in the hopes that there might be something he could do for her lover.

On 20th June Louise demanded that Neuda come to Döbling. She then showed Neuda a letter she had received from Géza together with a copy of his statement in Agram. Neuda was astounded. How had she succeeded in getting such a letter? Louise confided in him that she had for some time been in contact with Géza. Madame Ida Jelaćić was their intermediary. She was the sister of Artur von Ozegovics, a neighbour and old friend of Géza. Ida Jelaćić would slip the secret missives to Countess Marie Függer who would pass them surreptitiously to Louise. The replies returned via the same route.

This story panicked Neuda and he set about doing all he could to persuade Louise to stay away from Géza and to abandon all attempts to communicate with him. He promised Louise that Géza's prospects would be so much better if there were no contact between them. In fact, the situation for Géza was grim.

In December Géza was brought before a military tribunal where every effort was made to prove his dishonesty. He was found guilty, disgraced, stripped of all titles, expelled from the army and condemned to a six year prison sentence in the Möllersdorf Prison. His treatment there was particularly harsh and included whole days without food and two whole months each year in solitary confinement.

By the time Géza was taken down to face his sentence Louise had already been moved from the Obersteiner Clinic. Dr. Obersteiner refused to see her as mentally deranged and he no longer wanted her to remain in his clinic. On 21st November 1898 Louise was transferred to the Sanatorium Lindenhof in Saxony. This had been chosen because King Leopold II of Belgium refused to allow his daughter to return to Belgium and Philipp von Coburg did not wish her to be within the Austro-Hungarian Empire. The sanatorium was in the Purkersdorf region of Saxony not far from the capital, Dresden, and the nearest railway station was in the small town of Coswig. The head of the sanatorium was Dr. Rüdiger and Louise's care fell to Dr. Pierson.

Louise was taken to her new place of care without Countess Marie Függer who was retired, largely because of the part she had played in helping Louise remain in contact with Géza. The departure of Marie, who had for so long been such a friend to Louise, was crushing for Louise. Marie Függer was replaced by Anna von Gebauer, who was selected by Philipp. Philipp considered Anna «très bien». She was a spinster who had reached an age where she could consider herself on the shelf. No doubt, Anna was chosen as someone who would recognise that her duty was to the Coburg family but possibly Philipp also had an eye to whether she would suit Louise. At any rate, Louise took to her and liked her. Along with Anna von Gebauer a second lady-in-waiting was appointed for Louise, Olga Börner.

At this point it must have seemed to all that the whole matter had been sorted out and that the futures of Géza and Louise were certain and settled.

Chapter 91

Géza von Mattaćić was born on 19th December 1867 at Tomasevié. His father, Kalmán, was an alcoholic who would drink himself to death while Géza was still a small child. In fact, it is not certain whether Kalmán was his father. His mother, Anna (née Orsich), seems to have been able to introduce her lover, Count Oscar Kéglévić, into the family circle for some years whilst her husband was still around. However, the day came when Anna gathered up her two small sons, Béla and Géza, and left Tomasevié to go and live with Oscar Kéglévić in the family castle at Lobor, a few miles north of Agram. After Kalmán's death Anna married Oscar. Géza from the age of ten was sent to boarding school in Varaždin and from then on he only saw his family during the holidays. When his school years came to an end Géza joined the army and became a lieutenant in the 5th Regiment of Uhlans.

Géza had a playful personality and quickly won over his army companions. He was soon regarded by his officers as a natural leader. Early on in his life he showed unusual skill in getting people to do what he wanted. Few would have noticed it at the time but he was also good at getting people to do things they felt uncomfortable doing. He delighted in taking risks. He was especially good at leading his fellow officers astray and ending up in a whole variety of pranks. These usually resulted in large debts which Count Oscar Kéglévić ended up paying off.

There can be little doubt that Géza's mischievous character had enormous appeal for Louise in those dark years when she realised that her love affair with Döry had faded into nothing and he was gone from her forever. Géza brightened Louise's spirits and gave her a reason to look forward to the future.

But the surprising thing was that their lives should become knit in an indissoluble bond that was to last until their deaths. This was a bond that was strong enough to survive all the trials and tribulations that the two of them had to endure. As far as Louise was concerned, with Döry the attraction had been a dark, compulsive need. She had been caught up in a physical hunger for him that was all the more powerful because it could never be assuaged. Géza, on the other hand, could make her feel light-hearted and playful, warm and alive. This gave Géza enormous power over her. She just melted into obedience to him and loved the feelings that this provoked.

Géza was almost certainly drawn to Louise because she was royalty and presumably very, very rich. But for most of the twenty-five years that they were together she was completely excluded from her own family and there was never enough money. Many of those years were spent on the run. If what Géza wanted were the trappings and aura that went with wealth and connections with royalty he had turned to the wrong person.

Yet Géza supported her, he looked after her and he guided her through everything that happened to them. And he controlled her. More than that, he must have worked hard and endlessly to keep her spirits up. Did Géza ever have doubts about what he was doing? Or did he only realise where things were going when it was too late to turn back? Did he ever want to turn back?

The bond that kept them together was intense but was it one of love? Was either of them genuinely in love with the other? It is not even clear how much of an intimate relationship they had, and if they did, how long it lasted.

Géza was certainly not faithful to Louise. Increasingly he treated Louise like a child. And Louise began to regress into a childish mindset. She found companionship in the company of her dogs. For many years he seems to have had a normal man-and-woman relationship quite openly with other women. He made little attempt to hide this either from the other women or from Louise. The most significant of these other relationships was with Maria Stöger.

At the beginning of June 1899 there was a new employee in the prison canteen at Möllersdorf, a young woman called Maria Stöger. Her father was Rudolf Bog, a Czech soldier. Her mother was Croatian. Maria was married to a Viennese army officer, Karl Stöger, who was twelve years older than her. After six years of marriage to Karl their relationship was more a matter of form than reality. Maria soon separated from her husband and moved to the town of Möllersdorf where she found lodgings with a local postman.

In most of the literature Maria is described as having had her imagination fired up by all the stories she read in the popular press about the unfortunate Croatian officer and the Princess whose love for each other had led them to risk all... She is described as having decided she had to do something to help this ill-treated man, and this decision had led her to seek out employment in the prison. But how much was Maria committed to doing all she could for Géza before she ever came face to face with him? Given Géza's personality, it appears far more likely that he was able to inspire her feelings for him after she had started work at Möllersdorf and then he was increasingly able to control the way things were going.

The one thing that is certain is that she went to work at the prison. Once she had access to the prison she was able to go anywhere within its confines and she was soon drawn to Géza. They were able to communicate with considerable freedom because both spoke Croatian and few of the prison officers were able to understand them. And before long she had fallen into his arms. That it was possible for these two to do this and get away with it, even for a period, seems incredible but her affair with Géza was to result in a child.

On 21st July 1900 Maria gave birth to a son, Alfred. Maria already had a two-year-old son, Oskar. In later years Maria would insist that she did not enter her employment at Möllersdorf until January 1900 and that Alfred was also Karl's son. But Karl Stöger always refused to recognise Alfred as his son.

By the following year Karl Stöger had protested to the commandant of the prison that through her employment Maria's affections had been stolen from him. The prison authorities were already by then taking a particular interest in Maria Stöger. They considered her behaviour towards Géza inappropriate and she was being watched. She was suspected of passing extra food to Géza and also of smuggling letters out for him. But the chief cook in the prison, Frau Ilona Varga, begged the commandant to allow Maria to continue in her position in the prison canteen service. This turned out to be only a temporary reprieve. Maria lost her job there a year later.

Maria did not return to her marital home. Instead she took Oskar and Alfred to live with her and she earned her living as a seamstress. She also continued to do work for Ilona Varga. And all the while she was very busy seeking ways of helping Géza.

In October 1900 she had succeeded in winning the support of a Hungarian lawyer, named Polonyi, who offered to help without demanding any payment for his services. How much did Géza point the way and show Maria how to make an appropriate approach to someone of some standing? By the end of 1901 she had further succeeded in persuading Friedrich Austerlitz, the editor of the socialist newspaper *Arbeiter Zeitung*, to publish a series of inflammatory articles presenting the whole Mattačić affair as a miscarriage of justice. These articles attracted the attention of a socialist member of the Austrian parliament, Ignaz Daszynski, who was ready to speak out on behalf of Géza. Through Daszynski Géza was also able to draw upon the support of Albert Ignaz Südekum, from the German government.

All these people represented an immense driving force in support of Géza's cause.

But the immediate result of all this for Géza was a savage worsening of his situation because the Austrian authorities were furious about the publicity and particularly about the details that were made public. Géza's few privileges were removed and the commandant of the prison lost his job. The new commandant was a much harder man who unbendingly enforced a relentless rigour. Géza found himself locked in a dark cell without light for weeks on end.

Then suddenly and unexpectedly on 26th August 1902 Géza was released. He headed for Vienna where he found Maria waiting for him. Maria had installed her family in a small apartment in the Floridsdorf district and here she envisaged a future life for Géza, herself and her two boys. She imagined that she would continue working and Géza, too, would find work, such as running a tobacco kiosk or serving beer behind a bar. A working class life where money was always short but you got by.

Géza was appalled. Now, as had not been the case until this moment, it came home to him that he was no longer an elegant, titled officer in the Imperial Army to whom a special courtesy was ever due. What Maria imagined would be their future was one long existence of drudgery. Nevertheless, it had been his association with a royal Princess which had brought him to this and it seemed to Géza that his Princess would provide the way out of it.

By October 1902 he had arrived in Dresden and even been out to the sanatorium where Louise was being held.

There was a small café on an embankment alongside the railway leading to the station at Coswig. Here Géza and a friend of his sat drinking coffee and watching the sanatorium villa hour after hour. Once they went down to the road that led to the sanatorium and gazed at the huge iron gates that kept its inmates inside. The villa was surrounded by a high wall, in its own way a prison, too.

Then they returned to the café where they entered into conversation with the girl on the till. Cautiously they talked disingenuously about a mass of different things until Géza felt it was safe to make some throwaway remark about the 'mad Princess von Coburg'. The girl laughed and said, "What you don't know is that she is no more mad than we are!"

Then, according to Géza, at that moment the gates of the sanatorium swung open and a small carriage was driven out. Géza would not immediately have paid very much attention to this particular carriage but then he saw hidden inside was a lady dressed in black. It hit him at that moment that this was Louise. Géza held himself still, watching. He watched the carriage drive away down the road into the forest and later he watched it return. He watched the heavy gates swing open again and Louise disappeared inside. The girl in the café remarked that that was the Princess herself and she went out for a drive like that every afternoon.

The next day Géza and his companion were there again, this time with bicycles. They came upon Louise's carriage and rode past it. Louise was looking out the window of the carriage and suddenly she recognised Géza. He looked at her and she at him but both had the presence of mind not to show in any way that they had recognised each other.

Louise's heart must have been so aflutter! Did she sleep that night?

Not even her doctors ever suggested that Louise showed the symptoms and behaviour that could be described as mad. What one and all stressed was how childish she was and often they added comments about how passive she was and indifferent to the things they expected her to take an interest in.

She did ask to have a piano but never played it until Anna von Gebauer pushed her into taking a little interest in music and arranged for Louise to have some piano lessons. Her one pleasure was her little black dachshund called Kiki; Kiki replaced another dachshund called Wastl which was shot by mistake by one of the gardeners. Louise loved Kiki all the more because she was so upset about how Wastl had met his end. She cosseted and protected Kiki.

When you look back over Louise's life it seems that she had always led a very childish life anyway. When she first arrived in Vienna the impression she gave was of a delightful, playful and childish personality. When she wanted anything she demanded it and she got it. When she did not get it she seems to have sulked and taken umbrage over it – this is the impression you gain from her own memoirs. She had always been told what to do and had done it, often resentfully. When Philipp was not with her she was in the care of her mother-in-law, the Princess Clémentine, who, in fact, mothered her. When she was taken first to the Obersteiner Clinic in Döbling and then to the Lindenhof Clinic she was not mad but could she have led an independent life, taking control of her own affairs? The answer was almost certainly no.

Louise shocked her doctors when she showed absolutely no reaction upon hearing that her mother had died. Dr. Pierson broke the news to her while they were out walking in the grounds of the clinic. What followed was a strangely one-sided conversation – the doctor speaking of his sympathies for Louise's loss while Louise carried on talking about how wonderful Géza was and giving vent to all her bitterness against Philipp.

What were Philipp's plans for Louise? In one of Philipp's letters to Duke Ernst von Coburg, he made it clear that he and certain officials at the Imperial Court in Vienna were agreed that if Louise could be declared 'insane' this would prevent her ever being brought before a court of law by her creditors. Such a court case would cause a major scandal, not just for himself and his own family but also for the Emperor and the Habsburg family.

It is likely that Philipp envisaged Louise remaining in some clinic or other, written off as mentally deranged, just as her aunt, the Empress Charlotte of Mexico, was. He would have preferred it if Louise could have returned to Belgium to spend the rest of her days in a Belgian sanatorium. She would live her life in considerable comfort, cosseted and protected and spoilt and given everything she wanted if at all possible. She herself would be treated in much the same way that she treated Kiki.

Philipp had now reached the point where he wanted to wash his hands of Louise, especially since her debts had reached levels where his own wealth was painfully reduced. By April 1899 Philipp had paid out over a million gulden, an enormous sum of money. And he had no way of knowing how many more demands might be made of him in the future. Philipp had needed to turn to the head of the Coburg family to beg for some financial assistance. But he continued to try to sort out the mess that Louise's spending extravaganza had caused and he remained concerned about the difficulties faced by businesses which had extended credit to Louise.

Philipp was shocked to learn of Géza's release. Philipp suspected that Géza would set about seeking to get his conviction overthrown. Whilst still in prison Géza had already tried twice. If, now that he was out of prison, Géza succeeded in getting a retrial this would not be a military trial held behind closed doors but a civil trial in the full glare of publicity. Furthermore, if Géza succeeded in getting a retrial his lawyers would certainly want to call upon both Philipp and Stéphanie to give evidence. The thought of that made Philipp cringe. The only good thing, as far as Philipp was concerned, would be that after such a retrial Géza would be likely to leave Austria permanently.

All of this came out in a letter dated 4th September 1902 from Philipp to Stéphanie and at the end of the letter Philipp added that he did not believe that Géza Mattaćić would risk some sort of attack upon Philipp himself or attempt to get Louise out of the sanatorium at Coswig. He was wrong. Philipp, had he ever found himself in Géza's shoes, could never, ever have envisaged the kind of imaginative, risky, adventurous actions that Géza was willing to undertake.

Géza must have known that he was taking huge risks. Or perhaps he did not. Is it possible that Géza was a man with no sense of risk, or of danger, or of the possibility of losing everything? Nevertheless, although he had been released he had not been pardoned. He was still under police surveillance and that he must have known too, or at least suspected. He must have been aware that the authorities would not have hesitated taking him back into custody if they could have found some justification for doing so. His situation was precarious.

However, Géza was not just a man willing to risk everything but also a man who could win the total support of just about any woman and most men. Maria was the first of a number. If it had not been for these women it is hard to imagine how Géza could have succeeded in springing the trap around Louise.

Out there in Coswig Géza was busy. The next day brought heavy rain and, although Géza was back on the lookout for Louise's daily carriage ride into the forest, thanks to the weather there was no sign of her. On 12th October Géza – alone this time – saw Louise again. He had gone back to the place where he had seen the carriage and there he waited in hope. The rain had passed and the sky above was lit with sunlight. The woods were full of the moist scent of damp, autumnal leaves. It was pleasant waiting but Géza was impatient and barely noticed all the soft sounds around him. And it was not long before the carriage arrived. Louise herself was driving it and at her side was Anna von Gebauer. Louise pulled up the horses and she and Anna got out to walk away into the woods. Géza followed them at a distance. Then Anna turned and came back to him. She had precise instructions: he was to do exactly what she said and only that. Géza agreed.

"She was leaning against a birch tree. She held out her hand to me. Her eyes were full of tears and she cried out, 'There really is a God!' I found her completely unchanged from what she had been when we were torn apart. She was lucid. She moved in the same way she always had. She had the same playful air she had always had but her face was marked by her suffering. Yet the lines that pain had etched upon her seemed suddenly softened and her beauty struck me as never before. She had her dachshund with her and it was pulling at the lead she was holding."

But their exchange swiftly turned to their situation and the risks that each faced. Louise told Géza that until a few days earlier she had been living in hopes of being transferred to another sanatorium where she was not constantly under surveillance. Anna von Gebauer added that a telegramme from Bachrach had arrived at Lindenhof with the news that Géza Mattačić was out of prison and had left Vienna to travel to Dresden. So the hope of Louise going to another, less controlling sanatorium had been crushed.

Anna then pressed the pair to end their meeting but she promised that Louise would be at the same place at the same time the next day. Anna von Gebauer was supposed to be guarding Louise according to Philipp's instructions – yet, here she was helping Louise and her lover to meet. It seems that Anna, like Maria Stöger, had lost her heart to Géza and now, for him, she was prepared to risk anything to help him and Louise (though there were occasions when she may have had second thoughts). How had Géza in so short a time managed to bring things to this point?

Anna was the second of Géza's adoring women. In Anna Géza had the messenger he needed to take his messages to Louise and to bring hers to him. But for the next few days Géza was unable to see Louise. Anna brought him news that Louise, on returning to the sanatorium, was so agitated and upset that she had been confined to her room.

Louise during her time shut away in the sanatorium had been suffering from psoriasis. This unpleasant, painful skin disease caused her considerable distress. It worsened whenever she was upset or emotional and she would scratch away at the lesions on her skin until they bled badly. Sometimes she had scratched large areas completely raw so that she could not bear the feel of clothing against her skin. She also tore at her hair which often resulted in small bald patches. She could become enraged and demented with pain. Her guards frequently interpreted her restless behaviour as an indication of her mental abnormality. Clearly, with the arrival of Géza in the vicinity, her skin condition had flared up painfully. As Louise appeared more than usually worked up her supervision was increased.

Anna pressed Géza to leave the region because everyone was on the lookout for him.

It was six months before Géza made his next move. He and Maria Stöger arrived again at Coswig. This, in a way, was a calculated risk. Géza had won Anna's support and was confident that he could rely upon her to act as his messenger to Louise. But it seems unlikely that he had told her about Maria, and quite possibly he hadn't told Maria about Anna.

Géza remained in their hotel room because he did not wish to be tracked down too soon. Instead Maria went out to find out all she could. Maria managed to make contact with Olga Börner, Louise's second lady-in-waiting – had Géza instructed Maria to seek out Olga specifically? And Olga agreed to pass on a letter to Louise. Was this how Anna found out about Maria's role in Géza's plans?

Soon Anna von Gebauer was seen in the vicinity of the hotel where Géza and Maria were staying and there was something about this that raised suspicions. In the meantime Olga had turned up at the hotel. And there was something about Olga Börner that made Géza's antennae twitch – he did not trust her. He and Maria left the hotel upon the instant to hurry to the station and board the first train for Dresden. They did not even stop to pack their bags. It was fortunate that they moved so quickly because within minutes of their departure some policemen arrived demanding to search the hotel.

In spite of Géza's initial suspicions about Olga Börner, she was to become the third of Géza's adoring women, supporting him in his efforts to release Louise from her prison and willing to go with the pair of them wherever they went, living out much of the rest of her life in the small entourage of people who served Géza and Louise.

All this seems to imply that Géza had considerable confidence that he had the loyalty of his little team of adoring women and that they would do what he wanted them to do. He does not appear to have taken their individual feelings too much into account.

From then on Louise's permission to leave the grounds of the clinic and go for drives in the birchwoods around was severely curtailed. But it also seems to have been the case that Louise's psoriasis had got seriously worse and she was being treated with medicaments that contained arsenic. The arsenic may have been building up in her body.

At the end of 1902 Dr. Pierson reported that her mental state had steadily worsened. She gabbled senseless things, did not appear to know where she was, took no thought to her appearance or hygiene and sat endlessly scratching. She bit her fingernails and refused to wash. Pierson said bluntly that she was dirty. She would sit for hours on end, utterly immobile staring in front of herself with frozen wide eyes. Everything around her that was green or yellow had to be removed. She would not even accept these colours in the food on her plate.

She talked a lot as though she saw herself as almost perfect in every way, the flawless ideal in feminine form of purity, loyalty, magnanimity and noblesse. She saw herself as an untouched virgin, a holy bride, an innocent white lily who would pass into history along with Queen Elizabeth I of England or Mary Stuart.

Chapter 92

In the wider world Louise's situation continued to attract considerable interest. The newspapers showed her story in a sympathetic and romantic light. The popular press took a vehement stand against the harsh guardians who had seen fit to lock up this innocent and hapless Princess... This was embarrassing to the medical profession and to Philipp as more and more doctors were brought in to add their contribution to the assessment of Louise's mental state.

In September 1903 it was proposed that Louise should be taken somewhere in the south where the warmer weather would benefit her health. Dr. Pierson would go with her as her doctor; so too would Anna von Gebauer and Olga Börner. They planned to go to Venice. Certainly, Dr. Pierson gave some thought to the danger that Géza Mattaćić might make a new attempt to see Louise. But he was reassured that Géza Mattaćić had by now no money for travelling anywhere and if by some extraordinary chance he did succeed in reaching Louise Pierson was confident that Louise could be swiftly brought back to Lindenhof. It pleased Dr. Pierson that Louise received the news of this trip to Venice with enthusiasm and her mood was completely altered.

Even before their departure there were problems with Louise. She absolutely had to have forty-five pairs of silk stockings, twenty-five pairs of shoes and fourteen parasols. She also wished to take with her a large number of old blouses that in times of pent-up fury she had torn into strips and could never again wear. Olga Börner had to restrain her, insisting that she could only take with her two suitcases, a hatbox and a handbag.

But when they got to Venice Louise was annoyed to find that because their costs had to be kept under control she was not to be allowed to buy all the pictures and lace that she desired. Immediately she sunk into despondency and there in the street she crumpled into a ball sobbing her heart out. She could not believe that she was now expected to live in such a restricted way – she, a royal Princess! She believed that Dr. Pierson should have demanded more money for their journey – in any case, there was no need to pay the hotel bill. Louise could not understand why Olga Börner kept on so about paying the bills! This was a quite unreasonable idea, a mania with Olga, really, a disease!

One foggy evening she went out into the San Marco Square in a long white dress embroidered with little red sequins. She looked so extraordinary she attracted a great deal of attention which she revelled in. She wanted her photograph taken, and when the photographer told he could not take a photograph because there was not enough light, she lost her temper, waving her arms around and stamping her feet in frustration.

It was not long before Dr. Pierson began to think that this experiment was not a good idea. Louise's behaviour became ever more wild and unrestrained. She whined and complained the whole time. She would burst into tears at the smallest thing. She would collect up her used sanitary towels and place them with her underwear. She also caused huge embarrassment in public. She would suddenly stop and speak to complete strangers as though they were well-known to her. She would suddenly start screaming and shouting and end up sobbing loudly. If they went into a restaurant she would head for the trolley of patisseries and cakes and grab as many as she could, stuffing them into her mouth. She would attempt to steal sweets, sneaking them into her bag in the belief that her actions went unnoticed. At meals in the hotel she would squash her bread into little pellets and stick them in her nose and in her ears. Everywhere they went she complained about the food. And all the while she talked endlessly about Géza Mattaćić and kept looking around for him.

When they got back to Coswig Louise insisted that she had proved she could live perfectly well without all this supervision.

Dr. Pierson was a glutton for punishment – he agreed in August 1904 to give Louise another break from her life in the Lindenhof Clinic and to take her to Bad Elster for a cure – but extra guardians would be needed to assist in controlling Louise. The police in Bad Elster should also be informed and required to provide extra protection. So Dr. Pierson got the support of a second doctor, Dr. Mauss.

Somehow Géza Mattaćić got wind of this second trip. He and Maria Stöger were fired up with excitement. This, they believed, was the moment they had been waiting for. They were gripped by a now-or-never feeling, especially Géza. All those months he had felt watched and followed, and with good reason: he was watched and followed. But he was also not wholly confident that his adoring women were completely committed. Each of them was doing what she was doing because she was drawn to him and perhaps in love with him – and was there also some rivalry between them? Did his single-minded focus upon Louise not spark jealous doubts in them? He must have persuaded them that Louise no longer had any hold over his heart but she should one day be a source of money for them all. How did Géza manage his team so that they remained committed to their project?

He had by now decided to dispense with the services of Dr. Neuda and turned to a different lawyer, Dr. Siegfried Stimmer. The extraordinary thing was that the services these men rendered Géza were never paid for and they knew all along that they would never be paid. Géza's ability to get a team around him committed to his wishes and not expecting much or any reward for their services was astonishing. Dr. Stimmer later wrote how Géza had touched his heart and won his sympathy for the unfortunate Princess immured in a clinic for the mentally deranged.

Bad Elster was in Saxony and Géza was forbidden from setting foot in Saxony. This edict had resulted from some small remark let slip inadvertently by Anna von Gebauer which had excited the suspicions of Louise's guardians. Had this merely been an unfortunate slip of the tongue or perhaps Anna was indeed not entirely to be trusted? Géza was not sure but he chose to continue to give her the benefit of the doubt. This was a brave thing to do because he now intended to ignore that edict and enter Saxony. If caught, he would end up behind bars again.

There was a further risk he was willing to take: he believed that their chances would be far better if Louise was informed of their plans. On 28th July 1904 Dr. Pierson took Louise to an art exhibition in Dresden. When Géza found this out he too went to Dresden. The moment Louise came into the exhibition hall she saw Géza and rushed over to him. It says a lot about Dr. Pierson's character that he seems to have had no idea how to handle this situation. He decided that the one thing he did not want was a major kerfuffle in public. Instead he allowed the pair a short conversation together.

Short it may have been, but it was long enough for Géza to tell Louise what was afoot. At moments like this Louise was capable of pulling herself together and playing her part with some dignity. Yet the risk that Louise would give everything away must have been enormous. For months Louise had been regressing into an ever greater childishness. She was now not far short of her fiftieth birthday and she had been living imprisoned and cossetted at Lindenhof for some six years. How well did Géza understand her state of mind?

Géza now withdrew and laid low. Instead a friend, Joseph Weitzer,[21] travelled to Bad Elster to rent a house and find out the lay of the land. Weitzer also had to find out for Géza where and how it might possible to smuggle Louise over the border from Saxony into Bavaria. She was going to need to be smuggled out because she had no passport and would have been stopped at any official border crossing.

On 11th August Dr. Pierson and Louise drove in a motorcar the hundred miles from Coswig to Bad Elster. The dachsund, Kiki, went too. Anna von Gebauer, Olga Börner and Dr. Mauss came separately by train with all Louise's baggage.

We can imagine that Louise enjoyed making her entrance into the

---

[21] Joseph Weitzer may not have been his real name. It was later suggested that he was Géza's cousin, Count Orsich. Another suggestion was that he was from Wien-Floridsdorf where he was the tenant manager of a bar under the town hall.

Hotel Wettiner-Hof where the hotel manager, Julius Bretholz, stepped forward to greet her and welcome her to his hotel with all the obsequious courtesy due to a princess. This meant so much to Louise. A glow ran through her whole being.

Louise then went upstairs to her suite on the first floor, which consisted of a small salon, a bedroom and a balcony. There was only one door from her suite on to the corridor and opposite her suite was a room where a guard was posted at all times. To the left of Louise's suite were rooms for Anna and Olga. Every night Louise was locked into her room, the whole hotel was locked and police guards placed outside. Every morning Louise would leave the hotel to walk to the Badehaus to take the waters. Every morning she was accompanied by Anna and Dr. Mauss and two policemen followed behind. A police cordon surrounded her wherever she went and whatever she did. When she took the waters four policemen were present. When she took a mud bath[22] a policeman stood outside the door guarding her.

Rather less blatant was the gathering of Géza and his team, but they were gathering nevertheless. Two women together with a four-year-old child arrived to rent the Villa Jupiter. One called herself 'Maria Kunze', the other was Frau Schmidt. Joseph Weitzer was not hiding behind another false name and he had booked into the Wettiner-Hof quite openly.

Géza himself had left Dresden, driven by a certain Herr Thormann, and arrived on the outskirts of Bad Elster. He booked into a guest house and booked out the next day. He moved to another guest house nearby and booked out the next day. In the space of seven days he moved seven times, ending up at the Pension Wörgel. In the evenings he received visits from a 'Frau Schubert' who wished to go for drives around the town and enjoy the evenings. On these drives the coachman observed that 'Frau Schubert' was joined in the carriage by a number of different people.

In the Wettiner-Hof Weitzer had bribed the head waiter and Herr Thormann had slipped a sizeable sum of money to one of the guards whose job it was to watch Louise's suite from across the corridor. Each morning the head waiter delivered Louise's breakfast tray together with a copy of Le Figaro newspaper. One day between the pages of the newspaper there was an envelope for Louise. Géza's plan was about to take off.

But it very nearly all went wrong.

The conspirators had succeeded in making a wax model of the lock to Louise's room from which a second key was cut. But traces of the wax were found on the lock and orders given immediately to change the lock. The head waiter, however, managed to obtain another wax model of the new lock and another key was cut. All this meant that the day planned for

---

[22] Louise needed mud baths for her psoriasis; they did much to soothe her inflamed skin.

Louise's escape had to be postponed by twenty-four hours.

But now Dr. Mauss began to notice that Louise was becoming more and more nervous. He decided that it might be better to shorten Louise's stay in Bad Elster and to return to Coswig. Louise protested wildly and emotionally until finally Dr. Pierson agreed to stand by the original plan.

Wednesday, 31st August was a warm, sunny day. Louise was awake early that morning. This in itself was surprising since Louise frequently slept until midday. But on such a beautiful day she wished to have a game of tennis. From the tennis court she was accompanied to the Badehaus where for the last time she took the waters, followed by a mud bath. Back at the hotel she dressed herself all in white and in the evening she went to the theatre where – appropriately enough – there was a performance of Mozart's *Die Entführung aus dem Serail*. Before Louise returned to the Wettiner-Hof she had a short exchange with the Director of the Badehaus and promised him that on the following Friday she would attend a concert given by Hanna Proft, the famous singer.

Back in her room Olga Börner helped Louise undress and left her for the night, locking the door behind her. The moment she heard the key turn in the door Louise set about dressing herself again, this time in a brown dress. She stuffed her jewellery into a bag and picked up her shoes. For about an hour she waited beside the locked door. She became frightened that Kiki would realise that her mistress was dressed to go out and might get excited and start to bark. Louise had been told firmly that Kiki had to be left behind. The danger of him barking was too great.

Finally, the door to her suite very, very slowly opened and there was the head waiter. He took her shoes and hurried her down the corridor, down the backstairs and then before them a door opened. The head waiter gave her her shoes and pushed her through the door and then disappeared into the darkness. Waiting for her here were Joseph Weitzer and Herr Thormann. Weitzer helped her put on her shoes and then lifted her bodily on to the windowsill. He gave her a push and Louise fell to the ground where Géza was waiting to catch her. Weitzer and Thormann followed.

There was a full moon that night and the sky was lit with silvery shimmer – dangerously so, it was almost as bright as day. The four figures tiptoed around the edge of the garden over to some greenhouses where they paused for breath. They then continued, making their way down to the road.

Here they expected to find Maria Stöger waiting for them in a carriage. Instead there were two policemen hanging around engrossed in conversation. The little party waited and waited, hidden amongst the bushes. At last the policemen wound up their conversation and each went his separate way. Still they waited until they could hear the carriage approaching. By now the moon had gone behind a cloud and the night was dark around them. They drove away.

They headed for nearby Hof over the border where there was a station. It was necessary for them to take a long and roundabout route to Hof in order to be able to cross the border at a point where there was no border control. Thanks to the various delays when they arrived at the station the last train had already departed. This forced them to find a small hotel with a room where Louise and Maria could rest for the remainder of the night. The train they caught the following morning took them to Berlin.

They were free.

For the press this was the great story of the day and right across Europe the headlines blazoned their varying accounts of what had happened and everybody who had any part in it produced their own version. They played on all the romantic aspects of the story. It was all lush and florid, a great love story to stir the hearts of people whose own lives were drab and routine.

Yet when all the furore had died down, Louise and Géza were now faced with a precarious, rootless existence, zigzagging across Europe, endlessly moving on leaving appalling debts behind them, and there was to be no escape from this for the rest of their days. Again and again they found people touched by their plight, willing to help them, people in many instances who lost all they had.

One such couple were the Inhoffens. Walther Inhoffen was the son of a small businessman in Bonn. His father was a careful businessman who succeeded in building up a very tidy fortune which came to Walther when his father died in a car accident in 1907. Walther first met Louise when he was trying to sell some horses which Louise wished to buy from him. Louise offered him a credit note for the horses which Walther refused. In the end Walther gave way and Louise got the horses and promised that Walther would get his money in three months' time. Walther wanted to sell the horses in order to have the money to take his very new bride on a magical trip round the world. The journey was put off and put off. Louise was constantly with the Inhoffens, full of her pitiful story of how she had been treated. In a way, she blew their minds away. Here they were in the close presence of a Princess, a beautiful Princess, an unhappy Princess.

Walther Inhoffen: "She would recount in tears her desperate situation and she succeeded in winning our sympathy and our compassion. Little by little we came to have such confidence in her and every day we spent several hours with her... Every day we went out on excursions, we ate together or we went to the theatre. She painted a picture of her sad life and how all had abandoned her now."

So the Inhoffens kept giving Louise money and she promised them that they would get it all back. "Thanks to us she was able to relax for a few hours without financial worries." Walther Inhoffen felt a surge of pride that he was able to give her the help her own father denied her. Slowly Walther Inhoffen's capital disappeared. He told Louise he could no longer help her. Louise then turned to his wife and secretly persuaded her to pawn her jewels to help her.

The day came when Louise and Géza could no longer stay in Berlin and they decided that they needed to go to Hungary. Unfortunately they did not have the money for the journey. Walther Inhoffen was persuaded to borrow money against his business which Louise assured him would be repaid as soon as she had managed to get her furs which were in Hungary. Then she would sell them and repay the Inhoffens.

At this point Louise learned that her father was nearing the end of his life. Instead of going to Hungary she hurried back to Belgium. Ever since her escape from Bad Elster wherever Louise went she dangled the promise that when she received her inheritance she would be in a position to repay everything and more.

However, Leopold II had taken every step he could to ensure that she never got a penny when he died. And Louise then threw herself into various court cases against the Belgian nation in an effort to reclaim her inheritance. She also attempted to extract money from the new King of Belgium, King Albert (the younger brother of Baudouin who died in 1890). But what Louise never grasped was that her debts far outstripped by an enormous factor any inheritance she might have had a right to.

Louise's creditors were now never very far behind her. When they sniffed money they made their claims. To Louise's distress her mother's jewels were sold and she never saw anything. Her own clothes, jewels, pictures and everything she had still in Philipp's possession were sold in Vienna but nothing came Louise's way from it all. And still her debts went on rising.

Kiki, the dachshund, was black and longhaired. Louise made a great fuss of him and talked to him a great deal. Given how childish she had become after six years at Lindenhof it is somewhat surprising that she did not insist that Kiki come too the night she escaped. But no, when the door slid silently open and she was able to slip out into the hotel corridor, Kiki was left behind in the empty room. They were fortunate that Kiki did not start barking at that moment and alert the hotel staff. Louise's heart must have been thumping as she hurried along the corridor.

Her heart would have still been thumping when they reached the road and saw no carriage awaiting them. Here there was nothing they dared do while those two policemen stood below them in the roadway. But from the moment the carriage appeared in the distance, relief would have poured over Louise. She knew that Maria Stöger would be in the carriage. Louise had never met Maria until that moment but she knew about her and it is probable that she also knew that Géza and Maria had a son.

Towards the end of her life Louise said that from that moment on her relationship with Géza was like a brother-and-sister relationship. Clearly, it was no longer the love affair it had been up until the day they were separated at Lobor. This arrangement would have suited both of them. Louise in her childishness no longer wanted sex. She wanted to be looked after and she wanted an end to the restrictions imposed by Dr. Pierson. She did not want to be constantly told off in the way that she felt Dr. Pierson and Anna von Gebauer kept telling her off. She wanted to be allowed to play like a child.

Géza was no longer attracted to Louise. She was nine years older than him and she was losing her looks. She had put on a great deal of weight. Throughout the time she spent at Lindenhof those around her commented upon how much she ate. There were clearly occasions when Dr. Pierson feared that she was stuffing herself to the point where she might make herself ill. Her care of bodily hygiene was not good. She was no longer aware of how she was letting herself go but others would not have failed to notice.

Géza's affections had switched to Maria Stöger, who was eighteen years younger than Louise. Maria was energetic and engaged in life and eager to share a relationship to the full with Géza. Both Maria and Géza needed something that Louise stood for. Yet they probably did not want Louise herself. It is likely that they found Louise demanding and difficult to manage. Particularly Maria. Géza had presented Maria to Louise as her new lady's maid. What Maria thought of this is not clear but she certainly showed no skill as a lady's maid.

But Louise had an aura. With Louise in tow they could enjoy publicity and a high profile that they could never have had without her. Something of her royalness rubbed off on them and that was what they wanted from Louise. They received a royal treatment wherever they went that they would not have received without Louise.

When the little group arrived in Paris and moved into the Westminster Hotel there, Louise was persuaded to remain inside the building and to keep out of sight of journalists. It was, nevertheless, not long before a large number of shop owners and other salespeople appeared touting their wares for this royal Princess. Clothes and jewellery found favour, but it seems that it was Maria who benefitted from them, every bit as much as Louise. Maria received a long three-row pearl necklace from Cartier's. This had two pendants, each a ring around the numbers three and one, all set with diamonds. The three and one represented the date, 31ˢᵗ August, of their escape from Bad Elster. This was Louise's gesture of thanks for everything Maria had done for her. Her thanks were further expressed in the form of a three-and-a-half carat diamond ring. It is possible that Maria had talked Louise into making these gestures.

Maria had no difficulty getting accustomed to the grand life. She enjoyed oysters and champagne and dining in the finest Parisian restaurants. But Maria had her feet firmly on the ground. Around this time she learned that Ilona Varga in Möllersdorf had bought a plot of land and begun building a house on it. Unfortunately Ilona Varga had hit financial difficulties and Maria decided to take on the project. As a result Maria found herself the owner of a large house. On the ground floor were two shops, the rent from which provided Maria with a comfortable income. On the floor above Maria lived with her mother, her sister, Charlotte, and her youngest son.

Although she continued to see Géza and presumably continued to enjoy their relationship, from this time on she was spending time away from him, bringing up her son in Möllersdorf and managing her property.

Back in Coswig both Anna von Gebauer and Olga Börner had been dismissed summarily thanks to the suspected part they had played in Louise's escape. Both then wrote to Géza in Paris. Their timing was just right because Géza needed a carer for Louise. Géza sent Anna and Olga the money to get to Paris and he now had his three adoring woman around him.

It is unlikely that Géza felt particularly attached to any of them. Maria was already pulling away from him and building an independent life for herself. Anna was a rather elderly spinster whose love for him he found cloying, and he had once been suspicious of Olga and still did not really trust her. But each of the members in this rather strange and disparate little group needed the others if their act was to remain on the road. Anna in the end separated from the others leaving only Olga as Géza's true and trusted support right up until the end of his life.

At the outbreak of the First World War Louise, Géza, Olga and a French maid were staying at the Parkhotel in Vienna. Within days Louise had received a visit from the police telling her that she was required to leave the country. She, because she was Belgian, was deemed to be an enemy alien. Louise was stunned and shocked. She still considered herself a number of the Saxe-Coburg family even though Philipp had long since divorced her.

Louise's first thought was to reach Brussels and seek the support there of the King and the royal family. She only reached Munich. Here they were stopped and prevented from continuing on their journey. Here they stayed.

In August 1916 the Bavarian police entered their hotel and took away the whole group, leaving only Louise behind. The French maid was interned as an enemy alien. Géza was handed over to the Austrian authorities. Because they suspected Géza of being connected with Croatian conspirators against the Austrian state, he, too, was interned in a camp near Budapest. Only Olga returned to be with Louise.

Louise's situation was now pitiable. Without Géza there to see to her needs everything began to go badly wrong. Géza for years had been borrowing from Peter to pay Paul, staying in one place up until the moment when demands for payment became too pressing and then moving on somewhere else and all the while steadily selling off Louise's jewels and possessions in order to obtain ready money.

"During the war," Louise wrote, "it was often the case that I did not know where I would sleep that night or where I would find my next meal."

This was what Louise's life had come to. She turned to first one person and then another begging for help. Her prime targets were her daughter, Dora, and her husband, Ernst-Günther von Schleswig-Holstein, and, of course, Stéphanie. Günther was prepared to help his mother-in-law but only if she accepted very stringent restrictions which would limit any possibility of her squandering whatever she got from him. The essential condition imposed by Günther was that Louise never see Géza again. Günther also envisaged controlling her in order to prevent her running up further debts. He intended to keep her in some home or clinic where her physical needs would be assured. In a word, Günther's help came at the price of remaining for the rest of her life living as a prisoner just as Philipp had once intended.

Stéphanie's response to pleas for help was often simply silence. There were occasions when Stéphanie would welcome her sister as a guest in her house. But she would not give her money. Louise's family and relatives had learned that all the wealth in the world would not have satisfied Louise's demands. And in the end, this was Louise's problem: no one would give her money. She never understood how they could be so cruel and harsh. Why could they not see how unhappy her situation was, how great her needs were?

Louise and Olga found their way to Schleswig-Holstein with one thought only – to throw themselves on the mercy of Dora. But Dora's door was shut to them and remained shut. At this time in some extraordinary way Géza was still able to send them small sums of money. This came to an end when the German police held up Géza's post and started to return it to him unopened. With no money to pay their bills, it was not long before they were asked to leave the hotel where they were staying.

And then – yet again – miraculously, help turned up out of the blue. Louise and Olga found themselves sitting beside the road with their bags and cases around them, and with no idea what they should do next, when a car pulled up in front of them. The man who stepped out was a friend of Géza's and had been sent by Géza to do all he could to get the two women out of their difficulties and to bring them to Hungary. Since Louise did not have a passport this was not going to be a simple matter. But he proceeded to pay the hotel bill and then the three of them waited until nightfall.

Their journey took them to a small village not far from Munich from where they could actually see across the border into Austria. Louise and Olga took rooms with a local woman and from her window Louise could see the church tower the other side of the frontier.

Part of the frontier ran through woodland along a small stream, the *Weißbach*. A bridge crossed the stream but there were guards posted here day and night. Olga and Géza's friend had no reason to fear the guards – their papers were all in order. The problem was Louise. She was now, effectively, stateless. Austria no longer recognised her as a citizen and she had no papers.

One of the first things Louise did was go into Munich and bring back two of her dogs, a griffon and a German shepherd, which she had left to be cared for until her return. She then took to walking the dogs regularly within sight of the bridge but she would not go near the bridge. The dogs ran around without a care in the world, plunging into the water and crossing over into Austria and then racing back to her when Louise called. It was so easy for them. Louise watched helplessly.

Géza's friend was beginning to get anxious. He disliked the delay and he kept pressing Louise to pluck up courage and attempt to cross the bridge one night. Still Louise hung back. She would cross when she was ready. But day by day passed and she could not find the courage to make a move.

One morning she announced that she would cross that day at midday. During the course of the morning the other two went down to the bridge and crossed over without incident. And Louise remained behind with her two dogs. As midday approached, she set off with the griffon in her arms while the other dog bounded around her. It was early autumn and the day was hot under the bright autumn sun. The guard had moved away from the bridge to shelter from the sun. He was half asleep in the warm air. Louise wandered with a leisurely air alongside the water towards the bridge and then when she came to it she continued over. The guard did not even look up.

Louise's heart leapt inside her – she was in Austria! She kept steadily going until she was out of sight of the guard and then she began to hurry. She found the other two by the church in the village waiting for her. They had a carriage waiting and soon they were heading for Salzburg.

By the winter of 1918 everything in Austria was in a state of chaos. In so many ways civilisation was breaking down. There were demonstrations and riots, food shortages and starvation. Defeated soldiers were straggling homewards. The different regions were breaking away and grabbing their independence. The old Austro-Hungarian Empire was finished. There was nobody here concerned about Louise. All she could do was turn once again to her sister.

Hungary had now established itself as an independent country under communist rule. Throughout the land there were strong undercurrents of resentment against the landed aristocracy. As far as Elemér and Stéphanie were concerned this was a time for keeping a very low profile.

Stéphanie's attitude towards her sister had slowly hardened. She could no longer ignore the fact that Louise's debts were never going to be brought under control and if local tradesmen saw that Louise had the support of Elemér and Stéphanie behind her it was likely that they might be emboldened into extending her further credit. Stéphanie and Elemér, like everyone else, insisted that Louise had to separate from Géza if they were to become involved in helping her in any way. Elemér would have gladly washed his hands of Louise but this was not so easy for Stéphanie.

Once again, no doubt whining pitiably, Louise refused to be separated from Géza. Stéphanie showed her the door. Olga and Louise managed to get back to Budapest but here all hotels were closed. Louise made her way to the Coburg Palace where once she had spent time with Philipp. She found the windows boarded up but rioters had broken into the building and inside everything that could be taken was gone and what was left was broken, torn, and smashed. The Red Army had moved into the building. Soldiers watched these two forlorn, middle-aged women stumbling around but did nothing.

However, Louise then wandered out into the grounds and came across an old gardener who had once known her. His eyes lit up at the sight of her and the old man rushed forward and kissed her hand. "Yes, it really is our Princess!" He was so delighted to see her but in greeting her in this way he had given away who she was and within moments she was in the hands of the soldiers.

An hour later Louise found herself locked in a cell. It was dark and musty and she was alone. Olga had been allowed to go free. Louise had no idea what was happening outside her cell until one day a soldier walked in and announced to her that her case had gone to court and she had been found guilty of spying. Her sentence: death by firing squad.

Louise was transferred to a new cell. A week went by. Each morning Louise could hear the shots of the firing squads carrying out death sentences. And each morning she knew that one day it would be she herself who was taken out there to face that line-up of soldiers. Did you actually hear the sound of the shot before the bullet hit you, she may have wondered.

Each day she waited.

One evening the door of her cell opened and a guard entered to announce to her her fate: at dawn the following morning she would face the firing squad.

It was a long night. In the darkness Louise tried to prepare herself. There were moments when she was almost resigned, other moments when in a state of growing panic she went over in her mind every moment of what the morning would bring her. She thought of her family but they seemed so far away, so remote. She wondered when they would hear what had happened to her and whether any of them would stop to think of her when they did learn of her fate. She wondered where Géza was at that moment and whether he knew or whether he might still be wondering when he would see her again.

Finally the first light of dawn appeared. Louise froze, waiting in a state of tension. Was that the sound of the guards' footsteps coming for her? Why did the door not open? Already she could hear shots outside. Others were going to their maker – soon it would be her turn. The icy tension inside her grew.

And she waited.

The shots outside faded and a new silence fell upon the place. And she waited. Other noises rumbled and rattled, familiar noises she had heard each and every day she had been there but today they sounded grotesque, filled with foreboding. And she waited.

Louise already felt dead when the door did open. She didn't look up. She did not want to see them. She did not want to see anything. She could get through it if she didn't see anything. She hardly heard the voice. It could have been a million miles away. The announcement was dry, unreal – she was free, she could go. On one condition: she had to leave Hungary immediately.

(It later became clear that Béla Kun, Hungary's communist ruler, kept procrastinating over signing the actual death warrant; he was uncertain as to whether some powerful ally of this Belgian Princess might not cause him difficulties at some time in the future. In the end he refused to sign it and Louise went free.)

At the station Louise found a crowd in panic, jostling and pushing in an anguished bid to get on any train going westward. When a train heading for Austria came into the station the crowd stormed it, even piling on to the roof or sitting on the buffers. It would only go a few kilometres before grinding to a halt and then standing still, sometimes for days.

Gone were the days when Louise could take for granted that doors would be opened for her, a seat found for her, others would step back for her and all with much bowing and scraping. But Louise managed to reach Vienna. She was tired, dirty, cold, hungry and utterly crushed. But she found her way to the Parkhotel in Hietzing. She got some meagre help from the Belgian Embassy and somehow her little group of supporters, Olga, Géza and Maria Stöger, also found their way to her. Her creditors found her, too.

With the end of the war came the total break-up of the old social ways. For each it was a scramble to re-establish a footing in a strange world. How much Louise truly understood this is debatable but around her her little band of supporters were breaking up too.

Maria Stöger, ever practical, had already turned her thoughts to her commitments to her family and the need to hang on to her property. From the war her two sons had returned, scarred figures, needing support as never before. So she was ready to pull out of their 'arrangement'. This possibly came as a shock to Géza. He had had many relationships but he had always been able to depend upon Maria and it seems unlikely that it ever crossed his mind that the day might come when she was no longer there for him to depend upon. In many ways you could say that theirs had been the relationship that meant more to him than any other. It was not the frothy romantic fairytale he had shared with Louise – no, this was the grim and wonderful attachment that binds a man and a woman through the difficulties of life.

Quite simply, Maria did not need Géza as much as he needed her. She had admired him. She had gloried in their relationship. He had drawn her into exciting worlds she could never have experienced without him. But in postwar chaos Maria's instincts told her that she had to stand on her own feet and sort out her own affairs. They had been lovers; henceforth Géza would be her „*Bajtárs*", her comrade.

Géza would never have acknowledged that his own behaviour had any part in Maria's departure. He had always somewhat lorded it over his group of adoring women with the masculine confidence that assumed that they could never ever reject him. In the run-up to Maria's going there had been so many scenes, emotional flurries, slammed doors and hurt feelings – all because Géza was far from subtle and discreet in his relations with the women around him. Now he was left with just Olga Börner – and Louise.

More than ever he needed to play the aristocrat – at a time when being a member of the aristocracy was a dubious distinction. When Olga saw him her words had to be „*Ich lege mich zu Füßen Eurer königlichen Hoheit!*" ("I lay myself at your feet, your royal Highness!") and when she left his presence it demanded similar flowery etiquette. Perhaps here lay the basis of Géza's actions: a craving for the distinction accorded to royalty. With Louise some of her glitter and glory fell upon him.

Was Géza ever genuinely in love with Louise – or was the attraction always the glitter of royalty? As Louise's equerry he got a taste for it. From then on his craving was so strong that he was willing to leave the army (though he failed to inform the military that that was what he had done, which cost him his career, his titles, his good name) and for the rest of his life he clung to Louise and to the ever-diminishing glitter of associating with a Princess. In the end the Géza-Louise partnership was resonant of the organ-grinder and his monkey.

Géza had spent most of the war years in one prison cell or another and he had emerged physically broken, mentally utterly insecure and spiritually unable to cope with the world he now found himself in. During the long time he had spent in a Hungarian prison he had become addicted to morphine. It is not clear how he came by the drug but the likely explanation is that he suffered from a serious bout of malaria, for which strong doses of morphine were liberally administered.

Louise still meant something to her last hangers-on. She still talked about the money she would get when her aunt Charlotte died and the others clung to her, waiting for a share-out when this happened. Maximilian's wife had long been forgotten by the world but she was still alive. This was the last person from whom Louise could expect to inherit something. Her mother and her father had died and she had got nothing. In July 1921 Philipp von Coburg died. In 1906 the divorce between Philipp and Louise was finalised but Louise went on believing that he would leave her something. She got nothing from Philipp. Her aunt Charlotte was Louise's last hope of an inheritance. She got nothing.

In 1923 Louise and Géza moved to Paris. On the 1st October that year Géza collapsed in the street and died of a heart attack. He was fifty-six years old. Louise arranged for him to be buried in the Père Lachaise Cemetery and then, in true Louise style, she organised a requiem concert for him in the Madeleine Church with the choir of the Paris Opera company.

Louise did not outlive Géza by many months. She left Paris after Géza's death and moved to Wiesbaden in Germany and here in March 1924 she too breathed her last. She was buried in the cemetery in Wiesbaden and the only member of her family there to bid her goodbye was her daughter, Dora.

Chapter 93

Erzsi became the apple of her grandfather's eye. Franz Joseph came to love small children in his old age and he loved being surrounded by his grandchildren, but Erzsi was his favourite. Gisela had given him four grandchildren and in time Marie-Valérie was to give him nine, but both Gisela and Marie-Valérie did not live nearby. Erzsi, on the other hand, was there living in the Hofburg with her mother. Franz Joseph took to going up to Stéphanie's apartments for an evening meal with her and little Erzsi.

This is interesting because it is usually asserted with absolute authority that Franz Joseph did not like Stéphanie and that like the rest of the family he did not approve of her. But beyond the assertions there is little evidence of this. Of course, a man like Franz Joseph would never have stooped to express dislike if he had felt it; he was far too courteous towards women. But from his writings to her it would seem that he enjoyed her company.

In the spring of 1898 Stéphanie was very seriously ill and forced to stay on her sickbed for several weeks. In Franz Joseph's letters to Elisabeth he gave his wife a regular bulletin of Stéphanie's progress. He sounds genuinely concerned about Stéphanie. If he had disapproved of her so much would he have paid her as many visits or shown as much concern as he did? It is likely that Elisabeth barely flicked her eyes over those paragraphs. Elisabeth had never liked Stéphanie and Stéphanie's illness would not have bothered her. It was at this time that the scandal over Stéphanie's sister, Louise, broke and that would have interested Elisabeth far more. There is no evidence for this but it would have been in character for Elisabeth to have taken Louise's side against the court, which was shocked by the whole affair.

It does seem probable that it was during those years after Rudolf's death that Franz Joseph really got to know Stéphanie. He visited her regularly and it was not entirely because of Erzsi.

On 16th October 1891, almost two years after Rudolf's death, he wrote to Stéphanie to thank her for a pleasant evening and especially to thank her for bringing back for him the '*gute Cáffé Zuckerln*'[23] from Pressburg. Stéphanie had made a special effort to find for him what he liked and Franz Joseph was touched that she had thought of him. It is as if he felt touched by her little gestures of thoughtfulness towards him and then found he could come out of himself for a brief while and play with the child he adored.

Franz Joseph involved himself in every aspect of Erzsi's growing up; nothing was too small or insignificant. He corrected her when she misbehaved,

---

[23] These were coffee-flavoured sweets, a speciality of Pressburg, and Franz Joseph was particularly fond of them.

watched over her education, was interested when she had to have some dental treatment that involved a 'rubber machine'. He made a point of attending her first communion, a small intimate affair attended only by Philipp von Coburg and Louise, and their daughter, Dora, who was a playmate of Erzsi's.

Into the Josephi Chapel came Stéphanie, leading Erzsi in a long white dress with a long veil over her head. Franz Joseph noted how seriously Erzsi took it all and how sweet she was. He told Elisabeth that she was growing really pretty and he had been both upset and moved in that moment.

But as Erzsi grew older, the more her relationship with her mother turned sour.

In her imagination Erzsi had turned her father into a hero figure. She idolised him; she attributed every quality to him; in her imagination she wove romantic stories about him. Rudolf could never let his daughter down; he could never fail to show the perfect, intimate understanding she required of him; he could never topple from the pedestal she had placed him upon.

Erzsi came to blame Stéphanie for all her father's sorrows and difficulties. What was more, there were an awful lot of people around who blamed Stéphanie for all Rudolf's problems. Erzsi may have overheard many snide remarks about her mother's relationship with her father. Which would have confirmed her picture of her father and driven an even deeper wedge between Erzsi and her mother.

And everywhere Erzsi went there were the whispers about the 'poor little orphan', turning her into the heroine of a tragic melodrama. Erzsi was the sort of teenager who enjoyed feeling the heroine of some great tragedy. Later in life she was to show just how dramatic and imperious she could be. Erzsi grew into a difficult teenager, a mass of tensions, and full of disapproval for her mother.

In September 1899 Erzsi reached her sixteenth birthday, an age when thoughts would begin to turn to her future life and marriage. Stéphanie would have been conscious that the day loomed when her role as caretaker to her daughter would come to an end. That moment she had feared long ago in the early months after Rudolf's death was coming ever closer. 'What then?' she had asked Louise. She could have been forgiven for thinking that her position within the Imperial Court in Vienna had been difficult enough when she was Crown Princess and Rudolf was still alive; it had become considerably more difficult in the ten years since his death, but once Erzsi no longer needed a mother's close attention, it was likely to become even more difficult still. She dreaded that.

Stéphanie herself found the answer to that 'What then?' question. She had met the man she wished to marry.

There was everything to object to with this marriage (not least that he was not of equal birth) but in the end, what did it matter? Stéphanie had no real place within the Imperial Family and, if she was willing to accept that she would lose her titles, her rights within the Arch-house, her status, and most of her allowances, it did not matter. She would, of course, leave her apartments in the Hofburg and Erzsi could not possibly go with her to her new home. Nor would Erzsi be allowed to be present at her mother's re-marriage – not that Erzsi wanted to be.

There cannot have been many who realised just how increasingly meaningless Stéphanie's life had become. She had lost Rudolf in 1889. She had lost Count Artur Potocki in the spring of 1890. She had lost the job that had given purpose to her days and she had been forced – thanks to the difficulties of protocol her new position gave rise to – to remain away from almost all court functions for eight years after Rudolf's death. And now her daughter was growing up and growing away from her.

And she had also lost her sister. Since Rudolf's death she had seen less and less of Louise. And then in 1897 Louise ran away with her Croatian lieutenant. Stéphanie's relationship with Louise never returned to the easy footing it had had before.

Into this void came an unknown Hungarian magnate.

Stéphanie sprang her surprise in the early months of 1900 at a time when Franz Joseph and all his advisors were embroiled with the much more serious matter of Franz Ferdinand's wish to marry a lady not of equal birth. So it was that, with a heavy heart, Franz Joseph agreed to Stéphanie's marrying Count Elemér Lónyay von Nagy-Lónya es Vásáros-Namény.

Within the court, few had ever even heard of this Count Elemér Lónyay. The shock and surprise was all the greater. When the gossip about Franz Ferdinand and his lady-in-waiting briefly ran out of steam, questions swirled about this other shocking marriage! Who was he? How had she met him? How could she do this?

The emergence of the hitherto little-known Elemér Lónyay naturally sparked a good deal of curiosity. It sparked off disapproval, too, and sent shockwaves around Brussels. The reaction of Stéphanie's father was an utter refusal to countenance such a demeaning marriage. In Leo's eyes the marriage was all the more demeaning because he still nursed hopes of seeing Stéphanie as Empress of Austria. There had been some surreptitious negotiation to bring about a marriage between Franz Ferdinand and Stéphanie. Possibly, the fact that Stéphanie got on well with Franz Ferdinand had got back to Brussels and fed Leo's hopes and ambitions. The discovery that this was not to be must have incensed Leo all the more.

He flared up in anger and decided to have nothing more to do with his daughter. He expelled her from the Belgian royal house. He also forbade Clémentine to write or contact her sister ever again. Leo was one of those bitter men who never forgot a grudge. Years later, when Marie-Henriette was dying, he refused to let Stéphanie go to her mother to be with her in her last hours.

Stéphanie must have had a shrewd idea that it might come to this. She turned to her aunt, Queen Victoria, for help. Victoria had always had a very soft spot for Stéphanie and treated her with great warmth and affection. Stéphanie described her aunt as having an understanding, sympathetic soul. Would Queen Victoria put in a word for Stéphanie?

Victoria wrote back on 13th October 1899, "Poor child, you are so alone and it would make me so very happy if I knew you had found contentment and happiness." Victoria also told Stéphanie that she had always felt for her through all the difficulties and pain she had gone through. But Victoria had mixed feelings about Stéphanie's wish to marry again. She told Stéphanie that her letter had caused her considerable surprise. She only hoped that the step Stéphanie wished to take would really lead to happiness and that her future husband could really offer her what her heart needed so much.

But Victoria wrote to Leo, and Stéphanie also sent him a letter. In her letter Stéphanie wrote that she had lived an unhappy existence for a long time and that she saw little in her life ahead that might change its dreary tone. So she wanted to grab her chance at happiness with an honourable man from one of the best Hungarian families.

Stéphanie and her father were speaking at cross purposes. She sought understanding for her loneliness and the dreary tenor of her days and begged for a little bit of well-wishing as she went forward to build a new life for herself. Her father saw everything only in terms of status, prestige, protocol and rank in the world. Stéphanie's feelings were irrelevant.

There was no help from her mother. Marie-Henriette had long withdrawn from the world. She was no longer aware of what might be going on around her. A kind of fog of silence and isolation had enveloped her. It is debatable how much she really knew what was happening to Stéphanie. Mentally, she was drifting to the point where her image of her children was frozen in a far distant past. Leo had crushed her spirit and dementia was finishing the job. Now she was barely human any more.

Stéphanie was not aware how far gone her mother was when she wrote to her some pretty bitter words. "If I had ever found at home, whenever I came to see you and Clémentine, the love that anyone would need, if I had been able to visit you without restriction, then there is nothing I could have wished for more than to devote myself to you and your care, for in spite of everything I do love and honour you..."

Did Marie-Henriette ever read that letter? And if she did, did she ever understand it?

One aspect of Stéphanie's wish to marry again was a matter of some anxiety to her – money. As with Louise, her financial affairs had always been regulated by someone else. She had no money of her own, even though her wedding contract had stipulated down to the last detail all sorts of incomes and allowances, and when she became a widow the whole matter was gone over again and new arrangements made. Now that she was proposing to step away from the Imperial Family, she was more than a little concerned as to whether she would have an income at all.

And well she might have been, given that Leo's first step was to cut off the allowance of fifty thousand francs he paid her annually. Nothing mattered so much to Leo as money and he could never have enough of it, even though, having pillaged the Belgian Congo to the hilt, he was one of the richest men on earth. Franz Joseph was pretty outraged that Leo, who had contracted to pay Stéphanie's allowance for her lifetime, had suddenly withdrawn it. So it was with all the more gratitude that she recognised Franz Joseph's thoughtfulness when he saw to it that her future would be secured and her standing properly regulated.

Franz Joseph suspected that Stéphanie may have wanted him to accord further titles upon her fiancé and raise his rank within the aristocracy. But that was one step too far for Franz Joseph. When Stéphanie married Elemér Lónyay she would become Countess Lónyay. And she was to remain Countess Lónyay until Emperor Karl, soon after he became Emperor, ennobled Elemér Lónyay in 1917. But when Austria became a republic in 1918 all titles were abolished so that Karl's gesture turned out to be a hollow one.

Leo's reply to Stéphanie was a bitter accusation and he wrote in a similar tone to Queen Victoria. Victoria did not know what to do but she was concerned and upset on Stéphanie's behalf. She asked her daughter, Princess Beatrice, to write to Stéphanie and Beatrice wrote and explained how much her mother felt for Stéphanie but how helpless she felt and how difficult it was for her to do something about it. Beatrice said her mother had always felt so much sympathy for Stéphanie given all that she had gone through and she found the attitude of the Belgian Royal Family incomprehensible, but was glad that the Emperor was so supportive...

Deep down Stéphanie knew that all this was dotting the i's and crossing the t's. She had chosen and she was not going back. She might be pained at her parents' attitude but it would not deter her. On 8th March 1900 she left the Hofburg and on 24th March married her Hungarian magnate and she became simply Countess Lónyay.

It is highly unlikely that theirs was a flash-of-lightening love-at-first-sight affair. Both were level-headed people in their mid-thirties. And it was not just

Stéphanie who had to consider some of the disadvantages of the step they were taking. Stéphanie may have been a Princess of true royal blood but marrying her did not bring about a situation of unalloyed advantage.

In many ways, it would seem that Elemér had to give up more for his marriage than did Stéphanie. She, certainly, never regretted for one moment the step she took, but Elemér may have had secret doubts. If so, he was too much the gentleman to trouble her with them. Perhaps Elemér had expected social advantages and imperial favours if he won Stéphanie's hand. If so, he was wrong – when Elemér married Stéphanie he was required to leave the diplomatic service. Giving up his career was painful for Elemér and he was to find it hard to come to terms with this in the years to come. For her he gave up a career he loved and a very comfortable income, he ceased to travel as much as he had done or appear at Europe's finest courts as he had once done, and he settled into a country life that just may have seemed very dull to so cultured a man.

Elemér had a very distinguished air, one of those men who, in a crowded room, draws every eye to him, both men and women. This is not obvious from photographs of him. He had all the air of the elegant, fiery Hungarian aristocrat. He held himself with the easy, relaxed and noble mien of one who is assured of his place in the world. Leo, as far as we know, never met his new son-in-law, whom he used to refer to with scorn as that 'shepherd-boy'.

His family stood high up in the Hungarian aristocracy, and down the centuries various ancestors had shown great loyalty and bravery for Hungary. They had acquired wealth and lands. Doors opened to them wherever they went, they moved in the highest circles and they were at ease wherever they went. Young Elemér had studied jurisprudence at the university in Budapest and then gone into the diplomatic service. His diplomatic career had taken him to Bucharest, Rome and London. In St. Petersburg he was Legation Secretary; from there he went to Paris and then back to London. He and his brother, Gábor, had the title of Count conferred upon them in 1896.

With the title came the position of Court Chamberlain. This, later, was to be very important to him because marrying Stéphanie brought his career as a diplomat to an end. He was to remark with painful irony that, if he had not been Court Chamberlain, he would have had no entrée at court at all, he who had married the widow of the heir to the throne. But as time went on he rarely sought to appear at court.

History has tended to write Stéphanie off as such a plain and dreary personality. Elemér Lónyay saw something very different in her. Did he see

– and admire – the volcano hidden beneath the cloak of ice?

To everyone else it was all about rank and position. On 22nd March 1900 the *Neue Freie Presse* newspaper wrote that everybody in the land and especially the women were struck by this astounding move on the part of the Crown Princess Widow. She who had enjoyed the foremost female position after the Empress in the whole land was now willing to give it all up.

There was something of the romantic fairytale about it all! What made it all the more romantic was the fact that how she had met and won the heart of her cavalier was to remain Stéphanie's tightly-kept secret.

Various stories began to swirl around. There were those who were sure she had met him in London at a diplomatic dinner at which Elemér was Stéphanie's dinner partner; others said he was presented to her in Laxenburg; yet others said they first became acquainted while staying in Solza in Silesia with Count Heinrich Larisch. Mia Kerckvoorde, in her biography of Marie-Henriette,[24] states that Elemér Lónyay had a diplomatic position in Brussels during the 1880s and it was during this time that Stéphanie first met him. This implies that she first knew him when Rudolf was still alive.

Those curious had no idea either when she met him. In her memoirs Stéphanie said she met him in 1899 but Stéphanie's dates often got mixed up and it is possible that this was not the case. Elsewhere she is quoted as saying that she had stayed a number of times in Solza, occasions when Heinrich Larisch had invited a large number of guests for hunting parties. Here, possibly, Elemér had more than once been her neighbour at dinner.

If Stéphanie had met Elemér at a diplomatic dinner in London, at which he had been obliged to be her escort, how had they carried the relationship forward to the point where they both knew they wished to marry? The formality of the occasion would have worked against them. Subsequent meetings might well have been noticed. Similarly, if Elemér had been presented to her at Laxenburg. But in Solza the general atmosphere would have been a great deal easier and less constrained. So maybe it was at Solza.

It is not so much how they met that intrigues, but rather how they got to know each other well enough to know they loved each other. Stéphanie was not a stunning beauty for whom a man's heart would seem to stop beating. She had become a very elegant lady who exuded an aristocratic graciousness. She had acquired an excellent dress sense and she always took great care over her toilette and appearance. She dressed well. But she could not get away from having a face that was too pallid, too featureless. Men did not look at her with desire in their eyes. Mostly, they didn't look at her at

---

[24] *Marie-Henriette – Une Amazone face à un Géant* by Mia Kerckvoorde, (2001) translated from the Dutch by Marie Hooghe.

all. She must have been used to people looking past her into the distance behind. Stéphanie just was not the sort of woman who could make a man take one look and know that he wanted her. Women like Stéphanie tend to wear a neutral mask suppressing any hint in tone of voice or body language that might reveal her interest in a man, just to avoid humiliation, and men rarely see beyond the mask. With Stéphanie, remembering the pain she had felt over Count Artur Potocki, the need for reticence would have been all the greater.

Trust – that was the thing. They needed to trust each other. Perhaps in Solza there was time for Elemér to show an interest in her. There, there would have been time for her to get used to his paying attention to her – not the formal, courtly attention that she was used to, that she knew meant nothing but was merely the charade the people at court performed in the presence of a Crown Princess – but genuine, unforced attention. She may have slowly become aware that his attention was not simply conventional. Something in his body language, perhaps.

To begin with she would not really have noticed. She would have been wary when she did begin to notice. She would remember that in 1889 she had lost both her husband and also the one man she had ever deeply loved, her great secret.

Then slowly she would have found responses stirring within her that she did not expect and did not entirely know how to react to. This man heard what she said and listened to her – Stéphanie would have found that stunning and vaguely upsetting in a way she couldn't explain. This would have felt very strange to Stéphanie; she was not used to people listening to her. She was used to people half hearing her, their minds elsewhere, and then their responding with banal and largely irrelevant courtesies. Faced with understanding and real respect from Elemér Stéphanie would have opened up to him with a warmth that might even have surprised herself. And just possibly, through her confidences he came to see a woman who had warm and strong feelings, a woman whose happiness meant something to him. And a hard, little knot inside her began to melt. It was beyond her control to stop it happening.

In Solza the huntsmen went out day after day with their hounds. All day they would be out on horseback, only coming back as the long shadows of dusk spread across the landscape. Suddenly doors would be thrown open, the quiet stillness of the house shattered by the bustle of returning men, tired, dusty and hungry, full of the aftermath of energy and enthusiasm generated by the day's sport. Did Stéphanie start to listen for their return? In Solza informality reigned. Every evening at dinner the diners found themselves sitting next to someone different, so different from a dinner in Vienna where rank determined where you sat and rank ensured that your neighbour was almost always the same person. So, as the men bustled upstairs to get out of their muddy hunting clothes, Stéphanie may have wondered whether she would find herself sitting next to Elemér.

Trust – in the end she may have found she could not help but trust him.

At some point, a proposal was made. Nobody knows when; nobody knows how it was made; it is not even known which one of them actually made the proposal. Nor is it known whether time was needed before an answer could be given. It was such a big step, after all. But from that moment on, it could no longer be kept a secret and the wider world had to be faced.

Stéphanie may have hung back for a long time before bringing it all out into the open. She would have known that it would only attract Franz Joseph's disapproval. Rather like Franz Ferdinand, she may well have been eaten up with apprehension and doubts. Suppose Franz Joseph categorically refused her permission to marry Elemér? Approaching him would have cost her all the goodwill he had always shown her.

Stéphanie finally succeeded in screwing up her courage and seeking an interview with the Emperor to ask for his permission to marry Elemér. Franz Ferdinand's wish to marry the Countess Sophie Chotek had already exploded upon the court. Stéphanie could be grateful that it had. She knew that both her father and Franz Joseph had long hoped that a marriage could be arranged between her and Franz Ferdinand. With Franz Ferdinand fighting his battles for his Sophie, it may have been easier for Stéphanie to win a tired agreement from Franz Joseph.

Franz Joseph may not have liked the idea but Stéphanie had no place these days at court, her marriage would not upset the monarchy and there was little reason to refuse her. So, with huge resignation, Franz Joseph gave in. Even Erzsi provided no reason to refuse her, for Erzsi was now sixteen and she was already looking forward to marrying herself. Of course, Erzsi could not go and live in Hungary, but then Erzsi did not want to go with her mother to Hungary.

Chapter 94

On 9th January 1900 Erzsi attended her first court ball. She entered the grand ballroom on the arm of Franz Ferdinand and every eye was turned upon her. Erzsi appeared, head high, a stunning being according to the court reporter. She was wearing a white dress with scattered diamante-embroidered flowers; she was also wearing a brilliant diamond necklace that had been given to her by her adoring grandfather. Franz Joseph wanted his favourite granddaughter to appear at her very best and Erzsi did not let him down.

Stéphanie, too, wanted this, her first court ball, to be a great occasion for Erzsi. Perhaps she remembered her own first appearances in public and how awkward she had been and how, so often, she had been badly dressed and unbecomingly presented to a critical world. Over the years Stéphanie had learned the hard way just how important appearances were.

But that night both Stéphanie and Franz Joseph could, with real pride, watch Erzsi face the world. The court reporter gushingly described Erzsi as a combination of Snow White and an exalted Princess. Erzsi was every inch a Princess – she had already grown to be taller than Stéphanie – a Princess imbued with all the grace and charm of her position.

The reporter compared her to Snow White supposedly because of her delightful shy smile and her self-effacing modesty. But the Snow White description could hardly have fitted less well. To start with, Erzsi, like her mother, was as blonde as they come – no black-haired beauty she! Erzsi was like her mother; the shape of her face was Stéphanie's; her nose and mouth were Stéphanie's. Also she most certainly was neither shy nor self-effacing. On the contrary, she was a very self-assured young woman who knew what she wanted and was determined to get it.

And that evening, at her first court ball, her eyes never seemed to leave the handsome figure of a young officer from the Uhlan Regiment. She got the Master of Ceremonies to ask this particular young officer to dance with her again and again. For Prince Otto von Windischgrätz that request was an order. The whole court watched the turn of events with both curiosity and a certain disapproval, for Prince Otto was certainly not of equal birth to the granddaughter of the Emperor and to single him out so obviously was not considered wise. But Erzsi that evening set her heart on Prince Otto.

That ball was to be significant in another way – it was to be the last court ball that Stéphanie would ever attend. Already she had begun to say her goodbyes to her old life. In the days to come she would go to lay a wreath of orchids, roses and carnations on Rudolf's grave. On 4th March she gave a dinner for sixteen members of her household. Just as once she had had to say goodbye to every member of her family and Belgian household to marry Rudolf, now she had to say goodbye to those who had served her in Vienna for so long. There was a more formal goodbye for her household on 8th March when Stéphanie thanked them all with tears in her eyes and personally handed out gifts to each and every one. Many of those who stood around were moved and upset to see her go.

Earlier the same day she had gone to see Franz Joseph to thank him and to say goodbye. No doubt, this was a quiet and correct moment, but one suspects that both of them were moved beneath the masks they wore for the benefit of the other.

Then in the evening Stéphanie left for the station. Erzsi went with her – Erzsi was to accompany her mother on the train to Miramare but once there she would only stay a short while before turning round and returning to Vienna without having met Elemér and without attending her mother's wedding; it was not considered acceptable for her to attend the wedding. In any case, she did not wish to see her mother get married again. She resented Stéphanie's marrying again.

Stéphanie had suspected that this would be Erzsi's reaction and she had managed to keep her growing attachment to Elemér and her hopes of marrying him a secret from Erzsi for as long as she could. In the end, of course, Erzsi had to know.

The German newspaper, the *Berliner Lokalanzeiger*, seemed to be well-informed about the whole matter and published an article, telling its readers that Stéphanie had never discussed her own marriage plans or those that Erzsi herself nursed. Again and again, according to the article, the important discussions about these matters were put off and delayed. What made broaching the subject all the more difficult for Stéphanie was the fact that Erzsi, before she found out that her mother had hopes of marrying him, had once spoken out vigorously to Count Choloniewski (the senior steward in Stéphanie's household) about how much she disliked Count Lónyay.

This sounds as though Erzsi sensed that there was something between her mother and Count Lónyay and found the whole idea distasteful. How dare her mother! Erzsi throughout her childhood had placed the entire blame for her father's death at Stéphanie's door. Relations between mother and daughter had never been very good, and now her mother thought she could go dancing off into a new marriage and forget her father! How dare she!

So Stéphanie found herself in an embarrassing and difficult position. Stéphanie may have had suspicions that someone had already whispered the news to Erzsi which was why Erzsi was so against Elemér. On one occasion Stéphanie had mentioned Elemér and Erzsi had flared up and spat out that she hated him.

"You hate him? Do you know the Count? Have you spoken with him?"

Stéphanie asked unhappily. (This conversation took place in the presence of a lady-in-waiting who later reported it.)

Here Erzsi sounds like many a teenager. "No," she said, "but I can't stand him. I never want to see him!"

"But why? Has someone tried to put you off the Count?"

"No, Mama, I don't know why, but ever since I saw him for the first time a year ago, I took an immediate dislike to him. So please, Mama, don't ever mention him again!" Erzsi spoke with such vehement bitterness that Stéphanie did not know how to react. She had never heard Erzsi lash out so. According to the *Berliner Lokalanzeiger*, from that moment on there was considerable awkwardness between mother and daughter.

One effect of Stéphanie's marrying Elemér had upon Erzsi was to make her even more obstinately determined that no one was going to influence her and push her into marrying someone she did not love and admire. She asserted, "I will only marry a man I really love; I shall choose for myself!" And throughout those last days she spent with her mother Erzsi nursed within herself her utter determination to do just that. As she travelled with Stéphanie to the station she may well have been brooding ferociously over the whole – from her point of view – awful business.

Stéphanie rode to the station in a court carriage, the last time she would ever ride in a court carriage. At the station Franz Joseph was awaiting her; he particularly wished to see her on to the train. They had a few minutes together, no doubt saying nothing of any real importance, then the station master announced that the train was ready to depart.

Franz Joseph offered her his arm and led her across the platform. There was a crowd of people watching this strange little ceremony, fascinated. As always, Stéphanie held herself erect. She was wearing a dark green coat with a fur collar and a hat adorned with violets. Just before she stepped on to the train, Stéphanie sank into a deep curtsey before the Emperor and kissed his hand. Franz Joseph kissed her on the forehead.

The fascinated bystanders noticed that Stéphanie was clearly very emotional and there were tears running down her cheeks. Once in the train Stéphanie opened the window and leaned out to exchange a last few words with Franz Joseph. The cold was bitter but Franz Joseph refused to leave until the train had departed. And as the train pulled out of the station, both Stéphanie and Erzsi leaned out of the window to wave. Franz Joseph waved back.

Finally, they closed the window and sat back into their seats. One can imagine Stéphanie, lost in her own thoughts, staring out of the window watching the countryside roll by, still staring long after dusk had fallen and darkness had settled over the land. Did she find herself remembering another train journey that would bring her to marriage and a new life? Did she relive in her mind that departure from Brussels in 1881 when she left her childhood home forever? Did she remember how uncertain, yet excited, she had felt, how many questions had thronged through her mind as once before the train carrying her away chugged steadily across the countryside? Then she had been going to Vienna to a position of honour in the Austrian court, now she was leaving both honours and court behind, never to return.

She may suddenly have felt that there was so much she ought to say to Erzsi about this whole marriage business. There was – but she could not say any of it. Not to Erzsi, who was probably frowning, sitting there distracted with her own thoughts focussed upon marrying Prince Otto von Windischgrätz and so full of disapproval of her mother's marrying *that* Hungarian Count.

It may have crossed Stéphanie's mind that it was easy for the young to disapprove – they did not know what marriage was all about. She had known nothing of what marriage was about. Nor had Louise – if Stéphanie was honest with herself, she had to admit that. Over the years she had listened to one long litany of complaints from Louise about her marriage to Philipp, all of which Stéphanie had countered with her wary disapproval of Louise's reckless flaunting of the conventions.

Had Stéphanie's disapproval sprung from her stiff conformity or did it have roots in a deeper apprehension of what might happen if one over-stepped the limits? Louise had over-stepped the limits and her situation that cold spring day in 1900 must have seemed to Stéphanie to have reached rock-bottom. If Stéphanie had let her thoughts wander off to ruminate on Louise's prospects she would have assumed that Louise, shut away in the Lindendorf Clinic, was destined to remain there forever more.

Surely, Stéphanie's mind must have been a mass of thoughts and memories as their train rolled on its way. So many moments she must have relived, many of them painful but a few that filled her with feelings of warmth. Did she now have doubts about what the future would bring her? If Stéphanie had any doubts at all, not by so much as a flicker of an eyelash would she have let anyone suspect it. She was ever the staunch woman who would see things through to the end.

The spring of 1900 came late; the icy grip of a steely winter lingered on week after week. There was a good deal of civil unrest and strikes. Everything was changing and change was felt to be in the air. To the Viennese, musical as they are, this could be seen in their music. Brahms had died in 1897; the Waltz King, Johann Strauß junior, had put his violin aside, and at the Viennese Opera House there was a new musical director – one Gustav Mahler, whose music would be very different from what they were used to.

But on the Adriatic coast the spring weather was glorious. For ten days in Trieste Stéphanie and Erzsi were free to please themselves. They went out on bicycles together. They got out their sketchbooks and paints and went out to paint landscapes. Stéphanie's love of tennis came to the fore and she was seen playing tennis with various marine officers.

The plans for the wedding were put on hold because Elemér was not well; he had influenza which was the cause of a good deal of anxiety for Stéphanie who insisted upon sending for Dr. Auchenthaler to care for her fiancé. But the flu was not serious and Elemér was strong enough to travel to Görz on 17th March. He registered at the Südbahnhof Hotel under the name of Mr. Hudson. Elemér and Stéphanie were able to use the newfangled telephone to speak to each other. Finally Elemér travelled to Trieste where he was met by his older brother, Gábor, who had come from Budapest.

The following day, the 21st March, Erzsi returned to Vienna. Stéphanie accompanied her to the station and in tears she watched her depart. Then she returned to the castle alone. Her mind must have been full of swirling thoughts. There was so little she could be sure of. She must have wondered whether she would ever see Erzsi again. Erzsi could so easily turn her back upon her mother and refuse to see her again. Was this marriage worth that? Stéphanie could not have come up with an answer to that question at that moment. But there was no turning back. Nor did she want to. It was just that she would have liked to have had a clearer picture of her future and a little more confidence that she would find contentment in her new marriage.

Stéphanie married Elemér the following morning in the chapel at Miramare. Very punctually at eleven o'clock Stéphanie, wearing a silver grey dress adorned with delicate lace, joined her husband-to-be and the small group of wedding guests. It was all a very modest, low-key affair. It was conspicuous that there was no one from the House of Habsburg attending, nor anyone from Belgium, none of Stéphanie's family or former attendants. As Stéphanie entered the salon where the wedding party awaited her her emotion was very obvious and her face was very pale. At the moment of saying 'yes' there were tears running down her face, but her voice was firm and clear. Amongst the small group of people, mostly courtiers and servants, who were present that day, there must have been some who felt for Stéphanie as she took the step that would change the course of her life. At that moment the imperial flag that flew above the castle was brought down; from that moment there was nobody from the Imperial Family within the castle, only the Count and Countess von Lónyay and their personal entourage.

Elemér seems to have been touchingly concerned about his new wife. He had filled the rooms with flowers as if to hide the scarcity of wedding attendants. As a wedding present he had given her a pearl necklace which she was wearing. The only other jewellery she was wearing was a diamond diadem that Franz Joseph had given her. After the wedding mass there was lunch when all the telegrammes of congratulation were read out. These included a particularly warm message from Queen Victoria along with a ring that the Queen wanted Stéphanie to have in memory of her old aunt.

Back in Vienna the Emperor had ordered that the last links between Stéphanie and the Habsburg house should be broken. No doubt at the back of her mind Stéphanie would have known that this was happening, and that world must already have begun to feel rather remote and distant, yet just possibly at the moment when it did happen Stéphanie may have been intensely conscious of the change. Her life was moving forward and the old one had begun to crumble and fade into the past. From now on her life was linked, not to the Imperial Family in Vienna, but to a little-known, modest Hungarian Count and her home would be an estate in the Hungarian plains. For how long would everything she did provoke memories of the early days of her marriage to Rudolf and comparisons with those far-off experiences?

A week later Elemér and Stéphanie left Miramare on their honeymoon; they would never come back. Stéphanie never again returned to any of the palaces and homes she had known up until then. Nor would any of the Imperial Family attempt to keep in touch with her – the one exception being Franz Ferdinand and his loyalty meant a lot to her.

They headed for Cap Martin near Menton on the Riviera. Almost twenty years earlier Stéphanie had left Brussels forever, walking into a new life she knew very little about. On that occasion she had been allowed to take only a few personal possessions: a 'nécessaire de toilette' (a travelling case), an umbrella, her prayer book, and a few other small things, including a few little gifts from Rudolf, a music box, and the collar of a dog. What Stéphanie took with her this time is forgotten. She would have had a travelling case with her and her prayer book. Whether she was allowed to take all of her jewellery is not known. Almost certainly she would have collected up a few things that reminded her of Rudolf and her life with him. But the impression is that she walked into her new life very nearly as stripped of the things that had been part of her old life as when she left Brussels all those years before. You even wonder whether she still had the collar of the dog she didn't have.

Three months later Stéphanie received a letter – a long letter – from Franz Ferdinand. She was one of the people he wrote to, telling her that he, too, had married the person he wanted at his side for the rest of his life. He thanked her for her congratulations on his marriage and her best wishes for his future with Sophie.

Stéphanie had been one of the very few among his relatives who had sent any wishes at all. This was in character – she had supported him in his wish to marry the woman of his heart and she was delighted when he finally succeeded in doing so.

"I am deeply touched," Franz Ferdinand wrote. "I know what a warm and sincere interest you have shown me in this whole affair, how unwavering your friendship has been, and how kind you have been towards my wife!" It was a long letter and Franz Ferdinand ended up begging her forgiveness for going on so, but once again he reiterated how touched he had been to get her letter of good wishes. He called her 'his cousin' and it was clear that for Franz Ferdinand Stéphanie would always be part of his family.

Chapter 95

Five years after getting married, in 1906 Elemér Lónyay and Stéphanie bought Schloβ Oroszvár,[25] their final home. It was in a bad state of repair which pleased Stéphanie who eagerly looked forward to putting her own stamp on the place. Perhaps at that moment she remembered her efforts to settle and accept some of the grim rooms she had once occupied with Rudolf.

The palace stood in the Danube meadows not far from Pressburg, familiar countryside to Stéphanie, bringing back memories of her time with Archduchess Isabella. It was a wide, two-storeyed building with towers at the corners and balconies at first-floor windows. It had been built in 1840 by Count Emanuel Zichy-Ferraris who had a taste for English Tudor buildings and wanted to transpose the style to the Slovakian countryside. Stéphanie would have needed considerable imagination to discern any Tudor influence but, no doubt, she may well have added English touches to reflect the fact that she had invariably been happy when she was in England.

During those five years Stéphanie had discovered that she had an enemy in the Court Chamberlain, Prince Alfred Montenuovo, whose job it was to see that the ceremony of court life was always upheld and the dignity of the Imperial Family always preserved. Montenuovo was determined to ensure that, having married Elemér, she never sought privileges that were no longer due to her. Montenuovo would once not have dared to treat her in such a way but now he seemed to relish it.

Soon after her marriage Stéphanie began to experience the full extent of the petty humiliations that Montenuovo was now able to impose upon her, and she was shocked by them. Stéphanie grew ferociously angry when she realised that Montenuovo intended to emphasise in every petty way he could that she, who had been Crown Princess, was now no longer a member of the Imperial Family. Montenuovo went further and tended to treat her as though she was no longer royalty. Stéphanie's answer to this would have been 'I was born into a ruling royal family, a Princess, and a Princess I will always be!'

Yet having no status in the eyes of the world, away from official occasions she began to seek out a new way of life, one that was more relaxed, more easy-going and more out-going. Schloβ Oroszvár would symbolise that for her. Here Stéphanie's new life took root. The years passed. From now on she would rarely ever go back to Vienna. From now on Stéphanie

---

[25] Oroszvár means 'Russian town'; 'orosz' = Russian and 'vár' = town. In C19 it was named Karlburg. Today it is in the Czech Republic and called Rusovre.

could put behind her so many of the things that had once constrained her. Here at Oroszvár she wanted to create a life very different to the life she had lived in the Hofburg.

She wanted to greet people to her home without the constricting formality that ruled everything and everyone in the Hofburg. She wanted to offer warmth and welcome and she did not care too much whether she impressed her guests or not.

Viktor von Fritsche, who later became a chronicler of those pre-war years, wrote that the Lónyays opened their doors to a stream of aristocrats and royalty, not just Austrian and Hungarian but also English, French and Americans as well. Von Fritsche described how Stéphanie had achieved an elegance softened with comforts that he, an Austrian, regarded as English in style. Elemér Lónyay was a connoisseur and collector of art and antiques and every room reflected his skill in selecting objets d'art of value and taste. Stéphanie had found ways of displaying these with charm and elegance.

It was all generously welcoming. And yet it failed. Only a few of her guests could see past the almost universal preconception that Stéphanie was icily cold and distant so that while she talked of her wish to achieve the lifestyle of an English country house they saw the opposite. And Stéphanie, for her part, simply did not know how to be open and spontaneous; it was not something she had ever been allowed to be. She didn't know how to draw people closer.

Stéphanie found it particularly difficult to unbend with those younger than herself. Her eldest grandson, Prince Franz Joseph Windischgrätz (Erzsi's eldest son), described her as horribly pious and indescribably aristocratic and haughty, but what was important to him was whether a person was good "and she was very, very good." Franz Joseph, known as Franzi, and his younger brother Erni went to stay with their grandmother in September 1922. Their parents were locked in a bitter divorce and needed the boys out of the way. Both found their time in Oroszvár boring and longed to return to their mother. Yet in their letters home they expressed a liking for Stéphanie even while they could not endure spending too much time with her.

Another guest was the Nobel prize winner, Bertha von Suttner,[26] whose book *Die Waffen Nieder* ('Put Down your Arms') won the Nobel Peace Prize in 1889. She visited at Christmas 1906 when the changes that Stéphanie dreamed of had barely begun. Electric lights had yet to be installed but already Stéphanie had made the rooms gracious and elegant. What interested Bertha was the mixed collection of things that spoke of Stéphanie's journey through life up until that point. In Bertha's words, the decoration of the house illustrated a life that few acknowledged.

---

[26] Note 5 in the Notes Section.

And it amused Bertha how much Stéphanie particularly cared about her dogs. Like many a shy person, she found comfort in a close relationship with her animals. So there was Rollo, a wolfhound; Monsieur Björn, a Greland-Spitz; and a much, much loved Schnauzer, Lordy, who slept on Stéphanie's coat. To her dogs she related her innermost thoughts.

And here Franz Ferdinand could bring Sophie and be assured that she would be made welcome and cosseted with every comfort possible.

As he strode into the grand hall on their first visit Franz Ferdinand would have been feeling expansive and open. Stéphanie stepped forward and sank into a low curtsey with a demeanour of perfect submissiveness. Then Stéphanie turned to Sophie and put her arms around her, holding Sophie just a moment longer than mere politeness would have called for. Sophie was deeply touched.

Sophie, one step behind Franz Ferdinand, was observing his every tiny gesture and was glad for him. This was not a moment for her to admit even secretly to herself that she might feel a twinge or two of apprehension. First impressions of Stéphanie focussed upon her imperiousness. And nobody dared treat Stéphanie with familiarity – she was still accorded all the courtesies you paid the future Empress even though that was no longer what she was. How long did it take Sophie to realise that this might well be only a mask?

But ironically the situation was similar the other way round. "Like many outwardly controlled and reserved personalities, she hid a passionate emotional life beneath the mask of a great lady," wrote Stéphanie of Sophie. Thus, it took one 'volcano hidden beneath a cloak of ice' to recognise another. How long did it take them to recognise how much they had in common with the other?

At some point they would have gone out into the park. On the south side of the park there was a rose garden, beyond that a rock garden with a fountain flowing over the stones and down a rocky stream. There were many more gardens laid out in the grounds but this must have been the one that drew Franz Ferdinand and it would have been here that Sophie could watch her husband discuss roses enthusiastically with a fellow rose-lover. Perhaps that was when Sophie realised that there was another Stéphanie behind the remote, elegant figure who had been standing in the hallway to greet them, Elemér beside her and his scowling nephew, Carl, just behind them.

The days spent at Oroszvár were pleasurable. Franzi became jovial and cheery. He was delighted to find that his 'dear Cousin' was so passionate and knowledgeable a gardener and promised her a book by Freiland Stauden on propagating shrubs and trees "which," he wrote, "would certainly give her some new ideas for developing her park". And on her side Stéphanie was very chuffed.

Sophie relaxed. Her face softened. And here she found she could enjoy something she had largely lost since she married Franz Ferdinand. Sophie had always liked social get-togethers of like-minded people even if so often in the past she had had to enjoy them very much from the sidelines. Much as she loved her life at Konopischt, in many ways they were shut away from the rest of the world there. Whenever they ventured forth from there she was almost always on her guard. But as Bertha von Suttner described, Stéphanie always saw to it that her guests enjoyed a sociable ease, each day filled with many activities such as riding, boating, tennis, walking in the park when the weather allowed, time in the library quietly reading and evenings spent making music. More than most of the guests there, Sophie would have found special enjoyment at Oroszvár.

We can picture them sharing a glass of wine of an evening, waiting for the men to return. They would be gossiping over the ordinary family things that preoccupied them. And then they would talk about gardens and plants and flowers, for both Franz Ferdinand and Stéphanie were passionately fond of gardening. And, no doubt, they would cautiously mention the odd twinge or pain that afflicted them and discuss what was the best way of treating it.

They would have a laugh together over the latest fashion, and maybe one of them would say to the other, "You know, I really don't think it is very flattering – you'll never catch me wearing that!" Then almost wistfully would come the answer, "But it is nice to see young girls looking their best..." Perhaps Stéphanie would then confess how awkward she had felt when she first came to court, that she had known that people criticised her clothes and whispered behind her back how unattractive she was. Sophie would have known how to commiserate – Sophie was good at understanding how the other person felt. Then suddenly they would catch each other's eye and smile and relax.

And no doubt they would watch the shadows lengthen across the lawns as the light faded, and there would be memories, many of them painful. And all this would bring them closer together. Their liking for the other would strengthen and deepen. Did they ever reminisce about their childhoods? Stéphanie may have not wanted to talk too much about her own painful childhood. And Stéphanie would have refused utterly to speak of Rudolf – she froze if anyone ever mentioned his name. Nevertheless, it is unlikely that she could have found a better person to talk to about it all. Sophie had a serene understanding and a warm acceptance of people the way they were.

Sophie would have known how to listen with understanding to Stéphanie's account of her early years. Perhaps for the first time Stéphanie felt lifted from her mind a weight that she had never known was there.

Perhaps Sophie would respond by telling Stéphanie about her own childhood, the childhood of a diplomat's daughter constantly moving from one country to another. Sophie's childhood could hardly have been more different from Stéphanie's, not in the chaotic, wild-child way that Sisi's childhood had been, but rather in its supportive, homely ordinariness.

And then Sophie would tell Stéphanie about the time she spent in Brussels...

Chapter 96

Sophie was a minor figure who, according to all the conventions, ought to have lived a quiet life and been long forgotten. None would ever have expected that she might one day play so important a role in a world-changing drama.

She was born in Stuttgart on 1ˢᵗ March 1868, so she was four years younger than Stéphanie. Sophie was the fifth child to be born to Count Bohuslav Chotek [27] and his wife, Vilemína. There was already an older brother, Wolfgang, and three older sisters, Sidonie (known affectionately as Zdenka), Maria Pia (whose nickname was Rischel), and Karolina (Kara). After Sophie came Maria Antonia (Sophie's favourite sister), Octavia and Henriette, the youngest. And there was Therese who died in early childhood.

Sophie's mother, Vilemína, was a Kinsky, a very aristocratic Czech family. The Kinskys were among the most distinguished names of the Empire. They had several country estates and a fine baroque palace in Vienna. Anywhere in Europe the doors of the highest and most nobly-placed were ever open to them. They were cultured, cosmopolitan and travelled. Many had impressive military careers; it was said of them that no other family had produced so many brilliant soldiers. They were also patrons of the arts and Vilemína's grandfather had joined two others in 1808 in providing Ludwig van Beethoven with an annuity in order to persuade him not to return to Bonn.

The Kinskys did the things that the landed gentry did and they did them in fine style. They bred horses[28] famed for their strength. This was to draw a number of Kinskys into the inner circle of the Empress Elisabeth, in particular, Count Karel Kinsky who accompanied Elisabeth on her hunting trips in England in the 1870s. Most of the time Elisabeth had little liking for the Czech aristocracy but a number of the Kinskys enjoyed her interest in them.

Vilemína was the youngest daughter, a serene and gentle girl, who was extremely fond of music and played the piano remarkably well. She was described as very attractive, intelligent and clever, and she later helped mightily in her husband's career. She was always known affectionately as Mintzy. Sophie took after her.

In 1883 Karel Kinsky, riding his horse, Zoedone, won the Grand National Steeplechase at Aintree. The following year Zoedone collapsed during the

---

[27]   Note 6 in the Notes Section.

[28]   Note 7 in the Notes Section.

race, possibly due to poison. After that Zoedone was retired to the stud in Bohemia for the rest of her days. Sophie would have been fifteen when Zoedone first won at Aintree. No doubt she saw her mother glow with pride when she learned of her cousin's triumph.

The Choteks were not quite of the same standing as the Kinskys. But theirs was an old and respected family, one of the few whose ancestry was Bohemian all the way back beyond the wars of the Hussites and the Reformation. Bohuslav Chotek's father, Karl, had been the governor of the Tirol and Vorarlberg. Bohuslav himself was a diplomat.

Perhaps Mintzy felt that, in marrying Count Bohuslav Chotek, she had come down in the world. Count Bohuslav Chotek could not offer his high-born wife quite the standard of living that she was used to. He was not a wealthy man; the Chotek estates in Grosspriesen had all gone to his older brother. To support his large family, Bohuslav depended upon his income as a diplomat and it was never enough.

The impression one gets is that the Chotek family were down-to-earth, honest people. Mintzy bustled energetically to do the best for her children, trying always to present them to the world on a level that was slightly beyond the household finances but more than appropriate socially, given their aristocratic lineage. It is not hard to imagine that Mintzy economised on servants and household support but felt it incumbent upon her to see her daughters invited to the best dances and soirées even if sometimes it was not possible to have a maid accompany them. She would have pressed her daughters to become accomplished, elegant and cultured. Along with the usual accomplishments required of an aristocratic daughter, Sophie learned a number of languages. And along the way she must have learned a great deal about different European cultures. She may even have gained a shrewd grasp of European politics. Her enemies considered that she was formidably intelligent and in later years they would hold it against her.

Sophie was proud of her Czech antecedents but in some ways neither Sophie nor her family were very Czech. As a diplomat's daughter Sophie spent little of her growing-up years in Bohemia and the truth was that she spoke the Czech language only haltingly.

Mintzy would have required her daughters to help around the house, especially with helping with the younger children. No doubt there were scenes of family bustle full of chivvying good-humour. A girl calling down the stairs, "Rischel, Rischel, do you know where Mama has put her pelisse? Papa is already fretting. They will be late for the Embassy soirée and the baby is crying! Where could she have put her pelisse?" And a reply, "I don't know – don't ask me, I'm not ready either! Ask Soph, Soph will know!" And Mintzy, flustered, scurrying down, pausing only to check that her hair is in place and her dress straight, her mind half on the evening ahead and half on household matters she is leaving behind – "Girls, do make sure that the little ones have their suppers early and get to bed. Rischel, do you have to wear that ribbon? Now where is my fan?..."

Mostly Mintzy took the ups and downs her husband's lifestyle brought in its wake with gentle equanimity. But one can imagine Mintzy fretting over the image the family presented to the outside world, wishing that they could have just a bit more money so that the girls could go to more dances, more events, so that they could be seen more often at the theatre and the opera, so that they could have more toilettes and finer dresses. Sophie, particularly, loved and adored going to the theatre and opera but these were very rare treats because the family could not often afford them. The Chotek girls were invited often enough to the finest and richest houses in Europe, they met royalty, they could hold their heads high, but nevertheless, there was always a sense that they were Cinderellas at these events.

Mintzy also helped her husband with the long diplomatic reports that Vienna required from him. Many a long evening was spent preparing these reports; they had to be written by hand. It is doubtful whether they received more than a passing glance in Vienna, but they had to be done.

Since Bohuslav was a diplomat, the family led a peripatetic life. Sophie lived in St. Petersburg, Berlin, London, Madrid, Brussels and Dresden as well as Prague and Vienna. The family were not happy in Madrid. As well as finding life in Spain difficult they found it expensive. Bohuslav put pressure upon the authorities in Vienna for a change which, when it came, meant a move to Brussels.

The Choteks did well in Brussels. They were very well liked by the Belgian royal family. Marie-Henriette showed Mintzy special attention and almost regarded her as a friend. Mintzy returned the compliment by naming her youngest daughter, Henriette, after the Belgian Queen. And Bohuslav came to be on familiar terms with Leo.

Towards the end of May 1878 a new racecourse was opened in the Forêt de Soignies near Brussels. During the course of the celebrations on this occasion Leo left the royal pavilion to go over to speak to Bohuslav who was standing near the stables. Such a gesture from the King would have caught the attention of all around and singled Bohuslav out as someone who enjoyed the favour of the King himself.

Bohuslav sported the most enormous bushy sideburns, almost like a couple of unclipped hedges extending down from his ears almost to his chin. In the facial hair stakes the prize would have gone to Bohuslav. The picture we get of Bohuslav himself is of a somewhat fussy man, but he was a superlative courtier and knew how to make himself gracious towards those in high places. The Austrian-Hungarian Monarchy did not have quite the standing in Europe it had in the early years of the century, for the German Empire had risen and challenged that position, but the Austro-Hungarian Monarchy was still one of the most important states in Europe, whereas

Belgium was very much a newcomer. It is likely that Leo would have been glad of any chance to promote his standing with the Austrian powers. And in his fussy way, Bohuslav could be useful to the Belgian King.

But by all accounts, Leo's liking for Bohuslav went beyond the merely pragmatic. Whether Bohuslav liked Leo is not known – probably not. But if he did not much care for Leo, the only person he would have told would have been Mintzy.

Early in 1879 Bohuslav was summoned to Vienna from Brussels where he had a number of discreet meetings with the Emperor Franz Joseph, with Baron Haymerle, the minister of the imperial household and with Rudolf himself. Bohuslav returned to Brussels charged with the job of preparing the way for Rudolf's visiting Brussels in March – and the aim of Rudolf's visit was to decide whether he liked Stéphanie enough to marry her. It was a highly delicate task because Rudolf needed to feel that he could – if need be – walk away without repercussions or ill-feeling. Everything needed to be very discreet and hushed-up until Rudolf himself had made up his mind about Stéphanie.

In March 1879 Sophie had her eleventh birthday. She would have heard at home much discussion of events at the court. She would have picked up the atmosphere of excitement and eagerness that would have reigned while all this was going on. When, after it was announced that Rudolf and Stéphanie were to be married, there were dinners and gala evenings at the palace, and Bohuslav and Mintzy with their elder daughters would be invited.

Sophie was still too young to go to these sumptuous events. All she could do was wait impatiently at home for her sisters to come back, bursting with excitement, full of the evening's events, describing how grand it had all been. Perhaps she slipped into Zdenka's room and begged her to describe it all all over again – slowly, full of every detail and not miss anything out – "What was the salon at the palace like?" "What had the people there looked like?" "What were the clothes like?" And most important of all – Stéphanie "what was *she* like?"

Perhaps Zdenka took pity on her eager little sister. Perhaps she sat down before she had even fully unpinned her hair and tried to create a picture for little Sophie of what it had been like. Sophie could not get enough; her eyes big, she could have sat there till morning drinking up the images her sister was painting for her. Tiredness would suddenly have overwhelmed Zdenka; eyelids heavy, she would have started to yawn desperately. "Please, Zdenka, tell me!" "Go to bed, Soph, I'll tell you tomorrow. I'm too tired!" And a cross Mintzy would have looked round the door, exclaiming at the late hour, and chivvied her daughters to bed.

"But, Stéphanie, what was she like?" Sophie would not have let that drop; she would have wanted every last detail. And Zdenka would describe the light blue dress that Stéphanie was wearing, with a single string of pearls around her neck. Zdenka may even have giggled and said, "I don't think her maid knew what to do with her hair. It looked as though she had just pulled it straight back off her face!" Perhaps Zdenka then added thoughtfully, "She was trying so hard – it was funny."

Some years later Zdenka ended up as lady-in-waiting to Crown Princess Stéphanie. If she had really disliked Stéphanie that evening, she could have gone somewhere else, rather than join Stéphanie's household. So perhaps we can take it that Zdenka's first impression of the young Belgian Princess was a good one. All the Chotek girls knew what it felt like to be viewed as something of an ugly duckling. Perhaps Zdenka saw how very vulnerable and alone Stéphanie looked. Perhaps she told her little sister, Sophie.

And would she be happy, the Princess Stéphanie? Sophie would want to know that, too. What was he like, the Archduke from Vienna? It is likely that Zdenka could not satisfy her curiosity. At that gala dinner in honour of the betrothal of Princess Stéphanie and Crown Prince Rudolf, Zdenka almost certainly was never very near the betrothed couple and could only catch glimpses of them through the throng of elegant people. "But you must have noticed how they looked at each other?" Sophie surely pressed her sister. Zdenka thought. "They didn't look at each other much."

This little remark would stick in Sophie's mind. As the years went by, she would hear from time to time about the Crown Princess. She would see her picture in the papers. She would overhear unkind gossip about her. All the gory details of Rudolf's death would be blazoned across the country. A quiet, gentle-minded Sophie would think back to that day in Brussels and try to imagine what Stéphanie had really felt like behind the brave mask she was wearing for the outside world, and then she would wonder about how life had treated Stéphanie since then. Because of that little remark, Sophie would always carry around inside herself a special curiosity about Stéphanie and Rudolf, and also, by extension, about all the Habsburgs. Years later Sophie would find herself in the same room as Franz Ferdinand and her eyes would be drawn to him in some kind of demanding fascination.

Then in 1886 Mintzy died. Sophie was just eighteen and it fell to her to take over managing the household for her father. With most of her sisters gone on to lives of their own, Sophie was left to look after the small group of them left. Two of her sisters were on the point of getting married and Zdenka was serving the Crown Princess Stéphanie as a lady-in-waiting at the Hofburg in Vienna.

The death of Mintzy completely crushed Bohuslav who slowly withdrew from society. His last diplomatic posting was in Dresden and here he stayed with his remaining unmarried daughters. Since the unification of Germany, Dresden as the capital of Saxony was no longer of any great diplomatic importance. The move from Brussels to Dresden from a career point-of-view was something of a slap in the face for Bohuslav. Bohuslav had clearly expected some kind of honour or recognition for his work in facilitating the marriage between Stéphanie and Rudolf, but none had been forthcoming. Instead Bohuslav's diplomatic career had taken a backward step.

So the Choteks settled down to a quiet life in Dresden. Bohuslav missed his energetic wife and he did not feel that he had the courage to go on serving as a diplomat, but for financial reasons he could not retire and stop. However, now there seemed to be too much bureaucracy, too many reports, and he needed Mintzy's help with all those handwritten reports that Vienna demanded almost daily.

Mintzy died on 5th March 1886, just a few days after Sophie's birthday. Mintzy did not live to see Kara marry Count Leopold Nosticz-Rieneck which took place a few weeks later. Kara was just twenty-one. Her wedding must have been a much more subdued affair than Kara may well once have hoped for. Mintzy, in spite of weakness and illness, would have pushed herself to arrange for her daughter – the first to marry – the finest, happiest and most beautiful wedding possible. But she had not the strength to see it all happen.

About a year later Rischel (Maria Pia) married the Count Jaroslav von Thun und Hohenstein. Rischel was making a good marriage. Jaroslav's father was also a diplomat and had been posted to the Embassy in Berlin at the same time as Bohuslav Chotek. Berlin was changing out of all recognition and it was an exciting place to live. Jaroslav chose to study law at the university there. We can presume that it was in Berlin that Rischel and Jaroslav got to know each other and fell in love.

The whole Chotek family would have watched the growing love between the two young people with great satisfaction and pleasure. This marriage would have made Mintzy very proud if only she could have lived to see it, for the Thun und Hohenstein family came from the highest Bohemian aristocracy.

For Sophie, life settled into a quiet pattern. She did not go out as much as she had. Her father was no longer as interested in social events – he was old now, with no wife at his side to bustle him into action. There was no Mintzy to argue that going out to the theatre or opera occasionally was not just good for the girls but also good for promoting their chances of finding husbands. There was no Mintzy to fuss that Sophie and Henriette had the kind of elegant clothes in which they could face the highest in the land with their heads high. No doubt Bohuslav would say to them in puzzled tones, "But you have got wardrobes full of fine clothes – and very expensive they were, too! You can't say you haven't got anything to wear!" And Sophie would not know how to explain that, yes, she had plenty of clothes but she had had them a long time, they had been mended many times and her dresses were beginning to look a bit tired – and, besides, they were no longer quite the fashion and she could not help looking a bit frumpy in them.

But finances were horribly tight and within two years Sophie was looking for a position, like Zdenka, as a lady-in-waiting. She ended up accepting a position with the Archduchess Isabella. The announcement was given out on 10th August 1888 – Sophie was twenty-one, which was very young to become a lady-in-waiting.

The Archduke Friedrich was a cousin of Franz Ferdinand's; his wife Isabella had descended from the once royal family of Croy-Dülmen. She was one of those women who wanted everyone to know that the ancient house of Croy had once ruled and that that gave her a superiority no one should ever forget. Legend had it that the Croys were descended from the Arpads and the brothers, Antoine and Jehan, were among the first twenty-four Knights of the Golden Fleece created by Philippe the Benevolent of Burgundy in the year 1431.

Archduke Friedrich fell head-over-heels in love with the Duke of Croy's second daughter. He made no secret of his feelings which provoked the determined opposition both from his mother, who regarded a Princess of Croy as not being of sufficiently exalted a family for a Habsburg, and from his uncle, the Archduke Albrecht. Albrecht, whose own only son had died in childhood, had adopted Friedrich and intended to make him his heir, leaving him an immense fortune and a number of very fine palaces.

But in 1878 Friedrich announced his engagement and nothing was going to stop him marrying the girl of his choice. She was pretty in those days and high-spirited, too. Theirs was a good marriage and Isabella's energy went into creating a lively and interesting household where nobody could have found the time to be bored.

In later years Isabella grew very stout and she turned into a bulldozer of a woman. Frequent pregnancies did much to make her into what she became. Isabella gave birth to eight daughters before she held in her arms her one and only son, Albrecht.[29] Albrecht had strong acting talents that became very clear when the whole family got involved in amateur dramatics to while away the winter evenings. Albrecht, the high-spirited one like his mother, was the apple of his mother's eye.

---

[29]   Note 8 in the Notes Section.

If Sophie had ever had any dreams of a husband and home of her own they had slowly faded and once she had joined Isabella's household it is likely that she gave up such thoughts altogether. She would watch her sisters bring children into the world and focus her feelings on her nephews and nieces. It must have seemed as though life from now on would pass her by. Her future lay as a lowly member of Isabella's household.

In some ways it was a demeaning position for Sophie. A lady-in-waiting's role was to be an unobtrusive assistant to her mistress, always at Isabella's beck and call, there to remember on behalf of Isabella all the little things and to keep the social side of Isabella's household rolling smoothly. She was expected to forget who she was herself and to become an extension of Isabella.

Sophie, like many a lady-in-waiting, must many times have needed to bite her tongue and accept with a smile what was demanded of her. But would Sophie have seen this as so very different to running her father's household on not enough money, where there was often not quite enough on her plate and she often had to hide the fact that there were holes in her shoes? Sophie was bright and open-minded. She was the sort of person who looked forward to the future; she did not wallow in the past.

Chapter 97

The love between Franz Ferdinand and Sophie Chotek was a secret that they were to keep between themselves for years. There was only one person fully in the know, and that was Franz Ferdinand's personal servant, Franz Janaczek. Franz Ferdinand placed his trust wholly and entirely in Janaczek. It was not misplaced. Janaczek was to prove that he could be trusted absolutely. Even after Franz Ferdinand's death Janaczek refused to speak of any matter about which he had once promised to keep quiet.

And Franz Ferdinand treated his servant well, raising him from valet to major-domo of his household when he and Sophie settled down to live their lives at Konopischt Castle. Janaczek came to be one of the few who could act upon his own initiative, knowing that if he provoked the Archduke's anger it would only ever be a summer storm and soon over. Janaczek upon occasion was known to flout the Archduke's express orders. He could do even that. He only had to put on what Franz Ferdinand called his "offended Caesar's demeanour" to be restored to favour.

Without Franz Janaczek they could not have kept their secret so well for so long. It cannot have been a very easy secret to keep. Once their attachment for each other had taken root, both must have wanted to see the other as often as they possibly could. Yet each and every time they did meet there must have been a risk of something going wrong and their being found out. Of course, eventually something did go wrong and they were found out. But that was years down the road.

It cannot even be known with certainty when they first met. There are some who believe that first meeting took place as early as 1888. Rischel had married Count Jaroslav von Thun und Hohenstein in 1887 about a year after their mother's death, and they lived in Prague. Jaroslav was one of many with whom Franz Ferdinand went out shooting and hunting. It is possible that Franz Ferdinand first set eyes upon Sophie Chotek on some occasion when she was staying with her sister. But in 1888 Franz Ferdinand was twenty-four and Franz Ferdinand did not feel ready for marriage; also he had a mistress at the time so it is likely he would not have paid Sophie much attention.

The earliest hard evidence of them being together is a photograph taken at a shooting party held at Halbthurn in the winter of 1893. They are both in that picture.

By 1894 at the latest their feelings for each other had taken root. In 1894 Franz Ferdinand visited London, an occasion when potential brides were thrown at him on every side. Franz Ferdinand later wrote to Rischel, describing the discomfort he felt as he became increasingly aware of what their ploy was.

"I felt awkward," he said. The designated fiancées circled around him and they showed worrying degrees of persistence, he went on. Franz Ferdinand noticed the parents of one of them examining him with rapt attention, smiles plastered on their faces. Franz Ferdinand referred to the daughter as a "victim" and then went on to add "I cannot have made a very good impression". He studiously kept his conversation to matters like the weather, the economy and the likelihood of favourable harvests, allowing not a chink in his armour.

On one occasion at a luncheon given by the Prince of Wales, the Princess Hélène d'Orléans was suddenly planted beside him in a way that rather startled Franz Ferdinand. Princess Hélène belonged to the exiled French royal family; Her father was the Comte de Paris and a number of observers had great hopes that here was an excellent match, particularly from a diplomatic point of view.

She was beautiful and poised. Franz Ferdinand considered her the prettiest and most interesting of the prowling herd of would-be brides. But she insisted upon speaking to him in French and Franz Ferdinand found keeping up his side of the conversation a strain. It didn't help that he made mistake after mistake in French and she pointedly corrected each and every one of them – "with undying patience," he conceded. It can't have been an easy conversation.

Across the table the long-nosed comte de Paris made encouraging signs to his daughter. There was a champagne toast to her health which embarrassed Franz Ferdinand all the more because it felt like a toast to their engagement. By the end of the meal Franz Ferdinand felt a cold sweat dripping visibly down his forehead.

The irony here was that Hélène wanted him no more than he wanted her. Four years earlier Hélène had fallen intensely in love with the Duke of Clarence, Queen Victoria's grandson, and he with her. Religion made their marriage difficult, but she first offered to convert to the Church of England and then he offered to renounce his position in the line of succession to the British throne. Since he was Bertie's eldest son, this was a significant move. In the end the pressures against these two put an end to their hopes. The Duke of Clarence died before his father and his younger brother became the heir to the English throne and would one day become King George V.

Soon after all hope that she might marry the Duke of Clarence was gone, family matchmakers seem to have set about trying to engineer a marriage for her with Prince Baudouin of Belgium, the young man that

Stéphanie's sister, Clémentine, had been so in love with. Baudouin died young in 1891 and in 1892 Hélène learned of the death of the Duke of Clarence. So that in 1894 when Hélène found herself being engineered towards Franz Ferdinand it seems likely that she would have been every bit as wary of him as he was of her.

For Hélène romance was a fraught experience and it may even have seemed to her that any young man who showed an interest in her was cursed by the prospect of an early death. Hélène finally married Prince Amedeo, the second Duke of Aosta, and grandson of King Vittorio-Emmanuele II of Italy in 1895. Prince Amedeo died at the age of sixty-two in 1931, outwitting any curse emanating from Princess Hélène.

But for Franz Ferdinand, all these manoeuvres to find him a bride just increased the strain upon his love for Sophie Chotek.

The scandal did not break until 1899. So they kept their secret for a minimum of six years and possibly as much as eleven years. Even for six years to keep it secret and to keep it alive was a long time. The easiest way to keep it secret was not to see each other or speak to each other too much. The easiest way to keep it alive was to be in contact with each other as much as they possibly could be. For a large part of that time they could not see each other at all. Franz Ferdinand was seriously ill with tuberculosis and his treatment involved long periods when his doctors allowed him to do nothing at all for fear that it would overtax his strength. For much of the time many had already given up all hope of Franz Ferdinand's recovering from this terrible disease. The understanding between them needed to be firm and deep-rooted. They had to trust each other. And above all it had to be worth the risks each was taking.

Year in, year out, they made do with secret letters and brief meetings, often in the presence of others when each had to keep up the pretence demanded by their different positions. She had to play the part of the courteous, respectful, slightly retiring, insignificant Countess. He had to play the part of not showing any particular interest in her. He had to avoid being seen watching her, glancing at her, speaking with her any more than would be deemed appropriate given their different positions in society.

Keep it up they did, year in, year out, loving each other and hiding that love behind a mask of correct behaviour. No one knows whether they intended to keep it a secret forever, until love died, starved of oxygen. Or did they keep thinking that somehow they could work something out and be together? As it was something did happen and they were caught out and then they had to do something – either break it off completely, or fight for their love.

But how did the impoverished diplomat's daughter who had spent her life traipsing from court to court in the wake of her father's postings end up winning the heart of the man destined to become Emperor? How did the military Archduke, whose life appears to have been so constrained by protocol and whose social skills were always so very unsure, seek out and fall in love with so unlikely a partner? How did so staunch a love take root?

Franz Ferdinand was no Otto. There was a shy streak in him. Those he mixed with in the army had noticed that he was something of a loner, that he did not mix all that easily. Franz Ferdinand had had a mistress, but, unlike either Otto or Rudolf, there were no tales of his flirtations. There were no whispers about his amours in the same way there were whispers about Rudolf's.

It all sounds as though he did not find the courtly game of flirtation very easy. But he loved the company of his stepmother, Maria Theresia, and he was deeply fond of his sisters. He sounds as though he was the sort of man who wanted and enjoyed the company of women as friends. Never could he have treated them as adversaries in a mysterious erotic game the way Otto did. "Women," Rudolf had once said, "bore me to death when they are not laughing or singing. And, in the end, are they good for anything other than laughing and singing?" Never would Franz Ferdinand have spoken of women the way Rudolf did.

Franz Ferdinand was often described as „schroff". This means rugged, stern, gruff. A person who is „schroff" would tend to be abrupt and have a forbidding demeanour. And Franz Ferdinand was not always the most approachable person.[30] The young countesses who came to court balls and hovered gracefully in the vicinity of Archdukes would watch him a little warily. He was not like Rudolf. He did not charm them easily and then sweep them off into the dance. They dipped into deep curtsies, murmuring „Kaiserliche Hoheit" ("Imperial Highness") but his glance back did not make them turn to molten chocolate inside. No, he was „schroff" and that did not make it very easy for anyone to get to know him.

Franz Ferdinand himself was only too well aware of this. He knew he was not popular. He knew that he had acquired all sorts of reputations, mostly unflattering. He was said to be a miser. He was seen as difficult and dangerous, a threat.

---

[30] Hertha Pauli stressed this aspect of Franz Ferdinand's character in her book *The Secret of Sarajevo*. In fact, „schroff" did not have to mean objectionable – fans of Jane Austin might care to consider how „schroff" Mr. Darcy is as portrayed by Colin Firth in the 1996 BBC TV series of *Pride and Prejudice*.

His ideas about the future of the Empire he stood to inherit were viewed with great suspicion. In one sense he was intensely threatening: Franz Ferdinand always wanted to find out for himself and he would not just take someone else's word for anything. He wanted to learn all he could as far as possible straight from the horse's mouth. So the nobility, whether they were the Austrian nobility, the Hungarian nobility or the Czech nobility, felt that their unique position standing between the rulers and the ruled was under threat. Their ability to act as the conduit that translated edicts from on high into practice down below and advising as to what policy stance those on high should adopt was going to be under threat when this man became Emperor.

The Hungarian aristocracy particularly clung to this role. So it was no accident that Franz Ferdinand had acquired a reputation as a man who hated Hungary and the Hungarians. And yet, of the Hungarians, he would say, "How can one hate such a chivalrous nation? I don't know anyone more likeable than, say, the Hungarian peasant..." Franz Ferdinand's view of the Czechs was tempered by his awareness of Czech nationalism. He felt that the Czech nobility tended to be scheming. There were times when he decided that his Czech recruits were amongst the most dependable, but, he said, "Too bad we must work through the nobility..."

Franz Ferdinand knew that the officers' mess in Budweis called him "the ogre". They had difficulties dealing with a man who was, on the one hand, the harshest of martinets, causing his company commanders to wince under his tongue-lashings, and who, on the other hand, showed more concern for his men's welfare than they had ever known before.

There is a story which illustrates how Franz Ferdinand's concern for his men often made him so difficult to deal with for the officers. It came to Franz Ferdinand's ears that the funeral of a soldier serving under him had turned into a grim affair because the army band had been ordered to play at some social event instead of providing music to accompany the coffin to its final resting place. The dead man's family had been deeply hurt. Franz Ferdinand ordered the band to assemble at the church. He divided the musicians into two groups and had one group playing beside the grave and the other over in the far corner of the churchyard. Angrily, he told the officers that this was what they should have done: ensure that the soldier was properly honoured in death even if it meant that the other gathering had only a small group of musicians.

Few men welcomed the idea of joining Franz Ferdinand's staff, yet again and again they would find him so much easier to deal with than they ever expected.

His general staff aide, Baron Margutti,[31] was one hundred percent for

---

[31] Note 9 in the Notes Section.

Franz Ferdinand and he would not hear a word against a man whose affection and loyalty towards his men was not like any other. Margutti would have been the first to concede that Franz Ferdinand's outbursts of anger were explosive – but they passed over just as quickly, usually with a plea for forgiveness. Franz Ferdinand was quick to assess people, quick to decide who he could deal straightforwardly with, and from then on Franz Ferdinand's respect for those whose views he found worth listening to was unshakeable.

His private secretary, Count Paul Nikitsch-Boulles,[32] commented that there was hardly a topic one could not discuss calmly and openly with him. Nikitsch-Boulles added that Franz Ferdinand was the first to rue the violence of his outbursts and quick to make up with the person in question. Franz Ferdinand could cope with unpalatable truths and preferred to hear them openly and deal with them. He always preferred to be informed verbally and to his face which may have been an indication of his dyslexia.

Baron Andreas Morsey joined Franz Ferdinand's entourage in the last years of his life. Morsey was most reluctant about taking up the position and he cannot have found it reassuring when early on Franz Ferdinand bluntly insisted that however difficult Morsey might find it, he should always tell Franz Ferdinand the truth directly to his face – "even if you are afraid you might be thrown out for it!"

But nobody was ever thrown out for it. Morsey described how a certain Lieutenant Schwarz who had a lowly post running the administration of the gardens always spoke his mind completely unperturbed. Franz Ferdinand might explode but it never lasted. Schwarz knew that, in truth, he enjoyed Franz Ferdinand's highest esteem.

During the long years when Franz Ferdinand was fighting consumption, he was also trying to learn about the country he expected one day to rule. Franz Ferdinand's style was always crisp and to the point, so he did not come over as particularly emollient and he certainly did not give the impression that he would ever let anyone treat him as an easy push-over. But the picture of Franz Ferdinand being a mass of blinkered, unreasoning hatreds just does not ring true.

Faced with the most obstructive bureaucracy possibly ever known, where for each and every bit of information one bureaucrat had to ask another who had to ask a third, Franz Ferdinand exploded, "Are all these jobs sinecures? Are the gentlemen there only for dinners and medals? It is time for a change!" That did not make him loved; it made him resented and hated.

---

[32]   Note 10 in the Notes Section.

He would have fascinated the feminine half of society. Their gossip would have focussed upon him as a person, his relationships and flirtations or rather the apparent lack of them, and whom he might one day marry. Whispering together, young women may have conceded pity for whoever was unfortunate enough to become his wife, while shivering in delicious dread at the thought of the man who was such a mystery and so „schroff"!

Countess Nora Függer, who was a great confidante of his,[33] knew more about his feelings on the matter than most. She clearly had been pressing him to find a good, beautiful wife.

On 10th October 1898 Franz Ferdinand wrote back to her, asking, "whom then should I marry? There is nobody there. You say, Countess, that I should take a wife who is kind, clever, beautiful and good. All right, but tell me where I might find such a woman! Sadly, there is nobody to choose from the marriageable princesses; they are all children, „piperl" ['chicks'] of seventeen or eighteen, one uglier than the other..." Perhaps at that moment he was thinking of the circling herd of would-be brides he had had to fend off in London in 1894.

He was angry that "with us [meaning the Imperial Family], man and wife are related to each other twenty times over. The result is that half of the children are either epileptics[34] or idiots!" To Countess Nora Függer, he added, "I can imagine the kind of woman I would like, someone I could be happy with. She would not be too young, and her character and views should be fully formed. I know of no such princess..."

And that was the problem – back in 1888, ten years earlier, he had written to Rudolf that the only way of leading a pleasant, carefree life would be to ask for the hand of some princess or other, never mind who – a "wax doll" he called her. Ten years on he was no longer interested in whether there existed an appropriate "wax doll", he already knew exactly whom he wanted and was agonising over the likely outcome when the news came out.

In the autumn of 1894, a year after that photograph was taken in which Franz Ferdinand and Sophie are standing in the same group, the one in the forefront of the group, the other pushed to the back, a ball was given in honour of the Archduke by the imperial governor of Bohemia, Count Franz von Thun und Hohenstein, a cousin of Count Jaroslav von Thun und Hohenstein. It was held at the *Statthalterei*, the governor's mansion at the foot of the medieval Hradschin Castle. It was a sumptuous affair, all

---

[33] Nora Függer's close relationship with Franz Ferdinand lasted until he married Sophie Chotek after which an icy rift came between them. Note 11 in the Notes Section.

[34] It was widely believed in those days that epilepsy was inherited. There had been several instances of epilepsy within the Imperial Family, including Franz Joseph's uncle who was forced to abdicate. Epilepsy was much feared.

glittering chandeliers and lilting music, and the ballroom thronged with the highest and noblest families of Bohemia. To a ball for the great and the good of Prague given by Count Franz von Thun und Hohenstein there most certainly would have been an invitation to Count Jaroslav, together with his wife and his sister-in-law who happened to be staying with them. Thus Sophie was there that evening.

There are many who believe that this was the occasion when Franz Ferdinand and Sophie first became aware of each other. Adam Müller-Guttenbrunn in his diaries mentioned seeing Sophie for the first time on this occasion. He noticed how intently she was watching the Archduke. But he also suggested that Franz Ferdinand may not have been particularly aware of her interest, since he was preoccupied all evening with other people. Here he was wrong; if Franz Ferdinand appeared to pay Sophie little attention it was deliberate. He would not have wanted to draw attention to his interest in Sophie. He already knew her. The seeds of their love had already been planted.

Perhaps around about the time when that photograph was taken he had been out hunting with a group of his hunting friends. And in the evening after he had returned from the day's hunting, he had hung back, unable to control an agonising bout of coughing, as the whole household and the hunting party made their way to the dining room for dinner. Sophie, quietly observing as she always did, might have stopped to see that he was all right. She might have tilted her head and offered to get him a glass of water. Sophie invariably radiated warmth and calm and cheerfulness; she could show concern and understanding without being intrusive or officious. Perhaps then the warmth of her personality, her little gesture of thoughtfulness, touched him and he turned and looked at her. Yes, he had seen her before, fleetingly, but without paying her much attention – but this was different.

Maybe on another occasion he had found her alone reading a book while outside the rain lashed against the window pane. He might have enquired what she was reading and added that in this gloomy light she could hardly see to read. Could the book have been in Russian? Franz Ferdinand was the sort of man who would have been impressed by a woman with intelligence, knowledge and an interest in world affairs and other countries. He might have asked her opinion of the Russian situation and been interested when she gave it to him. She would have given it quite straightforwardly, neither affecting silliness nor pretending not to have her own ideas. She may even – almost imperceptibly – have contradicted him on some point knowing that he would rise to the bait. And when he assertively rebuffed her, he might suddenly have caught her eye and found there was an impish twinkle there. And as the gloomy evening drew on, perhaps they ended up sitting there in the half light, exchanging their thoughts in so free and easy a manner.

He just might have been a touch envious of her having lived in other countries and learned so much about them. Franz Ferdinand did not like travelling but he had travelled – he had travelled round the world. But he had never stayed long anywhere and he had found it difficult to fit into other cultures. He might have wished that he could have, like her, stayed for years in one place, getting to know it from the inside out and ending up feeling at home there. He would have admired her for that. She may have recounted little stories and anecdotes from her experiences in the different cities where she had lived. She had observed so much and now with a piquant detail she would lace her little account of something quite insignificant. She could use an amusing turn of words and make him smile.

His interest in her was really awakened in the spring of 1894. In April he wrote a letter to her, a very formal letter where he addresses her as „Verehrteste Gräfin" ('Most honoured Countess') and adopts a cool tone as befits a slight acquaintance. He mentions a meeting on the Italian Riviera. It is not clear when or how that occurred.

However, on 18th August 1894 he wrote again, recalling their having met at the palace of Count Heinrich Larisch in Vienna. This had been a masked ball which would have made it possible to let your hair down a little more than courtly behaviour usually allowed. Franz Ferdinand called it 'our Dervish Ball' which certainly suggests that behind the masks they had gone a long way towards getting to know each other. Had there been some rather exciting swirling around on the dance floor? Had Franz Ferdinand been able to draw Sophie very, very close? He wasn't the sort of man who found it easy to do that – he was no Otto – but with Sophie he could not help himself.

In the same letter he also mentioned "our last little dance at Sacher's". This suggests that he had been able to tempt Sophie away from the pomp of the Larisch Palace to somewhere where there were not so many eyes upon them. This letter was addressed to 'darling Sophie'. And by then Sophie was looking forward to the ball at the *Statthalterei*.

Since Franz Ferdinand was the guest of honour that night in Prague, many eyes would have been upon him. And what they would have seen was a slim young man, too thin and with a particularly pale face. Few who watched him that night would have doubted that he was a very sick man. Consumption had not yet been diagnosed but it was known that he had never been vigorous, that he was prone to throat ailments and that he was often warned against over-exertion. Before the evening was over he would look completely washed out.

He had not wanted to attend this ball at all and he did not expect to enjoy it but, according to the bureaucrats in Vienna, he was there to "tighten the bonds between the Imperial Archhouse and the high Bohemian nobility".

He was the focus of attention, but in a way he wasn't. They weren't interested in him. The glances cast his way seemed to turn away only too quickly as though he were negligible – one glance and you had seen what you needed to see and now could get on with throwing yourself into the evening! What was different about Sophie was that in her eyes he was not negligible. "She made eyes at the Archduke," wrote Adam Müller-Guttenbrunn in his diary.

It is just possible that Sophie wanted to be at this ball and had chosen to visit her sister deliberately in order to be able to accompany them. Sophie had always been the curious one. Perhaps she told Rischel, "I would just like to see what he is like!" This would have been a deception since she already knew what he was like and in her mind she had glowing memories of their 'Dervish Ball', but to keep up the secrecy little lies sometimes had to be told.

And Rischel would have told her how silly she was – "You know, he is not even very handsome!" Sophie would smile her wide smile, a slightly tilted smile, and Rischel would shake her head at her sister, who at twenty-six should have long since out grown her foolish imaginings. At twenty-six Sophie no longer had hopes of marriage herself. She would dress simply – a modest dark gown and no jewels to speak of. For Rischel the finery!

They would have entered that grand hall, their heads high, conscious that they had as much right to be there as anyone else. But Sophie, thinking of the impoverished state in which she now lived, would not have expected to be accorded much respect and even less attention. She was used to being brushed aside. She could remember an occasion when the Chotek girls had gone to to some soirée in Vienna and met with disdainful glances. They were alone and there was no maid to see to their needs and, worse, it was noticed that their shoes had been stitched up with thread to make them last longer.

So that evening Sophie stood somewhat apart from the throng. She did not seek to draw herself to anyone's attention. She was content to pass the time quietly, and she spent it watching the Archduke.

Looking intently at him, she would remember that time in Brussels when she had been too young to go with her parents and her older sisters to the palace at Laeken. She would remember sitting on the bottom step of the stairway waiting for their return, hardly able to contain her curiosity about the Princess and the Crown Prince. She would remember trying to picture it all from her sister's wholly inadequate descriptions of how it had been. Did Rischel, over there dancing with her husband, remember those times in Brussels? Rischel had never really understood her fascination. Sophie herself could not really explain – just, "they interest me; I wonder what they think and feel?"

Then, she had been still a child with a round face and long hair. Now she stood tall and straight, too thin for a society that saw prettiness in rounded curves. She was thin because in the Chotek household there was often only just enough food on their plates. She was thin because she often had to walk since a carriage could not be afforded. Her soft chestnut brown hair was piled around her face, a face best described as chiselled and fine rather than pretty. Her best feature were her eyes, large, intense, dark brown eyes. Those eyes that now were focussed fascinated upon the Archduke. And in her mind she wondered about him, his illness, his solitariness, his cautiousness.

But there was something else. At their Dervish Ball there had been brief flashes showing another side to him. They had been like the sudden bright flashes of sunshine penetrating the cloud cover on a dark, overcast day. The brightness of such flashes startle just because they are not expected. And he had startled her in an unexpected way. He had shown her at their Dervish Ball that he had humour and he could laugh and make her laugh, too.

Romantics have woven a whole romance into that evening at the *Statthalterei*, describing how Franz Ferdinand became aware of the beautiful woman standing a little away from the crowd, how he went over to her, danced every dance with her and then possibly slipped away to a quiet side room to be together. The trouble with this story is that it would all have been far too conspicuous. There is no way, if he had done that, that it would not have been noticed and commented upon. It is unlikely that he danced with her at all. It is unlikely that he danced with anyone at all. He wasn't feeling very well.

So many of the pretty young women who thronged around him at soirées and dances seemed to him to be nothing other than little minxes and Franz Ferdinand felt he could never relax in their company. They would glitter with jewels and sometimes with spite; their deep décolletages would reveal a spread of creamy flesh. They may have thought that appealing; they might have been surprised if they could have known how little he liked it. Franz Ferdinand had often been struck by a little mischievousness which would glint in Sophie's eye, but it was not the flirting glint of a society minx. Yet he could not have explained what it was that made the difference.

Sophie was lady-in-waiting to the Archduchess Isabella, wife of Archduke Friedrich. He was the typical hen-pecked husband, an unimpressive, nondescript man, short and squat, who in later years grew fat – though it is just possible that he was one of those so-called hen-pecked husbands who was only too glad to leave to his energetic wife all the organising and bossing around and keeping things running smoothly. Both Isabella and her husband were independently extremely rich. Many of

Isabella's critics accused her of letting riches go to her head. However, she did manage extremely adroitly both the fortune and the huge households and estates that went with it. A softer and more pliable woman would not have handled it all half so well.

Isabella was certainly neither soft nor pliable. She could be formidable and domineering. In photographs she looked for all the world like a female drill-sergeant and, it seems, she had the voice to go with it. There is a picture of Isabella with four of her daughters, having returned from a hunt. Isabella stands, hands on hips, bust thrust upwards and out, a feminine anti-mine tank.

She rode roughshod over her meek husband and terrified her servants and household. And it was all the more insupportable because she had a high-handed, condescending manner that made the recipients of her forceful energy cringe. When she got going her strident tones could be heard across the border. There were few who did not have some scathing comment about Isabella, no doubt spat out through clenched teeth. The officers at the nearby barracks called her 'Busabella' and they did not mean it to be a compliment!

All historians are agreed that the life Sophie now found herself leading was most disagreeable and not one she would have chosen if she had not been forced to accept it. They imply that Sophie was ever on the lookout for a way of escaping this life. Amongst other things, when Isabella was away from home travelling she economised on maidservants. Instead she required her lady-in-waiting to carry out "certain services of questionable propriety", that is, emptying chamber pots.

Why accept the position as lady-in-waiting to so unpleasant a woman? Quite possibly because there was another side to Isabella. But the voices of those who found a very much more warm-hearted woman than the name 'Busabella' would suggest have been drowned out by her vociferous critics.

This was a woman who involved herself in every aspect of the running of their estate and showed concern for every person on it (even if the manner of her showing concern appeared more like bullying). She could never rest.

When she was not running the estate or organising her husband's hunting parties or educating and bringing up her large family of daughters, all of whom had to be accomplished and well-presented, she was busy running workshops for the peasant women. The women who worked in those workshops at the traditional peasant embroidery[35] had good reason to be grateful to her. Isabella put all her energies into promoting an interest in their craftwork and she set about selling the products to couturiers in Paris. Her aim was to create and develop an interest in the beauty and originality of their work and to enable those who did it to earn a living from their skill.

---

[35]   Note 12 in the Notes Section.

She and her daughters liked wearing blouses with the traditional embroidery and around the house were hangings, again covered with embroidery. Isabella clearly liked and appreciated the embroidery of the local people.

With passion and enthusiasm she set about learning the new-fangled skill of photography.[36] She photographed everything and anything – the family, the children, the castles, the estates, the landscapes, the estate workers, the peasant people who lived around. And her photographs were good.

Somehow all this suggests that life under the wing of 'Busabella' was largely a comfortable and agreeable one, full of interest and activity, albeit a formidably well-organised one. In summer there were picnic trips, there was boating and riding and tennis; in winter there were brisk excursions in the carriage followed by cosy get-togethers around the fire, with conversation and amateur dramatics.

And all year round there was music. Isabella herself played the piano and Isabella's husband, Friedrich, would provide the rhythm on the drums. Isabella also played the cymbalom,[37] an instrument with a melancholy twang that was particularly fashionable towards the end of the nineteenth century. A number of Isabella's family were proficient players and so, too, was Sophie Chotek. Making music together of an evening was a popular way to spend the time and various members of the household would join in with piano, violin, guitar, cymbalom and drums.

There is a picture[38] of the family around the piano, with Isabella playing it, and behind the group, holding a violin, is Franz Ferdinand. It seems that Franz Ferdinand was a very passable violinist and only too happy to join in the evening's music-making. Making music all together gave Franz Ferdinand some of his best opportunities to stand very close to Sophie.

Yet, ironically, there are many descriptions of Franz Ferdinand where it is stated that he had no interest in music whatsoever and certainly no talent. This doesn't ring true. He clearly had enough of a musical ear to find that bad music making was enough to make him flinch. On his journey round the world in one letter home he wrote bluntly that he was going to have to set up a 'Clavierschutzverein', a society for the protection of pianos – too many indifferent pianists were mistreating the instrument! Furthermore the violin is a very difficult instrument to play and one does not arrive at even a

---

[36] *Photo Habsburg – Frederick Habsburg and his Family* by Vilmos Heiszler, Margit Szakács and Károly Vörös. This book is a collection of photographs taken by Isabella.

[37] Note 13 in the Notes Section.

[38] This picture can be found in *Photo Habsburg – Frederick Habsburg and his Family*, page 17.

passable level of proficiency without a reasonably good ear for music. And Isabella probably wouldn't even have allowed Franz Ferdinand to pick up a violin unless he could make a good showing in their music-making.

Sophie loved music passionately. As well as playing the cymbalom, she, too, was a skilled pianist. Music, surely, must have been one of the things that Franz Ferdinand and Sophie shared that brought them together. They just did not flaunt it. All those people who asserted with such assurance that Franz Ferdinand was utterly deaf to music cannot have known that side of him.

The Archduke Friedrich and his wife owned five truly magnificent properties but for the most part they lived in the city of Pressburg.[39] He commanded an army corps there. Their castle in Pressburg was an eighteenth century gem known as the Palais Grassalkovich created by one of the greatest of the baroque architects, Fischer von Erlach. Archduke Friedrich had inherited this castle from Archduke Albrecht, as well as the Palais Albertina on the Ringstraße in Vienna.

Palais Grassalkovich had beautifully proportioned wings, fine parapets and tall windows, crowned by a large copper dome. In certain lights the green of the dome seemed to blend with the colours of the surroundings. It has been said that this was a castle almost designed for romance. And Pressburg was not far from Budweis or Konopischt, Franz Ferdinand's own castle in Bohemia.

What more natural than for the Archduke Friedrich to invite his cousin, the Archduke Franz Ferdinand, for a few days' hunting? And what more natural than for the Archduke Franz Ferdinand to accept with alacrity? And then he would arrive, with entourage, and stay a few days, days to be spent out on the hills with guns and dogs. No doubt, he was often roped into many other activities as well and he certainly got involved in family music-making. And in the evening he would sit in the grand salon with Friedrich and Isabella and perhaps smoke a cigar. And when he reached for his cigar, that would be the moment for a lady-in-waiting to move delicately and unobtrusively forward to light it for him.

His appreciation of the gentle gestures of a particular lady-in-waiting did not go entirely unnoticed. In one of her invitations to Franz Ferdinand Isabella adds, "The Countess Chotek will be there," indicating that she felt that she could add to the attractions of the bare invitation by mentioning Sophie. Clearly she was aware that Franz Ferdinand was invariably happy to see her lady-in-waiting.

---

[39] In those days Pressburg was the city's recognised name, but the Hungarians called it Pozsony and the Czechs called the city Bratislava. It was a garrison town not far from the border between Bohemia and Austria.

No *coup de foudre* for these two. No catching a glimpse across a crowded room and falling hopelessly in love there and then. No great romance. No histrionics. Theirs was a love that grew very quietly and gently until it was unshakable. So very different from Franz Joseph's sudden love for a childish Sisi. So very different from Rudolf's formal political marriage. So very different from Otto's loveless marriage. So very different, in fact, from almost any imperial marriage at that time or earlier.

Chapter 98

Those meetings with Sophie must have seemed invariably all too short. In between they wrote to each other. Franz Ferdinand asked Sophie to write to 'Count Hohenberg' and her letters went to the post office to be picked up by Janaczek. And Janaczek took his replies to be posted. They trusted Janaczek but no one else. Franz Ferdinand was particularly wary of his equerry and chamberlain, Count Leo Würmbrand-Stuppach. Count Würmbrand was a tall, lean man, a down-to-earth bachelor, whose impressive whiskers usually seemed to be stuck into Franz Ferdinand's affairs. He was the last man that Franz Ferdinand wanted taking an interest in his new-found love for Sophie Chotek. This was of particular importance during the period when Franz Ferdinand was ill and it seemed to him that her letters were all he had to sustain him.

Franz Ferdinand had been a somewhat sickly child, never as robust as Otto. He had difficulties breathing which robbed him of energy. His mother at his birth had cried out, "Take it away! If it can't live, let it die now!" All his childhood had been clouded by strong, unspoken fears that he would not live long.

His health started to play him up in the early months of 1885 and when his breathing first began to give him trouble that year, Franz Ferdinand was relieved of military duties throughout the winter and spring so that he could convalesce. He spent the time sailing round the Mediterranean, from Alexandria to the Holy Land, Syria, Athens and finally ended up in Corfu where he spent some time with Elisabeth. When he returned from that trip it seemed that his health was fully restored and he returned to his regimental duties. But by 1892 it was clear that he would need to get away to a warmer climate during the winter months to conserve his energy. This time he wanted to take advantage of the fact that the new battlecruiser, the *Kaiserin Elisabeth*, was due to sail to eastern Asia.

Without the Emperor's permission he could not go. Although, with great reluctance, Franz Joseph allowed Elisabeth the freedom to travel where she wished, he hated anyone else in the Imperial Family leaving Austrian soil and kept the occasions when anyone did to a minimum. He did not like the idea of Franz Ferdinand travelling on the *Kaiserin Elisabeth*. Franz Joseph was not really very interested in the navy, nor was he particularly interested in Asia, and since he found it difficult to get on with his nephew, Franz Ferdinand, his inclination was to say no.

Franz Joseph may not have realised it, but a pattern was forming. Franz Joseph hated making decisions; when he had made a decision he hated having to change his mind. But Franz Ferdinand was sharp enough to realise that, with Franz Joseph, the answer was almost always going to be 'no'. However, with persistence he could be talked round. It would not be long before Franz Ferdinand realised that to get his way he needed to dig his heels in and refuse to take 'no' for an answer.

Franz Ferdinand got his way. On 15th December 1892 he boarded the ship in the harbour of Trieste. This was to be for Franz Ferdinand the adventure of a lifetime.

Karl Ludwig and Maria Theresia travelled to Trieste to see Franz Ferdinand off, together with Franz Ferdinand's brothers and sisters. They boarded another warship, the *Greif* which steamed out to sea behind the *Kaiserin Elisabeth* and followed as far as Pirano before turning back.

When the *Greif* put about to return to Trieste, a message was sent to Franz Ferdinand, "Happy journey; farewell and good hunting!" And then Maria Theresia and Margaretha-Sophie would have stood, leaning against the ship's railings, waving as they watched the *Kaiserin Elisabeth* fading into the distance. Long after the two figures would have ceased to be distinguishable, Franz Ferdinand watched the *Greif* disappear back to Trieste, and suddenly he felt the pangs of separation. In his notebook he wrote, "Deep inside me came the sinking feeling of an infinite longing for the homeland... it was homesickness, which I had never known before." He then set about arranging around his cabin a mass of family photographs.

What Franz Ferdinand hoped to gain from his travels can be seen by the people he chose to take with him. There was Dr. Ludwig Ritter von Liburnau from the Natural History Museum in Vienna. There was Count Heinrich Clam-Martinic who was a foremost exponent of some remarkable progressive ideas on agricultural co-operatives. Franz Ferdinand was planning to use his trip as a study tour in order to broaden and deepen his education. And, of course, Franz Janaczek was on board, too.

Someone else was on board that Franz Ferdinand would have preferred had not been. This was Archduke Leopold Ferdinand of the Tuscan branch of the Habsburg family. Leopold Ferdinand was five years younger than Franz Ferdinand. He was a thorn in the side of many a Habsburg, being largely undisciplined, unconventional and outspoken. He would end up being stripped of his titles and all his privileges as a member of the Imperial Family, and finally exiled to Switzerland.

He managed more than usually to be a thorn in the side of Franz Ferdinand on that trip. The two men just could not get on with each other. Leopold Ferdinand went around calling Franz Ferdinand the 'möchtegern-Kaiser' ('the eager-to-become Emperor') which needled Franz Ferdinand. Leopold Ferdinand's feelings towards Franz Ferdinand were bitter, and he assuaged them with some savage invective. He called him a cad and said Franz Ferdinand was "utterly lacking in even the remotest glimmer of sensibility or finer feelings". He said Franz Ferdinand called the Emperor a stupid old boy and wanted the old man out of the way. He said, too, that Franz Ferdinand was glad Rudolf had shot himself. He said each evening Franz Ferdinand drank himself into a stupor.

The feeling was mutual; Franz Ferdinand found Leopold Ferdinand's behaviour obnoxious. Leopold Ferdinand hated being on board ship at all and openly expressed his disdain with some very boorish behaviour. He showed considerable interest in some of the sailors on board and spent a lot of time locked away in his cabin with one particularly handsome young cadet. There is also a story that Leopold Ferdinand had smuggled his young mistress on board, disguised as a sailor. All this Franz Ferdinand found embarrassing and offensive.

There is another story which may not be true[40] that Franz Ferdinand's own mistress, the actress Mila Kugler, had begged to be allowed to accompany him on the voyage. Franz Ferdinand had refused bluntly but she succeeded in getting on board and it was not until the ship docked that she was put ashore.

If Leopold Ferdinand's mistress was on board pretending to be a sailor and Mila Kugler was on board pretending that Franz Ferdinand had wanted her there, the situation would have been decidedly delicate. It would have given rise to many an occasion for angry words between the two men. Leopold Ferdinand may have hinted that Franz Ferdinand was no better than he and if Franz Ferdinand had been completely taken by surprise when he found that Mila Kugler was on board he would have been all the more angry. Eventually, Franz Ferdinand complained about his young cousin to the Emperor who sent orders for him to return home to Austria. Leopold Ferdinand left the ship in Sydney while Franz Ferdinand continued his voyage.

As for Leopold Ferdinand, he went on being a thorn in the Emperor's side. He was posted to a regiment in Brünn. He took with him Wilhelmine Adamovicz, the daughter of a post office official. Wilhelmine, it is reported, was working as a prostitute in the Augarten in Vienna. The brazen way Leopold Ferdinand flaunted his new amour enraged both his own family and Franz Joseph. His falling in love with a prostitute caused his family much shame and they paid him 100,000 gulden on condition that he leave his mistress. This he refused to do. Instead he insisted he intended to marry her and set about educating her in the ways and manners of the aristocracy – not that there was ever much chance of the aristocracy accepting Wilhelmine in their midst.

---

[40] The source of this story seems to have been a short article in a Viennese newspaper.

When the Emperor learned of all this he had the young man consigned to a clinic for nervous disorders in Koblenz. Leopold Ferdinand ended up begging for a new posting within the Austrian Army which Franz Joseph brusquely refused him.

Leopold Ferdinand was something of a depressive and over time he became an alcoholic. Whether these were the consequences of his problems with the society in which he lived or the cause is not clear. But everything weighed upon his spirits and finally he and Wilhelmine travelled to Switzerland in 1902. He changed his name to Leopold Wölfling,[41] a name chosen after a peak in the Ore Mountains, and severed all ties with the Habsburg family. He and Wilhelmine got married a year later and became Swiss citizens. However, the marriage did not last and in 1907 Leopold Ferdinand married his second wife, Maria Ritter, whom he met in the red-light district of Munich. They moved to Paris but here Maria fell ill with what was called a nerve fever and the couple separated.

With the outbreak of the First World War he applied for a position in the Austrian Army but was refused. After the war he returned to Vienna. He was a superlative linguist – fluent in German, English, French, Italian, Hungarian, Castellano and Portuguese. With these languages he was able to work for some time as a foreign correspondence clerk. After more jobs he later opened a delicatessen store in Vienna where he sold salami and olive oil – hence becoming a grocer. He also tried his hand as a tourist guide in the Hofburg Palace in Vienna and was very well received by his audiences but not by some of the old families of Vienna. Unfortunately, he again ended up fleeing the city and returning to Berlin.

Here he was forced to do any work he could find and this included singing in a cabaret and writing articles about his life in Vienna when he still belonged to the Imperial Family. In 1933 he married for the third time to Klara Hedwig Pawlowski. The marriage only lasted two years because Leopold Ferdinand died utterly impoverished on 4th July 1935. Klara was thirty-four years younger than her husband and outlived him by forty-three years.

The *Kaiserin Elisabeth* sailed on to Port Said – it was here that Mila Kugler was bundled off the ship to find her own way back to Austria. Their voyage continued on to Ceylon and from there to Bombay. Franz Ferdinand

---

[41] In 1929 Leopold Wölfling wrote his autobiography *My Life Story – From Archduke to Grocer*, published in New York.. This was written in English and intended for an English-speaking readership. It is a highly readable book and it presents a fascinating picture of his world, one neatened up in subtle ways to ensure the approval of his readers.

arrived in India on 17th January 1893; he then spent six weeks in India before setting sail for Australia, via Singapore and Java. From Australia they made their way to Japan, with a number of ports of call along the way, including Singapore and Hong Kong.

In Japan Franz Ferdinand left the *Kaiserin Elisabeth* and continued his journey in a Canadian liner, the *Empress of China*. From the moment he set sail on 25th August 1893 he took a dislike to the *Empress of China*. He did not like the sailors – they were not "our own agile sailors" but "sulky Americans, stiff Englishmen and slant-eyed Chinese". He did not much care for his fellow travellers, the only exception being a charming American girl with whom he played deck tennis.

The *Empress of China* docked in Canada a month later and on 19th September Franz Ferdinand crossed from Canada into the United States. Here he got a shock. What had he been expecting? Whatever it was, the reality turned out to be very different – and disconcerting. Not feeling very comfortable in America, he took a dislike to all things American. The Americans, he decided, had become obsessed with the drive to exaggerate and to have the biggest of everything, "but they struck me as cold people and seemed to have no kindness in their hearts nor charm in their manners."

There was an awkward core to Franz Ferdinand. It went back to his difficult childhood when, despite his intense efforts, he could only do clumsily what others, and Otto in particular, could do easily and with grace. His dogged childhood efforts to learn had been hampered by some kind of invisible tripwire. He had so often felt uncomfortable and constrained by impediments that neither he nor anyone else could explain.

When Franz Ferdinand found himself feeling hampered, constrained and uncomfortable, those old feelings of shame would come flooding back. He would react by putting a distance between himself and whatever it was he felt to be the cause of his discomfort. He would hide behind his gruffness and stand on his dignity. And then he would decide that the problem lay with 'them'. It is very likely that his attitude towards the Americans was one such instance. He was interested in them, wanted to understand how it was that they were achieving so much, possibly even admired them, but was never comfortable with them.

Franz Ferdinand was more than a little shaken by the speed and force shown by Americans or Canadians when they played tennis. Franz Ferdinand loved playing tennis but after a visit to the Vancouver Tennis Club he wrote, "I would so much have liked to go and play, but my courage failed me when I saw the skill displayed."

When he set sail for Le Havre, he felt a wave of relief. He was going home. From Le Havre to Paris to Stuttgart and finally across the Austrian border on 18th October 1893 at St. Pölten. Here his family were waiting to accompany him back to Vienna.

Throughout his long ten-month journey Franz Ferdinand kept a journal which was published on his return. He asked Dr. Max Vladimir Beck, a lawyer and civil servant, to help him edit his book. Max Vladimir Beck had once taught Franz Ferdinand constitutional law and was one of his most trusted friends. This collaboration gave rise to the snide accusation that he did not really write the book, but his original diaries show that the book was only lightly edited – if anything Max Beck watered down the strength of the original. Franz Ferdinand's style was observant and acerbic and his comments reflected his intelligence.

And however much he may have disliked this or that on his journey, throughout it all he tried to keep an open mind and was quite prepared to learn whatever he could. He was interested in how the Americans – a pot-pourri of different nations – handled their different claims and cultures. He came to feel that something similar had to be brought about in Austria – also a pot-pourri of different nationalities. He admired the way the Americans tolerated quite big differences of culture so long as everyone in the country recognised the binding ties of a common language, a common currency and an army serving the whole nation.

For most of his trip Franz Ferdinand was representing the Austrian-Hungarian Empire and he was received as such with great pomp in the places his visited. But when he wanted some anonymity he would use the name 'Count Hohenberg', and this was to be the name he later asked Sophie to use when she wrote to him. It was to be of particular importance because the next time Franz Ferdinand was ill his cure was to be a great deal more stringent.

Doctors in those days could do little for a patient with tuberculosis – the treatment was clean air, rest, patience and prayers that the patient's own body was strong enough to fight off the disease. This was what faced Franz Ferdinand throughout much of the 1890s. Because of his ill-health during those years he spent a great deal of time away from Austria, most of it spent travelling around the Mediterranean.

This time he was to be separated from Sophie for a much longer period. Their love needed great strength to have survived the separations, as well as the underlying doubts as to whether he would ever come back at all, let alone as a healthy man. But through all of this Sophie's secret letters sustained him and during that time he came to depend upon her letters, the letters she wrote to Count Hohenberg, *poste restante*, for the faithful Janaczek to fetch for his master.

Chapter 99

Franz Ferdinand did all he could to hide the fact that he was not feeling well. But his chief of staff had inspected Franz Ferdinand's brigade in the spring of 1895 and during the course of the inspection he could not help noticing that His Imperial Highness looked pale and most unwell. Finally, the news found its way back to the Emperor.

Franz Joseph had scarcely ever known a day's illness in his life. He got up at the same time every day in the early hours of the morning; he followed the same routine every day; he ate his meals at the same time every day; he ate the same foods and in the same quantities every day, and he retired to bed at the same time every day. He lived a frugal life and he was never ill. Franz Joseph hardly knew what it meant not to feel well. Franz Ferdinand, on the other hand, had lived much of his life struggling to hide it when he did not feel well and refusing to let it get in the way of his life. Franz Ferdinand would have done much to keep his uncle from knowing now that he was always tired and often feverish. But people around him were becoming increasingly aware that all was not well with him.

When the Emperor sent his own personal physician, Dr. Widerhofer, to examine the Archduke, Franz Ferdinand could hardly refuse to see the doctor. Dr. Widerhofer found that Franz Ferdinand was pale and running a fever and that he was losing weight. He called in the lung specialist, Dr. Schrötter.

There was a fateful day in July 1895 – we can imagine the scene – when Dr. Victor Eisenmenger was asked to examine a sputum sample. His superior, Dr. Schrötter, stood by. Perhaps he moved over towards the window and looked out as his assistant placed the sample under the microscope. Perhaps he watched, distractedly, the people moving about in the street below, going about their business, rather like the bacilli on the microscope slide that Dr. Eisenmenger was studying. It did not take Dr. Eisenmenger long to straighten up and remark, quietly, "Unusually massive tubercle bacilli."

Dr. Schrötter nodded; he had seen these symptoms too often before. "I thought so," he said and paused. "The sputum comes from Archduke Franz Ferdinand," he added. He had also probably formed his own private opinion of the likely outcome, given such high levels of tubercle bacilli, but that he would have kept to himself.

To Eisenmenger he said, "I am suggesting you should be his doctor. Go and see him at once."

Dr. Schrötter ran a clinic specialising in tuberculosis and it was here that the newly-qualified Dr. Victor Eisenmenger had found what he believed to be his dream job. Victor Eisenmenger had never had terribly good health himself. Since he did not have talent enough to follow in the footsteps of his father, a highly successful artist, Victor chose to study medicine. Thanks to his uncertain health young Victor almost did not succeed in qualifying. So it seems rather surprising that Dr. Schrötter chose this particular young man for the position of personal doctor to Archduke Franz Ferdinand which was likely to be a very difficult position and also a dangerous one to Victor himself. In his writings[42] Dr. Eisenmenger hints that his position in the clinic was precarious, leaving him little choice other than to accept this new position, but he was reassured when Dr. Schrötter promised him that his position in the clinic would be kept open for him (it was not).

You are left wondering whether Dr. Schrötter had concluded that the Archduke had no chance of surviving and that, with a disease as infectious as tuberculosis, whoever he sent to take care of the Archduke faced a very real risk of losing his own life, too. Perhaps he had come to the conclusion that, with his precarious health, Dr. Eisenmenger could not entirely fulfil his duties in the clinic and Victor faced a steady decline toward's his own death. Dr. Schrötter had to find somebody for Franz Ferdinand. So quiet, modest, considerate Victor Eisenmenger was sent to Chlumetz where he was met by Franz Ferdinand's chamberlain, Count Leo Würmbrand-Stuppach.

Dr. Eisenmenger would have happily foregone the honour of treating the Archduke. But he did not get the chance of opting out. It is likely that Franz Ferdinand received Dr. Eisenmenger in his most brusque manner. He felt morose and discouraged. Dr. Eisenmenger was struck by his "droopy" air and his feverish eyes. He noted how pale and thin he was. "Extensive tuberculous lesions at the apex of the right lung, suspected implication of the left lung," wrote Dr. Eisenmenger later.

Dr. Eisenmenger did not tell his august patient the name of the disease and he insisted that it was curable. But – and this was the bit that Franz Ferdinand did not want to hear – the cure had to be followed rigorously and could not be interrupted for any reason at all until he was fully recovered.

Yet by the end of the cure – and heaven knows, Dr. Eisenmenger had a difficult enough time with his often recalcitrant patient! – Franz Ferdinand considered the doctor his friend, and clearly Dr. Eisenmenger had come to both like and admire his patient. There were plenty of explosions of impatience and frustration on Franz Ferdinand's side. Faced with these, the doctor needed to keep up his confidence and belief that a cure could be achieved. He needed to calm Franz Ferdinand down and reassure him that he would in the end pull through. Theirs was not an easy relationship, yet most of the time Dr. Eisenmenger had only respect for the Archduke's iron will-power.

---

[42] *Erzherzog Franz Ferdinand – seinem Andenken gewidmet von seinem Leibarzt* by Victor Eisenmenger, 1930.

Dr. Eisenmenger also stressed that the cure would last at least a year and would involve complete rest, pure air and a rigorously controlled diet, preferably in a sanatorium. Franz Ferdinand refused. Franz Joseph wrote to him a letter that for all its courteous tones was nonetheless an order:

> "I must stress that you now have only one duty, and that is to get well. As soon as possible you must go to a peaceful mountain resort, stay there absolutely quietly, and then move on to a southern climate (not Tunis because it is too dusty) where you must remain and rest for the entire winter, obeying your doctor's instructions. I know this will be extremely boring, but I hope that for my sake you will patiently persevere with it."

The Archduchess Isabella also wrote to him with her "grandmotherly advice" – was she consciously aware of the irony of that? For Isabella was a year younger than Maria Theresia and only seven years older than Franz Ferdinand himself. Isabella's letters to Franz Ferdinand were usually chatty and affectionate; they would begin with "Dear Franzi," rather as if she were writing to a dear younger brother.

Hearing that her 'dear Franzi' needed a complete change of air to cure his lungs, Isabella wrote, "I cannot tell you how depressed your news made me and how much this is on my mind all the time..." But she wants him to follow his doctor's orders to the letter. He must have called himself 'a wretched cripple' in a letter to her for she insists that even as 'a wretched cripple' he is always welcome in her house.

Dr. Eisenmenger told Franz Ferdinand that his cure would need a year of total rest and he had to start straight away. But Franz Ferdinand was allowed first to return to his regiment until after the summer manoeuvres. In the end he surrendered his command and left quietly and without ceremony. He told his general staff aide, Baron Margutti, one of the few wholly on Franz Ferdinand's side, that he would be glad to know before the Emperor did how the brigade was doing in the autumn manoeuvres. And then, with great reluctance, he travelled to where Dr. Eisenmenger had arranged for him to carry out his cure. With him went his chamberlain, Count Würmbrand, who invariably managed to make Franz Ferdinand feel uncomfortable, and also, of course, Janaczek.

Würmbrand's private opinion all along was that Franz Ferdinand would not stick with the cure. He warned Dr. Eisenmenger that Franz Ferdinand's restlessness was renowned, adding with a sigh, "The Archduke's accustomed lifestyle is the exact opposite of what you are demanding of him. Rarely ever does he stay in the same place for more than a day. For the last fortnight, I have not slept once in a proper bed, always in a railway carriage!"

The first part of Franz Ferdinand's cure took place in the Dolomite mountains. Dr. Eisenmenger had found a hotel in the Mendel Pass, not far from the city of Bozen, at an altitude of six thousand feet where the purity of the air seemed to him appropriate for a cure.

One issue that Dr. Eisenmenger had was dealing with other guests in the hotel. There were one or two whose company Franz Ferdinand would have gladly sought out – one of them were Wilhelm Röntgen, the discoverer of electromagnetic radiation (x-rays) and the writer and historian, Felix Dahn. But Eisenmenger feared that these two would be too interesting, would excite Franz Ferdinand. Some of the other guests presented Eisenmenger with a very different problem – they were like flies in a closed room, endlessly buzzing around and trying to get near the Archduke. They had a way of turning up wherever they went and some of them followed Franz Ferdinand throughout his cure.

What was more – as soon as the Archduke's health problems became public knowledge Eisenmenger found himself overwhelmed by those who were full of unsolicited and unwanted advice and those who knew better how to treat the patient for which, in every case, payment was sought. He was swamped not just with advice but with medicines of doubtful origin and a variety of treatments in an even greater variety of packages, bottles or boxes. Many of these experts could offer the Archduke the perfect place in which to receive the appropriate treatment. "I am not joking," wrote Victor Eisenmenger – they were invited, amongst other places, to "Siberia, South Africa and Mexico".

What made this more difficult to deal with was that it was part of Dr. Eisenmenger's brief to report back to Franz Ferdinand's father on every one of these unwanted offerings. Eisenmenger was also pressed to reply to each and every one of these offerings courteously – "because it was meant well".

Having at last been forced to face up to his illness, it hit Franz Ferdinand just how bad he did feel. He wrote to his friend, Countess Nora Függer, soon after arriving at the hotel where his cure was to take place and told her that he had a lung catarrh with some nasty complications and, "I... am feeling so weak and wretched that I am barely able to walk a hundred steps... and I am in terribly low spirits." For some indefinite period stretching far, far into the future he would have to accept that he could not do any of the things that make life interesting, no hunting, no riding, no travel. Further on he added, "Here I am lying all day long on a veranda in a reclining chair, living on milk and medicines and coughing continually. You can imagine the frame of mind I am in, and that I am already suffering from black melancholia..."

Dr. Eisenmenger wanted him to remain as near immobile as could be managed. He was to avoid all physical exertion and all mental agitation – pure agony for Franz Ferdinand. Such a cure would take immense will power. "Women are better," added Dr. Eisenmenger. Franz Ferdinand had started out, telling himself, "no more whining!" and he struggled to obey his doctor's orders but as his strength began to come back to him, Franz Ferdinand grew ever more restless and impatient. "You are locking me up like an animal," he would growl.

He was allowed to read light novels and to write letters. He also took to shooting small twigs off a larch tree which stood some thirty yards away. Apparently he knocked off hundreds of twigs and so neatly that the tree came to look as though it had been trimmed by a gardener's shears.

There was a little fox terrier called Mucki[43] who seemed to sense Franz Ferdinand's many moods. One thing Mucki did was chew the carpet in Franz Ferdinand's room. Dr. Eisenmenger thought the worn carpet was very much past its best but the hotel management insisted that it was extremely valuable and would have to be replaced at great expense.

Mucki liked to jump after the falling twigs. Mucki would leap around trying to catch each twig before it reached the ground and then bring his proud trophy back to Franz Ferdinand. For a man whose mind was often clouded by the dark side of life, any distraction was a good thing. Mucki with his bouncing energy and his droll expressions of enthusiastic delight in everything going on succeeded in amusing Franz Ferdinand. He was glad to have Mucki around.

It was not long before those around Franz Ferdinand became aware of his eager impatience for the arrival of the post each day. And when there was a letter his spirits would rise and he would submit more readily to the doctor's recommendations for his health. When there was no letter he would growl like a bear and his moods would be all over the place. This intrigued both Dr. Eisenmenger and Count Würmbrand. Dr. Eisenmenger was not particularly interested as to who wrote these long letters. Whoever it was was boosting the patient's morale and improving his chances of recovery. What was more the long replies that Franz Ferdinand wrote back occupied him and helped him to pass away the hours.

Würmbrand's reaction was rather different. He suspected that there had to be a woman behind the mystery and apparently he muttered under his breath that he knew who she was. "But I'll fix her," he added. But he failed to fix her. "For my purposes it was better so," wrote Victor.

Out there on the mountain high above the Etsch and Eisack valleys – a wonderful panorama that was no substitute for seeing Sophie – Franz

---

43   The name would be pronounced 'Mouz-ki'.

Ferdinand was forced to trust Janaczek. This must have been the time when these two built a relationship of deep affection for each other. Janaczek never left his master's side; he even slept in the same room as the Archduke. And Janaczek collected the letters from the post office and sent off Franz Ferdinand's replies, always discreetly. Without Janaczek it is more than likely that Franz Ferdinand and Sophie's love for each other could not have survived. Janaczek would have known not to give anything away to a man like Würmbrand. He may even have laid a few red herrings... He would have found that an amusing game to play on his master's behalf.

For a man who yearned to see the woman he loved the situation could not have been more dire. A whole year with nothing to do – enforced rest – and all he could do was think about Sophie, wonder what she was doing, who she was with, whether she was enjoying herself, and worst of all, wondering whether in his long absence she would start to grow away from him. In this agonising limbo Eisenmenger was to become more of a goaler than doctor, Würmbrand would need to be kept in the dark about what was going on and Franz Ferdinand would be forced to place all his trust in Janaczek.

Perhaps we can picture a man whose feelings were a tangled, awkward mesh. For as long as Franz Ferdinand had been busy and active and in the swim of things, private doubts and anguish could be stilled. Activity could carry him along and staunch any uncomfortable introspection. But now all sorts of doubts were free to crowd in upon his mind. He felt an overwhelming need to move, to hunt, ride, shoot, anything but lie still with his thoughts of inadequacy.

Did Franz Ferdinand doubt how long Sophie would go on caring for him? Tradition has it that it is the woman who waits in faithful longing, never certain that the man she loves will come back to her. But here the impression is that it was the other way round. It was not that Sophie had a stream of eligible men interested in her. On the contrary, she had reached the point where she could hardly expect to find any man interested in her ever again. There is no record of whether anyone before Franz Ferdinand ever had been interested in her – but there may have been. And if there ever was, clearly she had chosen to stay with her father and care for her younger sisters, in a word, putting others before herself. This seems to be the sort of person Sophie was – cheerful, good-humoured, easy-going, devoting her life to caring for others.

Historians seem to have some difficulty understanding how it could possibly be that this woman could be so alluring that Franz Ferdinand was ready to fight to the bitter end for her. They write about her striking looks and add that she was not conventionally beautiful, as if that were all there was to it. But it was never her looks he fell in love with.

Franz Ferdinand may well have doubted that Sophie would stay the course with him, not because she was a flibberty-gibbet of a girl, but because – with that thread of understanding acceptance of hers – she had the strength to love him and to allow him to fly free if he wanted to – or had to.

He may have sensed that she was capable of writing to him, bidding him to find love and happiness for his own sake and she would bless him and wish him well in his search. So just possibly, Franz Ferdinand on his mountain, staring across the sunlit valleys, may not only have been torn by the anguish of uncertainty over his health and whether he would live, but also by the anguish of uncertainty as to whether he would find Sophie when – if – he got back.

It would have been very easy for both fears to have grown in his mind and tormented him. Was he destined to die here without ever seeing her again? Perhaps it wasn't death that loomed but years of invalidhood and if that were so would he ever see her again? Uncertainty would have made him restless, not just inactivity.

A large part of his thoughts were taken up by Sophie but he had to keep it a secret. For the rest his thoughts revolved around politics, most especially, the political moves of the Hungarians to win more autonomy for themselves. This did not need to be a secret and he was free to write to his friend, Prince Karl Schwarzenberg, on the subject.

By this time the Hungarian nobility saw Franz Ferdinand as their sworn enemy and they felt that his ideas for the future of the Empire were particularly nefarious. Franz Ferdinand had for some time been wondering whether some aspects of the American system could be made to work in the Austrian-Hungarian Empire. He was beginning to envisage more autonomy for the different nationalities while keeping them welded into one unit by a common language for official purposes – German – and a single army.

This would have presented the Hungarians with some very considerable difficulties. They wanted greater autonomy, their own army and the right to use their own language for official purposes. But there was more to it than this. They laid claim to a region, Greater Hungary, the lands of St. Stephen, in which the Hungarians themselves were in a minority. The other nationalities living within the same area of land outnumbered the Hungarians. The Hungarians expected to be able, in claiming that region, to subordinate these other nationalities in much the same way that they felt Austria subordinated them. And the way the Hungarians treated the other nationalities within the Greater Hungary region certainly incensed many liberal thinkers of the time, for many Hungarian aristocrats could often be harsh and autocratic.

Franz Ferdinand's thinking was for breaking down that region into smaller ones and allowing the different nationalities equal degrees of autonomy. In such an arrangement the Hungarians would have ended up as a relatively small tribe among all the other tribes of peoples within the Empire.

Then one day there appeared an article in the Hungarian newspaper, the *Magyar Hirlap*, which had close ties to the government in Budapest. This article claimed that Franz Ferdinand had not much longer to live and there would be no mourning in Hungary when he died.

According to one source, Franz Ferdinand, when he saw this, turned "grey with rage". He wrote to Franz Joseph, saying that he knew he was not loved in Hungary and "I am in a sense proud of this, for I do not want to be honoured by such people." Franz Ferdinand also wrote to his friend, Count Nikola Szécsen, who was Hungarian. In his letter, after sounding off in the first few lines, he went on to apologise if his letter was "somewhat caustic". He added, "If death does not overtake me this winter... it will be a great pleasure, as soon as I am back in the Monarchy, to talk about these matters with your Excellency, a Hungarian whom I esteem and admire and to whose judgement I defer."

The effect of the *Magyar Hirlap* article was to galvanise him. He was determined to do anything to deprive the Hungarians of the pleasure of his death. He wanted to do something to speed his recovery along. He could not and would not endure that hotel half way up a mountain for more than a few weeks. The only thing that Dr. Eisenmenger could do to rein in Franz Ferdinand's forcefulness was to seek advice from Dr. Schrötter.

The very next day Dr. Eisenmenger was in a rubber bathtub taking a bath – in his 'Adam's suit' [44] – when the door swung open and Franz Ferdinand's father, the Archduke Karl Ludwig burst in, already halfway through a long protestation against Victor's treatment of his son. Yet again Victor could only stress that the only chance of a complete cure was if Franz Ferdinand submitted himself to the treatment until he actually was cured and for that the patient's commitment to the treatment was essential. As Karl Ludwig withdrew from the room he said, "My son will never be healthy again."

Dr. Schrötter arrived to back up Dr. Eisenmenger and finally Franz Ferdinand caved in, agreeing to carry on the treatment – but somewhere else, it had to be somewhere else. Eventually it was suggested that he go to Lussin-Piccolo, an Adriatic island near the naval base at Pola. Lussin-Piccolo

---

[44] Page 19 of Dr. Eisenmenger's book: *Ich war gerade im Adamskostüm in meiner Gummiwanne.*

proved to be an excellent choice. Dr. Eisenmenger was pleased to observe that Franz Ferdinand put on weight during the weeks that they were there. He no longer ran a fever and his appetite had improved. It was an excellent choice for another reason, too. The health of Victor Eisenmenger himself improved and he, too, gained weight and energy. In fact, he began to wonder whether he could return to his old job at the clinic. At the back of Victor's mind lurked a secret fear that if he was still in charge of Franz Ferdinand's health and Franz Ferdinand died then Victor's medical career would be over.

From there it was planned that he should go on to Egypt for the winter months.

Würmbrand wrote to Dr. Eisenmenger asking him to find out whether Franz Ferdinand wished him to go with them to Egypt. Franz Ferdinand's reply was an abrupt 'No'. Victor sought to smooth ruffled feathers but Franz Ferdinand was in no mood to change his decision. "If he is really so devoted to me, he would leave me in peace. I do not need someone who pokes his nose in my affairs and interferes. The only two I want with me in Egypt are you and Janaczek." And that, Victor thought, was the come-back for Würmbrand's meddling in the Sophie affair. (However, Würmbrand did accompany Franz Ferdinand to Cairo.)

But Franz Ferdinand did not want to go to Egypt and found a mass of reasons why he should not go there. His nerves were ruffled. He was on edge. He was restless and wound up. He did not know what he wanted. He knew only too vigorously what he did not want. He must have been extremely difficult to deal with.

Dr. Eisenmenger clearly learned how to handle Franz Ferdinand, and he knew when to call in others to back him up. It was Maria Theresia who succeeded in persuading Franz Ferdinand to leave for Lussin-Piccolo, after he had angrily rushed back to the family home, raging against the restrictions and restraints imposed upon him. He suspected those against him of using the doctors to isolate him and keep him out of the way, all on the pretext of curing his illness. In this view, he was probably not entirely wrong. The Emperor's own doctor, Dr. Widerhofer, was pressing for Franz Ferdinand to go to Madeira for his cure, a strange choice since Madeira was known for malaria.

Part of the problem with going to Egypt had to do with the Austrian Ambassador in Cairo, Ambassador Heidler von Eggeregg. Men like him too often sought private meetings with Franz Ferdinand simply to bolster their own standing and self-importance. Franz Ferdinand put his point of view across drily, "On my travels around the world I have had the worst imaginable experiences with Austrian official representatives abroad. Our ambassadors are all of them totally incompetent to undertake the duties expected of them; they are only interested in banquets and medals. If you need to get anything done you need to turn to the German ambassador.

"Heidler is a vain and ambitious man and he will want to drag me here, there and everywhere in order to make himself look important! I do not want to be seen anywhere! I want peace and quiet!" Those words would have been music to Victor's ears but Heidler could still be a problem.

For the crossing to Egypt the weather was fine, but the sea was rough and the passengers on board kept to their rooms. Victor saw little of Franz Ferdinand on the crossing. As the ship pulled away from Brindisi – next port of call, Alexandria – Janaczek sought a private interview with Victor. Janaczek insisted that what he was about to say must remain a secret and never revealed to anyone.

The Archduke had suddenly taken it into his head to seek a second medical opinion, possibly to bolster his wish to have as little to do with Heidler as possible. Dr. von Becker came from Vienna but was living and working in Egypt as the Khedive's private doctor. Franz Ferdinand had sent him a telegramme, asking him to be in Alexandria when the ship arrived. Victor was on deck as the ship tied up and he quickly picked out von Becker in the crowd.

Victor's handling of the situation speaks for the man he was. Medical etiquette demanded that Becker should get agreement from the doctor handling the Archduke's treatment before barging in. However, Victor speedily made his way over to the waiting Becker and said to him, "Don't stop to talk to me. The Archduke is standing over there; you should go straight to him."

For over an hour the consultation lasted. On his departure Dr. von Becker paused to speak to Dr. Eisenmenger, „Sie sind ein armer Teufel" ("Poor devil!"). He went on that in his opinion there was nothing that could be done – the Archduke was a lost man. Victor wanted to know whether Franz Ferdinand had been told how little hope there was for him. "Of course not!"

Dr. von Becker had, in parting, told Franz Ferdinand that the rigid constraints his cure imposed could certainly be eased. Hearing that Dr. Eisenmenger's heart must have sank. But the effect upon him was to convince him that Franz Ferdinand could be cured and that he wanted to be the doctor who brought it about. But, if anything, the constraints needed to be increased, not eased.

After Dr. von Becker had gone, Franz Ferdinand told Dr. Eisenmenger that he had just been told he was dying. At such a moment Franz Ferdinand's voice would be likely to go chillingly quiet, as though he were speaking from a thousand miles away. And Eisenmenger, who so often had to force himself to push away the unacceptable thought that he would be glad when this difficult patient finally died, would feel a stab of pity for him. Such a moment called for encouraging words, anything to bolster whatever hope of recovering Franz Ferdinand might have.

When they arrived in Cairo Franz Ferdinand was to stay a few nights in a hotel before boarding the houseboat, called a *dahabiya*, which would carry them slowly up the Nile. Franz Ferdinand was already tired as they came through the door into the hotel but suddenly he stiffened and grabbed Victor's arm. "There he is!" and without a word of greeting to anyone he rushed up the stairs as fast as he was able. 'He' was the Austrian Ambassador Heidler von Eggeregg.

The next day Victor went to the Embassy to explain the situation and there he was berated bitterly. Heidler insisted that Franz Ferdinand as heir to the throne owed him a certain courtesy and whilst he was in Cairo certain duties were expected of Franz Ferdinand which could not be pushed aside. Heidler was not going to get any of this because Dr. Eisenmenger set about getting his patient on to the houseboat as soon as possible.

And back in the hotel foyer Dr. Eisenmenger was faced with two surprises. Awaiting him stood Archduke Eugen, Franz Ferdinand's cousin. Of all the many members of the Imperial Family Eugen was the one Franz Ferdinand got on with better than anyone else. And here he was offering to accompany Franz Ferdinand up the Nile as far as Assuan, which would immediately put Franz Ferdinand in a good mood. Dr. Eisenmenger heaved a sigh of relief.

The second surprise was not a good one. Franz Ferdinand had left the hotel with Dr. von Becker and the pair had gone wandering round the bazaars and markets looking for interesting antiques and beautiful carpets. Nothing could have been worse for Franz Ferdinand's health than this. Had he decided that there really was no hope and that he might as well try to crush his fears and dread with distractions?

Dr. Eisenmenger went to have words with Archduke Eugen. He had to drive home to Eugen why Franz Ferdinand had to be got on to that *dahabiya* quickly and why it was his only chance of pulling through. He had to make Eugen see how dangerous Franz Ferdinand's situation was. He had to make him understand what a tightrope they were on. He got over-excited and Eugen had to tell him to calm down. Dr. Eisenmenger had one last card to play: if Franz Ferdinand could not accept the necessity of his obeying his doctor then Victor would give up on Franz Ferdinand's chances of pulling through and he would withdraw altogether.

Suddenly Dr. Eisenmenger knew he had to do the exact opposite of conciliating his patient. From then on Dr. Eisenmenger stopped avoiding the emotive word 'tuberculosis' and spoke bluntly about the illness. Dr. Eisenmenger also showed his patient a slide under the microscope with all the tubercle bacilli swimming around.

And finally, after a relapse due to the jaunt round the bazaars of Cairo, Franz Ferdinand took stock of his situation. Here he was and all the gains achieved on Lussin-Piccolo had been squandered. He became more co-operative and again set about doing what his doctor advised to build up his strength.

But it was all so, so, so boring, all the more so after Eugen had left the *dahabiya*. Weeks spent on a houseboat, called *Hope* (which could be thought of as being either appropriate or ironic) staring out at the monotonous flat landscape. When a sandstorm blew he had to stay below deck. When he acquired an infection of the larynx he was forbidden to speak.

There is nothing more conducive to brooding than enforced inactivity. It is not hard to imagine what Franz Ferdinand may well have passed his time brooding about. In those long relentless hours lying flat, staring at the sand, he went over and over in his mind the constant comparison with his brother, invariably to his detriment, the eagerness with which so many had been prepared to write him off, and his endless efforts to achieve something in his life and the doubts as to whether he ever would.

It would not be surprising if the thought of dying did not often preoccupy him. He may well have felt a failure. Perhaps there were times when anger was nothing less than a mask to hide his own private fears.

And through it all he wondered about Sophie and whether he would ever see her again. He probably went over in his mind every moment he had ever spent with her. Did he ever wonder for how long she would miss him if he never did come back? Did he ever think of her in the years to come when he was no longer around? Perhaps he saw her as a cheerful, kindly aunt to a growing brood of nephews and nieces, finding her satisfactions in life from her own family. And what he wanted was to have a family with her. He could not think how it could be done. There were so many impediments.

In all likelihood, during those long boring hours, the impediment that may have tormented him the most may well have been whether he would ever regain his health sufficiently to be a husband. He would not have wanted to impose a sickly cripple upon the girl he loved.

"It is not very pleasant to be regarded on all sides as written off and pushed into the background," he wrote to his old tutor, Dr. Max Vladimir Beck. Beck could only press Franz Ferdinand to be philosophical – "you understand so well how to rise above the unexpected in life!"

On and on the months dragged by. Franz Ferdinand complained of being locked up and Dr. Eisenmenger went on insisting that he would recover if he could only exercise "patience and good will". More than once Dr. Eisenmenger had to play his great trump card: if His Imperial Highness Archduke Franz Ferdinand did not co-operate with his doctors (Dr. von Becker had come along, too, on the *dahibiya*, *Hope*), then Victor Eisenmenger would not continue to be his doctor. On one occasion it almost came to his packing his bags and leaving his patient to his fate.

Evenings on the *Hope* gliding along that wide river when the men sat around the table drinking their inhibitions away and discussing the issues that gnawed at their spirits, the conversation often turned to issues that spiked their competitiveness, one against another. One such issue was the well-hidden fear of military men that if they should ever end up wounded whether the medical men attached to their regiment would be capable of giving them a chance of survival. The argument batted back and forth that evening was whether military doctors attached to the regiment were not finer doctors than civilian doctors. In general the opinion was that civilians were an incompetent bunch.

And on the edge of this group of military men with aristocratic backgrounds and impressive military careers sat Victor Eisenmenger, whose health had never been good, the doctor into whose hands the heir to the throne had placed his trust. Had he? Should he?

Accused of belonging to an incompetent bunch Victor spoke up. In fact, he argued that it was largely those who had little chance of shining in their profession who offered their services to the military. The surprising thing was that so many honourable and excellent doctors took up posts in the military. The argument grew ever more heated. Before leaving the room Victor said that a circus-rider could ride horses far better than many a cavalry officer. Victor returned to his sleeping quarters and began to pack. He wrote his resignation letter and gave it to Janaczek to deliver.

"Body and soul I am an officer," said Franz Ferdinand the following morning. "It is the finest profession of all. I beg you to put this matter aside and I will forget that it ever happened. I place all my trust in you as I have done since the beginning. I need you." And with that Victor Eisenmenger realised that he would never go back to Dr. Schrötter's clinic.

They returned to Cairo on the *dahabiya* where Karl Ludwig and Maria Theresia were waiting for him. Briefly they provided distraction and then they went on to Palestine. Franz Ferdinand went from Cairo to Monte Carlo. Otto joined him in Monte Carlo and from there they travelled together to Spain and Majorca and back to Monte Carlo. Again he was fretting to return home but was told that he must wait until the weather was warmer. So he went to Territet to visit the Empress Elisabeth who was staying there.

But before he even arrived in Territet, he received a telegramme telling him his father was dangerously ill.

Karl Ludwig did not live to see Franz Ferdinand declared cured. Karl Ludwig died of typhoid fever on 19th May 1896 while Franz Ferdinand was visiting Elisabeth in Switzerland. He had picked up the infection while visiting the Holy Lands. Karl Ludwig was a deeply religious man and he wanted intensely to see the holy places of the Bible before he died. As he got older, Karl Ludwig had withdrawn ever more into religiosity.

Franz Ferdinand arrived back in Vienna too late to see his father alive. Finally, then and only then, did his doctors allow him to return to his own home at Konopischt. But come the next winter there was again the battle over where Franz Ferdinand should go. This time it was to be Corsica, which Franz Ferdinand hated and then on to Algiers. When Algiers got too hot for him he moved on to Cannes.

Finally in March 1898 he was pronounced cured of tuberculosis. From July 1895 when his disease was indisputably diagnosed until March 1898 Franz Ferdinand had lived with the constant dread of dying. He had eaten his spirit away enduring enforced rest and inactivity. He had been an impossible patient. But in the end he was able to face the world and look forward without the weight of illness holding him back.

There was now no reason why he should not be acknowledged as the heir to the throne and treated as such. Before, there had been reluctance to proclaim Franz Ferdinand the heir-apparent because he was such a sick man. But now the reasons for not proclaiming him heir to the throne were disappearing. Yet still Franz Joseph made no move to acknowledge his nephew as his heir.

And Franz Ferdinand felt the slight. It was probably never meant. It was getting harder and harder to get Franz Joseph to make any hard and fast decision. Franz Ferdinand felt that there was a good deal of ground to be caught up on, and with renewed physical vigour he wanted to catch up as fast as he could. When no move was made to acknowledge him as heir he must have felt that his position was still in some doubt. But why? Could they still be thinking that he might be pushed to one side to make way for Otto? 'Der fesche Otto' with his prim, unhappy German wife, whose pinched lips repressed her misery?

Chapter 100

Franz Ferdinand hurried home to see Maria Theresia and tell her the good news. This before anything else. When Franz Ferdinand returned from his long cure, able to declare that he was now free of the tuberculosis that had blighted his life, Maria Theresia must have been almost more delighted than anyone else. Behind the facade of day-to-day life, she must have endured all those weeks and months and years of wondering whether he would pull through. And now here he was looking fitter and more robust than she ever remembered. Why, he had even put on some weight! And there was colour in his cheeks.

But then the other person he would have been impatient to tell was, of course, Sophie Chotek. One of the issues that had forced them to remain so much apart – his illness – was now resolved; but that did not make it much easier for them to sort out their future. And in their uncertainty, they continued the secrecy. This meant that they had to go on acting as though there were nothing more between them than a pleasant, casual liking.

Did Franz Ferdinand ever feel that the Sophie he found when he returned from his long convalescence had changed? Oh, not in her loyalty and her affections towards him! But in some other subtle way? In March 1898 Sophie celebrated her thirtieth birthday. She was settled in Isabella's household. No more constant moving around and no need to fear that she would be a burden upon her brother, Wolfgang.

It has always been assumed that life under Isabella's roof was almost intolerable, but the mass of photographs[45] that Isabella left behind do not suggest that this was so at all. They suggest a bustling, interesting little world where a crowd of young people enjoyed the activities of their time. In these activities the ladies-in-waiting were included even though they were expected to hang back. There are pictures of hunting groups; there are pictures of the family by the seaside; there are pictures of picnics; there are pictures of boating on the lake; there are pictures of musical evenings. In a great many of these pictures Sophie Chotek is there in the background along with the family.

What was more, Isabella had eight daughters, six of whom grew up to reach marriageable age, before she finally joyously brought into the world her only son, Albrecht. Sophie had grown up in a large family of five girls and three brothers, so this would have felt very familiar to her. She developed aunt-like feelings for Isabella's girls and shared their hopes and their dreams and their confidences. Sophie was ever discreet and she could

---

[45] *Ein Photoalbum aus dem Haus Habsburg*, editors: Vilmos Heiszler, Margit Szakács and Károly Vörös, 1989.

be trusted – the girls may well have turned to her in a hundred and one ways. And all of this would have made Sophie feel she belonged.

In most of Isabella's photographs, Sophie appears quietly serious and she is usually standing further back or to one side. But there is one picture of Franz Ferdinand and Sophie on the tennis court. Here Sophie is standing up at the net and she is smiling, and smiling broadly. The palpable happiness on her face in this picture is touching. Standing further back, Franz Ferdinand's face is half in shadow, making it hard to make out his expression, but he seems lost in thought and somewhat cast down. Sophie's smile is so warm, so light-hearted in that moment. This was the Sophie he longed for. The whole picture seems to tell the story of the easy-going young woman who is comfortable with her life and accepting of its limitations, and the man aching for her and not knowing how he might win her.

Perhaps Sophie just was the better actress, and she could play the charming lady-in-waiting who appreciated the Archduke's partnering her on the tennis court. It would have been most surprising if anyone had ever noticed anything about her that was anything other than deferential.

Franz Ferdinand may have found the acting harder to keep up. His thoughts at that moment might have been dark with brooding over the impossibility of the situation and his longing to be with Sophie and be open about it. And how long could this go on? He was not merely getting used to Sophie, he was thinking about her more and more. His need to be with her was growing and growing...

It has always been assumed that Sophie angled for the Archduke by every means possible. When the scandal broke, she was seen as an ambitious, scheming minx out to entrap him. When she withdrew this was interpreted as a ploy calculated to win him in the end. When she said she would renounce him, it was assumed that she was being duplicitous and deceitful. Above all, it was assumed that she knew what she was doing and that she was pulling all the strings.

It is easy to assume these things when we know how events turned out. But at the time nobody could be certain how things would turn out. Nobody could know the strength of Franz Ferdinand's love, not even Sophie. He may not have known it himself.

Sophie would have needed an enormous amount of confidence if that was what she was angling for. What if her bluff had been called? What if he had given in to family pressure? Where would she have stood then? She certainly would not have been able to go on living with Isabella. She could not have gone back to live with her father because Bohuslav had died in October 1896, making her situation all the more vulnerable.

Sophie had confided in her sisters and found that her family found the whole story improbable and very disquieting. They were far from ecstatic. They firmly believed that the Archduke who was expected to become the next Emperor of Austria would never marry outside his own circle of eligible princesses. For them the whole matter could only end in shame and tears.

For these reasons, no doubt, they, too, guarded Sophie's secret as closely as she herself. It seems likely that behind the scenes some of Sophie's brothers put pressure on her to end things quickly and as unobtrusively as possible. They may even have warned her that if she didn't, they would not support her financially when she found that she had nowhere else to turn.

Sophie must have spent plenty of time pondering over her dilemma and it is likely that she ended up ever more confused as to what might be her best way forward. She would have needed an extraordinary degree of assurance and a self-centred strength to see everything through if it had all been driven by calculated ambition alone. But there is nothing to suggest that Sophie had that kind of assurance. The smiling girl on the tennis court, smiling that soft smile, was not a self-centred, calculating person.

Yet one of Franz Ferdinand's friends, Count Sternberg, described in his diary how Sophie "lowered her heavy lids over glowing dark eyes". Count Sternberg was convinced that that was all that was needed to fascinate Franz Ferdinand and spur him on, because what royalty love above all else is the unreachable, rather than what is obsequiously served up to them on a salver. "Countess 'Sopherl'," wrote Count Sternberg, "met his approaches with the firmest resistance." People, like the Count, watching Sophie's resistance, came to believe firmly and insistently that she calculated every tiniest thought and reaction and manipulated them to her own ends. Thus, Sophie resisted and held back, and those who disliked her were certain that she must have been acting a part.

And Count Sternberg was probably right, that nothing was more likely to make Franz Ferdinand feel that she and she alone was the only person who could give him the companionship he wanted. She was the person who had written to him throughout all the long absences; she was the person who had shown she believed in him when he was most ill and others had only seen a dying man; she was the person whose warmth and affection had been so unwavering and of so much comfort to him in his moments of darkest despair.

And here she was – resisting. Because she cared so deeply about him, she would have told him. How often during those long months of inactivity had he suffered anguished doubts? But then there would be a warm letter full of her thoughts, reassuring him that she was still with him in spirit. All those accumulated anguished doubts may have coalesced together into one tight ball in his mind as he looked at her and came face to face with her resistance. And he had to respect her need for discretion and continuing secrecy. An ill-timed revelation would harm her so much more than him. So, impatiently and with difficulty, he reined in his impetuous nature while they hoped for the right moment. It must have seemed to him that Sophie had already accepted that it could never work out between them. He was the one who couldn't accept it.

Did they plan anything? Or were they leaving it to chance? How much did they discuss a way forward, or were they trusting to luck? No one knows. In the end scandal broke, ill-timed, unprepared for, and they had to deal with it.

Isabella had long been in the habit of writing regularly to her 'Franzi'. Her letters were warm, chatty and full of day-to-day family news, the letters of an energetic woman who is interested in everyone around her. Throughout 1898 Isabella wrote every few days. There were Christmas greetings at the end of the year and on it went through the first half of 1899. The letters came to an abrupt halt in July 1899.

There are varied stories about how it all happened.

The secret had been so well kept for so long. So much self-restraint! Such care not to let slip the slightest hint of their true feelings! One story is that, in the end, their discretion was not quite enough and that the little hints that slipped out began to accumulate and attract attention. And of all the stories this does seem the most plausible. It was likely that Franz Ferdinand had become more impatient than ever.

There is another story that the secret was blown out of the water one day in Abbazia and according to this one there was a violent scene between Franz Ferdinand and Isabella. Franz Ferdinand is supposed to have stormed out of the room with the ringing words, "Sophie is my bride!"

But one story has stuck. This is the story of the watch as related by Franz Ferdinand's private secretary in 1925, and it is also the story believed by both Isabella's grandchildren and by Franz Ferdinand's own daughter. However, after the deaths of Franz Ferdinand and Sophie in Sarajevo their children were to discover how little their parents had ever revealed to them the details of their own lives. In the picture of who their parents were there were huge holes. All the children could do was fall back on the stories that were circulated about Franz Ferdinand and Sophie and so often they must have found that those stories contrasted cruelly with their own personal memories of their father and mother.

Nevertheless, the story[46] of the watch has a fine drama about it.

---

[46] Beate Hammond in her book *Habsburgs Grösste Liebesgeschichte* states that the correspondence between Franz Ferdinand and Isabella came to an end earlier in December 1898, a time of the year when it would have been too cold for much tennis. Beate Hammond therefore questions the whole story of the gold watch.

Franz Ferdinand had spent a weekend at the castle in Pressburg with Isabella and her family, a warm weekend. During the day the sun was heavy in a brilliant sky and the leaves hung still on the trees. There had been a tennis party in the castle park but in the heavy heat, the air full of shimmering sunlight, their play had only been half-hearted, and at the end of the day Franz Ferdinand had departed for Konopischt. His leave-taking was as affectionate as usual and Isabella, as usual, pressed him to return as soon as he could. Was he slightly distracted that day? Had he not been able to play with Sophie or even get a few moments alone with her? Had this apparently never-ending need for secrecy and self-restraint weighed upon his spirit even more than usual that weekend? But nobody noticed anything out of the ordinary with him. There were smiles all round and Franz Ferdinand climbed into his carriage and waved as he left them all.

But on this occasion Franz Ferdinand had forgotten his gold watch and left it behind in the changing room. It was a heavy gold watch and attached to it were a mass of small trinkets that he had collected over the years, seals, medallions, cigar-cutters and the like – so-called *bréloques*. One of these was a flat round medallion with a closed lid, which would contain the miniature portrait of someone dear to the owner.

Franz Ferdinand was not a careless man and it would seem that this was the first time he forgot something. Such a watch, so heavy, is not easily forgotten but Franz Ferdinand forgot his and failed to notice that the weight of it was not there in his pocket.

It was a servant later that evening who found the watch. He took it the Archduchess Isabella. She had often seen Franz Ferdinand with it. Here it was in her hands and she looked at it closely and noticed the round medallion with its closed lid. She had to know whose picture was hidden in that medallion. She opened the lid.

Isabella had long been confident of seeing her eldest daughter, Maria Christina, one day become Franz Ferdinand's wife. True, he was sixteen years older than Maria Christina. He had known her since she was a child; he had watched her turn into an awkward and self-conscious girl and now, at nearly twenty, Maria Christina was turning into an attractive young woman. He had often shown her friendly attentions during her growing up years, nothing particularly obvious, nothing that went beyond ordinary, polite consideration, but Maria Christina was so obviously the right sort of girl of good family and of equal birth.

Maria Christina got on particularly well with Isabella's lady-in-waiting. Countess Sophie Chotek had proved a perfect companion for Maria Christina. Sophie, with her knowledge of the world and her quiet elegance, had been able to bring out in Maria Christina just the right kind of manners and openness. Sophie had done much to give Maria Christina confidence in herself. With Sophie discreetly in the background, Franz Ferdinand had spent much time with Maria Christina. Isabella had encouraged this.

Isabella was well aware that Franz Ferdinand was greatly attracted to her lady-in-waiting. She wouldn't have given it a second thought. Many a male member of the Habsburg family had enjoyed a passing flirtation with someone who could never be considered a possible wife. Such flirtations ran their course and were forgotten. If the lady in question or her family made difficulties they could be warned off with no difficulty.

Many, many years later in 1914 Franz Ferdinand invited his nephew, the Archduke Karl, and his wife, Zita, to stay with him at a favourite shooting lodge at Hahnenhort in Lower Austria. Franz Ferdinand took an interest in his nephew and liked him. The liking was mutual. So on that visit at Hahnenhort, Franz Ferdinand showed Karl and Zita a telegramme that Isabella had once sent him.

He would have stood there with a wry, humorous smile on his face as he watched the young couple read Isabella's words. She was inviting Franz Ferdinand to a shoot and she had ended up with the words 'Countess Chotek will be there'. Thus, Isabella was using Franz Ferdinand's liking for Sophie as a bait to tempt him to visit her and her family. Nor was that telegramme the only occasion where Sophie was the bait. In many of her letters to Franz Ferdinand Isabella emphasised how useful Sophie was to her, how diligent she had been or how thoughtful towards their visitors.

On one occasion when Isabella visited Konopischt to see and admire the changes that Franz Ferdinand was making to his beloved castle, Sophie was brought along too. Franz Ferdinand would have been able to point out how attractive a home his castle would make his future family, and he could watch to see if Sophie's eyes lit up or what drew her particular attention.

Franz Ferdinand kept that telegramme. He had it framed and hung it on the wall of his inner sanctum. He must have felt much mischievous pleasure when he looked up and saw it. In his eyes, it would have meant that Isabella knew he was not leading Maria Christina on.

But for Isabella a match between Franz Ferdinand and Maria Christina was a match to dream for. So much so, that Isabella would not have wanted to see anything that might suggest she was barking up the wrong tree.

It is just possible that Isabella had begun to manoeuvre things a little. Up till now she had been content to wait, both because of Maria Christina's youth and because of the uncertainty over Franz Ferdinand's health. Had Isabella, during that weekend, said something that had lodged disquieting thoughts in Franz Ferdinand's mind? Had she said something that had brought it home to him that he and Sophie were not going to be able to go on, as they had, keeping their secret and snatching brief, exquisite moments together when they could?

Perhaps we can see Isabella in her small salon, preparing to sort out some household matter, but pausing to look at Franz Ferdinand's gold watch first. Through the open windows she can hear the beginnings of a breeze in the trees. Behind her in the house are the familiar household noises, the girls are in the music room, laughing over someone's teasing rendition of a peasant song. Isabella turns back to the watch and opens the lid of the medallion. And she stares at a miniature of Sophie Chotek.

Because Isabella was a forceful woman, it has always been assumed that she immediately exploded with anger. There was a scene. Sophie was thrown out of the house. This is not true.

According to Franz Ferdinand's daughter, Sophie was not thrown out on the spot as though she were a disgraced scullery maid. Sophie had some leave due to her and she departed for the break that she was owed. During that break she wrote saying that she would not be returning. Appearances were kept up.

And maybe the actual confrontation between Isabella and Sophie may not have gone the way that is often described. It would be just as likely that Isabella suddenly turned stiff and haughty. She felt betrayed, both by Franz Ferdinand and by Sophie, betrayed and humiliated, and she would have felt it all the more keenly on Maria Christina's behalf. But even at this stage Isabella's reaction was more irritation than cold anger. Even at this point she would have assumed that the appropriate warnings would be given and the matter swiftly and unobtrusively brought to an end by some impassive court lackey.

But the picture of a volcanic Isabella would have appealed to a society that vicariously enjoyed explosive stories just like this one. So in the telling and the re-telling the drama had to be enhanced.

It was noted that Maria Christina shrugged off the discovery quite calmly. Maria Christina's feelings for Franz Ferdinand were at best very muted, but her mother had long been dropping hints in her ear, while exhorting her to behave in a way that would interest and appeal to Franz Ferdinand. It is just possible that Maria Christina was rather relieved to be let off the hook. Did she see Franz Ferdinand as rather old and gruff – in a word, *schroff*?

It is quite likely that Maria Christina had a sense of how things were between Franz Ferdinand and Sophie, far more so than her mother. She liked Sophie. Could Maria Christina have actually been pushing the two into each other's company? Did her sense of their secret appeal to a romantic streak in her? It may have been so. And after Sophie had gone, Maria Christina may have missed her a good deal, wondering whether it would all turn out well and hoping that it would.

As Sophie set about getting her things together, Maria Christina may have rushed up to find out from her what was happening. Sophie would have told her plainly. Sophie would also have tried to quell any wild outpourings of imagination. She did not know where she was going, or what was going to happen to her next.

Rather sadly, no doubt, she would have avoided making Maria Christina any promises that Maria Christina may have wanted her to make, just because she had no idea whether she would ever be able to keep them. She may have been touched, as she said goodbye to Maria Christina, at the look of anxiety in the girl's eyes.

So Sophie left Pressburg and she went to Vienna. Some say she went to stay with Zdenka, who was then a lady-in-waiting to the Crown Princess Stéphanie. Stéphanie, as a widow, was living a very quiet, retired life in the Hofburg when she wasn't away on her travels. She probably had no particular objection to Sophie's being there and she may have seen very little of her, if anything at all. Others say she went to the Hotel Elisabeth in Vienna.

She sent a brief note to the faithful Janaczek asking him to inform his master and then she laid low. Sophie did not stay long but moved on to stay with one of her Kinsky uncles at Kosterlitz in Bohemia. She later went to stay with her youngest sister in Dresden and then spent some time with another uncle in Grosspriesen[47] near Teplitz. Quite simply, Sophie had nowhere she could go to and stay; she was forced to keep throwing herself upon the hospitality of first one and then another relative.

---

[47] Today Grosspriesen is known as Velké Březno.

Chapter 101

They could not have handled him in a worse manner. They should have played for time. No ultimatums. Accept Sophie's presence in Franz Ferdinand's life.

Instead they could not have found a better way of driving Franz Ferdinand into digging in his heels and facing them all down. Backed into a corner with no way out, Franz Ferdinand was now forced to take a stand and fight for the girl he loved and fight he damn well would – fangs bared. He found himself almost alone in this battle. Lined up against him was the entire Habsburg family, the whole court and all the aristocracy. His most bitter opponent was the Court Chamberlain, Prince Alfred Montenuovo. Prince Montenuovo could not risk directly affronting a member of the Imperial Family but the gloves were off when it came to Sophie.

Isabella's first move was to demand an audience with the Emperor. She was extremely angry, but underlying her anger was fear – fear for her daughter and her chances. An indignant Isabella insisted that Maria Christina would now be the laughing stock of the court. Ignoring the fact that Maria Christina's reaction to the discovery had been very matter-of-fact, Isabella expounded on how her daughter's feelings had been awakened and her hopes raised, all under false pretences, all in order to cover up a shameful and illicit love affair.

Franz Joseph hated scenes and raised voices and angry women. They made him uncomfortable and he did not know how to react. His instinct was to smother everything and push it away as though it had never been.

Here he seized upon the point that Franz Ferdinand had never asked for Maria Christina's hand or declared his intentions towards her. There must be no further scandal and he would deal with the matter and then the interview was over. A ruffled and disconcerted Isabella had to withdraw and find peace of mind where she could.

Franz Joseph then sent Franz Ferdinand a telegramme commanding his attendance. This telegramme was dated 5th October 1899. We can only assume that between the summer when the gold watch was discovered and October Isabella had probably been pressing for intervention from the appropriate official to end the whole sorry business of a love affair between her lady-in-waiting and the heir to the throne. It seems likely that her anger sprang from the fact that several months on and the whole matter still had not been tidied up and filed away. The longer it went on the more harm it could do to Maria Christina's good name and marriage prospects. Franz Ferdinand, of course, had not ceased to insist that he would marry Sophie Chotek but it is likely that Isabella found that merely irritating. She would not have believed it could come about. However, she did need the matter cleared up, and quickly.

It was intended to be a short and inconsequential interview in which Franz Joseph would reassure his nephew that the matter with Isabella and her daughter could be smoothed over but he did not wish to hear anything more of the lady-in-waiting.

The interview was short, but not inconsequential. Franz Ferdinand listened and then he bowed. Then he formally asked for permission to marry Countess Sophie von Chotkova und Wognin.

The temperature in that room must have dropped several degrees. Franz Joseph was not used to being crossed or opposed, not even by his volatile nephew. He was a ditherer, a man with no strong persuasions, no committed attachment to any view or issue. And like many a ditherer he had a foggy sense of the whys and wherefores of what was happening around him, which was largely why he hated change. He was completely incapable of explaining his reasons for anything. Not that he considered he had to give any reasons for anything. He was the Emperor and he made the decisions, except that his decisions were almost invariably non-decisions. Which was why it was always so difficult for him to deal with Franz Ferdinand. Franz Ferdinand was the exact opposite. He made strong decisions. He thought things through and he had good reasons for whatever line he wanted to adopt.

All around Franz Ferdinand there were many struggling to maintain the status quo who saw real dangers in Franz Ferdinand's clear thinking. They weaseled and wheedled around Franz Ferdinand, seeking to contain and befog his view of things. It was a head-on clash hidden in polite foggy mists. But Franz Ferdinand seems to have had a brittle carapace. He found the weaseling and wheedling highly provocative and it could drive him to distraction.

So often those who fought Franz Ferdinand but who did not wish to see it in that light would have come to feel that it was Franz Ferdinand who was opposing them. In their minds his opposition came to feel bitter and angry. Franz Ferdinand came to be described as bombastic and belligerent. Perhaps this was when his reputation of being cantankerous, explosive and unreasonable began to grow up around him. It would not be surprising.

Those he bested tended not to forget it. Some of them flaunted their outrage. Those who knew how to meet the Archduke halfway were so often the quieter characters whose voices were not often heard.

Eventually the reputation would surround him so impenetrably that few seemed to see a human being behind the reputation. Eventually when any word or action, attitude or gesture, fitted this image of what he was like, it served to confirm his reputation all the more, and when any word or action, attitude or gesture did not fit then those around became deaf and blind to it.

Franz Joseph always seems to have felt a hidden, secret respect for those who could decide what to do. But he could not deal with such people. So with unfailing courtesy he held them at arm's length and he found his respect for them soured by a sneaking irritation because they made him feel uncomfortable.

If there is one thing that historians are certain about, it is that there was no love lost between Franz Joseph and Franz Ferdinand. Yet, oddly, one has a strange feeling that Franz Joseph may well have had a good deal of liking for Franz Ferdinand, even as he failed totally to understand him. There were things about Franz Ferdinand that Franz Joseph would have approved of. And it is even possible that Franz Ferdinand had considerable liking for the kindly old man, even as he deplored his flabby style of ruling.

But if there was ever any possibility of these two men working together, that interview put an end to it. The force of deep passion got bogged down in a quagmire. Franz Joseph told Franz Ferdinand to think it over and to return in a week.

Franz Joseph then turned to Prince Montenuovo.

This was the man whose task it became to sort out the whole Chotek affair. As *Obersthofmeister*, he had to uphold court protocol and he did so with a vengeance. He watched, hawk-eyed, for every little infringement of the long canon of rules and regulations (the Family Statute [48] that constricted the lives of the Habsburgs). It was as if he had a special mission to ensure that they did not slip the way his own grandmother[49] had slipped.

Montenuovo did not, of course, invent the rules of protocol he upheld so officiously. They dated back to the beginning of the nineteenth century, suffocating most freedoms and almost all spontaneity.

Nobody was more committed to them than Franz Joseph. To him a dynasty without protocol was a dynasty without a backbone. Montenuovo was only putting into effect what Franz Joseph wanted but he took things to

---

[48] This was effectively the Rules of the Habsburg Family, laying out what its members could and could not do and especially laying out the rules of status and precedence, as well as who could be accepted into the ranks of the family and who could not. Note 4 in the Notes Section.

[49] Note 14 in the Notes Section.

heights that Franz Joseph would not have done. What Montenuovo now stressed was that a marriage between the heir-apparent and a lady-in-waiting, whose family – although aristocratic – was not of equal birth, was impossible, or only possible if it were a morganatic marriage. Did he savour pressing a morganatic marriage upon people who, by breeding though not status, were his own close cousins?

There was one big problem: the Emperor, as head of the Habsburgs, had the obligation of upholding the rules of etiquette and behaviour of the whole family and his was the power, if anyone transgressed, to remove privileges or even expel them from the family. But the Emperor also had the power to change the rules of etiquette and behaviour. Franz Joseph had the power to forbid his nephew from marrying the Countess Sophie Chotek.

But Franz Joseph's power lasted only as long as his life. If Franz Ferdinand waited until Franz Joseph's death, then he would become Emperor and he would have the power to change the rules. And if he did so he could marry whomsoever he wished – an actress if he had wanted – and he could make her an Empress.

Franz Joseph was nearly seventy years old. He had virtually never suffered a day's illness in his life, but he was an old man and a tired one. Elisabeth's death only a year before in Geneva had knocked the stuffing out of him. It was still unspeakable to speak of the day when the old Emperor was no longer there, for an awful lot of ordinary people he had become virtually immortal, but there were those who found it necessary to start looking ahead. From the point of view of men like Montenuovo and Franz Ferdinand's other enemies in the government and at court, men like the then Foreign Minister, Count Agenor Goluchowski, there was an urgency to get the whole matter tied up and finished with.

When Franz Ferdinand went back to see the Emperor a week later he was faced with an ultimatum from Franz Joseph: he could marry Sophie Chotek but only if he gave up his right to the throne.

It would not have taken Franz Ferdinand long to realise that if he did agree to give up his right to the throne so that he might marry Sophie, there was a risk that he would not just be forced out of the line of succession but also expelled from the Arch-house, give up his lands and estates, probably obliged to take some other name and, as an exile, leave Austria for the rest of his life, never to return.

For a brief moment a memory of Gianni may well have flashed through Franz Ferdinand's mind. And Franz Ferdinand would have known what Gianni's fate had been. Of course, that shipwreck in a storm round Cape Horn – so very far away – had been a terrible accident; but for the monarchy it had been a convenient accident. For Franz Ferdinand nothing like that was going to happen. Did Franz Joseph see in his nephew's eyes a look he could not quite grasp?

Franz Joseph then dismissed Franz Ferdinand and told him to leave the matter be until the following spring of 1900.

Nobody could have known that Franz Joseph would live another sixteen years; they would not have thought that time was on their side. Time was not on Franz Ferdinand's side either. Sophie was already thirty-one and if Franz Ferdinand wanted to have not just a wife but a family as well, then they could not afford to wait too long before starting a family.

And time was not on Sophie's side. Sophie was effectively homeless and she could not count upon her family to keep on offering her hospitality indefinitely. She could not take another position as a lady-in-waiting because no one would have offered her such a position, and that left only the convent. Every indication suggests that Sophie was seriously thinking about a future in a convent and what it would mean to her. She was coming to terms with that inevitability.

When Otto died seven years later in 1906, Franz Ferdinand was deeply distressed, saying "in the past we were very close". Franz Ferdinand confided in a friend, "You can imagine what I went through and how I felt." And he thought back to earlier days and how they spent their whole childhood together. "Poor Otto suffered terribly during the last year and his death was a real relief – may God give him eternal rest."

Was he thinking of the time when they were both young men, just escaped from the schoolroom and still fancy-free? Was he remembering when they shared in escapades, together with Rudolf, when Rudolf was the next in line to the throne and neither of them had had any thoughts of becoming Emperor? Before men like Goluchowski and Montenuovo had insidiously promoted Otto at the expense of Franz Ferdinand?

And one memory would have sprung into his mind. In the early days, not so very long after Franz Ferdinand had first fallen in love with Sophie, he had mentioned to Otto how very much he was taken with the Countess. Later that year, 1894, Otto had made a caricature of Sophie and given it to her. Sophie seems to have been touched and found the drawing very amusing. She sent it to Franz Ferdinand, possibly with a mischievous note. That had been before things went so badly wrong between Franz Ferdinand and Otto and Franz Ferdinand would have remembered it with sudden sadness.

One thing is certain: no one was more against Franz Ferdinand and his dream of marrying the woman he loved than his brother Otto. Franz

Ferdinand was shocked and saddened. Did Otto's bitter feelings spring from the fact that, since he had had to marry someone whose very presence in the same room made him feel angry, why should 'Franzi' be able to do as he pleased? Otto's life was turning very sour all around him and, deep down, he may have resented the fact that 'Franzi' had found a love that satisfied him. Otto had never found a love that satisfied him, not within his marriage but not outside it, either, not even in an activity or interest that gripped him. His life was purposeless.

Otto's debauchery was to lead to his early death. It is possible that when the whole story of Franz Ferdinand's love for Sophie became public Otto was already experiencing serious symptoms. They may have made him resent Franz Ferdinand's surviving his illness and now being pronounced cured.

It was not just Otto who turned his back on Franz Ferdinand. Franz Ferdinand's younger brother, Ferdinand Karl, was also just as opposed. Of the three brothers, Ferdinand Karl most resembled their father, Karl Ludwig, with the same long lugubrious face. He was weak and dreamy. Franz Ferdinand was never as close to his youngest brother as he had been to Otto.

Katharina Schratt hated the whole idea of Franz Ferdinand's love affair with Sophie. Kathi would see Franz Joseph all wound up after some meeting with his nephew which had not gone well and Kathi would blaze in defence of her man. Kathi did not really know Franz Ferdinand but she had heard many stories about him and the image she had gleaned was of someone who deliberately aimed to upset and annoy the Emperor. Kathi would have instinctively taken Franz Joseph's view and made it her own. She certainly added her pennyworth of disapproval. She probably made Franz Joseph feel better by waxing vehement against the whole matter. Kathi's reaction when Franz Ferdinand and Sophie were assassinated was, effectively, 'good, now he cannot go on making life hell for Franz Joseph!'

Rudolf's widow and his daughter also become mixed up in it all but on opposite sides. Stéphanie had always got on well with Franz Ferdinand, so now she warmly supported him in his desire to marry the woman he loved. Stéphanie's support for Franz Ferdinand was all it needed for Erzsi to be opposed – ferociously so. Erzsi, with her passionate singlemindedness, was fiercely offended that Franz Ferdinand was willing to consider marrying someone below him in rank. Yet Erzsi herself had already met the man she wished to marry and he was not her equal in rank, either.

Some years later Sophie put her foot in it badly. She made the mistake of speaking to Erzsi. Sophie's path had crossed with Erzsi's during the time

Sophie had been lady-in-waiting to Archduchess Isabella and she also knew a great deal about Erzsi, having heard plenty about every member of Stéphanie's household from her sister, Zdenka. Sophie must have felt that she might be permitted a few polite words.

Fury flashed across Erzsi's face. We can imagine that Erzsi would have drawn herself up to her full height and when she did that she often towered above most men around her; she certainly would have towered above Sophie, physically putting Sophie in her place. Later that same day Erzsi spat angrily, "To think she thought she could speak to me!" From then on, Erzsi did all she could to make it impossible that Franz Ferdinand would be received by any of the nobility.

Years and years later a few of Erzsi's chickens may have come back to roost. One person who always did support Franz Ferdinand was Otto's eldest son, Karl, who would one day become Franz Joseph's successor and the last Emperor of Austria. We do not know how much or how little Karl's path crossed with Erzsi's but he must have known of her spite against Franz Ferdinand.

When, after the death of Franz Joseph, Erzsi turned to Karl for his support in her difficulties over her divorce from her husband, Karl was polite and considerate but also cool and distant and he lifted not a finger to help her. If Erzsi could not bring herself to be even coolly courteous towards Sophie then Karl could not bring himself to show any concern for Erzsi's wishes.

The battlelines were being drawn, people were being forced to decide on which side they stood and Franz Ferdinand was beginning to find that there were very few willing to take his side. The battalions lined up against him seemed to grow by the day. One person he did not turn to in vain was his beloved stepmother, Maria Theresia. She was not merely on his side, she was willing to enter the lists on his behalf. She sought interviews with Franz Joseph in order to speak up for her stepson. Anyone else coming to him to speak up for Franz Ferdinand would have got short shrift from Franz Joseph but Maria Theresia had a strange position at court that gave her more weight than she ordinarily would have had as the widow of one of the Archdukes.

Franz Joseph had come to like and appreciate his sister-in-law. Maria Theresia had a certain quality that won affection and respect wherever she went. And because of this Franz Joseph was willing to listen to her. She tried more than once to help Franz Ferdinand but in the end Franz Joseph was unyielding. No doubt, he found it hard to turn her away, harder than anyone else, but turn her away he did.

So Maria Theresia would return to a tense Franz Ferdinand and sadly tell him how little success her efforts had brought. And he would stare into the distance and the enormity of what he wanted to do would pass through his mind over and over again. He could not know how things would turn out and that gnawed away at him.

Franz Joseph could refuse him permission to marry Sophie. If he married her without that permission he could be stripped of all titles and rights and forced into exile. Franz Ferdinand could wait until Franz Joseph's death and he became Emperor but he could have no idea how long the waiting would be. He could, of course, hold this possibility before Franz Joseph – in fact, it was the *only* card up his sleeve. But Franz Joseph was the kind of man who was likely to adopt the view, 'I shall rule right up to my death according to what I hold to be right, and whilst I am alive I will not give in. But after my death, I can do no more and what will happen will happen.'

Because we now know the outcome, historians tend to assume that Franz Ferdinand was confident of that outcome. There is no reason to think he was. And there are a lot of reasons to think he may in his heart of hearts have been much more uncertain than he appeared to be. It is assumed that he was absolutely sure of Sophie. He could be sure of her love – he knew that. She had shown her love and been on his side in the days when so many had been canoodling up to Otto and building up his hopes of becoming the next Emperor of Austria. But could he be sure that she would marry him?

Sophie, just because she had won the heart of the heir to the throne, now found herself surrounded by a lot of enemies. Most of her enemies did not know her or what sort of person she was. They just wanted to denigrate her and crush her. They wanted to blacken her name and force her to crawl away into some corner, never to be seen again. They sought to find fault with her.

Sophie did not give them much to go on. She kept a low profile, said nothing, provoked nothing, challenged nothing. She was quiet and dignified and courteous. Her manners were flawless, her good behaviour unbending.

They, her enemies, leaned upon her family, which exacerbated the tensions considerably. Their situation was not a comfortable one and many of her relations were deeply opposed to her having a relationship with the Archduke. They worried for themselves but told her that they worried about her. And many of them must have told her, 'In the end he will not marry you, and the longer this situation drags on the worse it will be for all of us!' And that was a message she could not deny.

What was more, temporarily they were supporting her because she was one of the family, but they would not go on doing so forever. How often did Sophie retire of an evening, perhaps sitting brushing her thick hair, and went over and over in her mind that she was, in effect, homeless and penniless. Outside she may have heard trees and branches cracking as the cold of November nights bit hard, and she may have felt that they reflected her mood. She would not have been human if she had not had doubts.

We do not know how easy it was for Franz Ferdinand to see Sophie during those weeks and months after she had left Isabella's household. The faithful Janaczek must have done his duty in keeping them in touch with each other. But did Franz Ferdinand get the opportunity to be alone with Sophie? He would have longed to find some way to keep her courage up and to reassure her. He would have longed to dispel her doubts and to be sure that she would not waver.

So Sophie kept out of the spotlight, as much as she could. This was not easy because it was she that their enemies attacked. Early on she received a letter from Prince Montenuovo, a letter that was almost obsequious towards her but nevertheless commanded her to do her duty and release the Archduke from any promises he might have made towards her.

Franz Joseph turned to Franz Ferdinand's former religious teacher, Dr. Gottfried Marschall, who had recently been appointed auxiliary bishop of St. Stephen's in Vienna. Gottfried Marschall left his audience with the Emperor in an appalled and frantic state of mind. He is supposed to have exclaimed, 'which Emperor should I serve – the one of today, or the one of tomorrow?' However, he set about serving the Emperor of the day and got to work on all the various different individuals.

He had a meeting with Franz Ferdinand, building up to the moment of pressure, but apparently somewhere along the line Franz Ferdinand turned upon him and simply asked whether he was for him or against him. He could not give Franz Ferdinand a straight answer.

Gottfried Marschall turned to Franz Ferdinand's sisters, trying to win them round using Franz Ferdinand's well-known affection for both his own sister and his two half-sisters. He approached Sophie herself and spoke with her family. Gottfried Marschall was known to be a great persuader – here, he failed monumentally. A rift was dug between the bishop and his one-time pupil that was to damage the prelate's career irrevocably.

Throughout all this Sophie gave away very little. What her answers actually were is not known. How she handled the pressure inside herself is not known. Whether she felt confident about the road she was going down is not known. Into that silence others poured their assumptions. By and large, the picture that has come down to us today is what others assumed to be Sophie's feelings and intentions.

It seems that the worst fault that could be stuck upon Sophie was ambition. For the rest of her life she would be castigated for her ambition. When she was quiet and retiring, it had to be because she was haughty and ambitious. When she appeared ready to concede and give up all, it had to be because she was secretly playing a deceitful game. She had to be playing hard to get. She had to be leading the Archduke on. She had to be angling for the position of Empress. She had to be playing for the highest stakes. She had to be ambitious. Sophie's ambition is well-documented – by those who hated her.

Chapter 102

Marie-Valérie in her diaries recorded the family dinner on New Year's Day 1900 when, as every year, every member of the immediate family was invited (commanded) to dine with Franz Joseph. Year after year this ritual dinner demanded a charade of family felicity. Domestic tensions could not be allowed to be seen. Marie-Valérie, settled in her marriage with Franz Salvator, would watch the tense masks worn by others present. None more so than Otto and Maria Josepha, attempting to hide behind frozen faces the savagery of their mutual dislike. On this occasion their twelve-year-old son, Karl was with them.

Franz Joseph, who had found relations with his own children so difficult, adored his grandchildren. It was the presence of the youngest generation of Habsburgs that now gave him most pleasure. So, having raised his glass of champagne to toast the whole family, Franz Joseph then raised his glass again and drank to young Karl. It was as if the old Emperor was acknowledging the future Emperor.

The gesture was significant. Marie-Valérie glanced quickly at Franz Ferdinand and was caught off guard by the sharp change in his expression. He suddenly turned deadly serious and a hush fell upon the whole table. Possibly at that moment Franz Ferdinand felt a flash of fear that the Emperor somehow or other might succeed in eliminating him from the line of succession and maybe even forcing him into exile from the land of his birth. He would have told himself that this was ridiculous but something of the emotion he felt at that moment would have lingered with him.

It was a grim-faced Franz Ferdinand who later hurried away from the Hofburg.

For Franz Ferdinand the waiting was growing harder. He turned to his old tutor, Baron Max Vladimir Beck. Max Vladimir Beck had been an understanding and stable presence through his boyhood; he had supported him through his long illness; he had helped him with the editing of his memoirs from his trip round the world; and Franz Ferdinand knew he could trust Max Vladimir Beck.

Max Vladimir Beck was not entirely happy about Franz Ferdinand's wish to marry an insignificant Countess Chotek, but he was a pragmatic man and he preferred the idea of Franz Ferdinand being the next Emperor to the idea of seeing Otto on the throne. As the hushed chill of a cold winter night settled over the city, a gloomy Franz Ferdinand told Max Vladimir Beck that "no matter how long it takes" he would wait. Beck advised against waiting and realised that some kind of compromise had to be found. He also realised that Franz Ferdinand needed careful 'managing', for who knew what he might suddenly do?

Franz Ferdinand accepted Beck's guidance and, often biting his tongue, sought to adopt the conciliatory line that Beck advised. He wrote to Franz Joseph a letter full of submission and expressions of loyalty but nevertheless insisting that he could never marry anyone else. It was his loyalty, his unswerving, deep-felt loyalty, that Beck wanted Franz Ferdinand to stress in his letter, and he did, cost him what it might.

Beck also impressed upon Franz Ferdinand that he must not show any resentment towards either of his two brothers. Franz Ferdinand was called upon to inspect the regiments commanded by Otto and Ferdinand Karl and in his reports he stressed the skills and abilities of both his brothers. As far as Otto and Ferdinand Karl were concerned this did not change their attitudes by so much as one jot.

There was no reply to his letter from the Emperor, and the weeks rolled by. Winter faded into spring.

Since January 1900 Austria had a new government and a new prime minister. His name was Ernst von Körber, a dry bureaucrat whose opinion was that the marriage would be fatal. Franz Ferdinand sent for von Körber and while struggling to appear calm he told him how desperately he needed this marriage and that he would wait for as long as it took. But Franz Ferdinand was no longer able to face waiting for as long as it might take and at his second meeting with von Körber he got carried away and, impassioned, threw away his only trump card. If he could not marry, and soon, he would go mad or shoot himself.

They were words spoken in the heat of the moment. But they frightened von Körber. The repercussions of another Habsburg suicide could only do immeasurable harm to the Imperial Family. No one talked about it, but the sense that insanity lay hidden deep within the Habsurgs and the Wittelsbachs was an unspoken fear. It was only ten years ago that Rudolf had died by his own hand. If Franz Ferdinand should do the same... how much damage would that do?

In the adjoining room Dr. Rudolf Sieghart could hear the violent language. Dr. Sieghart was von Körber's most senior aide, a bureaucrat and one of those backroom figures who wield much influence but are rarely seen. Dr. Sieghart found himself with a pile of documents, including the Habsburg Family Statute and the relevant legislation with regard to a morganatic marriage. His job was to make a report which could be submitted to the Emperor. It would seem that von Körber was already considering the possibility of a morganatic marriage between Franz Ferdinand and Sophie. On the face of it, both Franz Joseph and Franz Ferdinand appeared equally determined not to concede, but perhaps men like von Körber and Sieghart had begun to sense that Franz Ferdinand's determination was of a more steely, driven, energetic kind. He was the one they dared not push to the brink.

Sieghart knew then – that 9th April 1900 – where this was going to lead. But once again there were so many issues that arose because the Hungarians could not be trusted not to use this as an opportunity to obtain further concessions. The problem was that Hungarian law was not the same as Austrian law and the Hungarians were capable of refusing to accept that a marriage between Franz Ferdinand and the Countess Chotek was a morganatic marriage. You could not have the wife of the future Emperor having no rights in one half of the country and being recognised fully and crowned Queen in the other half.

So when Dr. Max Vladimir Beck came to see Dr. Rudolf Sieghart in the afternoon of Easter Monday, 16th April, in many ways both men were beginning to speak the same language. It was the details they had to thrash out and Hungarian support and agreement that they needed to get.

And still the weeks rolled by.

On the other side Prince Montenuovo was equally busy. By 12th June he was ready and it was for that date that Franz Joseph summoned all the male members of the Arch-house of Habsburg-Lorraine, all the direct descendants of the great Queen Maria-Theresa. They gathered in the great audience hall where the Emperor and Prince Montenuovo were awaiting them. Otto and Ferdinand Karl arrived together; Franz Ferdinand stood slightly apart from the rest. Franz Joseph greeted them all and spoke briefly about the difficulties he had had to face because of his nephew's deep wish to marry a woman not of equal birth. Then Prince Montenuovo spoke in his slightly nasal voice. No doubt there was a heavy stillness in the room as he spoke, one of those silences where the buzzing of a fly suddenly seems incredibly persistent and loud.

What Prince Montenuovo was presenting to all the family – the family to which he himself was related by blood, and yet to which he could never belong – was an appendix to the Family Statutes, an appendix that would prevent Franz Ferdinand, if he ever married the Countess Chotek, from changing her status once he was Emperor himself. With this appendix agreed by each and every male member of the Arch-house, not even waiting until he became Emperor would enable Franz Ferdinand to make a woman of unequal birth his Empress and Queen. He himself would have sworn away that future freedom of action. All it needed was all their signatures.

What did that dry, fussy, little man feel as he made his pronouncement? One senses that he did not once look at Franz Ferdinand as he spoke, and in all probability Franz Ferdinand's eyes were turned away throughout. Prince Montenuovo must have believed that he had come up with a solution that would hold for all time and would preserve the continuing rule over the Austro-Hungarian Empire by the Habsburg family forever, unsullied by any improper marriage.

If he could have known that within only two decades the Austro-Hungarian Empire would be broken up and the Habsburg Arch-house expelled from Austrian lands... What feelings would Prince Alfred Montenuovo, great grandson of the first Emperor of Austria, Emperor Franz, have experienced then? Montenuovo would live through it all and end up living out his last years, stripped of his title, in an Austria that was a republic – anathema to everything he had always ever cared about.

But that June afternoon in 1900 Prince Montenuovo had the satisfaction of watching each one of the members of the Habsburg family sign this new appendix, with one exception – Franz Ferdinand.

His mind must have been racing. It would not have taken him long to work out that, just as Franz Joseph as reigning Emperor could bring in this new statute, so he, Franz Ferdinand, when he had become the reigning Emperor could repeal it – if he did not sign. But if he refused to sign he would have to deal with Franz Joseph's bitterness and hostility. And he would be faced with the resentment of every single member of his family as well. But if he signed it he would be betraying any children he might have.

He needed time to think, and to talk with Max Vladimir Beck. Beck's advice was to sign. Two weeks later, on 23rd June 1900, Franz Ferdinand went back alone. The meeting between uncle and nephew was short. Neither man said anything to the other that was not part of the script. The Emperor asked him whether he was ready to stand by his word; Franz Ferdinand assented.

Then, said the Emperor, he would consent to a morganatic marriage. Franz Joseph asked him whether he would swear to a renunciation barring any children he might have from succeeding him to the throne. Franz Ferdinand said he would sign a renunciation and swear to it.

Finally, Franz Joseph told him that he would bestow the title of Princess upon Sophie on her wedding day. Franz Ferdinand thanked him.

So Franz Ferdinand signed the amendment to the Habsburg statutes. Did he pause as he put the pen down? He was one step nearer to marrying Sophie but at the same time he had signed away possible rights and freedoms he might later have had, once Emperor. He may have been aware that a noose of restrictions was tightening around him. What he was not aware of – then – was how much more tightly that noose would be drawn around Sophie in the years to come. As he hurried away with the 'good news' he may well have been a thoughtful man.

Yet another put-down lay ahead before he could actually marry Sophie. On 28th June 1900 he had to return to the Hofburg to sign the renunciation document before the whole assembled family. Once again a throng of bystanders crowded round the entrance to the Hofburg to watch the carriages of Habsburg Archdukes arrive. The police had to hold back the throng. That morning was grey, overcast and damp but as the cortège of carriages started to roll through the great archway the sun broke through the clouds. Once again they all mounted the wide marble stairs to the Audience Hall. On this occasion there was a far bigger crowd, for the grand room was packed with high dignitaries as well as members of the Arch-house. As the clocks struck twelve, Franz Joseph entered and walked to Queen Maria Theresia's throne in the centre of the dais.

The renunciation was read out and Franz Ferdinand stepped forward and knelt before the Emperor. Then he stood. Cardinal Gruscha took the crucifix of Emperor Ferdinand II and held it up. With one hand touching the German text and the other touching the Hungarian text, Franz Ferdinand stared at the cross. He seemed to hesitate and then he repeated after the cardinal the oath.

"A grimly serious, mournful act," said one witness, as if far more had been renounced than titles and inheritance of unborn children. Far more had been renounced. Any future children would find, just like Prince Montenuovo, that they were closely related by blood to people who would not acknowledge them or allow them to know their own relatives.

Franz Ferdinand hurried away. He went first to thank Max Vladimir Beck and to say goodbye to him. Beck described the scene in his memoirs, how they said goodbye in the courtyard. Beck had watched him go into the Hofburg that morning looking very pale and drawn; now he was quite red in the face with emotion and misty-eyed. He promised Beck his friendship for the rest of his life, as they shook hands. And suddenly Beck was so moved, so carried away, that he kissed Franz Ferdinand's hand. Immediately he was struck that this was not a proper thing to have done but Franz Ferdinand let it pass and Beck felt that he had not been misunderstood.

Then Franz Ferdinand had to return to Schönbrunn Palace for an advance celebration of Franz Joseph's seventieth birthday before Franz Joseph left for his summer break in Bad Ischl. The first consequences of Franz Ferdinand's renunciation were already beginning to be felt at that celebration. Maria Theresia was no longer the first lady.

Because Otto was now the second in line to the throne, his wife, Maria Josepha, became henceforth the Archduchess closest to the throne. So it was Maria Josepha who entered on the arm of Franz Joseph. Otto stood grimly watching his hated wife in all her pudgy gracelessness walk forward to resounding cheers.

It may have crossed Otto's mind that when he became Emperor he would have to face so many, many occasions just like this one with his wife on his arm. The two of them no longer lived together, no longer pretended to have any sort of relationship, and they could do that so long as they both appeared at Hofburg functions and pretended for a few short hours still to be a pair. Once Emperor, Otto would have had to spend vastly more time in Maria Josepha's company. He would have had to take her on foreign trips with him and he would have had to allow her to set up her own court and play her role as Empress in whatever way she chose to play it.

Chapter 103

The next day, Franz Joseph left for Bad Ischl and his annual summer break. It is unlikely that he gave much thought to what Franz Ferdinand would do next. He knew that it would not be long before the distressing marriage took place. Franz Joseph himself would not attend, nor would almost all the Habsburg family. Franz Joseph had let it be known that their attendance would not please him and Prince Montenuovo had found a way of keeping almost all Franz Ferdinand's relatives away without appearing to do so. Prince Montenuovo had learned of the death of a Princess Josephine Hohenzollern, who did not belong to the reigning German dynasty, but to a side-line of the family. The court in Vienna had barely been aware of her existence but Prince Montenuovo had declared a period of mourning, which was to serve as an excuse for boycotting Franz Ferdinand's wedding. Franz Ferdinand had desperately wanted his brothers, at least, to be there. Neither was.

Sophie was staying with her uncle in Grosspriesen which made it hard for Franz Ferdinand to see her; all he could do was write or send telegrammes. Being impatient, he sent telegrammes.

Sophie was popular in Grosspriesen and local people were very happy to do things for her. One of these was Bruno Richter, the local postmaster. He later related that one day that spring he met the Countess Sophie in the town and she, with a flash of a smile, told him that she was going to stay for a while in Grosspriesen. Not long after there was a lengthy telegramme, signed Hohenberg, for Sophie. This was followed by several more. Sophie sought out Bruno Richter again and asked him specially to bring up to the castle himself any letters or telegrammes for her. And could he do it in the evening, please?

From then on Bruno Richter made the trip over to the castle and delivered her letters personally. Whenever he rang at the door, it was always Sophie herself who opened it and thanked him warmly. And sometimes when he got back to the post office, he would find an urgent service message announcing another telegramme for the Countess, so he would then turn round and go back up to the castle.

Bruno Richter had a pretty shrewd idea by this time that all these telegrammes were evidence of a romance. Then one day, the Director of the Post rang up himself and told him that the letters and telegrammes which seemed to be flooding in for the Countess were coming from a member of the Imperial Family. The director warned him to observe very carefully any special instructions and to refuse utterly to give any information to newspaper reporters. When Bruno Richter later saw Sophie, he told her about the call and she became very alarmed and worried. Bruno calmed her down, assuring her of his discretion, and insisting that they had spoken on an official line and no one could have listened in.

That same day as Franz Joseph was on his way to Ischl, Sophie again stopped in the streets of Grosspriesen to speak to Bruno Richter. Warm sunlight bathed her face. She glowed; she could hardly stand still; she was all smiles. Now you know who was the sender of all those letters and telegrammes, she told him, as if he did not already know. Buoyant with excitement and happiness, she rushed on to tell him that 'he' was coming that Sunday on the express train which, exceptionally, would stop at Grosspriesen. "If you are interested, go to the station, but don't tell anybody about it!"

Bruno's loyalty and discretion had been flawless up to that moment, but the crowd of civic dignitaries, local townsfolk and scores of holidaymakers that unusually thronged the station to watch the Vienna-Berlin express thunder through suggests that word somehow slipped out. They were not disappointed. To the surprise of most of the passengers on board, the train slowed and stopped. And every head must have been craned through the windows to watch Franz Ferdinand greet and thank with heartfelt warmth Count Karl Chotek and Countess Olga and their assembled family.

Sophie was not there at the station. She had already left. But one last thing she did before she left Grosspriesen was to invite Bruno Richter to the wedding. He straightened up and begged to be excused. Like a good official, he realised that the post office would be hectic over the next few days and he felt he could not be absent at such a busy time. He was right: on the wedding day, Bruno counted up some two thousand telegrammes for the bridal couple and almost a thousand letters of congratulation. But if Bruno could not be there, possibly his mother...? Sophie never hesitated, she beamed and Frau Richter became one of the most excited guests there.

Sophie had gone to stay with her sister in Dresden. This was her favourite sister, Maria Antonia, who was six years younger than Sophie but had been married for seven years to Carl Ludwig von Traugott Wuthenau-Hohenturm. No doubt, the two girls stayed up late that night, talking and chatting and discussing everything, too excited to go to bed. Perhaps, from her superior position as a long-married woman, Antonia was full of what Sophie should do and how she should do it.

All through the years Sophie had known Franz Ferdinand, the need for secrecy and discretion had been so great that Sophie had hardly dared to tell even her own sisters much more than she would have told anyone else of what was going on. And in recent months, everything discussed within the family would have been coloured by a certain apprehension, a sense of 'what if it all goes wrong?' Torn by her feelings for her own family, Sophie would not have wanted to rub in anything that might seem to them dangerous or unfeeling.

But now she could open up her heart, here with her sister. And Antonia must have wanted to know all the things that had needed to be suppressed for so long. Did Sophie talk of that ball at the *Statthalterei* in the autumn of 1894 given by the Imperial Governor of Bohemia, Count Franz Thun und Hohenstein? Did she think back to the thronged ballroom, the bustle and the glitter, the sparkling chandeliers and the lilting music, when she had stood slightly apart watching Franz Ferdinand, her dark eyes intently upon him, wondering about him?

She would have poured out to Antonia how she had thought about him from then on, worried over his health, prayed for him and waited for the letters from Janaczek. Perhaps her voice went soft, and she thought of the picnics in the woods around Pressburg where Isabella had brought the whole of her family, various ladies-in-waiting and a number of old retainers for a lavish – but, oh, so well-organised – meal on the grass not far from the river's banks. These would have been occasions when, unnoticed, Franz Ferdinand had somehow found himself alongside a lady-in-waiting. Did a little, mischievous smile twitch at the corners of her mouth now as she remembered a quick, furtive, sideways glance at him, a look that had spoken volumes about love and caring?

Antonia would have noticed a pensive pause. For a brief moment Sophie was far away. Then, maybe, she just chuckled. She wanted to tell her sister about one evening at the castle. When was that? Oh, it must have been one November evening back in the '90s. It had rained all day, the battering of raindrops against the window panes had never once let up. And Isabella had been at her most officious and energetic. She had been up and down the stairs between sorting out estate management matters and rushing back to her daughter, Maria Christina, who inexplicably that day was in the doldrums, could hardly stir herself, could hardly stop big, heavy tears from rolling down her round cheeks, as far as one could make out, for no reason at all. Perhaps it was just teenage tristesse. Sophie had found Maria Christina even more tearful after each time her mother had pounced in upon her. But Maria Christina had finally been chivvied into pulling herself together and coming down to dinner with the family.

The family could not be allowed to sink into despondency – Isabella took action. There would be music later in the evening. Were the cymbaloms in the small salon? Had Franzi brought his violin? Isabella's energy and drive often provoked suppressed groans but there was no resisting her. She had said there would be music later and there would be music later. Sophie had stayed close to Maria Christina, who was insisting between sniffles that she could not sing. In the end they had all sung, even Franz Ferdinand who usually refused.

And Sophie would have looked up at her sister and told her that she had often etched such events upon her mind because all along she had believed that that was all she would ever have. Just her memories.

The mood would have shifted then as both turned their thoughts to what lay ahead. What would it be like, being the morganatic wife of an Emperor?

Chapter 104

Franz Ferdinand and Sophie's wedding took place at Reichstadt in northern Bohemia. The castle and surrounding lands had been declared the Duchy of Reichstadt by Napoleon Bonaparte and Napoleon's only son, after he had lost his title as King of Rome, had ended his days as the Duke of Reichstadt. Maria Theresia had retired to Reichstadt to live out her life as a widow. Maria Theresia had done so much for Franz Ferdinand, fought his cause so persistently, and now his wedding would take place under her roof.

She was there on the castle steps awaiting him when he arrived that afternoon of 30th June. Sophie arrived soon after Franz Ferdinand and Maria Theresia then welcomed her with all the warmth and affection she had. A reporter standing by noted that Sophie was wearing a cream-coloured dress and a hat with ostrich feathers. There were a group of schoolchildren hanging around in the courtyard and they cheered when they saw her.

That Saturday night there was an intimate dinner in the castle and Maria Theresia gave Sophie her wedding present; this was a jewellery box with heirlooms left by Franz Ferdinand's mother, Maria Annunciata, whom Sophie had never known. It included the tiara that Viennese society considered Sophie should never have had and ought never to be seen wearing. Franz Ferdinand liked her to wear it.

Franz Ferdinand's own family stayed away. Neither of his brothers, nor his beloved sister, Margaretha-Sophie, had relented, although his two half-sisters, Elisabeth and Maria Annunciata, Maria Theresia's own daughters, were there. Right up until the last moment Franz Ferdinand had clung to the hope that his brothers and his sister would give way and be there to see him marry the woman he loved. He was deeply hurt that they were not.

It was a wound that never really healed and years later when Otto was dying Franz Ferdinand would refuse to visit the brother he had once been close to. And when it came out that his younger brother, too, had fallen in love with someone who was not of equal birth, Franz Ferdinand could not forget how Ferdinand Karl had been absent at his wedding. Ferdinand Karl would get no support from his brother when he turned to him to beg for it.

Franz Ferdinand's best man was Count Nosticz-Rieneck, his household chamberlain. The threat of Franz Joseph's displeasure had scared away every Habsburg, and even Sophie's older brother, Wolfgang, who feared for his position, chose not to see his sister get married. But Sophie's sisters and their husbands were there and so were her uncles and aunts, including, of course, Count Karl and Countess Olga from Grosspriesen. It was Maria Theresia's German cousin, Prince von Löwenstein-Wertheim-Rosenberg who led Sophie up the aisle in the castle chapel. A strange, modest group of people, each of whom personally cared for the bride and groom.

The day started out with brilliant sunshine in a cloudless, deep blue sky. When Sophie entered the chapel on the arm of Prince von Löwenstein-Wertheim-Rosenberg, she was very much the bride. She appeared in a dress of white silk with a train several yards long and a white veil that covered the whole of her body. She wore a diamond diadem intertwined with myrtles and orange-blossom, the symbols of innocence and virginity. The diamond diadem was a gift from Franz Joseph. There were embroidered myrtles and orange-blossom all round the hem of her dress and the flowers featured in her wedding bouquet.

Everything had been planned and arranged by Maria Theresia, and she seems to have carried it all out so meticulously, so lovingly, with such thought and care. All the while she must have hoped not just that it would go well but that it would be wonderful and touching. She had chosen the music for the ceremony and it was she who called for three cheers for the bridal couple at the wedding breakfast afterwards.

By the end of the day, when the carriages came to take all the guests away, it had begun to rain, and rain heavily. Sophie would not have cared – to her mind, happy the bride the rain rains upon. That evening they drove openly up to the front door at Konopischt. There she was greeted by the faithful Janaczek who had newly been promoted to the position of head of the household staff. Henceforth she would have a home and this was it. She had come home.

As the light faded Franz Ferdinand and Sophie went out to walk through the rose garden arm-in-arm, no longer constrained to hide their love for each other. It was a warm evening, the air, still soft and moist from the recent rain, was full of the scent of roses. Finally the two could relax.

But, as one Bohemian paper wrote, "Countess Sophie Chotek will never wear a crown upon her head, yet nonetheless she will feel its thorns."

Perhaps Maria Theresia watched from a window as the couple departed. She may have noticed how Franzi leaned tenderly over his bride. Perhaps his eye was caught by a loose tendril of hair at the nape of her neck and he felt tempted to curl it round his fingers, a tiny gesture of affection and delight. Most people would have thought she had caught him; Maria Theresia may have suspected differently.

And whatever Maria Theresia thought would have been confirmed a few days later when she received a rapturous letter from Franzi full of how happy he was. "We are so unbelievably happy and we have you to thank for our happiness."

He went on to confess that he had not shown the letter to Sophie and so he could say just what was in his mind: "Soph is my treasure, I cannot find the words to tell you how happy I am. She is so caring of me, I feel so much better, less wound up, I feel born anew... I know we will be happy together for the rest of our days," he wrote. His letter was also full of his gratitude, an overwhelming gratitude for so much support and understanding and love and kindness from his beloved Mama. Franz Ferdinand clearly knew without any doubt or hesitation that everything that had happened would not have come about without Maria Theresia's helping hand. "You have done such good work and made your two children happy for the rest of their lives!"

Did Maria Theresia wonder whether they really would be happy for the rest of their lives? She may well have smiled a wry smile. Did she suspect that Franz Ferdinand had not yet recognised or understood what was going to come their way? He was, in his own words, swimming in a sea of bliss after fifteen long anxious months. He was floating on air, over the moon, so ebullient, so excited. He was in no state to think about the slights and humiliations, the snubs and the hurts that would become an almost daily occurrence for the rest of his life.

Not long after they were married Franz Ferdinand and Sophie travelled to Lölling in the region of Carinthia where Franz Ferdinand owned a hunting lodge. Sophie's sister, Rischel, and her husband had property there, too, but on this occasion Franz Ferdinand wanted to be alone with his new bride.

The newly-weds enjoyed taking a picnic up into the mountains, usually alone. One time they were sitting back, relaxed on the ground under a clump of shady fir trees when another couple found their way to the same spot. Confident that the newcomers would assume that it could not possibly be the heir to the throne even if they noticed a resemblance, Franz Ferdinand jovially invited them to join him and his wife and he engaged them in a pleasant conversation. He went further and invited them to join their picnic. In the course of their exchanges Franz Ferdinand found that their guests came from Graz to which he cheerily remarked that he had been born in Graz.

Whether the guests ever realised with whom they were talking is not clear, but Franz Ferdinand would have assumed that they did not and, because for a brief moment he had been able to put aside the mantle of royalty, he had been able to open up and enjoy a friendly, uncomplicated conversation with them.

For a brief period of time there were sentimental newspaper articles celebrating the romantic triumph of love. It didn't last long. Within days the story of the moment switched to what was happening in Serbia where King

Aleksandar had just announced his engagement to Draga Mašín.[50] This shocking piece of news gave the scandalmongers and gossips a feeding frenzy. Draga was twelve years older than Aleksandar, had been a lady-in-waiting to his mother, and previously married to Svetozar Mašín. Draga could not even claim to belong to an aristocratic family. The world hated her from the moment Aleksandar claimed her for his wife, and none more so than the people of Serbia.

Behind all that was written about Draga lay a very sad story. She did not want to marry Aleksandar at all. She was taking on a very psychologically damaged young man. Throughout his childhood his parents had fought venomously with each other. Suddenly, when Aleksandar was thirteen years old, his father, King Milan, announced that he was abdicating his throne and he intended to spend the rest of his days living in agreeable places like Paris or Monte Carlo without any responsibilities or obligations.

For three years Aleksandar's formidable mother, Natalija Obrenović, acted as regent until Aleksandar announced that he was ready to take over the reins of government himself.

Aleksandar was a shaky, obsessed boy, frightened of shadows, who jumped out of his skin at the smallest sound. He saw enemies and assassins in every corner. He trusted nobody, and certainly not his own parents. He always insisted that the only person who had ever cared for him or understood him was his mother's lady-in-waiting, Draga Mašín. And it was certainly true that she had been kind to him and had given him what little warmth and affection he had ever received from anybody.

Draga never felt safe again from the moment she married Aleksandar. She was constantly aware that there were conspirators only waiting for the moment to get rid of Aleksandar and to put Petar Karađorđević[51] on the throne. All her fears came true barely three years later in June 1903 when a band of rebellious army officers dynamited the doors of the Royal Palace at midnight and searched its rooms until they found Aleksandar and Draga crouching terrified in their nightclothes in a cupboard. The officers gunned them down in a shower of bullets; then in a wild frenzy the officers mutilated and hacked their bodies into pieces with swords and threw them out of the window.

The leader of the conspirators was Dragutin Dimitrijević. He personally organized and participated in the coup against King Aleksandar and Queen Draga that resulted in their murders, though he was not present when they were killed. Dimitrijević did not retire quietly after he had achieved his aim of removing the Obrenović family from the throne of Serbia but in the shadows he maintained his conspiratorial network, the same conspiratorial network that would one day, eleven years later, be instrumental in

---

[50] Pronounced Mashin.

[51] Pronounced Kara-george-evich.

assassinating Franz Ferdinand and Sophie.

At the time it was announced that Aleksandar intended to marry Draga, the world's press frothed with indignation that a Prince could so lower the dignity of his throne. Franz Ferdinand saw hidden slights in all the pontificating about the obligations of princes to uphold royal dignity. Franz Ferdinand's sensitivity was probably entirely justified and he was all for complaining to Franz Joseph. For the first time Sophie had to exercise all her persuasive skills to calm him down and persuade him to let it go. "We have time," she said. It was to be the first of many, many times. She became good at it.

She came to understand her husband's character as did nobody else. She came to see all the signs of an impending outburst before it even happened and she may well have fended off many an outburst at the pass.

It was not long before Sophie discovered that she was expecting a child. Franz Ferdinand was immediately full of concern for her. Sophie was thirty-three and to the minds of many in those days bringing a first child into the world at such an elderly age was mortally dangerous. Franz Ferdinand hurriedly carried her off to Konopischt where she could be cared for and protected and away from snide gossip or any spiteful remark intended to frighten his Soph.

The great day came at the end of July 1901 and Franz Ferdinand found himself pacing up and down the castle corridors in a state of agonised tension. He couldn't breathe; his heart thumped; and on and on went the waiting. Franz Ferdinand was "half-dead from fright" throughout the unending hours. It was a long and difficult labour. Sophie after it all was confined to her bed for a week. On each of those seven days Franz Ferdinand would rush in to see her, his arms full of roses and flowers. He was flushed with gratitude and joy.

And there in the cradle was a little girl, little Sophie, already known as Pinki, who had tied his heart in a knot. When Franz Ferdinand, aglow with joy and pride, carried his tiny little daughter out of the bedroom for the first time, it was into the arms of faithful Janaczek that she was placed and the man who more than any other had brought her parents together was given a moment or two to look down at his new mistress. Janaczek must have been deeply moved.

"We are so thrilled with our little one, who is delightful and very strong," Franz Ferdinand wrote to Dr. Eisenmenger, apologising at the same time for writing in pencil but that was easier for him as he was sitting on Soph's bed at the time. "My Soph," he confessed, "is everything in the world to me."

Chapter 105

Elisabeth died in September 1898; Montenuovo was incensed that the actress Kathi Schratt continued to play a part in Franz Joseph's life even after the death of the Empress. Two years later the whole scandal of the love affair between Franz Ferdinand and Countess Sophie Chotek exploded on to the scene. In between Stéphanie had won from Franz Joseph permission to marry her Hungarian magnate. To a man like Montenuovo it must have seemed that the chipping away at the dignity of the Habsburg Arch-house was becoming more frequent and that the cracks in the flawless marble were growing deeper. It may even have seemed to him that his cousin, the Emperor, was dealing with it all too flabbily. Such feelings would have spurred him to greater vigilance.

Prince Alfred Montenuovo was one of the most powerful men within court circles. If Montenuovo saw fit then no one was either too high up or too low to feel his interference. Even Crown-Princess Stéphanie felt it. He played a part in the manoeuvres to bring Louise von Coburg back from Croatia and in getting her shut away in an asylum for the insane. He may possibly have stoked the fires of resentment against Gianni – this would certainly have been in character.

He cannot have approved of the Empress's behaviour, particularly her long absences from court. His lip would have curled in scorn at the very idea that the daughter of an actress (Henriette Mendel) could ever be received at court and by and large Marie-Luise was seen little at court; she might be received at Gödöllő or elsewhere but not so easily in Vienna.

Some years later, Archduke Otto died in the arms of another actress, Louise Robinson. Within the hour of Otto's death Montenuovo had ordered the actress out of the villa.

Montenuovo was all the more powerful because he did not exercise his power for his own benefit but to uphold the dignity of the Habsburg house. His enmity was not personal. If Kathi Schratt had never spoken to the Emperor, he might well have admired her as an actress. There was no personal animosity against women like Kathi Schratt, Sophie Chotek or Louise Robinson. No personal spite. But an actress! For Montenuovo no member of the Imperial Family should ever demean themselves by consorting with an actress. He could never accept Elisabeth's so-called friendship with Kathi and even less Franz Joseph's.

One of the ways in which Montenuovo intruded into the relationship between Kathi and Franz Joseph was to re-arrange interviews and audiences suddenly and at the very last minute in such a way that it became impossible for Franz Joseph to escape to see Kathi as he had intended. Since she usually had put herself out to make the arranged meetings possible Kathi came to resent these devious manoeuvres. In Franz Joseph's letters to Kathi sometimes there are apologies for those meetings that should have taken place and did not. His excuses were always that duty had to come before anything else – "in any case I am punished, for the hours I spend with you are the only happy hours I enjoy."

In his machinations against Kathi, Montenuovo's hand was strengthened when Elisabeth died. Up until that point everyone had paid lip service to the whole pretence that Kathi was Elisabeth's close and precious friend. This charade had worked very well while Elisabeth provided the smokescreen. Things were not quite so easy after her death. For some time there was something of a stand-off between Kathi and Franz Joseph after Elisabeth's assassination.

Furthermore, with Elisabeth no longer there, people polarised into those who were for Kathi Schratt and those against. Amongst court officials and servants opinions on Kathi Schratt had always been divided. There were many, possibly a majority, who were only too happy to accept her, knowing that she did much to put the Emperor in a good mood and also recognising that she was deeply important to the Emperor on a personal level. For every occasion when Montenuovo schemed to interfere with Kathi's meetings with Franz Joseph there must have been many more where someone else surreptitiously edged things in their favour.

As so often happens in these situations there were a few surprises; things had not always gone smoothly between Ida von Ferenczy and Kathi Schratt but after Elisabeth's death Ida was full of sympathy for Kathi. Ida, noting Montenuovo's little games, shared Kathi's discomfort and sought to engineer ways around Montenuovo's little games.

But after Elisabeth's death Montenuovo saw no further reason why the Emperor should demean himself by speaking to the actress. It is possible that, having in the past been unable to prevent this, Montenuovo was now all the more determined to put an end to Kathi Schratt having anything to do with the Emperor. Montenuovo now became more open and more determined to eliminate Kathi from court circles.

Kathi felt suddenly exposed. She and Franz Joseph had a row, the biggest row they ever had. Everything about this row suggests that it was one of those rows where the issue being argued over is secondary; the real issue from which sprang all the heat and hurt and exploding bitter feelings was never even mentioned.

The subject of the row was the Order of Elisabeth. When Franz Joseph had been on the throne for fifty years he had decided to introduce this new Order and Elisabeth had promised Kathi that she would receive it. But Franz Joseph felt that if Elisabeth had conferred the Order on Kathi the public would have seen it as a perfectly normal distinction coming from the

Empress. If he conferred the Order on Kathi it would be seen in a very different light.

Kathi did not agree. She said that it was well known that the Empress had drawn up the list of recipients herself. She felt that the order was due to her because it had been promised and she believed that the public would see it as a sign of friendship from beyond the grave.

Kathi was hurt and offended when Franz Joseph refused to confer it upon her and she made herself only too bluntly clear about the matter. But the real issue had far more to do with all those years when she had hung around for Franz Joseph and denied herself freedoms and friendships to please him. She conveniently forgot the other side of the coin – how much her position at the Burgtheater had been boosted thanks to Franz Joseph's protection of her. But in many ways they had not been easy years and now she felt pushed aside.

What made it worse for Kathi was the fact that the Order was being bestowed upon Mary Throckmorton who had once been a governess for Marie-Valérie. Elisabeth had ended up disliking Mary Throckmorton and would not have considered her for the new Order. Kathi's thoughts would have at once jumped to Marie-Valérie, who had liked her former governess and never lost touch with her. Kathi was only too well aware of Marie-Valérie's resentment towards herself. It would not be too surprising if she did not suspect that Franz Joseph's refusal to bestow the Order upon her was all Marie-Valérie's doing.

Suddenly it was all too much. Kathi exploded. She was hurt and humiliated. The long years trying to fit into the demands made upon her by the Emperor, along with his fussiness, his endless fussiness, came to a head. Franz Joseph was shocked at suddenly seeing her so out of control.

Franz Joseph needed Kathi then as he had never needed her before. He was a broken man. Just when he craved her company so desperately Kathi was standing off. He became painfully jealous of her new leading man in the theatre, Josef Kainz.

A new production of *The Spendthrift* was put on at the Burgtheater with Kathi once again playing her favourite role of Rosl. This was the play that Franz Joseph went to see in Ischl in the summer of 1885 when he first began to fall in love with Kathi. Now he could not or did not go to see her again as Rosl. In a state of gloom he read her letters describing it and praising Kainz to the skies. Kainz was the greatest living actor of the German stage and a star of international reputation. But Kathi admired him enormously as a man as well and did not bother to hide the fact. "Yesterday must have been a happy day for you," replied Franz Joseph, "since you were performing with a great artist." He noted how pleased she must be to act with a man she admired so much.

Neither could understand the other's point of view. Franz Joseph was wrapped up in grief for Elisabeth and completely failed to realise how much Kathi felt snubbed by not getting the Order of Elisabeth. Kathi was struggling, her nerves were in a bad way, and as a middle-aged woman she felt insecure and uncertain of her future. She was suffering from the pains and headaches of the menopause and had become extremely susceptible to the smallest slight. Franz Joseph wrote begging her to care for him just a little bit and to try not to be too angry with him. Once again he was abject before her.

Kathi cannot have known quite where she stood in the new arrangement of things. If Franz Joseph had come clean about how he saw their relationship continuing into the future she might have been able to come to terms with whatever difficulties the new situation had brought about. But she couldn't know.

In this weird situation Marie-Valérie came up with an extraordinary solution – her father should marry Elisabeth's younger sister, the now widowed Countess Mathilde Trani, whose husband had committed suicide, and then Kathi Schratt could be re-instated as the close and precious friend of the new Empress. By that time Mathilde, who had once been a bright girl called Spatz, had turned into a tired and wounded woman who presented a singularly unattractive proposition in marriage terms. Franz Joseph's reply was short and brusque.

"Every morning Papa goes for a walk with the Schratt woman, and when I see her I have to greet her with warmth and affection, but I don't feel it, yet I believe she has a true and generous soul. I think back to the many occasions when Mama insisted that if she died then Papa ought to marry the Schratt," wrote Marie-Valérie in her diary just ten days after her mother's death.

Marie-Valérie went on to muse over the situation. She could not envisage the Schratt woman taking Elisabeth's place but she felt torn as to how she should treat the person for whom she had for so long felt nothing but resentment. She watched her father and felt for him. Could she bring herself at this point to hurt him by pushing away the one person who genuinely cared for him and comforted him?

Gisela had no problems with their father's relationship with Kathi Schratt; she wanted it to continue and perhaps even flourish more than had been possible before. Gisela's husband, Leopold, told Marie-Valérie that "it was entirely natural". Marie-Valérie took their views as a rebuff.

Kathi decided to leave Vienna. She asked for a long leave of absence from acting.

Paul Schlenther from Berlin had become the new director of the Burgtheater that year of 1898. Paul Schlenther must have seen himself as the new brush that would not just sweep away what had for so long been hidden in dark corners but would inject new vigour into the performances at the theatre. He had no intention of bending to the demands of an ageing actress. And Paul Schlenther would have been aware that he possessed an independence from court interference in his decisions that his predecessor, Max Burckhard, had not had. There was also a new head of the imperial household. Prince Rudolf of Liechtenstein had handed over jurisdiction of the court theatres to the Second Chamberlain, Prince Montenuovo. So, Paul Schlenther found himself fully backed by Montenuovo as he set about showing who was boss.

Hugo Thimig saw that it was essential for Kathi to win round Schlenther and then go to the Emperor and tell him 'we've got the right man here!' Thimig was right but Kathi failed to see it. Instead she told Babette Reinhold, the wife of Max Devrients, "He [Schlenther] is a Prussian journalist and he has a nasty wife!"

In particular Schlenther intended to put a stop to Kathi's taking far more and far longer leaves of absence from the theatre than any of the other Burgtheater actors enjoyed. Kathi threatened to resign, wrote out her letter of resignation with a flourish. She was bluffing. It was a huge dramatic gesture that she never believed for one moment anyone could have thought she meant. But Prince Montenuovo presented Kathi's resignation to the Emperor and he signed it. It is possible that he did not even realise what it was that he was signing.

Kathi was utterly shocked and very upset over the way things had turned out. Did Franz Joseph not know that she was bluffing? From that moment on her career as an actress was over. She was not feeling well and she probably brooded over things. Soon she was caught up in a complete nervous breakdown and her doctors had ordered total rest. Suddenly into her mind came some of the things she had been denied because of her relationship with the Emperor; the other close personal relationships she might have enjoyed. Did she think about Hans Wilczek and his impassioned letter at the time when she first met the Emperor?

Then Franz Joseph wrote to her:

> "My dear kind friend,
>
> I have just got your letter which has depressed me all the more because I feel that it is my fault your nerves are in the state they are. Yet I want only to be good to you and am so terribly fond of you, more than words can say. I hope you will soon feel calmer so that I can see you again quickly, for the hours I spend with you are my only distraction, my only comfort in my sad and careworn mood. In the hope that you still care for me a little and not too angry with me,
>
> I am always your most devoted,
>
> Franz Joseph"

In spite of the efforts to persuade Kathi not to go, the efforts not just of Franz Joseph but also of others, Kathi went anyway. She was back in Ischl in the summer of 1900 for the celebrations of Franz Joseph's seventieth birthday but her plan was to leave soon after.

Towards the end of Franz Joseph's time in Ischl Marie-Valérie asked her father if he would like to go out that afternoon with her children. "No," he told her dully. He had to go over to Frau Schratt's villa to say goodbye to her. She was leaving him, perhaps forever; he did not know whether he would ever see her again.

Marie-Valérie was so bewildered. She had always wanted her father to split with the Schratt woman. She had schemed and worked for this. But he stood there, looking bowed, his face drawn with pain, his tired eyes dry with tears he could not shed. Marie-Valérie had never thought of what the relationship with Kathi gave her father, only that it was not proper and seemly. All along she had felt entitled to her disapproval. But now it seemed to her that almost overnight her father had aged by a decade.

What happened at that meeting is not known. But Franz Joseph wrote to her the following day, "Thank you for looking back at me so long yesterday after our parting, which was one of the most painful moments of my life." He called her „mein heiß geliebte Engel" ("my dearly beloved angel").

He may have spent a sleepless night. He wrote those words at six the following morning – he could hear the clock tower striking the hour. He went on to mention that he met a chimney sweep on his way back home the previous day. He knew that Kathi regarded such things as a sign of good luck. Perhaps it would bring him luck "and luck, for me, means seeing you again."

But it did not stop Kathi departing on her travels around Europe. By October a number of people were pressing Kathi to return to Vienna. These included her son, Toni Kiss, and Prince Ferdinand of Bulgaria and Prince Rudolf von Liechtenstein. Rudolf von Liechtenstein even twisted Paul Schlenther's arm and got him to write Kathi a glowing letter full of praise for her acting abilities. Kathi flounced off to appear as a guest artist in Stuttgart and then Munich. She was not going to crawl back to Paul Schlenther!

One of the most pressing of all was Gisela who was deeply worried about her father's health and state of mind. When Kathi came to Munich Gisela gave her the warmest welcome and she wrote to her father that she hoped Kathi's decision was not irrevocable.

But the following March Kathi sent no violets. One of Franz Joseph's great grandchildren had just died and Kathi did not even send him a word of condolence. Franz Joseph was hurt.

However, in June 1901 she finally returned to the villa in the Gloriettegasse. Kathi remained loyal to him for the rest of her life. Franz Joseph was now an old man. He enjoyed relatively good health right up until his seventieth birthday but into his letters to Kathi began to creep in mention of various aches and pains. "Age, particularly in recent times, is making itself felt and I feel so tired..." He was increasingly conscious of the difference in their ages – "You have a happy future before you. You can look forward with optimism but I feel shut out. In my loneliness I feel so downcast."

Increasingly, Kathi needed to jolly him along.

Ten years later, on 20th May 1909, Kathi found herself a widow. For many years she had seen little enough of her husband. Franz Joseph's reaction was a sensitive compassion for her shock and sense of loss, however much their lives had gone separate ways. Franz Joseph felt sure that she would wish to call off their arrangement to have breakfast together the following morning but he begged her to let him know what her orders were so that he could know when he might see her again.

There are those who believe that Franz Joseph and Kathi Schratt entered into a *'Gewissensehe'*[52] (a marriage of conscience) the following year or later. Some of Franz Joseph's descendants have expressed their belief that this secret marriage did, in fact, take place. Also, Peter Schratt, a great-nephew of Kathi Schratt, himself an actor at the Burgtheater, believed that his great-aunt could very well have been married to the Emperor.

The basis for their beliefs was a conviction that Franz Joseph with his keen sense of the 'right thing' would have wanted to do the right thing by the woman he had loved for more than thirty years. But there is more to substantiate their claims than just conviction.

The marriage is supposed to have taken place in the Andreaskapelle, a private chapel tucked away in the Archbishop of Vienna's palace, opposite the Stephansdom. Here a secret marriage could take place and all records of it kept from prying eyes. The only record that it had taken place would be a special book kept always locked away and protected by the Catholic Church. Unfortunately, this book in the aftermath of the Second World War has been lost. Nevertheless, there is reason to think that it may have contained the proof of that *'Gewissensehe'*.

On 30th June 1934 another marriage took place in the Andreaskapelle. Again the marriage had to be kept very secret, especially from the families

---

52 Note 15 in the Notes Section.

of the bride and groom. The groom, Otto Wagner, had not yet finished his training to be a doctor – which in those days would have debarred him from marrying. His very conservative family would never have given him their blessing. The family of his bride, Edeltraut Dobrucka – an old and aristocratic Polish family – would have been equally opposed to the marriage. So they had recourse to a secret marriage in the Andreaskapelle. Besides the priest and the bride and groom, the two witnesses were the only others there.

For a brief moment before conducting the marriage ceremony the priest was called away and the groom and two witnesses were left in the chapel with the book of secret marriages lying open on the table. They could not resist glancing at the entries in the book and there they read, "*Franz Joseph von Habsburg-Lothringen und Katharina Kiss de Ittebe, geb. Schratt*". This was a secret they kept down the years but before he died August Maria Knoll, one of the witnesses, told his sons, Reinhold, Norbert and Wolfgang, what he had seen that day. These three never had any doubts that the secret marriage between the Emperor and Katharina Schratt did take place.

Otto Wagner and Edeltraut Dobrucka celebrated a rather more conventional marriage in 1936 when Otto had completed his studies. They had a son and two daughters who also knew of the entry in the secret book and who were also convinced of the truth of the matter.

Did Montenuovo ever know?

Kathi's last visit to Franz Joseph was on 19th November 1916. This was Elisabeth's name day and as on so many previous occasions they shared reminiscences about Elisabeth. By then Kathi could not help but be aware that Franz Joseph's days were drawing to a close. She must have left him, as so often before, full of a certain dread and yet clinging to the possibility that they would still see each other again a few more times. Hope and dread, anguish and uncertainty. Something else Kathi clung to in those last days: a daily visit from Dr. Kerzl to tell her how Franz Joseph was doing. The day after Elisabeth's name day Kathi felt urgently that she had to see Franz Joseph but Montenuovo successfully managed to prevent it.

On the morning of 21st November Franz Joseph received his great-nephew, Karl, and his wife, Zita. Zita begged an adjutant to go in and ask the Emperor not to get up when she entered. For Franz Joseph not to stand when a lady entered the room was unthinkable and he struggled to rise as Zita came in. Franz Joseph had a high temperature and he was almost too weak to hold a pen but he was still at his desk, still working.

Franz Joseph died during the evening of 21st November 1916. It was Prince Montenuovo who rang Kathi to tell her that he had died. A little later

Franz Joseph's old valet was at her door with the message that His Imperial Majesty had bidden her to come to the palace. His Majesty? – but His Majesty was dead! And then she realised that His Majesty was the Emperor Karl. Kathi went out to the greenhouse to pick the last roses in bloom.

When Kathi arrived she was at first barred from entering the room where the man who may have been her husband lay dead. She was not a young woman and by now rather stout; she stood there looking shocked and shaken and in pain at the closed door before her. At that moment Emperor Karl appeared and offered her his arm to lead her through the door. Inside were only close family members.

Karl's young wife, Empress Zita, came over to Kathi. At this point something strange happened. Count Artur Polzer-Hoditz, who was now the head of Emperor Karl's household, recorded later how the new Emperor introduced his wife to Kathi and not the other way around. This suggests that Karl knew that the old woman at his side was his great-uncle's widow and courtesy demanded that Zita be introduced to her rather than she to the new Empress.

The rules of etiquette would always demand that the lower person be introduced to the Empress. Since Kathi was never crowned she was never in any way an 'Empress'. Those so strict conventions of yesteryear are today so irrelevant that it is hard for someone today to realise just how shocking it would have been for those standing around to see the new Emperor offer his arm to an actress or to introduce the Empress to her. But it makes sense if Karl saw in Kathi the widow of Franz Joseph.

Zita, when she recalled that evening, made no mention of this. She remembered how Prince Lobkowitz went over to Emperor Karl and, tears in his eyes, made the sign of the cross on Karl's forehead with the words, "May God bless Your Majesty". For the first time Karl was addressed as the Emperor he now was. But Zita had a very strong sense of her position in the world. It was all the stronger because as a descendant of the now exiled French royal family she had all her life seen herself as owed the courtesies due to members of a ruling family while faced with the fact that hers was not a ruling family and was often treated with a certain ambivalence. She may well not have expected to find herself being introduced to an actress nor greatly liked seeing her husband give his arm to Kathi. This amounted to according Kathi courtesies that put the actress above Zita. It seems likely that Zita was more than a touch ruffled at that moment.

And then Kathi was faced with another surprise. Marie-Valérie came forward, tears running down her face, and she put her arms around the woman she had so resented. She thanked Kathi for all the friendship and warmth she had given her father.

They all stood back then as Kathi walked up to Franz Joseph and placed two white roses into his hands. Those roses were buried with him; they were the only flowers placed in the coffin. She would have given him red roses if she could have but there weren't any. Red roses are a declaration of love...

But from that moment onwards Kathi was shut out. She asked about attending the funeral which was to take place on 30th November. Prince Montenuovo's reply was a cold, "No place has been arranged for *die gnädige Frau*." That upset Kathi a great deal. While the funeral was taking place she remained at home with her niece, Katharina Hryntschak, and there they quietly prayed for the soul of the man Kathi had loved so many long years.

For the remaining twenty-four years of her life Kathi remained in Vienna. In the hard times that followed the war she was as generous and as hospitable as she had always been. She was as adventurous and as curious to savour new experiences as she had always been. In 1929, when she was seventy-six, she flew by aeroplane from Zurich to Vienna. Did she think back to 1890 when she had gone up in a balloon with Alexander Baltazzi and provoked the wrath of the Emperor?

She died in April 1940 in a world that was once again at war.

Chapter 106

Prince Montenuovo had turned against Stéphanie from the day she married outside royal circles. From one moment to the next he ceased to accord her any respect. It was the same with Kathi Schratt; he had shown her cautious deference only as long as the Empress was alive but he had never been able to accept Kathi Schratt, just as he could never accept Countess Sophie Chotek.

Knowing that there were so many people, like Kathi, who were not on Franz Ferdinand's side, Montenuovo must have felt empowered to fight what was effectively an open battle with Franz Ferdinand, a battle well beyond the dictates of his position. Montenuovo was a man who could not trim his sails to the way the wind was blowing. After Franz Ferdinand had married Countess Sophie Chotek he would go to great lengths to draw attention to her inferiority – yet he must have known all along that the moment Franz Ferdinand became Emperor the bullets would be flying in his direction. Montenuovo knew that when the old Emperor died his own position would be seriously and adversely affected, but this would not have been enough to make Montenuovo change his behaviour in any way.

On 12th July 1914 *The New York Times* published an article by 'A Veteran Diplomat' vigorously defending his old friend Prince Alfred Montenuovo. Who 'A Veteran Diplomat' was is not known but if the tone of his article is anything to judge by, AVD was full of uncritical admiration for Prince Alfred Montenuovo. His article was a fulsome defence of Montenuovo, fending off criticisms by shifting blame elsewhere. Prince Montenuovo's battle to preserve the ancient ways sometimes seems today as ridiculously anachronistic even then, but in those times he would have been hugely admired for taking the stance he did. There would have been many defendents for Montenuovo's attitude. AVD was one of them.

When that article appeared – just twelve days after the assassination of Archduke Franz Ferdinand and Sophie – it would seem that AVD wanted to squash dispatches from Vienna suggesting that Montenuovo was to be forced out of office for "his failure to provide full Imperial honours for the remains of the ill-fated Duchess of Hohenberg". AVD went on to attack those insinuations in the press which were asserting "that any curtailment of the funeral ceremonies on Friday a week ago was due to the Prince's alleged spite and prejudice against the murdered Archduke and his morganatic consort".

To AVD Montenuovo was a most romantic figure. AVD and Montenuovo first got to know each other in 1877 and AVD clearly found the Prince handsome as well as romantic. AVD regarded Montenuovo's whole background as fascinating – from his great-grandfather, the Emperor Franz II down to the man who became, as AVD put it, the Cerberus[53] of the Hofburg. AVD insisted that the Imperial Family were all of them very close to Montenuovo and felt nothing but appreciation and gratitude for Montenuovo's vigilant support.

In 1864, when the title 'Prince' was conferred upon his father, Wilhelm Albrecht, Alfred Montenuovo was ten years old, old enough to have picked up what was, in all probability, a thread of bitterness running through the family. By blood and breeding Alfred was closely connected to the ruling Imperial Family in Vienna, but because the marriage of the Princess Marie-Louise and her lover, Count von Neipperg, had been a morganatic marriage he and his family enjoyed no standing whatsoever and the only status they could lay any claim to was what the Habsburgs chose to confer upon them. Was Alfred Montenuovo very conscious that, if his grandmother's marriage had not been morganatic, he would have had a place at court as the Emperor Franz Josef's cousin? He did have a place at court, but only as *Obersthofmeister* (Court Chancellor – literally: highest master of the court), in effect, a bureaucratic position.

He had to live with the inherited stain of that morganatic marriage. He turned it into a twisted badge of honour and made it his life's work to ensure that nothing might ever impinge upon the dignity due to the ruling Imperial Family. Protocol was everything to him. It was the form that mattered, whatever it hid behind the mask. In the process he made bitter enemies and stirred up huge troubles.

Princess Marie-Louise lightly and unthinkingly had sown the seeds that would grow into a plant of strangulating bitterness. But she did not know she was doing it.

However, AVD was at some pains to prevent anyone thinking that Montenuovo himself sprang from a morganatic marriage. He was convinced that Princess Marie-Louise's marriage to Count von Neipperg was not a morganatic marriage.

AVD pointed out in his article that Montenuovo owned one of the finest racing studs within the Austro-Hungarian Empire and that he was President of the Austrian Jockey Club. (This would have brought him into contact with

53   Note 16 in the Notes Section.

the Baltazzi brothers which surely must have been intolerable to Montenuovo.) Montenuovo only resigned his position as president when there was a scandal of reckless and massive gambling in the Jockey Club and the press was demanding to know why the laws against gambling were not being upheld at the Jockey Club. (Nobody dared suggest that Montenuovo himself was involved in gambling.)

However, after his resignation he continued to breed and race horses and (according to AVD) the only stud in the land to better Montenuovo's horses was that of Karel Kinsky, which gave piquancy to the situation, for Montenuovo's wife was a Kinsky and so was Sophie Chotek's mother. AVD wanted to stress that Karel Kinsky's support was for Montenuovo rather than for the Duchess of Hohenberg.

No, not even a woman who was a relative of Montenuovo's own wife[54] and who was the wife of the future Emperor could win favours to which she was not entitled – not while Montenuovo was the Cerberus of the Hofburg. Montenuovo believed that Sophie was bent on securing prerogatives at court to which she was not entitled. It was Montenuovo's bounden duty to limit what he perceived as her constant encroachments. He was so convinced that position at court was what she was scheming for that he saw in her every move and every gesture confirmation of his beliefs about her.

There was a battle that raged in Montenuovo between power and helplessness. He needed to win against Sophie and to win meant a kind of final bringing down the curtain where events had been tied up and brought to a close. In contrast, the situation he found himself in, a situation of constant vigilance against perceived manoeuvres to get Sophie accepted, was on-going and he could never relax. Montenuovo wanted to press home the point that Sophie did not belong. AVD almost purred with approval.

Much of the aristocracy in Vienna did not expect the marriage between Franz Ferdinand and Sophie to last. They waited and watched for signs that the rebellious pair had bitten off more than they could chew. And in a way Montenuovo felt impelled to speed up the whole process by intensifying the restrictions he imposed upon Sophie.

He had entered into combat with her. It is possible that Sophie did not realise that she was engaged in a battle with no holds barred. When a concession in the rigid rules that dictated what Sophie could or could not do was made it was done in such a way that her unequal position was emphasised and attention was drawn to it. Montenuovo saw to that.

Yet, before Sophie married Franz Ferdinand, she – as a Chotek – had been entitled to appear at court. After her marriage she lost that privilege along with so many others. After marriage she carried the title 'Princess Hohenberg' and later she was elevated to 'Duchess of Hohenberg' – both

---

[54] Note 14 in the Notes Section.

titles significantly higher than that of 'Countess Chotek', yet she was stripped of honours that had been due to her as 'Countess Chotek'. Montenuovo saw to it that privileges she had been entitled to before marriage were taken from her afterwards.

The lines had been drawn. Franz Ferdinand and Sophie remained well back from their line; Montenuovo pushed his ever further out. They withdrew; Montenuovo began to feel that he was winning. Franz Ferdinand once confessed to his priest that he avoided social gatherings in Vienna, especially as the Viennese aristocracy had never forgiven him his marriage. In a way, it was as though the exile he had feared had come about anyway.

To AVD all this could be taken as evidence of Montenuovo's integrity of character. Montenuovo was unbending. Montenuovo would not even have paused to consider what it might one day cost him personally. It would never have occurred to Montenuovo or to AVD that he was over-officious.

It is likely that officiousness sprang from an unspoken fear. The fear of revolution lingered. Only a society so closely bound together in its structures that no chink might be perceived could feel confident of its ability to fend off revolutionary pressures. Rudolf's death had shaken Austrian society more than anyone cared to admit.

But Franz Ferdinand wanted his beloved wife at his side if at all possible and even when that could not be, he wanted people to acknowledge her and treat her with respect as a human being. Whenever Sophie was treated with courtesy and consideration, Franz Ferdinand would relax. What he could not take was seeing her crushed while he was helpless to prevent it. He could not stand seeing her being pushed around and sneered at. Everything he could do for her to prevent such treatment he did do.

Anyone who brought tears to Sophie's eyes was making a lifelong enemy of Franz Ferdinand. His helplessness to ease things for Sophie made him all the more angry. Part of Franz Ferdinand's difficulties lay in the fact that Montenuovo had such power to humiliate Sophie. This wound Franz Ferdinand up far more than it could ever wind Sophie up. Yet Montenuovo remained convinced that the animosity of the Duchess of Hohenberg towards him knew no bounds, and furthermore that she had succeeded in embittering her husband against him.

But there were so many, many snubs intended to rile her and put her in her place. If she was allowed to be present at all at any court event no one would have considered her comfort. At every function where Sophie appeared at all – there were few enough of them – Sophie had to take her place behind the last and youngest Archduchess. She would enter any court function the very last of all, and her escort would be a court chamberlain. As she approached the two doors through which the whole court procession had passed one would be shut in her face, forcing her to move awkwardly around it.

When she did reach her place it might be that she had been squeezed into some chilly corner or no seat would have been provided for her, leaving her standing when no one else in the room except the servants were standing. Whoever failed to provide a sufficient number of chairs must have known that he had Montenuovo's tacit backing.

Sophie ended up on many an occasion almost in tears. She had no idea how to handle the situation. Yet as time went by she learned to handle it all with quiet gracefulness and a gentle demeanour. She held herself very erect, the perfect embodiment of regal dignity. Her air and her manner made many of the ladies there appear common.

On her wedding day Maria Theresia had given Sophie Maria Annunciata's jewels and she was often seen wearing a diamond tiara from the collection. Was it Sophie who picked out that tiara or had Franz Ferdinand pressed her to wear it for his sake? Franz Ferdinand in his longing to have his wife at his side may well have pushed her to face head-on all those put-downs and to rebuff them in a way that Sophie was reluctant to do. What it all cost her they would never know. On every side of her were harsh eyes watching and waiting for the moment she tripped up. They watched in vain. None knew better than Sophie what she might or might not do, and she came to use submission to the restrictions imposed upon her with such quiet dignity that it was her detractors who were caught out.

On one occasion Sophie found that not only was one of the double doors shut in her face but no escort had been designated for her. Sophie hesitated, unsure as to what she should do, and then she turned and left the palace, pleading a headache. When the same thing happened a second time, Sophie quietly walked into the room alone and unescorted. One of the younger Archdukes was appalled at this and hurried over to her side to offer her his arm. This shocked many of the others there who saw it as evidence that Sophie was beginning to find a way around the restrictions imposed upon her. There was a groundswell of anger at the fact that Sophie had taken the arm of an Archduke, violating imperial etiquette. Montenuovo was swamped by complaints. He can't have been entirely clear whether the complaints were against him or against Sophie.

Far more often she was not allowed to be present at all. There were occasions when Franz Ferdinand would receive foreign dignitories at the Belvedere Palace, his official residence in Vienna, and Sophie would be required to shut herself away like a servant so that all could pretend that she was not there and did not exist.

Her detractors ended up twisting her every move or action. One would whisper to another about her "small-minded fury" and compare her to a drill sergeant. And the thread that ran through all of it was that her only thought was how to gain the upper hand and win an Empress's crown. The stories went on circulating, painting a picture of Sophie's intense ambition, her relentless determination and her harsh single-mindedness to attain ultimately the position of Empress and open the way for her eldest son one day to become Emperor in his turn.

Yet the one who raged against all this was Franz Ferdinand. Sometimes he threatened to go to the Emperor. But Sophie would pause, turn and look at him, putting her hand on his arm, and murmur, "The Emperor is old and feeble." Franz Ferdinand's bluster evaporated.

Franz Ferdinand and his family simply dropped out of all social events at which they might have been expected to appear. They stayed away from Vienna and retired to Franz Ferdinand's country home at Konopischt. They loved Konopischt and they loved the easy-going, informal style of living that they enjoyed there. A largely reclusive existence was a relief. They preferred it and came to enjoy it.

Montenuovo would have seen that as entirely appropriate. They were not wanted in Vienna.

But there were subtle consequences that few recognised. One was that few came to know Franz Ferdinand well. He had been noticeably retiring before, but he became more so afterwards. The Franz Ferdinand who emerged on to the official scene once he had been acknowledged as the heir to the throne was, to so many, very much an unknown quantity. Except for the few who really knew him he tended to come across as remote and distant, an aloof bear of a man who sent shivers of dread through so many who did not know him.

People found him a puzzle. They interpreted his quietness as suspiciousness. They became wary of his sudden, unexpected changes of mood. A picture of an irascible monster grew and spread wider and wider. There was nothing to contradict or counter such a picture. Franz Ferdinand, when he did appear anywhere without his wife, was stiff and cold – which merely confirmed the story that gossip had created. When he was at all rattled or wound up, Franz Ferdinand could be prickly and abrupt.

However, the extent to which Franz Ferdinand could be short-tempered and irascible tended to be exaggerated. He was still, behind the mask, a rather shy man. If he had been a lot more hail-fellow-well-met, he could easily have been fairly short-tempered and often loud and yet few would have taken very much notice of it. But Franz Ferdinand was more reserved so that when his anger did arise it tended to take those around by surprise. And they feared his anger because they could not predict it. They became wary. And out of this Franz Ferdinand came to be seen as always angry.

Sophie could calm him. She had a delicate palate of moves that could change Franz Ferdinand in a flash from a tense and wary being into someone jovial and generous. She might catch his eye and imperceptibly half raise an eyebrow. The corner of her lip might twist delicately. She might glance sideways with a tilt of her head and a questioning look and Franzi would read the question and his expression would become briefly rueful. A quick smile. Then she only needed to murmur "Franzi, Franzi" in a low voice and Franzi's frown would disappear. Just one of these tiny messages and Franzi's response was instantaneous. But she was so seldom there and so very few saw this other softer side of 'the monster'.

Franz Ferdinand became so good at dividing himself up. He could be the heir to the throne, the future political leader, the regal authority in one place and then cast it all off like a cloak to become the easy-going family man in his own home.

Everything suggests that Franz Ferdinand had no wish to see either of his sons seek positions within the Imperial Family. This meant that none of his children could ever expect to receive an apanage[55] from the Habsburg Family Fund. Instead, Franz Ferdinand did all he could to ensure that they would have independent means to live well when he himself was no longer there to provide for them.

He envisaged Max living out his life at Konopischt and Ernst owning Chlumetz; Sophie, he hoped, would make a happy marriage. He wanted his sons to become landowners, able to enjoy life without material cares but nothing more – "The Habsburg crown is a crown of thorns," Franz Ferdinand insisted. In fact, he gave every impression of envying his children the future he envisaged for them, a quiet, useful future as country squires able, according to Ottokar Czernin, to enjoy an anonymous life away from the centres of political life.

But however much Franz Ferdinand insisted that nobody should desire the throne who had not been born to it, much of the Austrian aristocracy continued to believe that Sophie was working on him so that her ambitions might be realised.

An article in the French newspaper *Le Figaro* in May 1909 acknowledged that her situation was exceptionally difficult and that she nevertheless succeeded in ignoring humiliation after humiliation through miracles of quiet tact. She faced the world with great sweetness. There was nothing sharp about her. All who met her were seduced by her warmth and intelligence.

That may have been the impression picked up by a French journalist, but in Vienna resistance to Sophie barely wavered. And that resistance flowered because increasingly Sophie stayed away from the limelight and public attention. When she exercised those delicate manoeuvres that

---

[55] An 'apanage' was a personal allowance paid to a member of the Imperial Family.

defused Franz Ferdinand's explosions of emotion, she was seen as having far too much influence over him. When she emerged to meet other heads of state her calm manner seemed to confirm that she had ambitions to being in that position all the time. She seemed just too assured.

Who was to blame? The Austrian aristocracy who seemed so blind and deaf to any other interpretation than the one they enjoyed believing in? Franz Ferdinand for his emotional explosions? Or Sophie, whose presense, whose voice and gestures had an effect so potent?

The more they stayed away from Vienna the more other weird, exaggerated stories began to circulate. One of the most persistent was that while society in Vienna was being fobbed off with reports that the Archduke was at Konopischt, in reality he had been taken to an asylum for the mad and secretly locked away. Behind locked doors he mumbled inanely all day while playing with toy trainsets. He clutched his revolver and shot at everything and anything, and he liked to shoot at the face of a clock. His servants were terrified and would not go near him and his care came from maniacal psychiatrists with little pointed, goatee beards and tiny, iron-rimmed spectacles perched on their noses.

Such stories got back to Franz Ferdinand. He shrugged his shoulders and commented drily, "Those who know me would never believe any of this, and the rest will certainly one day get to know me." He made no attempt to seek out popularity.

There were two Franz Ferdinands but only one of them is ever remembered.

Chapter 107

Franz Ferdinand made no secret of how happy his family made him. "When I come back to my family from my daily business and see my wife sitting with her needlework and my children playing around, then I leave my cares at the door and I can hardly believe how much happiness is around me." His children – little Sophie (Pinki), Max (Maxi) and Ernst (Bululu) – were his entire delight and pride. For all of this he would look at his "Soph" with a look that seemed to say he could not wholly believe she was real or that she had given him so much.

This was the kind of family life that Franz Ferdinand had always wanted and for the rest of his days he never quite got over his luck at finding it.

This was an age when most aristocratic children were shut away with nursemaids and tutors, mini households almost entirely separated from their parents' lives. But Franz Ferdinand and Sophie played an unusually large part in the lives of their three small children. As far as possible the children were included in their parents' activities and interests and they built close personal relationships with both their parents of a kind that might have made Rudolf or Stéphanie sick with envy.

At Konopischt they shared all their meals with the children. They spent their evenings with the children. They took an interest in the children's lives and knew everything they could about their children and their thoughts, interests and activities. When it came to his children's upbringing, perhaps Franz Ferdinand thought back to his own grim schooling. He certainly did not want his children let off learning the skills, knowledge and culture necessary for their future lives but he did not want them to spend the long hours in the schoolroom that he had had to endure.

Franz Ferdinand loosened up far more than most Archdukes ever did with their families. He enjoyed an intimacy and a camaraderie with his children that few would ever have suspected him capable of. He played with them. With no intrusive eyes upon them, Franz Ferdinand could get down on the floor with his sons. He would be goofy and the boys would howl with laughter.

At home at Konopischt, each morning the first thing that Franz Ferdinand would do was head for the children's rooms to be there when they woke. He liked to have breakfast with them in the nursery and he would linger there until their tutors came to lead the children away to their lessons. He would watch the three small figures, dressed in matching sailor-suits, depart reluctantly. Sometimes his private secretary, Paul Nikitsch-Boulles, would bring the morning's post up to him there.

Their mornings were spent with their tutors, but their afternoons, or at least part of them, were out-of-doors. Often they would accompany their parents walking through the forest or out driving in a carriage.

They learned to love the countryside. Franz Ferdinand would glow with pride when his children could name each of the trees, shrubs and flowers in the park around Konopischt. Visitors were often surprised at how practical and involved the children were in the upkeep of the estate. Filtered through their father's enthusiasm, the business of managing a country estate was presented to them as a game but what they were learning was serious.

They enjoyed playing tennis, too – but, of course, tennis was special for their parents since it must sometimes have seemed to Sophie and Franz Ferdinand that some of the best moments of their own courtship had taken place on the tennis court. When the ponds froze over in winter they spun round on the ice and when the land lay beneath a deep covering of snow they would get out their sleds and race down crisp, white slopes. In summer they swam. All three enjoyed riding and became skilled with horses.

They would return to the castle rosy-cheeked from their exertions feeling pleasantly tired. There they would join their mother for tea. And the evening would spread out as Franz Ferdinand and Sophie would watch their children playing together. Franz Ferdinand would smoke or read out loud to the family and Sophie focussed upon her needlework. "Evenings at home, when I smoke my cigar and read the newspapers, Soph knits and the children tumble about the room and throw things on to the floor and it is all wonderfully cosy," and a remote look would come into Franz Ferdinand's eyes. Little Sophie was soon showing that she had inherited her mother's love of music and often she would go to the piano and perform for them all.

An ordered, largely contented world. Years later Pinki would look back with a lump in her throat, full of nostalgic longing. "We were brought up knowing that we were not special." "Konopischt was home." "We were always taken along with our father whenever possible." "He was stern but never harsh or unfair." Pinki always remembered that her father's wish was for her to marry a Bohemian Count. And their mother was the heart of the family, its peace-making core. They became known as the best behaved and the best brought-up children in the whole Habsburg family. They were required to treat those who served them with respect and to make their lives as easy as it could be.

From the moment she became a mother Sophie was so much more involved in her children's care than almost any other aristocratic mother. She nursed and bathed her children herself. Every night she put the children to bed. They would say their prayers with her and then she would turn out the light. Her children were her life. It was presumed that this was all that she could have wanted. And so it was – but might she have added a "Yes – but..."? Sophie was very isolated and spent a lot of time alone. If Sophie could have opened up in utter frankness to a very close and very, very trusted confidant, what might she have revealed?

But Sophie was very reticent and whatever she thought she kept to herself. And Sophie was a product of her world and to her mind the life she now found herself leading encompassed all that a woman could wish for. She would have allowed herself a wish that some of the humiliations could have been avoided but that is as far as she would have gone. She regretted that they had not been able to have more children but after Ernst she suffered a still-birth and her doctors firmly advised the couple never to try for more children after that.

Sophie was a good deal more isolated than Franz Ferdinand. Her contact with her own family, her sisters, had become so rare. This would have distressed Sophie but it sprang from the fact that Franz Ferdinand never had a particularly good relationship with Wolfgang Chotek or with his sisters-in-law and their families. The only exception was Sophie's youngest sister, Henriette, but the rest he held very much at arm's length and they found him somewhat cold and imposing. An icy patina of formality prevented their finding any common ground with Franz Ferdinand. He would not have given this any consideration but it was Sophie who paid the price.

Franz Ferdinand also felt cut off from his own family. He missed his two brothers who would never speak willingly to him again, and he was aware that from the day he got married he would have to find with Sophie all the emotional warmth and support that he needed so badly.

The children as a result saw very little of their relatives and tended to behave rather formally with them when they did. There were no big family gatherings, something that Sophie would once have considered an essential part of family life. Now she had to accept that the kind of family life she was leading with her Franzi was little like what she had once assumed she might find if she ever married.

On such occasions as she did spend time with one or other of her sisters, Sophie might well have tried to persuade them that Franz Ferdinand could be a jolly, warm-hearted man. Then perhaps she would catch the look of disbelief on their faces and sense a momentary clamming up. So she would smile and drop the subject.

Yet there were some occasions when the house was full of guests and company. These were people that Franz Ferdinand was pleased to welcome to his home and Sophie would go to great lengths to make them welcome and ensure that they enjoyed themselves. Sophie also did her best to get to know their guests and try to like them.

Guests at Konopischt often found the grim, intimidating Archduke relaxed, telling jokes against himself and laughing outrageously in a way that none could resist. He could even see the humour in the situation when a German Prince who had not recognised that he was speaking to the master of the house remarked that he was expected to go shooting with "that tiresome Franz Ferdinand".

Once at Konopischt a record was put on to the gramophone turntable and the Archduke urged the assembled guests to follow him in a conga line, dancing from room to room throughout the castle. The line wove its way into one room and came face to face with a strange piece of drapery over the chandelier. There were anguished squawks of embarrassment from the middle-aged lady there who cringed away appalled and red-faced. It must have taken a moment or two for the assembled party to realise that the drapery was an intimate article of lady's underwear which had been washed and hung there in order that it should dry more quickly. Franz Ferdinand found this wonderfully funny and laughter shook through him until he could not catch his breath.

Sophie must have related such anecdotes to her sisters but found that they barely believed her. At such moments she may have felt strangely bereft.

The strain of her situation took its toll upon Sophie's health. She was taking a variety of medications for symptoms that may well have been psychosomatic or indications of stress and possibly also of low-key depression. These included migraine tablets, laxatives and tranquillizing drinks. She also drank a good deal of red wine because it had been suggested to her that this would help correct an iron deficiency which left her easily tired and often drained of energy.

Certainly the passing years had changed Sophie. She was no longer so skinny-thin. She had endured four difficult pregnancies and they had affected her health. There were concerns about her heart; she suffered from palpitations of the heart and shortness of breath. Arsenic drops were prescribed when these symptoms were particularly noticeable. In the spring of 1914 she took to her bed for several weeks.

There were whispers and rumours that her health suffered as a result of life with a difficult husband but these were more likely to be the malicious views of those who disliked her.

Chapter 108

For all Montenuovo's tight control over the lives of Sophie and Franz Ferdinand there was one area that was problematic. Montenuovo had no direct power to dictate to foreign courts. By and large all that was needed were quiet messages from ambassadors in other capitals to the effect that any acknowledgement of the 'morganatic one' would distress the Emperor and might cause unpleasantness and tension between countries. Thus, Montenuovo exercised his power even outside Austria. Visiting royalty were allowed to pay their respects to Franz Ferdinand and Sophie in private; they were not allowed to invite her to any public occasion where salutes and formalities would be accorded and it might appear that she, by her presence, was included in the honours.

But Montenuovo could not command. And sometimes he was to find that foreign courts refused to accept such restrictions. If there was an explicit invitation to Sophie the situation became delicate. For Montenuovo the easiest way of dealing with such situations was to prevent Sophie from travelling with her husband. In January 1902 Franz Ferdinand travelled to St. Petersburg but he was obliged to travel alone and leave Sophie behind.

The following year the German Kaiser Wilhelm visited the Archduke Friedrich and Isabella and from them heard all sorts of insinuations about Sophie. His reaction was to join the general chorus and refuse to acknowledge Sophie.

Wilhelm then travelled on to Vienna. He was accompanied by his Chancellor, Bernhard von Bülow. Von Bülow had a reputation for being as slippery as an eel, a devious man who made a secret of everything, an amusing man, charming and clever. He was pasty-faced with a permanently ingratiating smile on his face. He could sweet-talk just about everyone and he came to manage Wilhelm most successfully by showering him with fulsome praise.

In the train, von Bülow pressed Wilhelm to avoid annoying Franz Ferdinand. Wilhelm flushed with irritation and retorted that he risked opening the door to his own sons marrying ladies-in-waiting and maids.

The train pulled into the station at Vienna and there were the Emperor and his heir waiting to greet the Kaiser. As Wilhelm moved to step down on to the platform, von Bülow whispered quietly behind him, "Your Majesty now has a choice. For the rest of your life the future Emperor of Austria will be your enemy or your friend." Did von Bülow, knowing how contrary his master could be, think to himself at that moment, 'He won't do it!'? But von Bülow was in for a surprise.

Wilhelm greeted the Emperor with great bonhomie and then he turned and greeted Franz Ferdinand, adding, "And when can I have the honour of greeting your wife?" Franz Ferdinand relaxed visibly; Franz Joseph tightened up.

And Wilhelm? He was a man who desperately craved respect, admiration and liking. He had never felt genuinely welcome in Vienna. He did not understand Vienna. When he was there he felt as though he himself knew he was there but no one else was aware that he was there. Germany was now the more powerful nation but it was still a smaller country and a relatively new one and Germany needed the close relationship with Austria-Hungary that apparently existed but sometimes seemed a little shaky.

The old Emperor was aloof and withdrawn, but with those few words Wilhelm felt he had henceforth the liking and warmth of the future Emperor. He did and he didn't. To Wilhelm's mind he had become Franz Ferdinand's best friend. He would write to his daughter and tell her of 'his high regard' for Franz Ferdinand and how incomprehensible it was that so few in Austria recognised his cleverness.

But Franz Ferdinand was a man well able to keep his thoughts to himself when it suited him to do so. Franz Ferdinand would allow Wilhelm to witter on and on while largely keeping his own thoughts to himself. Wilhelm took this to indicate respect and admiration and he remained unaware just how ambivalent Franz Ferdinand was about him. The subtle difference in their attitudes towards each other was expressed in how the two men addressed the other. Wilhelm always called Franz Ferdinand 'dear Franzi'; Franz Ferdinand's '*Du, Majestät*' was not quite so intimate.

However, anyone who was courteous to Sophie could count upon Franz Ferdinand. Franz Ferdinand would have been glad that he had Wilhelm's support. He always made Wilhelm welcome from that moment on. Wilhelm's loudness, his cheeriness, his over familiarity, all created the impression of great closeness. Franz Ferdinand's slight coolness just got caught up in the loud swirl of bluster. Historians present the relationship between the two men as mutual and close. But Franz Ferdinand's feelings were more nuanced than that.

In 1909 King Carol of Rumania invited Franz Ferdinand and his 'consort' to honour him and his wife by visiting them. This put Vienna in a spin but a rebuff would have been too public and obvious. The Emperor found that he had little choice but to agree to their both going. But the invitation was not to the capital city but to King Carol's summer castle, Peleš Palace, which would have made the invitation just acceptable to Montenuovo. And Sophie would have been delighted for this was a wonderful place in the Carpathian Mountains – Franz Ferdinand's private secretary, Paul Nikitsch-Boulles, overwhelmed by the beauty of their surroundings, described it as "a magical fairy palace, seemingly part of the incomparable landscape".

It was a private visit. Nevertheless, this was the first time that Sophie travelled with Franz Ferdinand to a foreign country not using an alias but under her own name. They were both met at the station by the Crown Prince Ferdinand and his wife, Marie. There was a guard of honour and a regimental band played the national anthems of the two countries as Franz Ferdinand stepped down from the train on to a red carpet with Sophie at his side.

Princess Marie was uncomfortable with the situation but when they all reached the castle they found the welcome with which King Carol and Queen Elisabeth greeted them could not have been kinder. Sophie tried to curtsey to the Queen but found herself caught up in the arms of Queen Elisabeth who was kissing her effusively. The Rumanian royal couple were delighted with their visitors – Sophie was absolutely charming, Carol later wrote, and there were no problems about her difficult position. They treated Sophie like royalty which Sophie found bewildering. At the banquet in their honour Sophie was seated beside the King and not at the bottom of the table.

Franz Ferdinand relaxed completely. He knew her well enough to have guessed at some of the thoughts and feelings going through her and then he would have looked across the table at his wife's modest manners and gentle charm and felt deeply proud of her.

The aftermath of that visit cast an unpleasant shadow over what had been a delightful stay. Franz Ferdinand, having noticed on the journey there that the train rushed, unstopping, through the region of Transylvania, ordered for their return that the train should be stopped at various stations along the way so that local people could greet them as they passed through. Transylvania was ruled by Hungarians but by far the largest part of the population in the region was of Rumanian blood. The Rumanians were severely oppressed by the Hungarians and Franz Ferdinand was well aware that they had high hopes that when he came to power he would hear their pleas for better treatment.

Franz Ferdinand's orders were overruled. A Hungarian officer boarded the train at the border and insisted that the safety of the heir to the throne demanded that no stops be made in Transylvania. So the train raced through while police officers forced the excited crowds back at sword point. Franz Ferdinand fumed. When they had left the region and passed into central Hungary the train stopped at every station, but now he had the curtains of his carriage drawn, refusing to acknowledge their greetings.

Back in Vienna there were feelings of rage and resentment that the visit had been allowed at all. Why so much resentment? But it was fear that underpinned it, fear of change and the unknown and Sophie had somehow come to stand for change. More than any other western European country, Austria-Hungary could not face the changes that other countries were beginning to embrace. Yet, in spite of the tensions, that was the year that Franz Joseph chose to raise Sophie's rank. She now became the Duchess of

Hohenburg and entitled to the title 'Her Highness' instead of 'Her Serenity'. What Sophie thought of her new status she kept to herself, but Franz Ferdinand was almost boyishly excited over the achievement. Full of eagerness, he insisted that when the servants forgot the new title a fine would be imposed, the money to go to the poor. But the very first person to forget was Franz Ferdinand himself. He burst out laughing and paid up, with interest, delighted to be the first sinner to be caught out.

Wilhelm was one of the first to send Sophie a congratulatory telegramme and he then went on to invite Franz Ferdinand and Sophie to Potsdam. This was rather more tricky than the earlier visit to Rumania because Franz Ferdinand did not know how the German Empress would treat Sophie. Thus, in November 1909 Franz Ferdinand travelled to Berlin. Sophie was on the train with him, though expected to remain in the shadows. Franz Ferdinand descended from the train as bands played and flags fluttered and a guard of soldiers snapped to attention – all the honours due to the heir to the throne of Europe's oldest monarchy. But when Sophie appeared Wilhelm bowed before her and kissed her hand and then pressed into her arms a bouquet of exquisite orchids. Sophie rose to the occasion with elegance and grace. Few would have noticed a blink or two hinting at a twinge of embarrassment.

Just as in Rumania, in Berlin some subtle sleight of hand was needed to prevent any awkwardness. Thus, it had been arranged that the long banqueting table should be replaced by a number of smaller round tables and Wilhelm announced that he and his wife and their Austrian visitors would share one of these. Wilhelm even took Sophie's arm and led her to the place of honour at his right side.

In some ways what happened in England was of particular significance. When he had travelled as a young man round the world his first impressions of the English were not good. Franz Ferdinand clung to the views and attitudes he had formed then and they were very much against the English.

He found them arrogant. He considered them inflexible and determined to impose on others their way of doing things. Little things stuck in his mind – when he was in India at an official banquet given in his honour by the British Governor of Bombay, Franz Ferdinand was startled and offended when the first toast was made to Queen Victoria and not the head of the country from which came the official guest, himself. Things like this, to Franz Ferdinand's mind, were evidence that the British regarded themselves as superior to all others.

In 1897 it was Franz Ferdinand who was sent to London to represent the Habsburgs at Queen Victoria's Diamond Jubilee. Franz Ferdinand had not yet been proclaimed cured of his tuberculosis but two years of fighting the disease had gone by, two years during which Franz Ferdinand had been very isolated. He must have grown used to the isolation and the quiet that had enveloped him. London, with all its bustle, must have come as a shock to Franz Ferdinand. He had also spent a great deal of time brooding over what possible outcome his love for Sophie might have and his broodings kept him constantly despondent.

By that summer he was feeling stronger and better and the matter was very much on his mind. Alone in London (he only had a small suite with him, and this included Dr. Eisenmenger) he felt jostled by the crowds, overwhelmed by all the events, and crushed by all the noise and bustle. Queen Victoria's daughter, the Empress Frederick, wrote home to tell her daughter that Buckingham Palace was like a beehive, so full of people was it. Franz Ferdinand was not staying in Buckingham Palace but there were many banquets and receptions there that he would have attended.

He seemed so unsure of himself and lost in his own thoughts that he did not make a good impression. He was seen in England as morose and withdrawn. This was not the occasion that might have made Franz Ferdinand change his mind about the English, nor they about him.

Five years later Franz Ferdinand was again in London attending Queen Victoria's funeral and then again the following year he was at Bertie's coronation in 1902. By then Franz Ferdinand and Sophie had been married for two years and the extent to which Montenuovo intended to keep them apart was becoming clear to Franz Ferdinand. Sophie was not allowed to go to London and without her at his side it is unlikely that Franz Ferdinand opened up much.

The Sophie problem was beginning to cause a certain discomfort in London. England had no history of morganatic marriages. England had also had in Queen Victoria a ruler whose husband was not given equal status but was, barring a few very small distinctions, always treated with the same honours and distinction accorded the Queen.

According to Henry Wickham Steed, the correspondent of *The Times* in Vienna, the English took it for granted that when Franz Ferdinand was Emperor Sophie would be treated by them as if she were Empress. Wickham Steed reported that Bertie had remarked that sooner or later everyone would have to face the fact that Sophie would become Empress when Franz Ferdinand came to the throne. And Emperor Franz Ferdinand would have found that his wife would have been accorded the same courtesies as himself had they ever travelled to the United States. It would not just have been the little countries like Rumania that would have had little truck with complications over how to treat Sophie, rather it seems likely that everywhere outside Austria Sophie would have been treated as though she were the Empress.

One person who was not happy about this was Princess Mary of Teck who had married the future George V. She had no wish to rub shoulders with Sophie. The morganatic status was a sensitive issue with Mary – she herself came from a morganatic marriage and she was acutely aware of the difficulties that came with morganatic marriages. She did not wish to meet Sophie. But she was to find that she would get no support from her husband over this. And in 1904 Mary had to meet Sophie. The newly-married British royal couple paid their first state visit to Vienna that April, where, of course, Sophie was pointedly kept away from all official functions.

However, George insisted upon visiting Franz Ferdinand and Sophie privately. This meeting seems to have gone very well. Very slowly, unobtrusively and largely unremarked, something like a real friendship grew up between George and Franz Ferdinand. They found that there were many similarities between them. They both preferred to retreat into their own family circles. They were both interested in the navy and they both liked being out of doors, shooting or even just striding over the hills away from crowds and the constant social demands of their positions.

Neither spoke the other's language very well. George never spoke German and his French was a clunky, wobbly matter where communication was hard to achieve. Franz Ferdinand's knowledge of French and English was always very stilted. Yet these two understood each other and came to like the other's company.

There was a set-back over Bertie's funeral in 1910. Franz Ferdinand wanted Sophie to come to London with him, staying incognito in a hotel until after all the ceremonies were over and then they hoped to remain a few days longer. The authorities in London had no problems with this, but Vienna did. The British Embassy in Vienna was forced to contact the Foreign Office in London and the message was passed on to the Austrian Ambassador, Count Albert von Mensdorff.

Mensdorff had arrived in London in 1889 and he became ambassador fifteen years later in 1904. He had family connections with the British royal family because his grandfather had married one of Queen Victoria's aunts[56] and his father had been a cousin of Prince Albert as well as a close personal friend. As a result, Albert von Mensdorff enjoyed a welcome and popularity in London that few others could ever have hoped to attain. He was a personal friend of both Bertie and George and he had been invited as a friend

---

56 Queen Victoria's mother, Marie Louise Victoire von Saxe-Coburg, was the fourth daughter of Franz Friedrich von Saxe-Coburg. Her eldest sister, Sophie, married Emmanuel von Mensdorf-Pouilly.

and not in an official capacity to Sandringham. George would sign his letters to Mensdorff 'Your affectionate friend and cousin'.

He got great satisfaction out of his special relationship with the British royal family and was prepared to go to considerable lengths to preserve it. When Mensdorff got the news that any plans for Sophie to come to London with Franz Ferdinand had to be thwarted, he hated the manoeuvres needed to prevent her coming. But it had to be done. Mensdorff wrote to Franz Ferdinand begging him to understand that Her Majesty Queen Mary was unable to receive half the royal ladies she would have liked to receive and she could not include the Duchess of Hohenburg. Franz Ferdinand insisted that Sophie would arrive separately and would maintain the strictest possible incognito and never go near Queen Mary. But Vienna was determined to prevent it.

It was a very disgruntled Franz Ferdinand who came to London and, being in a bad mood, he found fault with everything. The funeral was too long; no chairs had been provided in St. George's Chapel so that the guests could sit through the service.

He fumed about the 'arrogant English', remarked that the President of the United States had distinguished himself by 'an exceptional lack of any courtly manners' (possibly a case of the pot calling the kettle black), and made personal comments about almost everyone else – Crown Prince Alexander of Serbia looked like a 'bad gypsy' and Foxy Ferdinand looked like 'a pig' on horseback (which he probably did, given the poor horseman he was, but it was hardly tactful to say so.)

Franz Ferdinand also mocked some of the little quirks that were traditional to the English. Nobody had told him that it was traditional at the funerals of English kings and senior officers for their horses to follow the cortège with their riding boots in the stirrups the wrong way round, facing backwards, to indicate that the dead man's riding days were past. Franz Ferdinand noticed the boots and found it ridiculous their facing backwards.

(Clearly, Franz Ferdinand had never heard of a special arrangement at the funeral in 1865 of Belgium's first King, King Leopold I. Following the funeral cortège was the King's horse which had had its legs strapped in such a way that the animal was forced to limp. At Baudouin's funeral his favourite mare, Irlandès, followed the cortège but without the same constraint.)

Most of Franz Ferdinand's spluttering was due to ruffled feathers and the ill-ease he felt in the midst of so many people and so much ceremony. So, when not long after, he should have gone to London again for George's coronation, he refused and in his place went Archduke Karl.

This was Karl's first important opportunity to represent Austria abroad. He was twenty-three and had only recently become engaged to Princess Zita of Bourbon-Parma, so it was a rather inexperienced young man who found himself caught up in the swirl of celebration in London. In character Karl was shy like Franz Ferdinand; but whereas Franz Ferdinand's shyness expressed itself in a gruff, stand-offish manner, Karl's shyness was expressed as a self-effacing gentleness. Karl, too, did not enjoy crowds and noisy celebrations. What he enjoyed the most during his time in London was a visit to Spithead where there was a naval review and great steel ships from all the nations were lined up in all their might.

Karl immediately made a very good impression on the new King and Queen, all the more so because the English royal family secretly felt that the Habsburgs were rather a queer lot – the old Emperor impossibly rigid and unyielding, Rudolf's death had wiped out the good opinion of him that had once existed, and in public Franz Ferdinand was too withdrawn and morose. But Karl did the right things. People were particularly delighted with the obvious warmth he felt towards his new fiancée. The fact that he did not dance with anyone at all and behaved with becoming restraint met with approval. And he proudly showed the new Queen Mary a picture of his fiancée.

Time went by but in unobserved ways Count Albert von Mensdorff was still trying to smooth the way to more contact between the English King and the future Emperor of Austria. King George also wanted to see Franz Ferdinand and Sophie again. He sent Franz Ferdinand his warmest thoughts and suggested that they might make plans for Franz Ferdinand and the Duchess of Hohenberg to visit England.

The best possible opportunity for this came in May 1912 when the English Horticultural Society intended to open its first international flower show, the first Chelsea Flower Show. Everything about the invitation would have eclipsed any ruffled feathers Franz Ferdinand still had. He would be coming to England as a horticulturist and not as royalty, Sophie was explicitly included in the invitation and the chance to attend the flower show provoked all Franz Ferdinand's interest and love of plants and flowers. The invitation, too, was a subtle recognition of all the work Franz Ferdinand had put into his own gardens at Konopischt where his rose gardens were legendary. Franz Ferdinand felt appreciated.

It would have amused Sophie to watch him bubble with pleasure and satisfaction, and she could relax, too, and look forward to their time together in England. Few ever noticed how much their way of life put a strain on Sophie. She hid the stress she experienced behind an apparently serene face of calm acceptance. But she once wrote to her sister, Octavia, admitting that it was difficult.

The truth must have been that it was more than difficult. There was a real strain that never went away. There must have been many times when

Sophie went to bed and found that she could not sleep. Thoughts, always the same thoughts, went round and round in her head. She was constantly wary of what might be the next thing to wind Franz Ferdinand up. She also worried about his health.

Sophie's worrying was quiet and unobtrusive; Franz Ferdinand more than made up for her apparent calm with his own hypochondria. He knew he was a hypochondriac but he could not prevent each and every little thing sparking great anxiety in him that it might mean something serious. A coughing fit would immediately raise fears that his tuberculosis had returned.

On another occasion Franz Ferdinand called in Eisenmenger to inspect a small lesion on his tongue. Eisenmenger's assurances failed to reassure Franz Ferdinand who went on worrying that it might indicate cancer. As he neared his fiftieth birthday he became increasingly aware that his hearing was deteriorating. Sophie wrote to Octavia to tell her that the doctor had only found his hearing slightly worse, which was a relief for Franzi.

Sophie's anxieties had to be suppressed and kept hidden. Maybe she had told him many times that really and truly none of Montenuovo's needle jabs got to her, so why couldn't he shrug them all off in the same way? She may even have laughed and asked him, "What do you think would have been the alternative for me?" and pointed out that she hadn't really had greater freedoms as Isabella's lady-in-waiting. Couldn't he see that the life they had was, for her, so much better than she could ever have hoped for? And she loved him.

Yet there might have been a tiny, niggling thought at the back of her mind that in spite of those so-called difficult times, life in Isabella's household had always been full of activity and very sociable and Sophie had enjoyed being in the middle of it all. Life was a lot quieter now. Sophie had always been sociable, she enjoyed having people around her, and now she missed that. But that would have been a thought she kept very much to herself. Such thoughts she would have pushed hurriedly away with a sudden stab of guilt. How could the thought even come into her mind that she had lost something in marrying this man she loved?

Few saw the strain. Few noticed that something of Sophie's twinkle had gone out of her. They did not see that her calm and serenity had a taut quality to it. That girl in the picture of her and Franz Ferdinand on the tennis court where she is laughing with such unashamed delight, that girl had gone.

But she would enjoy going to England, particularly since they would be the 'Count and Countess of Artstetten'. They arrived in London to be met by Sophie's niece, Countess Elisabeth Baillet-Latour, and drove to the Ritz Hotel where they stayed in a suite that overlooked Green Park.

On 23rd May 1912, thanks to the efforts of Count Albert von Mensdorff, they were invited to Buckingham Palace to a lunch with King George V, Queen Mary and the Dowager Queen Alexandra. This was ideal. Franz Ferdinand was at ease and he opened up. George was struck by how charming they both were – they made themselves very pleasant, he noted in his diary. And the thing was they were not even trying to. They were comfortable here in this small circle and interested in everything and that made them interesting. Much of Queen Mary's dread of them evaporated like morning mist. Sophie was flawless, so agreeable, interesting and charming. She never put a foot wrong.

They spent a fortnight in England during which time they not only went to the flower show but also visited several country houses. Elisabeth Baillet-Latour was living in England at that time and it was she who arranged a number of these visits to people she knew, particularly to people who would make her aunt feel very much at home. In spite of the wealth they found in England, they did not find the same formality that they would have found in Vienna and Sophie might well have felt very much at home if only she had not been constantly thinking of the children back at Konopischt.

The visit that they enjoyed the most was to Welbeck Abbey in Northamptonshire. Here William Cavendish-Bentinck, Duke of Portland, was particularly cheery and open-armed. He insisted that they should return in the autumn and Franz Ferdinand could go out shooting with him.

Franz Ferdinand found the flower show fascinating. He was like a small boy in a toy shop. You hope that Sophie was wearing comfortable shoes because once through the doors of the showground she could not have dragged Franz Ferdinand away from all these displays of plants, some exotic, some ordinary, some arranged in miniature gardens, some set out as massive displays of perfect blooms. He could pretend that they had no idea who he was (and he probably wasn't far wrong about that) and talk to them about the difficulties of propagating this plant or that, or what kind of soil and climate conditions produced the best blossoms, and he could discuss his own experiences and learn how to deal with the problems he had met with. The best of it all was that he could forget about courtly protocol.

So Sophie would stand there and watch as he got animated over a particular rose. Her eye might catch him biting a lip and she would know that he was wondering whether this rose could even put his own roses in the shade. And she would shake her head in amused despair. But he was happy that day and so was she.

Together they also visited the Botanical Gardens at Kew and Hampton Court Palace. They went to the Wallace Collection and enjoyed an evening at the recently-opened Victoria Palace Theatre – here they watched Anna

Pavlova dance, something that Sophie particularly would have enjoyed. In a letter to a friend Franz Ferdinand commented on how much he had enjoyed their time in London, revelling in his two favourite activities: art and horticulture.

There is no recorded evidence that these two teased and joked together. However, all the evidence suggests that Sophie had a teasing, mischievous streak to her character and perhaps this may have been the most important reason why he had fallen so deeply in love with her. Her eye could light up with a glint of impish delight. But in public she kept a very tight lid on any expression of her feelings. And a man like Franz Ferdinand would have kept a very tight lid on any expression of his feelings – he knew that there were those who whispered that he was a jabbering idiot whose entourage consisted of psychiatrists and doctors.

But when they were together behind closed doors away from spying eyes? Did she tease him that he had been envious of the man who had grown that particular rose with the wonderful graduated colours? Me, envious? Of course not. Did she giggle a little? And hadn't he hung on every word of that man who explained that plants were like human beings, some shy and retiring, others brash and boisterous? Well, she knew somebody who was a delicate, tender plant, didn't look it but was. And it would amuse her that it took him a moment to realise what it was she was saying. And then she would listen and listen as he told her all the things he had learned or found interesting or had given him new ideas for their gardens at Konopischt.

We will never know whether it was like that.

In November 1913, Franz Ferdinand took up the Duke of Portland's invitation and returned to England for the shooting. Mensdorff had told King George about the proposed visit and George immediately suggested that Franz Ferdinand and Sophie should combine a visit to Windsor with their visit to Welbeck Abbey. Again, Franz Ferdinand was delighted and he asked Mensdorff to tell the King how 'exceptionally enchanted' he and Sophie would be to accept the invitation. He was all the more glad that it was to be a private affair without "terrible banquets and toasts". He was now talking about "beautiful England" and his special gratitude to the King.

The British royal family extended a warmth and welcome that must have blown away any lingering resentments Franz Ferdinand might still have harboured. King George greeted them on the station platform at Windsor when they arrived. And Queen Mary was completely won round by them. She wrote to her aunt, the Duchess of Mecklenburg-Strelitz, to relate how changed the Archduke was. He had been so very anti-English but was now so much changed for the better, she wrote. Sophie curtsied low to Queen Mary. She won Mary round as she won almost everyone round who actually met her. And Mary's approval was unstinted – "her influence has been and is good, they say, in every way." Mary was happy to add that Franz

Ferdinand had been most enthusiastic over his visit to them and to England. Mary must have felt very glad that any fears of future difficulties she might have felt had totally ebbed away.

King George and Franz Ferdinand made the most of the shooting and afterwards George noted in his diary that "on Tuesday, we got over a thousand pheasants and four hundred and fifty ducks." That particular Tuesday there were high winds and beating rain which did not make conditions easy for shooting. The hunting group was small and exclusive, consisting of King George, Franz Ferdinand and three English dukes. It could have been an awkward moment for Franz Ferdinand because he was not used to the English way of shooting, where the beaters drove the birds into a much higher and faster flight than was the custom in Austria. Far greater skill was needed to perform well. It is likely that Franz Ferdinand was well aware that he was not up to the standard of those he was shooting with. But he was no Wilhelm – he always wanted his rewards to reflect his unaided skill and achievements.

And after Windsor Franz Ferdinand and Sophie travelled up to Northamptonshire for more shooting. The Duke of Portland was to write of the occasion, "The Archduke proved himself first class and certainly the equal of most of my friends... Given enough practice in this country, he would have been the equal of any of our best shots."

Franz Ferdinand almost did not return to Austria. It was a cold, wintry day. Snow had fallen early that year and was thick on the ground at Welbeck. One of the gun-loaders slipped on an icy patch and fell. As he did so the gun he was holding went off. Two shots from both barrels of the gun flew past Franz Ferdinand. A few feet to one side and Franz Ferdinand would have ended his days in England.

Every eye must have swung round to the Archduke – was he going to explode with anger as he was so wont to do? Franz Ferdinand could not have been more relaxed. He jovially shrugged his shoulders and brushed the incident aside as a natural sporting hazard.

Franz Ferdinand got something else that November visit. Instead of largely pretending that they did not know Franz Ferdinand and Sophie were in London, the Austrian Embassy extended an invitation to them both to a dinner party in their honour. The Princess of Hohenberg was being treated to the honours due to a future imperial consort. Here was no hiding behind an incognito – she was there in her capacity as the wife of the future Emperor. One wonders how Montenuovo ever let such an event take place but perhaps he was not fully kept in the loop. One suspects the hand of Mensdorff here. He loved England and seeing the growing easy friendship that the British royal family were showing the imperial couple, Mensdorf would have wanted to do anything he could to promote it.

But as far as Franz Ferdinand was concerned, none of that mattered; all that mattered was that every single precedent acknowledging Sophie as his wife was grist to his mill. He took the bold step of asking whether Sophie might go with him to a play in an ordinary public theatre. This was a step too far. Montenuovo, in all his usual convoluted and obsequious, sycophantic language, firmly refused.

Of course, this gave rise to murmurings that he might go back on his oath once he was Emperor. And there were comments that gave weight to the murmurings. The Pope pronounced that in the eyes of the church a man could not swear away the religious rights of his unborn children. With the Catholic Church backing him, might Franz Ferdinand feel that his oath had been forced out of him and was invalid? Princess Zita was secretly convinced that he would and that prospect disturbed and upset her. She wanted to be an Empress and she never entirely trusted Franz Ferdinand.

Back in Vienna Franz Joseph grew to dislike the marriage more and more and increasingly wished he had never agreed to it. Possibly, by 1913, the thought may have crossed Franz Joseph's mind that if Franz Ferdinand had had to wait thirteen years to marry Sophie his determination might have wavered. In 1900 neither Franz Joseph nor Franz Ferdinand could have known just how long the Emperor would live on.

However, by 1913 Franz Joseph was growing increasingly frail. He no longer wanted the stress that went with the surreptitious battle against Sophie. By now he was not just courteous towards Sophie on a personal basis, but he was charming and invariably kind towards her, too. In February 1914 Sophie attended the Vienna Court Ball. She sat at some distance from other members of the Imperial Family but it was noticed that she spent much of the evening talking with Marie-Valérie.

Franz Joseph as usual started the dancing by leading the first waltz with Princess Zita which emphasised that Zita was the first lady in the room that night. Franz Ferdinand watched stiffly. But after the dance Franz Joseph turned to Franz Ferdinand and asked whether Sophie would have the kindness to come and sit next to him for a while. Such a little gesture but to those around it was momentous. It was interpreted as indicating that Franz Joseph's opposition to Sophie might be waning. More likely it meant nothing more than that he found it easier to accept her presence when she had been allowed to be present.

Increasingly senior figures within Austrian society were focussing on what changes would come when Franz Ferdinand became Emperor. Unobtrusively, attitudes had to be shifting ground in preparation for the day. One person whose attitude had softened was the Archduchess Isabella. Isabella wrote inviting Franz Ferdinand and Sophie to a dance in June, adding that she would be really pleased if they would like to come. Perhaps Isabella did not want to be barred from court life when Franz Ferdinand became Emperor, or perhaps, quite simply, she had come to recognise that there never had been a relationship between Franz Ferdinand and Maria Christina and now the whole matter was too far in the past to go on making a big issue over. And deep down Isabella had always felt great fondness for Franz Ferdinand and with the passing of time it was getting easier and easier to brush aside any tensions that had existed between them.

No doubt there were some who were quietly glad to note that Franz Ferdinand seemed to be building rather better relationships with fellow rulers which would bode well for Austria-Hungary in the future. That last visit to England had been a happy occasion. And in March 1914 the Duke and Duchess of Portland accepted an invitation to Konopischt. Konopischt was Franz Ferdinand's own private property and what happened there was outside Montenuovo's jurisdiction. Clearly Franz Ferdinand had come to see that there were ways of cementing future relationships without his every effort being soured by Montenuovo's machinations. The Duke and Duchess departed having agreed that King George and Queen Mary should visit Austria in September for some private autumn shooting. Then there was talk that maybe Wilhelm should also be invited. The tree of friendship was putting down roots.

Chapter 109

Otto never got a chance to become Emperor. He never did have to watch Maria Josepha preen herself as she played the Empress. He never did have to ascend the highest position in the room with Maria Josepha at his side. He died more than ten years before Franz Ferdinand.

Within a short period from their marriage Maria Josepha effectively separated from Otto and lived apart from him, determined to protect her two sons from their father's influence. Otto threw himself into an aimless, feckless, debauched life. It may have been around the time when Franz Ferdinand renounced all rights on behalf of his future wife and possible future children that Otto first became infected with the syphilis that would kill him some six years later. Ironic this – that he acquired what would prevent his ever being a possible heir to the throne when that possibility might have become a reality.

When Otto had retired from public life to die slowly of syphilis Maria Josepha refused to come to his side. Right at the end of his life he was brought to a secluded villa in Vienna. Here Archduke Otto died a long drawn-out and very painful death, largely isolated and hidden away from the world. He was only forty-one when he died on 1st November 1906 in the presence of his spiritual adviser, Bishop Gottfried Marschall.

Some of Otto's old friends and a few chorus girls he had once flirted with came to visit. But they came only once, horrified by what they found. Most could not stomach the stench that pervaded his sickroom. By the end of his life syphilis had so eaten away at his face that he was forced to wear a leather nose to conceal what lay beneath. Finally, the disease attacked his larynx and he had to endure a tracheotomy. A tube was inserted into his throat to prevent him dying of suffocation. Otto suffered torments of agony every time the cannula in his throat had to be changed and he had to be watched the whole time because there was a danger that the cannula could move and choke him.

For the last two years of his life, he was nursed by his last mistress, Louise Robinson, and by his stepmother, Maria Theresia. Louise Robinson was the daughter of a Jewish music teacher and when she first got to know Otto she was riding high as a young starlet who shone particularly in operettas. But for more than two years she had not been seen on the stage. However, she was still acting a part. In order to nurse her lover she had put on a nurse's habit and taken the name 'Sister Martha' and she had done this because the disguise was needed to conceal the fact that a mere actress was spending time in the close company of a member of the Imperial Family.

Here, too, Maria Theresia showed her thoughtfulness for others.

Stéphanie wrote, "She sacrificed herself for her predecessor's children. She poured over them the riches of her heart – hers was the most generous heart ever to beat in this house and this family." Maria Theresia was the only one of his own family to come to his side when Otto was dying.

But Maria Josepha had long had no further connection with him. At some point – probably after the disease that would kill him had begun to ravage Otto's body and force him into quasi-hiding – Maria Josepha met the German actor, Otto Tressler, who took pity on her. It was not long before these two were meeting discreetly but regularly and soon their relationship had deepened into an affair. Despite the fact that she was very pious, Maria Josepha was clearly no nun.

It was the First World War that finally brought an end to Maria Josepha's affair with Otto Tressler. And at the end of the war Maria Josepha accompanied her son and daughter-in-law, Zita, into exile. Otto Tressler went on to become a film actor and a very prolific one, appearing in over forty films right up until 1962, shortly before his death.

Otto's eldest son, Karl, learned of his father's death late at night on 1st November 1906 in the railway station in Milan. Karl, with his mother, had been to a family wedding in Cannes and they were on their way back to Austria.

Karl all along had taken his mother's side. His was a dutiful character and he clearly disliked his father's behaviour. He was close to his mother and felt protective towards her – at least until Otto Tressler came on the scene.

Karl found he could appreciate Franz Ferdinand's knowledge of the country's problems and his sharp ability to seek out possible solutions.

When Otto died Franz Ferdinand insisted that he would do everything in his power to bring Otto's children up as good Christians, Austrians and Habsburgs. Franz Ferdinand paid special attention to Karl. Karl became a frequent visitor who enjoyed spending time with his uncle. He also spent holidays with Franz Ferdinand and Sophie. These were opportunities for Karl to discuss the problems and tensions within the country with his uncle. The two got to know each other well and Karl came to recognise Franz Ferdinand's concern for his well-being. Franz Ferdinand wanted to do what he could to make Karl's preparation for his future position as Emperor easier than his own had been.

Franz Ferdinand had an age-old dislike of paperwork and reports. His method was to discuss the issues and problems of the moment with almost everybody or anybody, regardless of their competence. These conversations often cannot have been very easy for the other person. Franz Ferdinand could be so intimidating, he could also spurt out in anger when he disagreed, only to apologise a moment later. Underneath it all Franz Ferdinand lacked self-confidence and always had. When he was summoned to a meeting with Franz Joseph, his secretary, Paul Nikitsch-Boulles, would watch the Archduke on the long drive to Schönbrunn shaking as nervously as a schoolboy who is not ready for an impending examination.

Franz Ferdinand was not just supportive but also proud of his nephew and glad to think that one day this young man would succeed him. There was a clear divide in Franz Ferdinand's mind. His own sons would be aristocratic landowners with no part in the ruling of the country and no greater interest in its problems than any other educated landowner might have. His nephew was to be his successor and when Franz Ferdinand came to be Emperor it was his intention to prepare Karl for the role and educate him in all the skills he would need in order to be a good Emperor.

Karl's picture of where Austria was going came from Franz Ferdinand and it must have been coloured by Franz Ferdinand's growing frustration with Franz Joseph's refusal to acknowledge the need for any sort of change at all. Franz Ferdinand was trying to work out how the bomb of change could be defused without setting it off in the process. When Karl came to the throne himself all his aims and instincts turned in the same direction.

As the future Emperor, Karl could not have chosen a better future Empress than the young, impetuous Princess Zita of Bourbon-Parma. After the outbreak of the First World War, she became the target of a good deal of spite and was inappropriately often referred to as "the Italian woman". Zita herself regarded herself as French by birth and fiercely Austrian after marrying Karl. She was descended from the Sun King. She took a vivid pride in being a Bourbon and signed herself 'Zite de Bourbon'. She hankered after the magnetic grandeur of the French royal family. She longed for a powerful role in life. As an Empress? That thought would have thrilled her through and through.

Zita seems to have started out admiring Franz Ferdinand but later she grew somewhat ambivalent about him. What Franz Ferdinand thought of Zita has not been recorded but he would have been delighted that Karl had been able to find someone to be a future member of the Habsburg family who ticked all the boxes and, more importantly, someone that Karl was genuinely deeply in love with. However, privately Franz Ferdinand may also have found Zita a bit too forceful for his own liking.

Princess Zita Bourbon-Parma was born on 9th May 1892 in the Villa Pianore in Tuscany.

The region of Parma had been batted back and forth from one

illustrious Italian ruler to another for centuries but when Napoleon Bonaparte was defeated, it became the home of Napoleon's widow, the Austrian Princess Marie-Louise and her second husband, General von Neipperg. After her death in 1847 the region returned to the rule of the Bourbon family who had ruled there before Napoleon Bonaparte had brought the duchy under French rule. But in 1859 Parma was swept up into the new unified Italy.

In 1859 the ruling Duke Roberto di Parma was still only a boy. He had come to the throne of this tiny principality six years earlier when his father was assassinated by a fanatic on the streets of Parma. He and his younger brother and two sisters fled with their mother to Switzerland and after her death the children passed into the care of Henri Chambord.

Henri Chambord[57] was a claimant to the French throne who could trace his ancestry back to the last ruling kings of France, and he was known as Henri V to all those who wanted to see a King restored to the throne in Paris.

However, Henri Chambord was barred from living in France and he had made his home in Frohsdorf, south of Vienna. The castle where Henri lived may have been in Austria but within its gates everything was ultra-French. And when Henri died in 1883 all his estates, including the family castle of Chambord-sur-Loire were inherited by Roberto.

Roberto appears to have regarded his life's mission as one of producing as many children as possible. He had two wives and twenty-four children. His first wife was Princess Maria Pia and she was the daughter of King Ferdinand II of Naples and the half-sister of King Francesco of Naples and the sister-in-law of Marie-Sophie, the heroine of Gaeta. Maria Pia had twelve children in thirteen years, several of whom were mentally handicapped, three of which died in infancy and the last of them carried his mother with him to the grave.

Roberto then married the youngest daughter of the King of Portugal and she gave birth to a further twelve children. When Princess Zita was born she already had twelve half-brothers and sisters, two older brothers and two older sisters.

Duke Roberto's little army of children lived their lives as one of the gang. Each learned to assert themselves as best they might. Zita had no trouble doing this. She was small and determined. Her aim in life was to make sure that she never got overlooked. She was talking at a very early age and words spilled out of her. Even if Zita had not been so set upon being in the forefront of all the children's activities, her adorable little face with its abundant mass of curly golden hair would have attracted much attention. She could upon occasion be a bossy little thing.

---

[57] *Le Comte de Chambord et son Mystère* by Jean-François Chiappe, 1990. Note 3 in the Notes Section.

For Karl, whose childhood had been very different, this aura of being caught up in an ebullient bunch of youngsters was an important part of Zita's charm. The tensions between his mother and father had made Karl self-effacing and modest and he never found it easy to assert his own point of view. Zita, throughout her childhood, saw Karl as one of a wider circle of children, related one way or another, who belonged in her world.

"But I remember noticing one nice thing about him when he came to visit us," she reminisced in old age. Karl was always so concerned about his little brother, Max. Karl worried that Max had on the right clothes and that Max was getting enough to eat. "That was something which stayed in my mind."

This enormous clan spent half the year in Italy and the other half in Austria. But Schwarzau rather than Pianore was 'home' for the family. Early in July as the heat of summer in Italy built up to uncomfortable levels, the whole caravanserai, some sixteen coaches on a special train with two engines in order to get it over the Semmering Pass, would journey into Austria to spend the next six months in Schwarzau. Then in early January when the winter's bite in Austria made itself felt Italy and Pianore once again beckoned. The family with all its entourage was like a small township. For the children there was little distinction between schooling and other activities within the whole group. And the attitudes of Duke Roberto and Maria Antonia were that everyone had a role to play which imposed discipline as well as an adherence to patterns of activities none was allowed to question. In many ways the rules set down for what you did and when and how were as strict for the ducal family, though less onerous, as it was for their servants.

This was thinking that Zita would never question. It was particularly appropriate for Zita herself. The story has it that the Bishop of Lucca had in 1891 asked Duke Roberto as a personal favour to name his next daughter Zita. Zita was the patron saint of servants and Saint Zita was much venerated in Tuscany. The concept of serving others was drummed into all the girls. While they were in Austria the girls were required each year to collect remnants of cloth from a nearby textile factory and make them into garments for the poor of the town of Neunkirchen. Visits to the poor and the sick were expected of them. In Italy the girls were required to set out an array of clothes and food along the roadside to be handed out to the local poor. Because consumption was a good deal more rife in Italy than in Neunkirchen, when the girls returned home they had to change out of everything they were wearing and disinfect their hair with spirits. And in the background they might hear their mother saying with a laugh, "Love for your neighbour is the best disinfectant!"

At the age of eleven Zita was sent to the convent school at Zangberg, south of Munich. For Zita this new world came as a shock and she found it difficult to settle into school life. On the face of it strict discipline, a timetabled pattern to her days with few opportunities to escape being permanently surrounded by others, and a strong emphasis on religious belief had always characterised her life and would characterise her schooldays.

Yet there were subtle differences that shook Zita. At home Zita was used to standing out and winning special favour. At school she seemed submerged amongst the other schoolgirls. Zita performed well in her studies but never stood out from the others. Her biographer,[58] Tamara Griesser Pečar, put the difference down to the fact that a French spirit and culture reigned at home but not here. Zita distanced herself from her classmates. One teacher commented, "Not everyone understood Zita's reserve," and added that Zita's learning was driven more by a sense of duty than by a drive to achieve.

Her teachers soon found that there was another side to Zita, an enjoyment of some slightly doubtful jokes. On one occasion she mixed ink in the consecrated wine which resulted in the holy sisters going around all day with blue smears on their faces. There was a lot of distress and embarrassment as a result. It became clear, too, that Zita tended to attract people into her orbit or to push them away.

One of the main aims of sending Zita to Zangberg was to build up her knowledge of German and thereafter even during the holidays at home her mother spoke to her in German. In spite of this Zita's mastery of German did not improve much. But during the time that Zita was there, French came to be spoken, particularly amongst the girls who were Zita's close friends.

In 1907 Duke Roberto died suddenly and totally unexpectedly from a heart attack as he was reading the newspaper after lunch. Zita's studies clearly suffered from the loss of her father and a year later she left Zangberg. Zita's education was rounded off in a Benedictine nunnery on the Isle of Wight which had been set up by Zita's grandmother. Her older sister, Adelhaid, had come here and taken the veil. And the niece of Zita's other grandmother was also a sister of the order. All this gave rise to hints that Zita, too, would take the veil.

But there were other rumours that it had been Adelhaid who was expected to marry the Archduke Karl and she, the most beautiful, the most lively, vivacious and high-spirited, had suddenly shaken her whole family with her decision to enter a nunnery. Zita, next in line, was still too young for marriage plans. However, her stay on the Isle of Wight lasted only six months – not because of any proposed marriage but because Zita did not like being there and her health was affected by the climate. Was Zita the sort

---

[58] *Zita – Die Wahrheit über Europas letzte Kaiserin*, by Tamara Griesser Pečar, 1988.

of girl who exaggerated her ailments to attract attention? Certainly her health had become an increasing cause for concern.

In 1909 she was suffering chronic ill health and was sent to the Bohemian spa of Franzensbad to recover. She stayed with the Archduchess Maria Annunciata, the younger sister of Franz Ferdinand and of Otto. In the background was Maria Theresia – stepmother of Maria Annunciata but also the sister of Maria Antonia, Zita's mother. And Maria Theresia had begun to take an interest in the feelings and inclinations of the younger members of the family. Archduke Karl, whose regiment was based at Brandeis on the River Elbe, some two hundred kilometres distant from Franzensbad, enjoyed frequently visiting his relatives in Franzensbad.

It was here that Zita and Karl really got to know each other. The last time that these two had met each other had been before Zita was sent to Zangberg when they had both been children. Now things were very different. Their meetings, however, were strictly controlled and their getting-to-know-each-other barely proceeded given the need to evade gossiping tongues. Karl's natural reticence did not help here, either. But there are also hints that Zita, too, hung back somewhat. Zita seemed to find Karl's cool manner off-putting.

All clues suggest that Karl was more taken with Zita at this stage in their relationship than she with him. Years later Zita remembered, "We really got to know each other and became friends. We were always glad each time we met up together."

Early in 1911 the gossiping tongues were spreading rumours of Karl's wish to marry Princess Bella Hohenlohe. These rumours reached Franz Joseph's ears and Karl was immediately summoned to Schönbrunn. Karl found himself facing an old man already prepared to bring the full force of his authority down upon his great-nephew. There must have been a surge of relief all round when it became clear that the rumours were only rumours.

The tension went out of the old man and Franz Joseph drily asserted that he could never have consented to such a match, so it was just as well that Karl was not harbouring thoughts along those lines.

For the Hofball on 16th January 1911 Zita had been receiving special dancing lessons and a particularly important dress had been designed and made for her so that she could impress all who saw her at the most important ball of the season. When the great doors opened and the Emperor entered with the Imperial Family in line behind him, Zita over to one side watched intently. For the first time it was beginning to come home to her that if Karl... then perhaps one day she would not only be in that cortège but at its head, too.

It was all very impressive, regal and romantic. And then when the Emperor had retired the guests all fell upon the buffet with almost animal-like greed and Zita was shocked at what she saw. Only some of onlookers took particular notice of her, while both Karl and Zita maintained a cool demeanour. They danced and were seen as a charming pair but no more than that could be read into their behaviour. Perhaps some of those who became aware of what a delightful pair they were wanted to read more into it than that.

The truth was that since Rudolf's death Vienna had felt that absence of an attractive young couple embodying all that was admirable about the Imperial Family. Year after year Franz Ferdinand and the Duchess of Hohenberg had sent prickles of annoyance and frustration throughout society, and these had built up to the point of causing an angry tension across Vienna. What the Austrians needed was for the young, charming Archduke to step into the void and be their new Prince Charming.

They wanted Karl to become the new Rudolf. But there were certain aspects of Karl that the Viennese found disappointing. They would so much have loved it if he had been '*fesch*' and gallant – after all, his father had been '*der fesche Otto*', how could it be that the son lacked gallantry? Still, his was the task of expunging all that Rudolf's last days had done to harm the glory of the Habsburgs. And for this he needed a princess at his side – a true princess, one who would have felt a pea through twenty mattresses.

Some months later this ball was followed by another, this time given by Maria Josepha. This may have caused a small shiver of surprise since very rarely indeed did Maria Josepha host public entertainments of any sort. Furthermore, since she had become involved with Otto Tressler she had withdrawn even more from the public eye. But for her eldest son she would put on a ball.

From the moment of her arrival Karl was at Zita's side insisting that she dance the cotillion with him. She hesitated. She had cause. Officially etiquette demanded that Karl should dance this most important of dances with Zita's older sister, Francisca (Cicca, as she was known in the family). If he danced the cotillion with her he was publicly advertising his love for her. Effectively, if she had any hesitation about committing herself to him, from that moment on she would find it difficult to withdraw.

Did she hold him at a distance? There are hints that that evening did not end on the best of notes. Karl afterwards felt that Zita had adhered too strictly to the demands of etiquette when he longed for her to concentrate all her thoughts and feelings upon himself.

And Karl had recently learned that there were a number of contenders for Zita's hand in marriage, amongst them Don Jaime of the Madrid Bourbons. Karl was shaken to learn that Don Jaime's suit was serious. He did not know whether Don Jaime had formally proposed to Zita, nor whether she was seriously considering accepting Don Jaime. The 1911 winter season of dances and balls in Vienna increased Karl's anguished uncertainty. They met, they danced, they smiled, they laughed together, but still Karl could not know whether she was willing to look his way.

It speaks much for Karl's natural modesty that he entirely ignored the fact that he was the most eligible bachelor in Europe. There were others angling for him. Because he was such a desirable catch there was much speculation over this possible *partie* or that. Many a gossip sparked off a delightful frisson as some well-bred young woman caught the attention of the gossips and her every move or expression came under their scrutiny. Franz Joseph was taken with the possibility of Karl's marrying his granddaughter, Ella, one of Marie Valérie's many daughters, but this proposition was severely stamped on by Maria Josepha who disliked the fact that Karl and Ella were far too closely related to each other. Franz Joseph was then drawn to the idea of Princess Margarete of Denmark.

Archduchess Isabella (Busabella) certainly seemed to be after Karl for one of her younger daughters. Karl was serving as an army officer not too far from Isabella's castle in Pressburg. Just as she had been ever ready to invite Franz Ferdinand, she now frequently invited Karl. It became widely believed that Isabella became a furnace of bitter resentfulness when Karl married Zita but this may very well have been nothing but exaggerated gossip.

What was surprising was that Zita was not one of the young women attracting the gossips' attention. It seems that Zita herself was more concerned to evade any possible scrutiny than she was to win Karl's interest in her. Finally, Karl must have gone to his mother and sought her advice. Maria Josepha did not know what to do and she ended up appealing to her step-mother-in-law. There could have been no better person to turn to than Maria Theresia.

Once again Maria Theresia found herself trying to bring about the happiness of her family. She had supported Franz Ferdinand in his battle to marry Sophie Chotek. She had nursed Otto when all others kept away from him. And now here was Otto's son in love and unsure how to win the hand of the girl he had set his heart upon.

Maria Theresia knew exactly what to do. She arranged a hunting party for capercailzie. Stalking capercailzie during their mating season was the custom and since the birds hid deep in the forest the stalking had to be both silent and stealthy. Presumably in the stillness of a wooded glade Karl found the courage to speak his heart. And Zita admitted that, yes, Don Jaime had proposed to her and she had prevaricated. And she had been growing desperate because her mother was not going to let her hold off for ever. They walked back hand-in-hand.

You wonder whether Zita had been pushed into a corner and there was no way out other than to accept either Don Jaime or Archduke Karl but neither had sparked flashes of ecstasy through her heart. Karl was so nice and one day he would be Emperor. He was very sincere but just a touch earnest. When he spoke each word came out one after the other with a kind of heavy tread. He smiled at everyone and everyone liked him but he didn't spark excitement.

In June 1911 Karl travelled to the Italian coast where Maria Antonia, Zita's mother, and her children were enjoying their regular Italian break. Here on 13th June the engagement was officially announced and a special service in the family chapel was held to bless the newly-engaged pair.

It was noticed that Zita seemed rather shy and embarrassed; her manner had a nervous, birdlike flutter. When Karl presented her with the engagement ring she hurriedly slipped it into her pocket whispering almost inaudibly „*Danke vielmals!*" As they left the chapel Karl turned to his fiancée and said something that surprised her – "Now we must help each other reach heaven." She had always known that his religious beliefs went deep but this seemed somehow over-exalted.

When the news of their engagement broke it came as a huge surprise everywhere. On every side people were caught out by the announcement. The gossip and the newspaper articles all turned to an assessment of the new future Empress that rather went along the lines of 'she is not exactly beautiful... but so charming, so delightful, so tactful, biddable, courteous, considerate – and gives off hints of spirit and passion that speaks of the true Viennese sparkle.' „*eine echte süsse Madel; ein weanerisches Blut!*" Zita certainly looked the part that she was going to be called upon to play. There were hints of a resemblance to Elisabeth that lifted the spirits of the Viennese.

And then Karl returned to his military duties.

He also seems to have been concerned that Franz Ferdinand should have no reason to dislike the marriage he was entering into. In August 1911 he wrote to Franz Ferdinand, "I will continue to be true to you, as I always have been. Both you and Aunt have always been so kind to me." And after they had got married Karl wrote again an impetuous letter of warmth and gratitude. The letter was written in pencil on a train (for which Karl apologises) but he could not wait to send his thanks for everything Franz Ferdinand and Sophie had done for him, "especially for the very kind welcome which you gave my bride, and for your kindness and love." Karl went on to tell his uncle just how happy Franz Ferdinand had made him by approving the girl he had chosen to be his wife. And once again he reiterated his thanks: "I assure you again that I will do everything possible to come up to your expectations."

The wedding took place on 21st October 1911. It was an event to take the breath away from all who attended it. Monsignore Bisletti took the ceremony which was held in French. Zita looked out of this world in her ivory Satin Duchesse dress with its three-metre-long train embroidered with Bourbon lilies. Because her father could not lead her up the aisle it fell to Don Jaime to lead the bride to the altar. Just before he stepped away as they were approaching the altar steps, Zita turned and teasingly whispered that he had always wanted to lead her up the aisle and now he had got what he wanted. And then she turned her eyes to the waiting Karl. Zita was moved by intense emotion and more than once the spectators noticed tears in her eyes.

There was a small hitch over the rings. The moment came when Monsignore Bisletti looked round expecting to receive the rings to bless them. But nobody had the rings ready to pass to him and there was a moment of surreptitious fumbling as each member of the little group searched for them. A moment later a shamefaced smile appeared on Maria Josepha's face and she awkwardly reached over to her son and handed him the small red velvet étui that she had been clutching fervently without realising that it contained the rings. The awkward moment was passed and very few in the audience were aware that it had happened. But it had ruffled Zita's composure.

Then Monsignore Bisletti made his address to the bride and groom, this time in Italian, ending up with the blessing that "in the bitter hours that even these two blessed young people would not be spared they might find true support in their belief in God and comfort in a happy family life." The Monsignore then went on with the expected words of blessing for the newly-married pair, wishing them long lives and the hope that their children and children's children would reign over Austria far into the future.

This, of course, was painful for Franz Ferdinand. Franz Ferdinand was there that day but not Sophie. Karl would have liked Sophie to be there but that could not be.

Franz Joseph was also there looking unusually cheerful and relaxed. He had not looked so jovial for many years and nobody would ever see him looking so cheerful again. It was Franz Joseph who proposed the wedding toast with many references to Karl's father, Otto, whom Franz Joseph kept calling "my favourite nephew". He spoke of his confident hope that Karl and Zita would both find the happiness that they were destined to achieve. Destiny, of course, had rather different ideas but on that day there were no clouds of doubt.

Chapter 110

In the background overhanging Karl and Zita's wedding there was a shadow. It had emerged that two years earlier in 1909 Franz Ferdinand's youngest brother, Ferdinand Karl, had married in secret and without the Emperor's permission.

Bertha Czuber's father had disliked his daughter's attachment to the young Archduke every bit as much as Franz Joseph had been opposed to Franz Ferdinand's marrying Sophie. Only if Ferdinand Karl did the honourable thing and married his daughter would Professor Czuber allow her to go on seeing him. And Ferdinand Karl could see no way out of this dilemma. Just as his brother had insisted he could not live without the woman he loved, so Ferdinand Karl could not give up the woman he loved.

Underlying it all for Ferdinand Karl was something more – the feeling that he could not do the Habsburg thing. He did not really fit in. All those ceremonial occasions when they all came together to perform a majestic mummery in which human beings were turned into robotic figures in a pomp that was dehumanising. Ferdinand Karl's only wish was to have nothing to do with them. He cringed inside at the very thought of them. He must have thought that perhaps what he did was cowardly, but he could not act differently.

All of this was ironic, given Ferdinand Karl's bitter opposition to Franz Ferdinand's marriage back in 1899. Ferdinand Karl's opposition to Sophie had been so very implacable and then only a few months later he himself met Bertha Czuber at a popular ball in 1900 and fell in love with her, just at the time when the opposition to Franz Ferdinand was building up to its most intense. Suddenly everything had turned round but Ferdinand Karl could not bring himself to go back on his previous stance. His situation was all the worse because he had so angrily refused to have anything to do with Sophie. Yet he was marrying the daughter of a mere university professor, a young woman who would provoke even more outrage than Sophie Chotek. And when the secret marriage came out into the open in 1911, Ferdinand Karl was forced to crawl to the Emperor and beg his forgiveness.

What most shocked Franz Ferdinand was that his brother had lied to the Emperor. Franz Ferdinand did not feel like supporting Ferdinand Karl in his bid for forgiveness from Franz Joseph. And along with all the rest, Franz Ferdinand did not like Bertha herself at all. She was a commoner and one who, on top of everything else, had a 'past'. From the moment Franz Ferdinand came to know of her existence the thought that his brother would want to marry her had gnawed away at the back of his mind. In a letter to Max Vladimir Beck, Franz Ferdinand wrote that he feared his brother might lose his head and do the unforgiveable thing.

Just like his brother Ferdinand Karl turned to Maria Theresia to intercede for him but this time Franz Joseph refused to give way. Franz Joseph increasingly disliked Franz Ferdinand's marriage and increasingly he wished he had never given way over it. So now his intransigeance towards Ferdinand Karl was rock solid. Franz Joseph wrote to Franz Ferdinand a letter that revealed that what had shocked Franz Joseph most was that Ferdinand Karl had broken the promise he had made seven years earlier.

In the end Ferdinand Karl was stripped of all rank, titles, privileges and decorations and cast out of the Arch-house completely. He was forced to leave Austria as plain Herr Burg and he left to live in exile for the rest of his life. On only one occasion was he allowed back on to Austrian soil and that was to attend the last blessing for his assassinated brother in 1914. Ferdinand Karl died of tuberculosis a year later in 1915.

Thus, a third Archduke was forced out of the family and exiled from his homeland. It must have seemed to some that the cohesion of the Habsburg Arch-house was showing the first signs of cracking up. To men like Franz Joseph and Montenuovo this could not be allowed and the answer was to clamp down even harder upon any sign of independent thinking. Those who refused to abide by that had to be pushed as far away as possible, out of sight and out of mind. In comparison Karl's demeanour and loyalty to the Arch-house was all the more commendable.

Karl was now no longer able to maintain his role as an active soldier in the Imperial Army and in August 1912, ten months after his marriage, the newly-wed young couple returned to Vienna to make their permanent home there. And this drew them into a rather different life. They were expected far more than before to play up to their royal role.

Karl was content to place his trust in his uncle. Zita was not so sure. Zita felt doubts about their ever becoming Emperor and Empress. Supposing Sophie died before Franz Ferdinand? Franz Ferdinand could marry again and produce legitimate heirs. Darker thoughts turned to the possibility that, once Emperor, Franz Ferdinand might find some way of overturning the statute that prevented his own sons from inheriting the throne. Since nothing that Franz Ferdinand ever did or said suggested that he was envisaging such moves, and all his actions pointed to his preparing his sons for a quiet life far from the throne, this shows how deeply embedded was the thought amongst so many that Franz Ferdinand could not be trusted. An undercurrent of paranoia rippled throughout the court.

When Zita married Karl in 1911 Franz Ferdinand was just two months short of his forty-eighth birthday; he was now healthy, strong and vigorous and could be expected to live another twenty-five years, if not more. Zita could expect to live these years sidelined while Franz Ferdinand sat on the throne, but she expected to be very much in the public eye as Empress-to-be.

She may have told herself that this was all she wanted for both herself and her husband. And yet the whole question of whether Franz Ferdinand really would stick to his word or whether he would, as Emperor, seek to bring his own sons into the line of inheritance seems to have gone round and round in her mind. Zita was the sort of person who needed to know one way or the other but uncertainty rubbed her up the wrong way.

Zita felt pulled in different directions which made her uncomfortable. She chafed. If she was wholeheartedly for Franz Ferdinand and Sophie it felt awkward facing others who remained intransigently against them. When she heard the stories and gossip about Franz Ferdinand and Sophie she found herself wondering whether she shouldn't believe some of them.

Also she was beginning to find that although Karl always came across as so mild and easy-going, in reality he could not be pushed around. Karl never made any show of opposition but if he didn't agree he wouldn't budge an inch. Zita perhaps wanted him to be openly more vigorous and assertive towards others and a little more yielding with her.

In particular, where his uncle was concerned Karl would not give way. Karl's attachment to his uncle went back far and was deep-rooted. Over time Zita came to find that fact galling. Franz Ferdinand had too much influence over her Karl. She did not seem to have enough.

But then Zita, the girl who felt keenly that she was a descendent from the royal family of France, may have felt that in some way the throne was owed to her.

During the grand summer army manoeuvres Karl was thrown from his horse and badly hurt. Severely concussed, he was brought to Vienna for medical treatment.

By this time Zita was already expecting their first child and wanted to set about establishing a family home. The baby boy was born in the early hours of 20th November 1911 and he was named Otto after his grandfather. One newspaper report looked ahead optimistically to the day around the 1980s or 1990s when the Emperor Otto would sit on the throne of an Austrian Empire that had been in existence for centuries and had every reason to expect to continue for centuries more. Emperor Otto would have matured into a well-established and loved ruler, enjoying "calmer times". Little did they know.

Franz Ferdinand and Sophie[59] attended little Otto's christening. They arrived quietly and did not stay too long. It was not until after they had left that all the festivities to celebrate the new Prince really began – open-air concerts burst into music despite the cold and wind, there were mountain-top bonfires lighting the skies and torchlit processions through the chilly streets. Perhaps Franz Ferdinand glanced back to see the lights filling the dark November skies, but Sophie did not. She would have been thinking about that little baby. Her thoughts may then have turned to Zita. Sophie could not help but be aware of how different was Zita's welcome into the Imperial Family to her own rejection. Yet she would not have envied Zita her position.

For her part, Zita would have wanted to see brought to an end this whole game that surrounded Franz Ferdinand and Sophie – a game of smoke and mirrors, of pretending to do one thing while doing the exact opposite, of watching the couple as though they were sleep-walking to a waiting guillotine. Zita herself disliked playing the game. It made Zita feel uncomfortable seeing how her new uncle and his wife could not go to the theatre and sit in the same box together; they could not attend the races together, nor could they be seen in public places side-by-side.

Early on in their marriage Karl and Zita attended the theatre one evening. Franz Ferdinand and Sophie were there but in separate boxes. In the interval Zita rushed up to Sophie and warmly kissed her hand. When Zita came to recount the incident[60] she pointed out that she was still very young and she saw this as a courtesy due to an older woman.

Sophie was startled. She recoiled visibly as though she had been stung. Zita was astonished by her terrified expression.

Zita would always remember how she whispered imploringly, "Please – in public – never do that again!" It was just what the people wanting to make difficulties for her were looking out for, Sophie explained. Sophie looked around anxiously to see who had noticed. She admitted that she had even had letters threatening death after incidents like that. "Please never do that again!"

The last time Zita saw Franz Ferdinand alive was in May 1914 when she and Karl were invited to a family dinner at the Belvedere Palace. Franz

---

59 On her wedding day Sophie was given the title Princess, not a royal title within the Habsburg Monarchy. In 1909 the Emperor raised her rank again and Sophie was accorded the title Duchess of Hohenberg. As the Duchess of Hohenberg she was permitted to appear at more functions, such as this one.

60 From *Archduke of Sarajevo – the Romance and Tragedy of Franz Ferdinand of Austria* by Gordon Brooke-Shepherd, 1984. Gordon Brooke-Shepherd knew the former Empress Zita personally and she recounted this to him in 1976.

Ferdinand was due to attend the army's summer manoeuvres in Bosnia the following month and arrangements for his journey and stay in Bosnia were going apace. Franz Ferdinand was very uneasy about the whole project. He knew that the whole region was a hotbed of revolutionary thinking and reports and rumours of a possible assassination attempt had reached Vienna.

That evening, however, was relaxed and agreeable. Franz Ferdinand and Sophie were charming and Zita could see Karl enjoying himself more than he did in most other Habsburg settings. Sophie came out of herself more than usual. Some of her old wit and sparkle appeared.

It was with a warm smile that she excused herself for a few minutes while she took the children upstairs to bed. Little Ernst was sleepy and she bent over him with motherly warmth as she guided her small brood through the door.

Franz Ferdinand watched them, his face very still and impassive. There was a moment's silence as the door closed behind them and then Franz Ferdinand was suddenly galvanised.

"I must speak quickly," he said, "as I don't want your aunt to hear anything of this." Very steadily he went on to tell Karl that he would soon be murdered. He knew this. He indicated the desk. In it were papers which would be of great importance to Karl after his death. "When it happens," Franz Ferdinand said, "take them; they are for you."[61]

Was this a joke? No, Franz Ferdinand insisted he could not be more serious. And then Sophie reappeared and all three had to do their best to carry on as if nothing had happened.

But Karl and Zita were stunned and neither knew quite what to think. Surely, he was exaggerating the dangers. All royalty faced dangers but you didn't brood over them. Franz Ferdinand would return from Sarajevo. He would be full of grumbles about the heat, which he disliked, and the impossible lack of organisation which he disliked even more. Sophie would be full of descriptions of those strange eastern people they had seen and met there. She would talk with twinkling animation of the colours and sights and scents on the hot southern air. And both would delight their children with all their experiences. Perhaps even before Karl and Zita had reached their own home these were the thoughts that they reassured themselves with.

And life went on. Karl and Zita left Vienna for a summer break at the Villa Wartholz. Here life could not have been more relaxed. On warm, sunny days the young couple liked to take their midday lunch in a wooden summerhouse in the grounds.

---

[61] These accounts came from Zita towards the end of her life. She spoke openly to Gordon Brooke-Shepherd and he related it all in his book *The Last Empress*.

On one of those warm, sunny days the meal was a particularly long, drawn-out affair. Perhaps Zita was leaning back, letting the sun bathe her face with its rays. She paid little attention to the servant who approached. He had a telegramme from Baron Rumerskirch, Franz Ferdinand's aide-de-camp. Karl glanced at the sender's name and remarked lazily, "That's odd. Why him?" then he read out the message aloud. His face went white.

Karl and Zita hurried back to the house to find out whether this awful news could possibly be true.

Chapter 111

The spring in 1914 was brilliant, sunny and warm, unusually so, and it brought with it the promise of a hot, languid summer full of blue skies and heavy sunshine. That delicate green of fresh buds shimmered in a silken light. Perhaps sometimes it may have seemed to some, looking back with all the hindsight of what was to come, that the weather mockingly was showing the world just what it was about to throw away in a destructive bloodbath.

Franz Ferdinand was unusually restless that spring. Kaiser Wilhelm was due to visit in June – for that, house and garden had to appear at its best. The gardeners at Konopischt had rarely been as hard driven as they were during those weeks; they must have longed for the German Emperor's visit to be over and past so that some of the pressure on them might be lifted.

On 12th June at nine o'clock Franz Ferdinand, accompanied by his valet, Andreas Morsey, was at the station at Beneschau to greet Wilhelm. As the arrival of the train was announced Franz Ferdinand moved to pull on a pair of white gloves. He suddenly realised that he had brought with him two left-hand gloves and he turned to Morsey who quietly and discretely passed his own pair over to him. A smooth, unobtrusive little gesture. Then Franz Ferdinand turned his attention to the Kaiser.

Wilhelm stepped down from the train with a cheery, "*Na, Kinder*, here we are again!" Franz Ferdinand always expected Wilhelm's bluster but inside he may have felt a slight wince. He had to suppress a further wince when, having reached Konopischt, Wilhelm's two smooth-haired dachshunds, named Wadl and Hexl, escaped into the grounds. When the two dogs came back they were proudly carrying their trophy. They had hunted down and killed a pheasant. But this wasn't just any old pheasant. It was Franz Ferdinand's prized golden pheasant, a bird that was there for show only and enjoyed the freedom of the park without reason to fear for its life. It was the only golden pheasant in the park at Konopischt.

Wilhelm would have brushed the incident aside with a casual, thoughtless apology. Franz Ferdinand had to bite his lips.

When they reached the castle there was a further slight hitch causing lunch to be delayed. Wilhelm, because of his deformed arm had to have specially designed cutlery and this had somehow been packed away in the depths of his luggage where it was not easy to find. However, from the moment after the meal when Wilhelm and Franz Ferdinand were able to go out into the gardens, all ruffled feelings were forgotten. And come the evening, the two men spent an hour alone, the last time they were ever to do so.

There are many who are convinced that this meeting turned into a conference on military matters and what strategy would be needed for the impending war. For the previous ten years there had been much rumbling about war, so it would not have been unusual for talk to turn to war matters. If so, Franz Ferdinand's fierce determination to deflect all possibility of war would have come out. Wilhelm tended not to hear what he didn't want to hear. It would have been in character for Wilhelm to make grandiose pronouncements about the glories of war and Germany's foremost position on the battlefield. But it also would have been in character for Wilhelm then to do a complete U-turn and end up with pious statements about the importance of maintaining peace.

Wilhelm returned to Berlin on 13th June very pleased with himself. After war had been declared with Serbia, stories whirled around spreading the myth that Franz Ferdinand and Wilhelm had held a war conference with both eager to kick-start a new war as soon as possible. This was one of the little assumptions that soon became fact after Franz Ferdinand's death.

In fact, after Franz Ferdinand's death in Sarajevo there were many little details of his ordinary everyday activities that those who were around at the time would remember afterwards. Some would remember such details with poignant sorrow. Some would remember them with a numbed ultra-intense awareness of their significance. Some would build all sorts of assumptions upon these details and they would become heavily imbued with a significance that they would not have had if nothing had ever happened at Sarajevo. Those details fed into the myths about Franz Ferdinand that were soon flourishing on every side.

Out of these small details it has been suggested that Franz Ferdinand had a sense of impending doom, an impression that something terrible was going to happen. Franz Ferdinand did have a feeling of doom, but mostly because he disliked travel, he knew he would suffer in the heat and most of all because everything was so very badly organised. And Franz Ferdinand tended to have a sense of impending doom all the time. He had long taken it as a given that he would be assassinated one day and that if he was not assassinated then he would have been very lucky. Most of the time, although he could never quite eliminate the thought of assassination from his mind, 'one day' was nice and vague and hopefully far-off.

But for Andreas Morsey who accompanied his master to Sarajevo, that tiny incident with the gloves at Beneschau Station would later be imbued with significance. He took those same gloves to Sarajevo and he was wearing them as he cradled a dying Franz Ferdinand.

Franz Ferdinand, from when the trip to Sarajevo was first proposed, seemed to be unusually aware of possible dangers and a number of those around him heard him remark upon the risks. It has been suggested that he was in some way aware that he was going to his death in Sarajevo. Certainly, his words to Karl and Zita telling them that he knew he was going to be murdered point to that. What we do not know today is whether after the event Karl and Zita's memories of exactly what Franz Ferdinand said that evening may have been subsequently spiced up. Zita particularly had a dramatic streak and it would have been in character for her to slightly dramatise Franz Ferdinand's words.

Franz Ferdinand was a courageous man. He regarded the risk of assassination as one of the prices that men in his position had to accept and shrug off. There had been a number of instances within his own lifetime. The Italian King Umberto had been a victim of assassination in 1900, the Duke of Braganza in 1908, the Greek King in 1913. And, of course, soon after his marriage there had been the brutal murder of King Aleksandar and Queen Draga of Serbia – but people tended to brush that aside because Serbia was viewed as a dangerous and backward country.

In 1906 Franz Ferdinand saw an assassination attempt at first hand and it made a big mark in his mind. He was attending the wedding ceremonies of King Alfonso of Spain. As the newly-wed couple were returning from the church, from a third-floor window a Catalan anarchist named Mateu Morral threw down to them what appeared to be a bouquet of flowers. It hit a balcony below and then the bomb hidden amongst the blooms exploded violently. Down in the street a lady's head was blown off, a horse and its rider were killed and the front of the royal carriage was shattered. King Alfonso and his new bride, a grand-daughter of Queen Victoria, were shaken but not harmed, although Ena's wedding gown was drenched with blood.

King Alfonso showed a cool that impressed itself upon Franz Ferdinand. Alfonso whispered to the girl trembling and gasping for breath at his side, "Heads up! Don't appear afraid!" Not until they reached the palace could they begin to relax and Ena fell sobbing into Alfonso's arms. For Franz Ferdinand this was the first time he saw for himself all the aspects that were usually glossed over; he saw faces blanched by fear; he heard the screams and the whinnies of wounded horses; he saw close up the panic that went through the crowd. He was struck by the sight of a shocked young girl in a white dress bespattered with blood.

Sophie had accompanied him to Madrid but she was not there on the day of ceremonies itself. The events of that day marked both of them – Franz Ferdinand had come face to face with a very real assassination attempt; it must have come home to Sophie in a way that she had refused to dwell upon up until that moment that this was a threat that they, too, had to live with – and even more so once Franz Ferdinand became Emperor.

It is likely that from then on Sophie did try far more than before to be at her husband's side when he was on public duty and might face such a danger. In June 1914 she insisted upon being alongside Franz Ferdinand as much as she was allowed to do.

And if Franz Ferdinand had ever thought bullet-proof carriages and large escorts of police officers would preserve him, he only had to remember the death of Czar Alexander II of Russia in 1881. Alexander II, Russia's great reformer, saw a number of attempts upon his life. Finally, on 13th March 1881 he was returning to the palace, having made his regular visit to the Mihailovsky Manège for the military roll call. There were three assassins among the crowds that lined the streets. The first bomb wounded several people and killed one Cossack but only damaged the bullet-proof carriage which had been a gift from Napoleon III. The Czar climbed down from the carriage, shaken but unhurt, and he resisted his guards' attempts to hurry him away from the scene. A moment later the second bomb hit him.

Franz Ferdinand certainly refused to allow danger to limit his movements or his activities. Rather, he often chose to joke about the assassin's bullet. He once insisted that precautions were useless – why, out of that bush over there someone could bring him down at that very moment! "I whistle at all of that! ...If you let worry and caution take hold, living becomes paralysed. Fear is a dangerous business!" He found he could cope with the uncertainty and the danger more easily if he joked about it. Gallows humour. An inner tension that could be relieved by laughter, grim, gruff laughter which was anything but humorous.

There was one precaution he did take: he went to confession before any journey that might involve danger. "One must place one's trust in God," Franz Ferdinand said many times and perhaps confession made him feel somehow safer. Before he left for Sarajevo that June 1914 Franz Ferdinand spent so long in the chapel praying that his travelling companions feared he would miss his train.

Earlier he had had a few quiet words with Janaczek. Here were the keys to his private desk at the Belvedere Palace in Vienna. If anything should happen to him then Janaczek was to make sure that the keys reached the Archduke Karl. And he had a request: would Janaczek look after his children if anything should happen? Then Franz Ferdinand placed a gold watch in Janaczek's hands. It was as if he was tidying up the loose ends, Janaczek felt afterwards. In retrospect it was all so much more significant than it had seemed at the time.

When they got to the station there was a problem with Franz Ferdinand's imperial carriage on the train – one of the four axles was burnt out and unsafe so that another first-class carriage had to be found at the last minute. The kind of damage that had occurred to the imperial carriage was normally only likely to come about with old carriages that had not been maintained, neither of which could be said about any carriage designated for a member of the Imperial Family.

Franz Ferdinand drily commented as he waited for the necessary changes to be made, "Na, this journey is setting out to promise us some surprises." At such a moment Sophie at his side would almost instinctively put out her hand to touch his arm. But to Baron Morsey he said, "This is the way it starts," and he went on to say that from a problem with the railway carriage things would escalate into a murder attempt in Sarajevo and finally "if that does not kill me, there will be an explosion on board the *Viribus!*" Gallows humour!

But when Franz Ferdinand and Sophie got to Vienna their routes separated. The arrangements were that Franz Ferdinand and Sophie should have separate itineraries to Bosnia. Both left Chlumetz together and travelled by train to Vienna. From there Franz Ferdinand travelled by train to Trieste and then boarded the battleship *Viribus Unitis*. He sailed down the coast to Dalmatia. Sophie travelled in a separate train to Bosnia.

Just as the Trieste train began to pull out of the station, all the lights in Franz Ferdinand's carriage went out. The electricity system had failed and the Archduke found himself sitting in a dark carriage with only a few candles to light it.

"Like being in a tomb, isn't it?" he laughed loudly. It was a hollow sound.

In the shadows it is likely that those around could barely make out his expression. Afterwards, with hindsight, the memory would come back to them. When people came to look back they would remember these little incidents with a shiver and it must have come to seem that in those last weeks there hung in the air a certainty of disaster.

The fact was that Franz Ferdinand wished the trip to Sarajevo was over so that he could return home and take up his day-to-day life. It wasn't fear that made him reluctant. He may not have known himself how much he wanted it behind him but it was clear to Paul Nikitsch-Boulles that "the whole trip appalled him from the beginning".

In his book *Vor dem Sturm* Nikitsch-Boulles mentioned how shortly before their setting off he took a telephone call from Colonel Karl von Bardolff, who was on Franz Ferdinand's staff as Head of the Archduke's Military Chancery at the Belvedere Palace in Vienna. Full of apologies Bardolff had to explain that Franz Ferdinand's train departure would have to be brought forward by an hour if the Archduke was to reach Trieste in time. A little matter, but Franz Ferdinand was so wound up that he began cursing that if Bardolff kept on messing them around with irritations and difficulties then he would leave the whole matter of attending the army manoeuvres to Bardolff and have nothing more to do with them. What caught Nikitsch-Boulles' eye was the way Franz Ferdinand's hands twisted and twisted a handkerchief until the linen was torn. Franz Ferdinand's tension had infected Nikitsch-Boulles who increasingly could not take his eyes off the Archduke.

To Eisenmenger Franz Ferdinand confided how much he would have preferred it if the Emperor had sent someone else in his place. When Franz Joseph was brought down by a bout of bronchitis Franz Ferdinand sought permission to cancel his attending the manoeuvres in order to remain close to his uncle.

One thing that would have been at the back of Franz Ferdinand's mind was that only four years previously in May 1910 Franz Joseph himself had visited Sarajevo. The contrast between the concern shown for Franz Joseph's safety and the almost total lack of concern for his own safety now must have been foremost in Franz Ferdinand's mind.

Before Franz Joseph ever set off, Vienna had received warnings that there might be an assassination attempt. Consequently, during the three days the Emperor was in Sarajevo the most stringent security precautions were imposed and all possible suspects removed from the city. Soldiers lined the roads Franz Joseph travelled along and the crowds were infiltrated with more soldiers and policemen. Franz Joseph returned to Vienna safely.

But a few days later there was an assassination attempt on the life of the Governor of Sarajevo, Marijan Varešanin. The assassin, Bogdan Žerajić was a Bosnian Serb student in the Faculty of Law at the University of Zagreb. Žerajić's attempt on the life of Varešanin and his subsequent suicide when it failed made him a martyr to the growing number of young men in Bosnia who deeply opposed Austrian rule over them. Later Gavrilo Princip would be one of many who took inspiration from Žerajić. Gavrilo Princip began to visit Žerajić's grave, swearing to avenge him and to kill one of the oppressors of their people.

Now, four years later, Franz Ferdinand was getting nothing but conflicting advice. The Croat vice-president of the Bosnian government saw dangers on every side and urgently pressed Franz Ferdinand to stay away. The Serbian envoy to Vienna, Joca Jovanović, had sent a warning to the Austrian Finance Minister that it might be dangerous for Franz Ferdinand to go to Sarajevo. This warning was so vague that little attention was given to it. It is quite likely that it was never passed on to Franz Ferdinand and even if it had been, without more details and facts, Franz Ferdinand would have brushed it aside without wasting time over it.

The Governor of Bosnia, General Oskar Potiorek, was so determined that Franz Ferdinand should come to Sarajevo that he could not even consider any possible impediment, and he breezily brushed away all the objections that were raised. Potiorek was a man driven by a compulsive ambitious force. There had been a moment a number of years earlier when his name was put forward as a candidate for the position of Chief of the Imperial Staff which would have made him Franz Joseph's righthand man. Franz Ferdinand's reply to this suggestion was a terse "Out of the question". This may well not have reached Potiorek's ears but it is likely that he was aware that he did not stand in good stead with Franz Ferdinand.

But Franz Ferdinand was not a man lightly swayed by others pressing him to do this or that. Soon after the proposals to hold army manoeuvres in Bosnia had been put forward he had agreed that he would be present at those manoeuvres. He did not like going back on his word.

He was well aware that ill-feeling towards all Habsburgs was welling up both in Bosnia and in neighbouring Serbia and he expected anti-Habsburg political demonstrations in Sarajevo. It is possible that some of the subversive literature circulating in Bosnia had been kept from him but he was under no illusions about the extent to which his presence would inflame the feelings of some of the young hotheads there. In one pamphlet Sophie was described as 'a monstrous Bohemian whore' and Franz Ferdinand was referred to as an ogre. As far as possible Franz Ferdinand's entourage would have tried to keep such cruel remarks from him.

As the date drew nearer feelings of reluctance tormented Franz Ferdinand but the reasons for his reluctance had little to do with the subversive literature. Within a few weeks of the manoeuvres Franz Ferdinand decided to approach the Emperor and see if the whole exercise could be called off. On 7th June 1914 he had an audience with Franz Joseph. Here he sought to get out of going on account of the great heat to be expected in the Bosnian valleys at that time of year.

Franz Ferdinand tolerated heat, especially humid heat, very badly. He suffered from asthma and he dreaded an attack of breathlessness. Even after so many years since he had been declared cured of tuberculosis, he continued to try to avoid putting a strain upon his weakened lungs. Certain areas he would be called upon to travel through whilst on these manoeuvres were infested with malaria – a request not to take the risk of becoming infected would have been entirely justified. For health reasons he felt he could withdraw without loss of honour.

Franz Joseph indicated that the final decision lay with Franz Ferdinand but he also made it perfectly clear that he wished his nephew to attend the army manoeuvres. This amounted to an order. Not surprising, then, that Franz Ferdinand dealt with each mishap with a morose quip.

Sophie, too, was wracked with dread. She once said to her priest that if her husband was risking his life her place had to be at his side. About this particular trip she said it was dangerous and she would not allow the Archduke to face it alone. Sophie struggled to hide her growing apprehension. Fear gnawed away inside her during those weeks before they set off.

Chapter 112

However, from then on everything seemed to run according to plan. When Franz Ferdinand arrived in Mostar for the first formal ceremonies on 25th June he was in high spirits. At half past eight in the morning he was greeted with a flowery speech welcoming him to the capital of Herzegovina and assured of the "faith and loyalty" of the people. Franz Ferdinand beamed and attempted a sentence in Serbo-Croat which he had been practising relentlessly for some time. The crowd loved it and roared their delight at his mispronunciation.

From Mostar he travelled to Bad Ilidže, arriving in the early afternoon. Sophie was already there, eager to see him. She had arrived quietly accompanied by Baron Morsey, Baron Rumerskirch and her lady-in-waiting, Countess Vilma Lanjus von Wallenburg. In the time between her arrival and that of Franz Ferdinand Sophie sent their son, Max, a telegramme to reassure the children that she was safe and sound and the journey had gone very well.

Sophie was on the steps of the hotel awaiting Franz Ferdinand when his car came to a halt, eager to embrace him. After Franz Ferdinand had joined her the first thing he did was send another telegramme to Pinki who, with her two brothers, were staying at Chlumetz. Franz Ferdinand's and Sophie's plan was to return to Chlumetz after they left Sarajevo, sweep up their children and head off on holiday – probably to Switzerland. They often went to Switzerland on holiday.

Pinki would have been expecting that telegramme but that would not have dented her joy when she got it: "Safely arrived and found Mama very well. Very beautiful and pleasant here. Our quarters are splendid. Weather nice. Fondest embraces to you and your brothers." Franz Ferdinand sent another telegramme to Pinki first thing on the last morning before he and Sophie set off for Sarajevo. Again he assured his daughter that everything was going well for 'Papi' and 'Mami' and told her how much he looked forward to getting back to Chlumetz to be with them all again. It was the last thing she would ever hear from her father.

Having sent his telegramme Franz Ferdinand suggested that he and Sophie should go for a drive. His idea was that they should go to Sarajevo and visit the old Turkish market. He was interested in visiting a particular oriental store in the Bas Carsija which belonged to the man who had furnished their hotel in Ilidže, Elias Kabiljo. That was where they headed.

Relaxed and happy to be together, Franz Ferdinand and Sophie pottered through the store, admiring the brightly-coloured motley of goods. Exotically crafted gold and silverwork was on display. Linens, silks and carpets were arrayed, a mass of brilliant colours. Carved and finely-worked furniture inset with mother-of-pearl decoration and old antique weapons jostled alongside. A crowd soon surrounded them, curious and fascinated to find themselves so close to the Austrian heir to the throne. It was astounding to them to see him wandering around, interested in everything that was on display, just like any other person. There were shouts of *"Zivio"* ('Long may you live').

Paul Nikitsch-Boulles stood tense and jittery nearby. He could not make out any police protection in that crowd. True, the faces surrounding his master were open and welcoming, but...

Franz Ferdinand and Sophie bought a few things that caught their eye; Franz Ferdinand wanted to take some carpets back to Konopischt while Sophie studied with care and delight some embroidered pieces and oriental jewellery, buying a few, before turning her attention to gifts to be taken back for the children. And all the while they treated the crowd that gawped at them and pressed in upon them with genial smiles and gentle appreciation.

Little did they know that, by pure chance, in that crowd glowered Gavrilo Princip, the boy who was set upon killing them, who had sworn to avenge Bogdan Žerajić. He had a pistol in a pocket and he could have killed Franz Ferdinand there and then – but he made no move to do so. His excuse to his friends later that evening was that there was a policeman nearby, but when he was interrogated a week later he said he hung back because he had not wished to harm Sophie. No one knows whether either excuse was true or whether there was something else that held him back. It may have been that there wandering through the shop Gavrilo Princip saw Franz Ferdinand and Sophie as ordinary people rather than as an ogre and a Bohemian sow.

Nedeljko Čabrinović, another conspirator who was well known to the police, was also there in that crowd. A policeman saw him and recognised him. The policeman went after him, but Nedeljko Čabrinović escaped into the night. The policeman then telephoned police headquarters in Sarajevo to report that Čabrinović had been seen stalking the Archduke. However, that warning was brushed aside because the man who took the phone call assumed that the Čabrinović referred to was Nedeljko's father. Nedeljko's father had opened a café in Sarajevo and for this he had required a permit. The Austrian police had refused to give him the necessary permit unless he acted as an informant for them. The older Čabrinović was an unwilling informant and there is little evidence he did much for the Austrian police. More likely, the little he did for the Austrian police only exacerbated his son's resentment against Austria.

The army manoeuvres in the Bosnian hills went well. The heat had not been either as intense or as clammy and humid as Franz Ferdinand had feared. The mock battle was entirely successful. Franz Ferdinand was grateful for the fact that it had all gone so well and he readily told the troop commanders how pleased he was with the day's efforts. He also assured them that he would have nothing but praise when he reported back to the Emperor, which he did in a telegramme to Franz Joseph that same evening.

Towards the end of the manoeuvres a figure leapt out of some bushes with what looked like a long black tube directed straight at Franz Ferdinand. Various officers immediately grabbed the intruder. Franz Ferdinand turned to find out what the kerfuffle was all about and then, when he recognised the man, burst out in a throaty laugh. He then called to the officers to let the man go. "That's the court photographer. He's only doing his job. A man has to live!"

It was a jovial Franz Ferdinand who returned afterwards to the hotel in Ilidže where Sophie awaited him. Her quick eyes would have picked up his good humour and she would have felt pleased for him. Sophie, too, was tired. She had spent the two days Franz Ferdinand had been attending army manoeuvres seeing the sights of Sarajevo. She had been to the Great Mosque, the carpet factory that Sarajevo was famous for and she had visited a number of different schools and distributed generous sums of money to them which came from Franz Ferdinand's private purse. Both of them had done what they could to honour Bosnia and show its people how important Bosnia was to them.

And now it was almost over – they would be home tomorrow. They must have sat down to dinner that evening tired but relaxed and looking forward to seeing the children as soon as they got back.

Sophie lightly reproved Bosnia's president, Dr. Josip Sunarić, for his pessimism. Now that it had all gone so well she felt she could say that wherever they went they were welcomed, and even the Serb people had greeted them with such heartfelt warmth. And it all touched and pleased them so much. Clearly, Sunarić was not entirely convinced. He turned to Sophie with a dark face and replied, "Your Majesty, I pray to God that tomorrow evening when I have the honour to see you again, you will repeat those words to me. A stone would be lifted from my heart, a very large stone." Perhaps Sophie thought, "and a stone would be lifted from my heart, too." But she didn't say it.

They very nearly changed their plans and wound up the trip that evening. A number of the officers were leaving and Baron Rumerskirch, the head of Franz Ferdinand's household, suggested that it would be a good idea if they all returned to Austria in the morning, giving the visit to Sarajevo itself a miss. After all, they had completed what they came to do and all had gone well. Rumerskirch pressed the point that there was a danger of hostile demonstrations in Sarajevo. Franz Ferdinand's expression revealed his feeling of relief and his personal eagerness to go along with Rumerskirch's proposal.

Immediately, the officers on General Potiorek's staff were disconcerted by this turn. Erik von Merizzi, General Potiorek's adjutant, argued forcefully that if the Archduke left a day early it would cause enormous offence amongst the population. So Franz Ferdinand backed down and agreed to remain. And then Franz Ferdinand pushed back his chair. Glasses were refilled and the company sat late into the night discussing the day's events. The cognac flowed freely and Franz Ferdinand mellowed.

The following morning, in full dress uniform as General of Cavalry, Franz Ferdinand with Sophie at his side set off to drive through the streets of Sarajevo to the Town Hall where the governor of the city would welcome them. In the crowds that lined the streets were six would-be assassins. If all six fanatics had stuck to their plans, shots would have rung out from six pistols, six bombs should have been thrown at the passing cavalcade and the six excited young men should have swallowed their cyanide pills, dying at the scene of their attack.

But from the moment their vengeful attack had been first conceived everything had been a chaotic mish-mash of bungling. At every turn the plans of the conspirators ought to have stumbled and they should have been prevented from carrying through their intentions. The six conspirators who lined the route the Archduke's cavalcade would take must have been very nearly the most disorganised and the most inept group of assassins that ever came together. The greatest mystery remains that they succeeded at all.

The powers in Belgrade who wanted to foment rebellion nevertheless never had much confidence that Gavrilo Princip and his companions were capable of achieving very much and their support had been spasmodic and minimal. It would have only needed the smallest thing to have prevented Gavrilo Princip and his friends, Nedeljko Čabrinović and Trifko Gravez, from reaching Sarajevo. It would only have needed the smallest thing to have brought about the discovery of their activities and the weapons they had brought with them from Belgrade. It would only have needed the smallest thing to put paid to their attempts on the life of Franz Ferdinand and Sophie.

Yet, in spite of the bungling, as the cars passed, Nedeljko Čabrinović managed to throw his bomb. It bounced off the hood of the Archduke's car and landed in the gutter. The car drove on. On the ground the bomb lay smoking for several seconds and then exploded. It was the car behind Franz Ferdinand's which took the blast. And it was Erik von Merizzi who was badly hurt. He was helped to a nearby doctor's surgery where his wounds were bandaged and then taken to the local hospital.

The conspirators scattered, terrified. Nedeljko Čabrinović leapt into the River Miljacka and there tried to swallow his cyanide powder. He failed, spilling most of the powder in the muddy waters of the river and was dragged from the water by several shocked gendarmes who had suddenly realised what was happening.

The whole cavalcade was utterly disrupted. The damaged car had to be removed and its other unharmed occupants found places in the cars behind. This would have been a perfect moment for the other conspirators to throw their bombs or shoot the Archduke. Instead, they scuttled away.

The Mayor was in the first car in the convoy. This car was driven on ahead hurriedly so that the Mayor was there on the steps of the Town Hall ready to extend a formal welcome to the Archduke when he arrived. The Mayor heard the explosion but he assumed that it was a salvo of welcome from a nearby artillery regiment. He reached the Town Hall not knowing that the sound he had heard had been the explosion of a bomb.

Franz Ferdinand may well have believed that he had risen above fears of assassination attempts but that bomb that exploded only feet away from him must have shaken him to his core. Perhaps as his car raced away from the scene he could feel his blood pulsing in his temples. His mind may even have flashed back to Rudolf and his not-always-successfully suppressed nerves. Or maybe he suddenly saw with strange vividness the scene in Madrid when a bouquet of flowers containing a bomb was thrown at King Alfonso and his new bride. But more important for him at that moment than anything else had to be Sophie. He could feel her at his side trembling slightly.

When they got to the Town Hall, still shaking, the Mayor stepped forward from the little reception committee and launched straight into his well-prepared unctuous speech totally unaware of what had happened. "Your Imperial and Royal Highness, we are carried away in our hearts by your gracious visit..."

But the Mayor was not allowed to continue. Franz Ferdinand burst in with his anger. A bomb had been thrown at him, he protested – it was scandalous! Then he caught his breath and, rather calmer, added "Now you can carry on with your speech!"

So little care had gone into ensuring Franz Ferdinand's safety while he and Sophie were in Sarajevo.

General Potiorek, Governor of Bosnia, had all along insisted that the full responsibility for all the arrangements for the Archduke's visit should be his and not Vienna's. But he had done nothing. None of the young hotheads who could reasonably be expected to make trouble had been kept away from Sarajevo. No extra police had been brought into the city. Only the normal day-to-day deployment of police officers were there on the streets of Sarajevo that day. No attempt to keep the crowds back from the Archduke was made.

The story of how Franz Ferdinand's assassins – young, ill-trained, unprepared boys – got from Belgrade to Sarajevo is a long catalogue of bungles, any one of which should have resulted in their being apprehended and prevented from carrying through their murderous plot. And even after Nedeljko Čabrinović had thrown his bomb and been dragged off to the police station, so very, very little was done to increase protection for the Archduke.

There was a force of some two hundred and fifty soldiers in Sarajevo itself who could have been quickly brought out on to the streets. No one seems to have thought of calling them out, although Major Höger, an officer on General Potiorek's staff, insisted afterwards that he had pressed for the military to be called upon to clear the streets before Franz Ferdinand left the Town Hall. No move was made to clear away the crowds, or even hold them well back from the Archduke's person. Within the Town Hall they took the reassuring view that the worst that could happen had happened and they could now all relax. As a result, all that was done was to suggest that they take a different route than the one originally planned.

Franz Ferdinand himself seems to have been strangely indifferent to his fate at that moment. His gallows humour had not deserted him. He was heard to mutter caustically that, with true Austrian *schlamperei* (muddle), the man who had thrown a bomb at the head of the heir to the throne would be honoured with some important and meaningless decoration and "perhaps end up as a Privy Councillor". He was also heard to say in his grim sarcastic way that it was likely they might get a few more pot shots that day. Had it hit home to him that he could one day feel an assassin's bullet? He pressed Sophie to stay behind and not drive through the streets of Sarajevo at his side. Her reply was simple: she would not leave him – 'where you are I go.'

Yet he was determined to go out to that car and drive back through the streets of Sarajevo, making a detour to the hospital to visit Erik von Merizzi and find out how he was. He was equally determined that Sophie should not go with him in spite of her earlier insistence that her place was beside him. He sent Baron Morsey up to the room where Sophie was receiving some of the Turkish ladies of the town. His orders were that Baron Morsey should accompany Sophie back to Bad Ilidže in a different car.

Sophie would have stiffened. She was there not for self-aggrandisement but because she had to be with her husband when he was showing himself in dangerous situations. Once again she insisted that she would not leave his side. She was adamant. It would be surprising if her heart were not thumping at that moment. No doubt, she and Franzi had privately talked about the risks that they took and when they did Sophie would remember Franzi's description of the attempt on the life of King Alfonso in Madrid. They would have agreed between them that together they would face what life threw at them. Both were strongly religious and they would have found strength in their belief. And perhaps with that they would have put the thought of danger aside.

But that day it would have hit home to them both that nothing really prepares you the first time for personal danger.

In almost every book about Franz Ferdinand a particular photograph appears. Franz Ferdinand and Sophie are walking down the steps of Sarajevo Town Hall. There is a space around them; they look isolated and exposed. Those few steps must have taken courage. They are about to settle into the open car that would take them back to the station. They look anything but heroic. This is a picture of two middle-aged people feeling the strain and the tension, crumpled and wearied by the blazing heat. The expression on Sophie's face can barely be made out; Franz Ferdinand's face is completely lost in a dark shadow. Both must have been longing to get through the day. Surely their thoughts had already turned to the three children waiting for them at home?

Colonel Bardolff went out to give Sarajevo's Chief of Police, Dr. Gerde, the altered plan for their route back through the town. Bardolff was heard emphatically telling Gerde the changes that had been agreed. Witnesses to this were never sure how much Dr. Gerde had really been paying attention but the police chief did acknowledge the instructions and then hurried out to pass them on to the drivers. However, the driver of the car in front of Franz Ferdinand's was not informed of the changes, and when the cavalcade set off he was still under the illusion that the route was the original one.

Once again the convoy of cars proceeded down the Appel Quay along the river bank. They passed the third conspirator from Belgrade, Trifko Grabez, who was still armed with both his bomb and his fully-loaded pistol. Grabez made no move to attack the Archduke. Later he would insist that he was only carrying the bomb for his friend Ilić but he had wanted to use the pistol, only the safety catch was on so he could not.

Then at the point where it had been agreed that the convoy should continue straight on, the car in front of Franz Ferdinand's slowed and prepared to turn right according to the original plan. The driver of Franz Ferdinand's car followed. General Potiorek shouted out to the driver and told him to reverse back on to the Appel Quay. So the car came to a stop. There was a grumbling of gears. And at that moment Franz Ferdinand was a sitting duck.

It was chance yet again that made it possible for Gavrilo Princip to fire his shots. He was not expecting to have that opportunity. He believed that the morning's attempt had ruined all their plans. Somewhat disconsolate, Princip crossed the road and as the cars showed to a halt he was standing on the very corner that Franz Ferdinand's car had been turning into. Princip raised his arm and looked away and he may even have closed his eyes at that moment. Eyewitnesses later confirmed that he was not actually looking at his victims at the moment when he pulled the trigger.

Two shots rang out. The first hit Franz Ferdinand in the neck. The bullet entered Franz Ferdinand just above his collarbone and pierced the jugular vein, ending up lodged in one of his neck vertebrae.

With his second shot Gavrilo Princip hoped to kill General Oskar Potiorek but a bystander, seeing what was happening, knocked into Gavrilo Princip and the bullet hit Sophie in the stomach instead. This resulted in massive internal bleeding. Sophie lurched forward and slid off the seat on to the floor of the car with her face pressed to Franz Ferdinand's knees. She is supposed to have cried out, "In Heaven's name, what has happened to you?" A stream of blood began to flow from Franz Ferdinand's mouth and all immediate attention was turned upon him.

Count Harrach, who was riding on the footplate, saw more than anyone else what was happening in the car. Count Harrach did not realise that Sophie had been hit and when he saw a thin stream of blood flowing from Franz Ferdinand's mouth Count Harrach ceased to be concerned with Sophie.

Count Harrach famously reported Franz Ferdinand's last words. "Sopherl, Sopherl, don't die. Stay for our children!" And when he asked Franz Ferdinand if he was in great pain he got the distinct answer "It's nothing," which Franz Ferdinand repeated several times more as he slowly lost consciousness.

Certainly, if Franz Ferdinand was able to speak, these words ring true. But many doctors have since argued that the bullet had severed Franz Ferdinand's neck artery which would have made it impossible for him to say anything at all. The full force of arterial blood would have filled his mouth and throat and he would have lost consciousness very quickly as his blood pressure plummeted.

Neither Franz Ferdinand nor Sophie regained consciousness; both were dead before help could have reached them.

Chapter 113

There had been many occasions when Franz Ferdinand had remarked how glad he was that he had stuck to his guns and married the woman he loved. Before setting off for Sarajevo he had pondered how often one does things in life that you look back to in later years and think how you would act differently if you were faced with them again – but "if I had to marry again I would do exactly the same in every way as I did". And Sophie, too, had never had any doubts about marrying him. To one of her ladies-in-waiting who accompanied her to Sarajevo she remarked that on 1st July it would be exactly fourteen years since she and Franz Ferdinand had got married. She wished she could live each and every day over again.

Reactions in Vienna to the news of the Archduke's death could not have been more different to the reactions that had greeted Rudolf's death twenty-five years before. A second heir to the throne had died a brutal death, leaving a very old man on the throne. You would have expected a much more shocked reaction than came about when the news broke.

On Monday 29th June 1914 the diarist Joseph Redlich wrote "No mood of mourning in the city... music everywhere."

It was the sudden silencing of the music which startled the Viennese from their activities and made them realise that something serious had happened. Yet even as the news rippled through it interrupted little. There was no special shock or dismay on the faces of the crowd. The day was too hot, the air too sultry. Franz Ferdinand had not been liked and for a great many in Vienna that day the immediate thought was that now they had the popular Archduke Karl as the next heir to the throne – so everything would be alright.

Baron Morsey turned to Sophie's lady-in-waiting, Countess Vilma Lanjus von Wallenburg, to decide how to break the appalling news to the various members of Sophie's immediate family. Telegrammes were sent to Sophie's brothers and sisters. Her brother, Wolfgang, was in Karlsbad at the racecourse when the telegramme was handed to him. He was so shocked by the news he fainted to the ground.

Baron Morsey also succeeded in telephoning Sophie's sister, Henriette, who was in Prague. Before Henriette had had time to collect her thoughts there was another phone call for her, this time it was Dr. Stanowsky,[62] the

---

[62] It is not clear whether Henriette received the call from Baron Morsey first and the call from Stanowsky second or whether it was the other way round.

children's tutor, begging her to come to Chlumetz as soon as she possibly could. The children needed her support and comfort. But Baron Morsey did not want Henriette to actually tell the children of their father's death.

Baron Morsey and Vilma Lanjus finally agreed to enrol the services of Dr. Stanowsky in breaking the news to the children. It is interesting that they felt that it needed to be a male figure to break the news to the children rather than their Aunt Henriette. The telegramme to Dr. Stanowsky begged him to tell the "poor dear children as gently as possible" that "the exalted personages have fallen victims to the brutal hands of a murderer".

Dr. Stanowsky knew how excitedly the three children were waiting to see their parents. He knew that they had spent the time at Chlumetz preparing a small theatrical piece, a tableau, to welcome Franz Ferdinand and Sophie when they arrived. He had watched them moving furniture around, preparing costumes for their parts, even bossing each other around in their determination to get it right. Dr. Stanowsky could not think how to break such news to them.

Sophie, the eldest, was now almost thirteen years old. She was just reaching an age where she was increasingly aware of her parents as individuals. She was growing conscious of how her mother juggled the difficulties of her position. Her father and mother had never talked very much with their children about their whole situation. It cannot be known whether they ever intended to do so – when the children were old enough to understand – but in all likelihood they probably did not intend to do so. But just because her parents drew a curtain over the more difficult aspects of their lives did not mean that a child like Sophie was not very much aware of them.

Sophie had been working things out for herself. She had begun to understand what all those unspoken things all meant. She had also begun to form her own views and feelings about them. She was beginning to feel drawn into a conspiracy with her parents, a conspiracy that gave her an understanding of how they in the Hohenberg family behaved. Henceforth she would need that understanding. Henceforth, in the secret depths of her mind, she would constantly refer to her parents for guidance as to how a Hohenberg behaved and she would guide her younger brothers, too.

At lunch that Sunday Sophie was slightly surprised when Dr. Stanowsky was called away to take a telephone call. Her immediate thought was that it had to do with his mother who happened to be ill. As a result when he returned to the table looking stunned and shaken, she assumed that he had received bad news about his mother. He sat down again at the table white-faced and said nothing. The children were too well brought up to ask.

By the middle of the afternoon their Aunt Henriette unexpectedly arrived at the castle. The children ran out to greet her eagerly but were shocked to see tears in her eyes. As soon as she could Henriette took the children aside away from any observers and told them straight-forwardly that there had been an attack on their parents at Sarajevo. She told them, too, that Franz Ferdinand and Sophie were both injured but she could not bring herself to tell them that they were dead.

Immediately little Sophie exclaimed that they had to visit her parents in hospital. Henriette restrained them. Did she assure them that as soon as it was possible they would see their parents? But she still could not pronounce the word 'death'. Instead, she told them that they should all go to the small local church where they could pray.

We can picture them going into the old quiet stone building, out of the hot sunshine into the shady coolness filled with centuries of prayer. Here the three children would have begged a kind Lord to save their parents and bring them home safe to them. They still did not know what exactly had happened. But they must have been picking up all the signs of shock and pain in their Aunt Henriette. As they floundered in uncertainty their anxiety must have been growing by the minute.

The idea of praying had come from Baron Morsey. He knew that at half past five that afternoon there was to be a service in Sarajevo for the victims of the assassination. In Sarajevo prayers were being intoned for the souls of Franz Ferdinand and Sophie while in the village church near Chlumetz a little girl and her two brothers prayed for their recovery.

Years later Sophie would remember how they had let the children pass the night still not knowing and largely unable to sleep. It was not until early next morning that they learned the truth. Dr. Stanowsky broke the terrible news to the two boys. Max went berserk with grief. Sophie learned the truth from her uncle, Count Karl von Wuthenau, who, with other members of Sophie's family had travelled through the night to Chlumetz to be with the children.

"The anguish was indescribable, and also the feeling of total bewilderment," remembered Sophie. Suddenly, they could not imagine what would now become of them. Nothing of the future can have been clear to them. They were lost and felt totally at sea.

Quite possibly there was something else that Sophie would remember. From that moment on she stopped being Pinki. That was a family name, used when the whole family had been gathered together at Konopischt.

The following day the children were taken to Vienna where their step-grandmother, Maria Theresia, awaited them. From the station they drove to the Belvedere Palace; the road they drove along was lined with schoolchildren standing in silent sympathy as the carriage passed. Here they waited, knowing that over at the Hofburg lay their parents' coffins in the court chapel. But the court for them was a no-go area.

The most vindictive gesture of all was Montenuovo's excluding Franz Ferdinand's children from the very few funeral ceremonies accorded their father and mother.

Chapter 114

A massive thunderstorm ended the summer sultriness. Like some kind of Wagnerian ceremony of Valhalla, in the dark hours of night it would seem as though the elements were trying to obliterate the Archduke and his lady-in-waiting wife. A kind of last vindictive gesture from Montenuovo.

Even in death Montenuovo could not allow these two the smallest iota of dignity if he could prevent it. His initial plan was for Franz Ferdinand's coffin only to be brought to Vienna for the lying-in-state, while Sophie's would be hurried away to Artstetten Castle where she would be buried. But Montenuovo had reckoned without Maria Theresia and Archduke Karl. Montenuovo received direct orders from the Emperor for both coffins to be brought back to Vienna.

The train carrying the two coffins arrived in Vienna after night had fallen. A dim but full moon hung still in the warm night sky, creating an eerie light. Montenuovo had wanted there to be only a few officials at the station to oversee the transport of the coffins from the station to the Hofburg Chapel. But again he reckoned without Archduke Karl who was determined to be there for his uncle and with him came a large crowd of mourners.

The following morning there was a shockingly short lying-in-state and everything was done to restrict the number of people able to pay their last respects. In the afternoon there was a short funeral Mass which lasted no more than a quarter of an hour. The traditional hymns and the usual prayers had been cut from the service. Franz Joseph was there but few other members of the Imperial Family.

Paul Nikitsch-Boulles, Franz Ferdinand's secretary, watched Franz Joseph closely throughout the short ceremony. He later described how Franz Joseph's stony expression revealed not the smallest hint of feeling. No sorrow, no grief there. Rather an overwhelming indifference. The Emperor's frozen demeanour made an unforgettable impression upon Paul. It seemed to Paul that Franz Joseph's haughty expression was what he might have worn to face some underling upon some matter-of-fact, day-to-day affair. Paul slowly came to the feeling that Franz Joseph viewed the proceedings with a sense of relief. Franz Joseph could breathe more easily as though a fraught and turbulent dream had faded away and could now be forgotten.

When the service came to an end, Paul described how Franz Joseph left the chapel in his typical hurried way. Franz Joseph never looked back, never cast a glance at the remains of his nephew, never even tilted his head in their direction. For him it was a perfunctory procedure.

Various foreign royal families sent wreaths and so had Stéphanie – she was the only member[63] of the Imperial Family to offer a symbol of her grief and sorrow. Franz Ferdinand and Sophie's three children had also sent flowers – a wreath of white roses and a ribbon inscribed "Sophie, Max, Ernst" – but they themselves were not allowed to be there. As the children of a morganatic marriage they were not deemed worthy to be present in the same chapel as the Emperor. Sophie's brother, Wolfgang, was also prevented from being present. Only after the Emperor had left the chapel were the children allowed in to see their parents' coffins.

Paul Nikitsch-Boulles was enraged over Montenuovo's edicts with respect to which officers, which regiments, what troops should be present to honour the dead Archduke. What particularly incensed Paul Nikitsch-Boulles was the fact that Montenuovo – a mere 'functionary' – should be ordering around the army, especially given that the Archduke had been the chief of the army and second only to the Emperor in authority over the army.

However, here again Montenuovo did not call all the shots. Montenuovo had ordered that the officer corps should be forbidden to salute the funeral cortège on its way from the Hofburg Chapel to the station, but this provoked an outrage. According to Paul's memoirs, he was overruled by Count Ernst Rüdiger von Starhemberg who brusquely informed Montenuovo that nobody was going to stand in his way when he paid his last respects to the Archduke.

"And if it came to it, I would rather resign from my position in the Emperor's household than lower myself to be the blind puppet of a Montenuovo!"

Von Starhemberg then led a large contingent of army officers and aristocrats of the highest order to make up the cortège that accompanied the hearses, again after dusk had fallen, through Vienna to the West Terminus Station where they were put on the train for Pöchlarn.

This was the nearest station to Artstetten which was where they were to be interred. Montenuovo considered his job done when the coffins reached the station and from then on he washed his hands of all further arrangements. Paul Nikitsch-Boulles quoted his words: "I will take charge of the bodies as far as the station, get them into the train, and once the train has moved off, you can do with them whatever you like!" Montenuovo also wiped his hands of the cost of transport to Artstetten – that, in his opinion, fell to Sophie, Max and Ernst to pay. Again, protests to the Emperor ended up with Montenuovo settling the bills. (Thus, when AVD in the *New York Times* set about counter-attacking insinuations that Montenuovo had acted with spite and prejudice against the murdered Archduke and his morganatic

---

[63] Strictly speaking Stéphanie was only an ex-member of the Imperial Family. You wonder whether she would have been allowed to send a wreath if she had still been a Habsburg.

consort, it is unlikely that he convinced anyone who had actually been there at the funeral ceremonies.)

In the decades since, many books describing the unfolding of those events have emphasised how paltry and undignified were the procedures. They often imply that it is only with hindsight that such a view has come about. But there were at the time many rumblings of complaint. There was resentment too, and indignation and anger. Representatives of other European royal families were deliberately kept away, which caused in many cases bad feelings and offence, all the more so because most of those other European royal families had been prevented from attending Rudolf's funeral.

Margutti remembered afterwards how there had been uncomplimentary comments, not just directed at Montenuovo but also hinting at the Emperor's lack of respect towards his own nephew. Many journalists, particularly foreign journalists reported the ill-feeling. One French journalist commented upon the ripples of indignation in Vienna and went on to say that the ostracism faced by the Duchess during her life was all the more disgraceful and disrespectful in death. The view spread that the Imperial Family had no respect, not even for the dead. The Archduke, the heir to the throne, was buried with less consideration than would have been shown to a junior employee in court service.

It was in the early hours of the morning that the train arrived at Pöchlarn carrying the coffins. The station was in no way prepared for an imperial funeral party. There were no black flags to indicate mourning, no police contingent to show appropriate respect for the two in those dark coffins, but most important of all, there was nobody to oversee what should happen next.

Even the weather seemed to have entered into Montenuovo's humiliating arrangements. Suddenly the heavens opened with a violent thunderstorm. In the wind and the rain it proved impossible to get the coffins to the nearby church where priests were waiting to conduct a last service of respect.

A service of sorts was held in the dingy station waiting room. The words of the bewildered priest could hardly be heard over the battering of torrential rain on the roof. The mourners, as many as were able, crowded into the constricted room, crushed up against each other. On the walls there were train timetables and advertisements for holiday trips, as if mocking the solemnity of the moment. (Afterwards the press described a wholly-fabricated story of how the two coffins were used as buffet-tables in the waiting room at Pöchlarn Station.)

The cortège decided to wait until the rain began to ease a little. Between Pöchlarn and Artstetten Castle lay the River Danube and the coffins would be taken across the river by ferry. The sombre cavalcade, drenched and bedraggled, arrived at the quay as dawn was breaking. It was still raining and the winds were whipping up the waves on the river. This was never going to be an easy crossing. With the greatest difficulty the horses were coaxed on to the ferry.

The animals by this time were fretful and jittery, tossing their heads and pawing the deck of the boat with their hooves; they shifted around and jostled each other restlessly, growing ever more nervous and wild. Men scurried around, their heads bent against the steady rain, trying to control and calm the animals. The horses were in the worst possible state for a ferry crossing.

Suddenly there was a violent flash of lightning followed by a clap of thunder. Some of the horses began to rear up and struggled to get away. The hearse bearing Franz Ferdinand's coffin slipped awkwardly over the edge of the boat and the coffin was almost launched into the depths of the river. On the wet, slippery boards of the boat it was almost impossible not to slip and slide yet somehow the men managed to haul Franz Ferdinand's coffin back on deck.

Somehow they got across to the other bank. Somehow terrified horses were calmed and brought back to their task of carrying the two coffins up the hill to the castle. Somehow the bedraggled mourners led by Archduke Karl found their way to the castle chapel for the final blessing. Dr. Viktor Eisenmenger was to say afterwards that the ceremony was "simple but dignified".

One unexpected figure was present at that last blessing: Franz Ferdinand's youngest brother, Ferdinand Karl. His had been one of the first telegrammes of condolence sent to little Max: "Desperately shocked by the terrible misfortune. I am with you and your brother and sister in thought. May God protect you."

As a man exiled permanently from Austrian soil, it had needed Franz Joseph's permission for his appearing there to say goodbye to his brother. Franz Joseph's initial response to Ferdinand Karl's request had been to refuse. With her usual determination, Maria Theresia saw to it that this edict was overturned. She probably also saw to it that the unfortunate man was not treated in the way that Franz Joseph insisted. He was not spoken to as 'Herr Burg' as prescribed by Franz Joseph but rather by one and all he was given his full erstwhile title of "Imperial Highness".

Ferdinand Karl was a broken man whose wish to marry for love had robbed his life of all meaning. In the two years since his marriage to Bertha Czuber bitterness and regret had gnawed away at him and he had become a shadow of his former self. There was a gaunt and haunted look on his face which shocked the surprised crowd as he descended from the train at Pöchlarn. But here, for a few brief hours, he was an Archduke. Franz Ferdinand had rejected his brother when Ferdinand Karl's marriage was discovered, and the two had never seen each other again in life. But they were still brothers and in death Ferdinand Karl needed to be there for the last time.

When the service was over he returned to the station to board the train for Munich – to return to his exile and his isolation and, as it turned out, an early death only a year later.

The children – little Sophie, Max and Ernst – had not been allowed to attend the service at the Hofburg Chapel – only after Franz Joseph had left were the children allowed in to see their parents' coffins for the first time and to say a prayer over them – but they were allowed to be present at the last blessing at Artstetten.

Maria Theresia brought them to Artstetten. She had taken on the role of ensuring that the children were not pushed aside as if they were irritating detritus of the whole affair. She it was who bundled them up and made sure that they were there and had a chance to say goodbye to their parents. She it was who embraced them and comforted them. And they were there, solemn and isolated, staying as close as they could to Maria Theresia, holding her hand.

At the end of the service they took each others' hands and moved up to the two coffins. They kept their heads down but observers noted how their bodies shook with suppressed sobbing. They wiped away the tears surreptitiously but constantly with their handkerchieves. The three children followed the coffins down into the crypt. At the last moment, Max, no longer trying to hold back his tears, stepped forward and placed a small photograph of the three children on his father's coffin. Had Maria Theresia helped him find the photograph and made sure that he brought it with him, keeping it from getting bent or creased? Then, hand-in-hand, the three small figures turned and went back up into the daylight.

Little Sophie found a moment to say, "God wanted Mami and Papi to join Him at the same time. It was better that they died together because Papi could not live without Mami and Mami could not have gone on without Papi."

However, after the burial at Artstetten Franz Joseph wanted to see the children privately to express his personal sorrow at their loss.

This was not the first time the three children had come face to face with him. In 1912 certain repairs and renovations needed to be carried out at the Belvedere Palace and in consequence when Franz Ferdinand and his family came to Vienna rooms had been found for them in the Hofburg until they could return to the Belvedere.

During their stay Franz Ferdinand was required to inspect the guard. Upstairs the children found a window in a corridor where they could eagerly watch what was going on in the courtyard below.

None of them paid much attention to what was going on around them and barely noticed the sound of growing bustle in the corridor. Ernst's nose was pressed right up against the window pane. Max and Sophie struggled to get a good view. And then suddenly there was the Emperor himself bearing down upon them. Within the blinking of an eye all three rushed frantically away back to their rooms, hoping that the Emperor had not seen them.

Later Franz Ferdinand decided to ask his uncle whether he might introduce his children. This took great courage on Franz Ferdinand's part. As always, the big, strong man could be reduced to a state of shivers at the thought of speaking to his uncle. You wonder whether he had heard about the morning's little incident and felt a need to show Franz Joseph that his children were courteous and well-brought up and nowhere, not even in the Hofburg, were they out of place.

So, during the afternoon Franz Ferdinand brought Sophie, Max and Ernst down to present them to the Emperor. Sophie curtsied low. The two boys made several deep bows.

Did the hint of a smile wrinkle the corners of Franz Joseph's eyes? With so much facial hair it would have been hard to tell. Franz Joseph looked at them and remarked drily, "We saw each other this morning, didn't we?"

On that occasion they had had their father standing by them, but on this occasion they were alone. The meeting must have been a tense and awkward one. Long ago the old man had lost all ability to express emotions or feelings. The children would have found themselves face to face with a stiff and daunting figure and found it all the more intimidating because of who he was, not just because he was the Emperor but because he was their great uncle.

Yet, young as they were, the one thing the three children had learned was dignity. Franz Joseph would have found himself gazing upon three childish figures who looked back at him with a kind of regal calm that spoke of a maturity they should not yet have had and did not feel.

There is no record of how that meeting went. We do not even know whether the children stood throughout or were invited to sit. It is hard to imagine that either side found words easy. Franz Joseph had long since ceased to communicate with anyone; he had a repertoire of phrases that said nothing but served when some sort of pronouncement was expected of him.

None of them served here. The children would have waited to be spoken to. All the old man could offer them were a few platitudes of apparent sympathy for their great loss. Their only response would have been to acquiesce, a mumbled, uncomfortable acknowledgement. They would have avoided looking at him and maybe little Ernst fidgeted. Maybe Sophie clutched his hand the tighter.

And Sophie? She was very much her mother's daughter. Sophie Chotek had known how to be reticent and unobtrusive but behind the mask she had been neither a fool nor a pushover. And maybe here her daughter saw the old man, shrunk and growing wizened, rather than the Emperor. Where all the world saw dignity and worthiness, did Sophie? Perhaps at that moment into little Sophie's mind sprang a memory of some remark from one or other of her parents, or a sentence suddenly broken off, or a tone of voice and something began to make sense to her.

When they turned to leave, it would have been with a sense of relief that that was over. They would never see Franz Joseph again.

Chapter 115

Immediate care for the children came from Sophie's two sisters, Rischel and Henriette. Rischel and her husband, Count Jaroslav von Thun und Hohenstein, had been accorded guardianship of the three children. Henriette became almost a second mother to them. She, it was, who tried to comfort the children, her aim to give the children a joyous youth as far as was possible, at least. It must have caused Henriette's heart much pain as she watched the children struggle to come to terms with their loss.

Ernst, the youngest, was especially badly affected. He suffered from loss of appetite and serious bouts of depression and for a number of years his health was not good. The other two, being older, sought to suppress the outward signs of their own pain.

Back at Konopischt there was some continuity and their lives continued much as before as far as day-to-day activities and education were concerned. Janaczek and most of the servants stayed with them, even though there were attempts from the Hofburg to sever their employment. Yet this must have made the absence of their mother and father all the more painful. Once evenings had been spent together as a family group; once Sophie had tucked up her children each night and heard their prayers before they went to sleep – now, there were shadows and silences and echoes and all too many nights when the children could not sleep.

All around them the most terrible war the world had ever seen was being waged. Food was in short supply, here as everywhere else. By the spring of 1918 throughout Austria-Hungary, just as elsewhere in Europe, there was growing discontent and strikes, food shortages and starvation. The war years imposed a special kind of strain upon the growing children at Konopischt. As discontent and anger fermented all around them, they would have known that much of it was focussed upon them. They would have known that people who did not understand the true situation would have seen them as enemies just because of their blood relationship with the Imperial Family. They would have known that they were in danger.

Sophie, Max and Ernst were not Habsburgs, and they retained the rights to their properties in the Austrian half of the country. But the new nation of Czechoslovakia seized all Habsburg property within its new borders and in that move they declared that Konopischt and Chlumetz had been Habsburg property. They ignored the fact that Max owned Konopischt and Ernst owned Chlumetz and both of them were private citizens. It was all illegal but there was nothing that they could do about it. And once they had left Czechoslovakia the new government there insisted that they could not return without a special visa.

It had for some time been growing clear that the children were at risk if they stayed at Konopischt. Angry feelings against Franz Ferdinand had been fermenting and were now at the point of explosion. There were marauders and trespassers whose activities became increasingly menacing. There were rumours of revolution. The children would hear stories of homes being looted and of lives being threatened. Henriette did her best to reassure the children, comforting them as much as she could.

Count Jaroslav von Thun und Hohenstein chose not to tempt fate. He sent his brother-in-law's younger son, Friedrich, who was always known as Fritz, to fetch the children and bring them safely to his own home at Tetschen.

Fritz was one of Kara and Count Leopold Nosticz-Rieneck's sons. He was twenty-six years old when he arrived at Konopischt. He had fought in the war and returned home a war hero. He insisted that he could not stop thinking about Sophie, Maximilian and Ernst and worrying about their situation.

Fritz caught Sophie's attention in particular when he came to Konopischt in the spring of 1919 to escort Franz Ferdinand's three children away to Tetschen. She would have been aware of how kind, supportive, reliable he was, taking into his own hands the authority to deal with what for a young girl must have been a frightening situation. He must have seemed to lift some of the constant dread that weighed upon her.

For as long as she could remember she had felt responsible for her little brothers. She needed to be strong for them – that was what her mother would have expected of her. But there had been nobody she felt she could lean on, until this tall, young man walked through the door and took charge with a firm voice and an air of confidence. It was during the time that Fritz was with them that the Czech police arrived and ordered them all to leave. They were told that they would be allowed to return once law and order had been re-established but that never happened.

They were not allowed to take with them anything, not even childhood toys, personal possessions, mementos, letters, diaries or photographs. As they were leaving the Czech guards insisted upon searching their luggage. They were only allowed to take their clothes and their school books.

Fritz could not prevent their luggage being searched before they left the house but he would have been able to do something to prevent the guards insulting them. There was a comfort in his presence. For weeks, months and years they had been living in a state of growing apprehension – there must have been such relief when Fritz arrived. He stirred in Sophie's heart a feeling she had never experienced before.

Konopischt had been home. In future they would feel homeless. They would each of them in his or her own way mourn its loss. Years afterwards they would get worked up and upset when memories came flooding back. Sophie, Max and Ernst spent only a short time in Tetschen. From there they travelled to Vienna to spend some time with their grandmother, Archduchess Marie-Theresia and then finally to Artstetten Castle where their parents were buried. This was to become their new home. Max had never liked Artstetten but this was where they now spent a large part of their time.

A year later Sophie vowed to Fritz her lifelong love and loyalty. Ever since they left Konopischt Sophie and Fritz had kept up a correspondence out of which blossomed their love for each other. On 8th September 1920 Sophie and Fritz were married in the Chapel of St. George at Tetschen. They were allowed to marry there because Fritz was a Czech citizen. Max and Ernst were allowed to attend the ceremony but they were ordered to leave Czechoslovakia immediately afterwards. From then on the Czech authorities made it as near impossible for the two brothers to return to the country ever again.

Sophie never liked her wedding photographs. Almost none of the figures in them seemed to be able to relax and enjoy the occasion. Ernst, particularly, looked angry and tense. Max's expression was dazed. Sophie herself looked withdrawn.

Marrying a Czech meant that Sophie, at least, was now able to return to Czechoslovakia. One thing she did when she could was visit Konopischt. The castle had been turned into a tourist attraction and it was as a tourist that Sophie went round her old home. It was an awkward, unreal experience for her. But she was allowed into her old rooms and there the guards turned a blind eye as she gathered up a few small, treasured things. What she would have liked would have been to take away mementos of their parents, but the guards insisted that she could not touch any of the photograph albums, the letters and diaries that Franz Ferdinand and Sophie had left behind.

What would Franz Ferdinand and Sophie have thought if they could have seen their children's choices in marriage? It is just possible that they might have been slightly surprised at Ernst's choice, but there was nothing surprising in the choices made by little Sophie and Max and both would have won their parents' unreserved approval. Sophie would have been so glad to see her daughter marrying Friedrich Nosticz-Rieneck and settling in the new Czechoslovakia. Max's choice would have warmed her heart perhaps even more.

Sophie Chotek and Princess Sidonie-Zdenka Lobkowitz had enjoyed a close friendship that went back to their girlhoods. In due course Princess Sidonie-Zdenka Lobkowitz had married Count Waldburg zu Wolfegg und

Waldsee and later, of course, Sophie had married Franz Ferdinand.

Their paths had diverged and they had not seen each other for many years, until in 1912 both found themselves among the guests at the wedding of one of Franz Joseph's granddaughters, the eldest daughter of Marie-Valérie, Elisabeth Franziska. Here the two of them rekindled the old friendship with renewed warmth. There was so much to catch up on, so much had happened in the years since they had last seen each other. One little detail caught Sophie's attention when her friend remarked that she had a picturebook-pretty little daughter at home. Sophie came back with the remark that her own son, only a few years older than the picturebook-pretty little girl, was also handsome and well-grown. And then a little sigh and the almost wistful comment about how nice it would be if their children could end up one day knowing each other.

But twelve more years would go by before the handsome little boy and the picturebook-pretty little girl finally did meet each other. This occasion, too, was a wedding. Max Hohenberg was there among the guests to see his cousin Adelheid Schönberg marry the brother of Elisabeth-Bona von Waldberg zu Wolfegg und Waldsee. Max's eye was caught by the groom's attractive sister.

Max was a considered man. He took his time and weighed his decisions. He did little on the spur of the moment. That meeting may have been love-at-first-sight but Max wasn't the man to plunge ahead without careful thought. Max felt unready to offer his hand to any girl. He needed to feel assured that he could offer her security and comfort. Until he had finished his studies and gained his legal qualifications he could not do that.

How open was he was with Elisabeth-Bona as to his hopes and intentions? Perhaps he kept his hopes to himself. After the wedding he left Germany to study jurisprudence at the University of Graz, fired up with determination to gain the best qualifications he could.

In the end the legal profession did not suit Max much. He disliked its adversarial nature, nor did he like being in the public eye. But the law was a good, settled career – all the more important after the war and the massive disruption it had caused.

Two years later, when he graduated, among all the congratulations was a telegramme: „Herzlichsten Glückwunsch! Alle Wolfegger" ("Warmest congratulations from all the Wolfeggs.") Then, and only then, could Max declare his love out in the open. Years later Maximilian would one day point out to his son, Georg, the grassy bank where he had actually proposed to Elisabeth-Bona. Perhaps, too, it crossed his mind how much his mother would have liked to see this moment come about. Sophie, with her strong sense of family, would have felt that things were on the right path.

They got married on 16th November 1926 in southern Germany where the Waldberg-Wolfegg ancestral castle stood. There was a happy family reunion. Sophie and Fritz arrived from Prague and Sophie, watching her brother beaming, found this wedding a much happier event than her own wedding had been.

It was not until 1936 that Ernst got married, some ten years after his brother and sister had settled down. The picture we get of Ernst is that he was always slightly, imperceptibly, distanced from his brother and sister. Sophie and Max were separated by only a year in age and in photographs of them as children they look very similar. Ernst came into the world two years later and he always had a rather puckish look with his curly hair and a smile that hinted at mischief. You wonder whether Ernst didn't have a secret, well-hidden, special corner in Sophie's heart. She had wanted a larger family but a miscarriage and a stillbirth had put paid to that. So Ernst had turned out to be her youngest and possibly her dearest.

Whilst the two older children had grown up with the assumption that they would belong to the landed gentry and did achieve that as much as they could, Ernst always seems to have been less sure of those assumptions. In some way, he belonged slightly less and went his own way slightly more. The curly hair slowly disappeared. His childishly slight figure thickened into the shape of his father. The puckish spirit turned into an independent energy that disliked being told what to think. And it took him a long time to find the woman he could love for a lifetime. The girl who won his heart had much in common with him. Both were outsiders looking in.

She was the daughter of the rakish Captain George Wood and the fiery Hungarian Countess Rosa Lónyay von Nagy-Lónya es Vásáros-Namény, whose father was distantly related to Stéphanie's husband, Count Elemér Lónyay. These two must have genereated so much energy, spark, brilliance, verve that almost any child would have been overwhelmed by it all.

Lucian Meysels [64] described Captain George Wood as a pimpernel character who might have stepped out of an Ian Fleming thriller. There was an air of mystery about Captain George Wood. He belonged to the highest echelons of the British aristocracy and was related to Viscount Halifax, the British Foreign Minister. In the years before the First World War Captain George Wood turned up in Vienna with the interesting title of 'Honorary Military Attaché'. He let it be vaguely understood that he had something to do with the diplomatic service but he was never too explicit. It is not clear whether he gave himself this title and it is probable that he was never

---

[64] *Die Verhinderte Dynastie – Erzherzog Franz Ferdinand und das Haus Hohenberg* by Lucian Meysels, 2000.

formally anything to do with the diplomatic service.

His boss, the genuine Military Attaché, Colonel Francis Teck, was related to Queen Mary, had grown up in Austria and done his military service in the Austrian Army and then emigrated to England. But then Francis Teck had found his way back to Austria as a diplomat. Francis Teck and Captain Wood immediately took to each other. And in the last years before the outbreak of war both enjoyed Austrian society to the full.

It was not long before Rosa, flashing colourful sparks wherever she went, danced into Captain Wood's circle and he swept her up into marriage. These two quickly became known as the "most charming pair within Viennese society". No two people could have been more romantic. With the outbreak of war Captain Wood took his new bride back to England.

After a time in England he and Rosa reappeared in Vienna at the beginning of the 1930s. Again they charmed their way through society – that drab society of the new shrunken and belittled Austria of the interwar years – with a sparkle and vivacity as if they wanted single-handedly to reawake the glory of Franz Joseph's vanished Empire.

George might so easily have been a model for James Bond but his daughter was no James Bond adventuress. George rather kept his daughter, Maisie, in the background. She was just a little too mouse-like, a poor shadow of her flamboyant mother, and she may have cramped his style. She was very pretty but in a homely way with none of her mother's exuberance. The more her parents shone, the more Maisie shrank into the shadows. Maisie was an awkward figure, something of a misfit. She found life in Vienna something of a struggle, because, although she spoke English and Hungarian fluently, her German was a mangled mess which made it difficult for her to enter into social activities. She was also beginning to go deaf. She became rather withdrawn and despondent.

One evening the idea came up that an evening at the theatre would lift Maisie's spirits. This proposal was put forward by a close friend of Ernst Hohenberg, a friend who seems to have sensed that Ernst and Maisie were likely to hit it off together. Ernst may well have accepted his friend's suggestion with thoughts that he was willing to make the gesture but probably wouldn't want to repeat it. Maisie may well have been reluctant, too, given that she was not going to understand very much of what was going on on the stage.

However, Ernst Hohenberg must have awoken in Maisie an interest in the theatre – for many more such theatre evenings followed. Other interests were being awakened as well. They found that they had a lot in common. They opened up to each other. But there was no rush to the altar. A secret understanding led to private promises to each other and then to an official engagement, but it was a long, slow surreptitious process.

However, in 1935 with full pomp their marriage was celebrated in the

Karlskirche in Vienna. It all harked back to the glitter and glory of pre-war days. Maisie looked particularly lovely and happy as she came down the steps of the church. To be frank, in the photographs Ernst looked as though he had been forced to face some ordeal of an unpleasant physical nature.

Had Sophie ever met Maisie she would have quickly sensed what they had in common. It seems likely that Sophie would have quickly taken Maisie to her heart. Sophie would have understood that Maisie's life had been coloured by the ups and downs of the diplomatic world her own father had worked in.

Franz Ferdinand would have had difficulties with Maisie's father, disliking his flamboyance and bravado. It might have needed a twinkling defence from Sophie to win him round.

Now that she was married to Ernst, Maisie henceforth would look forward to a future life in Austria. From then on she would be Austrian and Austria would be her home. The Second World War would drive a wedge between her and the land in which, to a large extent, she had grown up and, also, between her and her father.

With the outbreak of war George Wood was forced to return to England to join his regiment. By the end of the war, much of which he spent in the Bahamas in the suite of the exiled Duke of Windsor, George Wood had been drawn into the murky shadows of various secret service activities. His official role was that of 'King's Messenger'. He also had business activities – he had established a brewery in Africa which does not seem to have been a great financial success. George confessed to a friend, "Sadly the blacks don't really like drinking beer!"

While Max was a quiet and self-effacing man whose greatest energies were focussed upon his wife and six sons, Ernst deep down had a fiery streak which came to the fore when the Nazis threatened Austria. And Ernst went around tearing down pro-Nazi posters and pictures of Hitler. Before too long he was caught and forced to apologise. But his actions had caught the attention of the Nazis.

However, it was Max Hohenberg who belonged to the Frontmiliz, an amalgam of military groups bitterly opposed to Hitler and everything the Nazis stood for. It claimed to be a non-partisan movement whose aim was to defend Austrian independence. The worst thing that could happen to members of the Frontmiliz came about on 12th March 1938 when Hitler's Germany annexed Austria into Nazi Germany. On 13th March the Frontmiliz was officially banned.

One evening a few days later Max returned home late still wearing his Frontmiliz uniform. It had been an overcast day, the sky heavy with dark, damp cloud which perhaps set the mood. Max burst in upon Elisabeth-Bona, his wife, with a desperate, "It's all over now!" He went out and changed out of his uniform and came back with his decision that they should all wait and see how things turned out.

Elisabeth-Bona refused to listen. She insisted in a voice that allowed no argument, "The only thing is to get away from here." Max didn't argue. He was too shaken by the realisation of what things had come to. He allowed Elisabeth to take charge. She collected up her children who were already abed and then found a taxi driver willing to drive them away – the man must have been aware that he was running a great risk. He drove the family to Gmünd because they believed they would get across the border there more easily.

Perhaps they might have done so. The border control officer who stopped them was drunk. He never even sought to look at their papers but growled that they could not cross that night. Crushed, the family returned to Artstetten.

The following morning Ernst and Maisie arrived. Sophie had been on the phone to them desperately begging them all to leave while they still could – but not, most definitely not, in the direction of Prague; rather they should head towards Hungary. Maisie, however, had other ideas. Her father, Captain George Wood, was English and a member of the British diplomatic service. Unfortunately, George Wood was not in Vienna at that time but in the south of France where he was engaged in talks with the Duke of Windsor and his wife, Wallis.

Believing that seeking help from the British Embassy was a better course of action, Maisie was confident that this was where they should turn. Once more they packed all their children into the car and set off, this time for Vienna.

The events of those days left a deep impression upon Max's second son, Georg, then eight years old. Twinges of guilt would linger long after – totally and utterly unjustified, yet a ruffled sense of how much pain might possibly have been avoided if they had acted differently. Georg recounted later how they had all assumed they would be safer in Vienna.

They took young Georg with them, a bewildered small boy, all too aware of the atmosphere of danger and uncertainty. They had to drive past the German Embassy where Nazis were wildly celebrating, filling the street with shouting and noise. Once through the door of the British Embassy the huge, heavy door closed behind them and suddenly Georg was overwhelmed by the stillness and quiet that reigned inside.

Georg remained downstairs with his mother and watched as his father, his Uncle Ernst and Aunt Maisie went up the stairs. He waited. In due course the grown-ups appeared again. They were utterly shocked. It seemed that the British, or those in Vienna, could assert with straight faces that the

Hohenbergs had nothing to fear – they were civilised Germans outside in the street.

However, Michael Palairet followed up with a report to his boss at the London Foreign Office. Very bluntly Palairet stated that he had offered the party two nights' asylum in the Embassy. Palairet's words offered no sympathy for the family, nor did he put forward the smallest argument for the British to be in any way concerned about the welfare of these people. But he was well aware that Marie Therese (Maisie) was the daughter of Captain George Wood who had been the Military Attaché at that same embassy and so she was half English. In 1938 the British government was still hoping that appeasement would ensure peace and were most unwilling to offer help even when those seeking help could produce clear proof that they were in real danger.

On 14th March the family left the building. From there they returned to their hotel only to find that the Hotel Imperial demanded that they leave immediately. They then went to stay in the house of Captain George Wood where they believed they would be safe – the Nazis would not force an entry into the house of a prominent Englishman. They could not have been more wrong.

On 16th March the Gestapo turned up with a warrant for Ernst's arrest. He was accused of the deaths of a number of miners who had been working in a mine that did not belong to Ernst and had nothing to do with him. Ernst was carried off into the night, leaving his wife aghast with their tiny son. Max was allowed to remain but he had been threatened by the Nazis and he reasoned that if he fled the country Ernst might be killed. He chose to give himself up to the Gestapo two days later. Within days both men had been taken to Dachau concentration camp.

The two wives were left behind in fear that they might never see their husbands again. They were in a state of anguish over how they themselves along with their families of small children would cope. Maisie, particularly, had strong reasons for fearing for the worst.

Chapter 116

Back in 1935 Hitler had sent Franz von Papen to Vienna on a mission to nudge the Austrian government towards acceptance and agreement with Nazi actions and ideals. Von Papen was a slippery character and much disliked by almost everybody who ever came into contact with him. He acquired the name 'Satan in a Top Hat' and a reputation as a powerful, evil genius. He had been a politician with the Catholic Centre Party until, in 1932 in a way that astounded those around, he switched to become a close collaborator with Hitler, betraying his own party and many of his former friends. He became German Ambassador in Vienna and played an important part in over-riding any opposition in Austria to the country's being annexed into a Greater Germany. At the start of the war he was sent to Istanbul where on one occasion in 1942 a bomb was thrown at the car he and his wife were travelling in. It was not the only attempt on his life.

During his time in Vienna, von Papen had met Captain George Wood's striking and charismatic wife. She assaulted his senses in every way. He had courted her and left her with the impression that secretly he would do anything for her.

So, Rosa Wood, as soon as she learned of what had happened to her son-in-law, went to see von Papen. As soon as she came through the door he was all over her with effusive greetings and many promises. It was, he insisted, all a regrettable misunderstanding and he would make sure that everything was put right in the twinkling of an eye.

In fact, von Papen was none too sure whether a noose was not tightening around his own throat and the last thing he wanted to do was make waves. He most certainly did nothing for Ernst Hohenberg. Perhaps he knew that Hitler felt particular animosity against the Hohenberg brothers. Both Max and Ernst were treated in Dachau with especial harshness and cruelty.

By the end of that month Sophie's husband, Friedrich Nosticz-Rieneck had travelled to Vienna and brought Maisie and her baby back with him, after Rosa had left Austria to join her husband in the south of France.

Immediately he learned of the danger facing his son-in-law Captain Wood flew back to London and presented himself at the Foreign Office where he received a very cool reception. He sought to reach Lord Halifax and win his support but his messages were almost certainly pushed aside and filed before they ever landed on Lord Halifax's desk.

However, he was not one to give up lightly and he clearly touched a nerve. Even so, the British authorities were reluctant to get involved. Queen Mary pressed for action but it is unlikely that she achieved much either though it is thought that her pressing for action on their behalf may have attracted attention in Berlin.

From then on the battle to get the Hohenbergs freed was taken up by Max's wife, Elisabeth-Bona. She managed to get an interview with Hermann Göring at the Hotel Imperial in Vienna that the Nazis had largely taken over. Afterwards, long afterwards, she would describe that meeting in tones of humour and derision – but that was long afterwards.

First of all she was made to wait because, according to an extremely polite young Luftwaffe officer, the Viennese would not let Göring leave the balcony where he was being overwhelmed by their warmth and welcome; again and again with more jubilant cries Austrians loyal to the Nazi cause called him back out on to the balcony. Elisabeth-Bona had arrived early but she was made to wait hours. Seated alone in the grand entrance hall of the hotel, her isolation in all the bustle and stir of uniformed men around her making her feel very conspicuous, she waited. The morning passed and then much of the afternoon as well. Elisabeth-Bona never moved from her seat.

When at long last Elisabeth-Bona entered the room she still found herself alone until Hermann Göring stepped through the high windows from the balcony into the room. He was dressed entirely in white and the image that immediately came to her mind was that of a village butcher. What no village butcher would have worn were the massive gold signet ring and the monocle he kept fiddling with, drawing attention to an artifact he had no use for but fancied because he considered it a symbol of nobility. He sat down at the huge desk and immediately swung round turning his back to her.

He treated her with a strange mixture of imperious obsequiousness, making it obvious that he did not know how to treat her. He had never before spoken to somebody whose father-in-law had been an Archduke and heir to the throne of an Empire. His opening words were offensively inappropriate:

"I know that you have come to plead for your kinsmen. I have for some time been considering whether I should leave them indefinitely in the concentration camp where they belong or whether I should have them hanged straight away."

Elisabeth-Bona held herself still and said nothing. She had, when she wanted to make use of it, a regal stance. The silence began to weigh heavy on the air. Göring swung back to face her again and went on to tell her that there was nothing he could do for Ernst Hohenberg. Elisabeth-Bona had the impression that decisions about Ernst and Max's fates were not his to make.

"How can you defend Ernst Hohenberg?" he fired at her.

Göring had some story about how some time ago Ernst had had a Nazi tortured over a hot fire. According to Göring, Ernst had personally branded the man with a swastika symbol on his chest. In reality the man had stumbled and fallen against a brazier and suffered severe burns but Ernst had not moved a finger to cause it. He had leapt to the man's aid.

Elisabeth-Bona remained calm, outwardly at least. Her thoughts in turmoil and her heart pounding in anguish, she maintained her aristocratic bearing. There was no greater snob than Göring and Elisabeth-Bona's standing as a member of the old nobility of Germany (which Göring pretended to scorn) and her aristocratic bearing impressed him.

The interview over, Göring shook her hand and said, "Head high, German woman." And then after a pause, "Write to me, keep writing to me. One day you will open the door for your husband."

And six months later Max was allowed to go free. He was convinced that his wife's efforts had done much to bring this about, that Göring had been so impressed by Elisabeth-Bona that he was prepared to ignore Hitler's orders and secretly grant Max a conditional release.

But what Göring had said to Elisabeth-Bona was very different to what he was saying to the Foreign Office in London where finally moves were afoot to find out what was happening not just to the Hohenberg brothers but also to various members of the Austrian nobility who had been transported to Dachau. Berlin justified what was happening because of unspecified "acts of brutality".

Further pressure from London resulted in the British Ambassador to Berlin, Neville Henderson, obtaining a meeting with Hermann Göring on 20th April 1938. Here Göring made no bones about his wish to see the Hohenberg brothers rot in prison until the end of their days. Hitler himself had personally ordered that the "Hohenberg boys" should be treated with the utmost severity and Göring personally passed on the Führer's wishes to SS-Oberführer, Hans Loritz, the camp commandant.

"They are sadists, like their father," Göring informed Henderson and he expounded at length on the story of Ernst torturing a Nazi colleague over a hot fire. Göring's last words were, "If you knew everything, you wouldn't lift a finger for these people." Almost everyone in Britain was still hoping that war with Germany could be avoided and Henderson was in no position to do anything other than to go along with that. It is highly improbable that Captain Wood knew of Henderson's meeting with Göring when he arrived at the Foreign Office to plead for his son-in-law, or he would have made a much bigger fuss.

On Hitler's orders Max and Ernst were singled out for every particularly humiliating assignment. They were forced to empty and clean the latrines. They were harnessed to a cart and whipped and beaten when they failed to move fast enough. They were taunted by SS guards as they worked. Stones were thrown into the cesspits causing the foul ordure to splash up into their faces. And they were mocked and called "Imperial Highnesses".

Yet Max and Ernst maintained a dignity that seemed superhuman.

There are many reports of the supremely noble presence the brothers maintained throughout their ordeal. There are also many tales of the generosity and self-sacrifice they showed others. Unflinching and undaunted, "an awe-inspiring example" was how one fellow prisoner remembered them. They were "gentlemen". What stood out about them was how they seemed wholly focussed upon the care of those around them. If one or other of the brothers had succeeded in obtaining a lump of sugar, they, in their thin, ragged clothes, skeletally thin and struggling as much as anyone else for survival in those desperate conditions, would share this 'bounty', offering fellow inmates of the camp more grains of the sugar than they kept for themselves.

Max one day noticed how the attention of one of the SS guards had been caught by a gypsy. Within moments the guard was chasing the gypsy. Max succeeded in grabbing the man and hiding him in a box of sand. When finally the search was called off Max went back to help the terrified man get away. This little incident would never have been known about had a young gypsy lad not turned up many years after the end of the war at the castle of Artstetten. The lad was herding two geese before him and he had brought this offering to thank the man who had saved his father's life.

Among the inmates of the camp was Leopold Figl who was later to become Chancellor of Austria. From the moment he arrived at Dachau Figl's attention was particularly caught by Max and Ernst, their air of inextinguishable authority even as they stood wretched and shivering, silently enduring the jeers of their Nazi guards. "They suffered the most excruciating humiliations," Figl said later, but never did their inner fortitude waver through it all. Figl was struck that they did not behave with the stoical pride of noblemen but rather with an unshakable humility as men who saw their role in life as serving others. They treated prisoners who came from the common folk with the same courtesy and consideration that they accorded other political prisoners of higher social standing.

It was on 24th September 1938 that Max was taken from the camp and pushed on to a train heading for Vienna. He was told that he was free to go home on condition that he did not take part in any kind of anti-Nazi or any other political activities. He was required to report weekly to the Gestapo. That was it.

Max was stunned and overwhelmed with disbelief, convinced that all this was some kind of charade, such as the SS were known for, which would end up with his execution. Yet he found himself in Vienna and made his way to his old apartment. The apartment was empty. It had been empty since the family had left for Artstettin, explained an elderly porter, Franz Salava. All this felt unreal to Max as he stared around at all that had once been so familiar and now seemed so strangely remote from reality.

Fortunately for Max the telephone had not been cut off and he was able to ring his family and tell them that he was still alive and coming home. Embarrassed and confused he was then forced to turn to the old man at his side and beg him to lend him the money to get to Artstetten because he had no money.

Back at Artstettin the children were holding their breath and listening for the car that would bring their father home. They waited painfully, eagerly, yet were still not sure that they could believe that he was actually really coming home to them. Then "we heard the car and ran out and suddenly he was standing there," remembered Georg. The thing they noticed first was that he no longer had a moustache.

And then someone broke off and asked, "Where was Ernst?" All Max could tell them was that Ernst was still alive. A stillness settled over them. The exuberance was dampened. The family that went inside to try to return to their former way of life found that the shadow of not knowing Ernst's fate hung over them. Silently they each came to believe that they would never see Ernst alive again.

A shadow hung over Max, too. He knew that he could be hauled back to prison at any time it pleased the Nazis. Throughout the war he lived his life as quietly and as unobtrusively as possible. Elisabeth-Bona found that harder to achieve. Local Nazi officials were pressing her to become a member of the Nazi Women's League. She dealt with that skilfully. She travelled to Vienna to the Gestapo office and announced that she feared that there were problems here. She felt, she said, that it might be somewhat embarrassing for committed and loyal Nazis if the wife of an ex-prisoner were to join the Nazi Women's League. She then waited for a reply. Finally, it came: "Tell them that the Gestapo has forbidden it."

On another occasion she found herself under pressure to buy two busts, one of Hitler and the other of Göring. A refusal to take the busts was impossible but Elisabeth-Bona could not help remarking that she had personally made the acquaintance of one of those gentlemen. She had to buy them but what subsequently happened to the two busts no one knows. They had disappeared before the war was over.

Elisabeth-Bona brought into the world twelve children, six of them sons. For this she was 'honoured' with the *Nationalsozialistische Mutterkreuz* (the Nazi medal for mothers who had large families). In Germany her father, Prince Maximilian von Waldburg was incensed by this 'honour' and sent it back with the curt explanation that she was not a cow and she did not merit a medal.

But the boys could not get out of becoming members of the Hitler Youth Movement. The younger boys refused to treat this seriously which resulted in a summons to their father to attend a committee where Max had to promise that his sons would in future show more respect and attend meetings without fail. Max returned to impress on his boys the need for a demeanour that no one could find fault with. He pointed out and stressed to the boys just how precarious their position was and he would have thought of Ernst, still a prisoner, still in the camp. It must have weighed upon him that there was nothing he could do to help Ernst.

Around the time that Max was let out of Dachau Ernst was moved to another concentration camp: Flossenburg. Then, at the beginning of 1940, he was moved to Sachsenhausen-Oranienburg where he was held until April 1943. His family started to receive letters marked with: Absender: *„Schutzhäftling Hohenberg, Ernst, Nr. 17.739, Block 5, Konzentrationslager Sachsenhausen-Oranienburg bei Berlin."* Ernst now had this small concession: he was permitted to write a letter home once a month, a strictly censored letter, but still it meant contact. Each letter ended with "Every day and every hour I think about you and I only hope that you are not suffering from great worries and difficulties. I hug you and send you a thousand kisses, Your Ernst."

Month after month Maisie waited for those letters. They must have awoken some hope in her. She was desperate to increase her efforts to get him home.

Her father could no longer do anything for him. Captain George Wood had become an adjutant of the Duke of Windsor.[65] In 1940 after the fall of France the Duke and Duchess of Windsor (ex-King Edward VIII and Wallis Simpson) fled to the south of France amongst thousands of others all fleeing to find a way out of the country. The Duke of Windsor was offended that the British government had not sent a destroyer to collect them and then decided to sulk and sit it out. Captain George Wood was one of a whole chorus of voices pressing the Duke and Duchess to leave while they still could. George Wood accompanied the Duke and Duchess to the Bahamas and there he spent the rest of the war.

In her desperation Maisie was finding new courage, more than she

---

[65] Andrew Morton in his book *Wallis in Love* suggests that Maisie, along with Max and Ernst, had been taken to the concentration camp. It would not be surprising if in the chaos of war George Wood did not know what was happening to his daughter.

would ever have dreamed she was capable of. It didn't feel like courage, not to her. It felt more like anguish. This terrible war was making her wonder who she really was. The way some people did not see her as fully Austrian was sowing insidious doubts inside her. But, of course, she was Austrian. She had been born in Vienna on 9th May 1910 and, apart from much of her childhood, she would live all her life in Austria. And despite his nationality her father had always loved Austria more than anywhere else in the world.

When the family arrived back in Vienna in the early 1930s it had felt almost triumphal, a strange feeling for Maisie who had heard so much about her 'home' in Vienna, a home she had little memory of. But after the outbreak of war Captain Wood found himself serving in an elite regiment of the British Army. So if Maisie sensed some uncertainty around her, if she sensed that people might not be wholly convinced that her heart was indisputably Austrian, perhaps it was not surprising. But their doubts made her uncomfortable. She was always inclined to hang back.

Yet she found the courage to seek out Karl Scharizer, the head of the SS Brigade in Vienna, in an attempt to arrange a meeting with Heinrich Himmler. Scharizer had no objection but no meeting came about and it is likely that Maisie's English connections stood in the way. They certainly did not dispose anyone in her favour.

Sophie, however, had more freedom than the Hohenbergs in Austria, largely because she had no history of political activities. She set about trying to get Ernst Hohenberg transferred to the custody of her husband. Friedrich Nosticz had supported the annexation of the Sudetenland which stood him in good stead with the ruling Nazis. As a result Scharizer was willing to endorse this proposal. But as wind of these plans got back to Berlin, and in particular to Hitler and to Göring, they were blown out of the water. Hitler's long-standing animosity against the 'Hohenberg boys' exploded.

This did not stop Maisie and Sophie writing endless letters. They also turned further afield in their attempts to find someone else who would speak for them. They hit upon Count Friedrich Schaffgotsch. He was a very remote relative of Sophie Chotek's family. His grandmother had been a Kinsky, just as Sophie's grandmother had been a Kinsky. This was a tenuous connection but better than nothing. It helped that Friedrich Schaffgotsch had unwittingly found himself very much hand-in-glove with the Gestapo.

How does someone find themselves unwittingly hand-in-glove with the Gestapo? It certainly was not what Friedrich Schaffgotsch would ever have intended, and particularly not with the Gestapo officer over whom he came to have some influence.

Friedrich Schaffgotsch for most of the year lived a rather retiring life on his estates not far from Breslau in Silesia. He was one of the richest landowners in the region and he belonged to the highest aristocratic ranks in Silesia. By the time Maisie and Sophie turned to him he had grown old and forgetful. Increasingly he lived in the past. He was settled in his ways, a tired old man who meant well by everyone. From time to time he liked to travel to the Hotel Metropolhof in Breslau. Here in the hotel lounge he could hope to find neighbours and acquaintances with whom he could share a drink or few and exchange congenial gossip.

The war had not changed his habits. Indeed, he remained largely in the dark on all matters of politics or what was happening in the world around him. He was now elderly and he didn't want to know what was happening, it all made him feel too downcast.

So, one afternoon there he was in the lounge in the Hotel Metropolhof, his stein of beer before him, his deafness impeding his hearing very much of the conversations going on around him, his thoughts somewhere else. His daughter, Mia, was with him. Someone walked past their table and greeted Schaffgotsch most politely, bowing his head towards the old man.

Friedrich Schaffgotsch had no idea who this person was, but no one of his breeding would rebuff such old-fashioned courtesy. Schaffgotsch did not like the way the world was going and anyone who clung to the consideration and courtesies of yesteryear immediately appealed to him.

„*Komm, setz dich zu uns,*" ("Come and join us."), he said, graciously indicating the adjacent chair. Mia's head shot up but her father did not notice. It was his habit to invite people he knew to come and join them; he was a sociable old man and always glad to extend hospitality to someone he knew.

Nor did he notice that all around them a sudden silence fell upon the company, that heads turned away, while others shot sharp, angry glances towards the old man. Mia fidgeted in embarrassment, not knowing quite how to handle the situation. When they were alone again together, she burst out, "Are you completely mad? How could you speak to him and even invite him to our table?" Spluttering she had raised her voice and now every head in the room was turned towards them.

Friedrich looked confused and bewildered. "What's wrong? I know him from somewhere? I can't remember where but he greeted me as though he knew me and of course I invited him to sit down!" Mia dropped her voice and leant forward to explain just who their guest had been. Friedrich finally ended up saying that what had happened he could not undo. And Mia flashed angry looks – as though *that* put things right!

The following day there was a telephone call and their guest was effusive in his thanks. He wound up with, "If you ever have the smallest difficult with the Party or the Gestapo, please turn to me. You can always trust me!" and with that Udo von Woyrsch hung up.

Schaffgotsch pushed all thought of ever having any further contact with his 'friend' of the previous day out of his mind.

Udo von Woyrsch had never been much liked by the local aristocracy and landowners. They barely tolerated him and did all they could to hold him at arm's length, but he had risen high in the Gestapo where he enjoyed considerable influence and power, so it suited the inhabitants of Breslau to conceal their antipathy as far as they could and to avoid him.

This did not prevent a swirl of gossip about him and it was widely believed that he was involved in the death of his sister-in-law. Perhaps he had actually murdered her himself. Perhaps his part in a rather shady affair had simply consisted in covering up what had actually happened.

Udo's brother, Siegfried, had married Consuela Nathan, the daughter of a rich Jewish banker in Frankfurt. This connection had not prevented Udo from excelling in his career with the Gestapo but Consuela, who was actively involved in anti-Nazi activities, was becoming an embarrassment for Udo. About a year after the Nazis came to power in Germany Consuela, along with a large number of other anti-Nazi activists, was rounded up in Frankfurt and arrangements were made for them all to be taken to Berlin on a special train. Udo von Woyrsch was responsible for their transportation.

Consuela never reached Berlin. Her body was found beside the railway line. Little was done to investigate her death and it was not long before, locally, it was widely assumed that Udo had something to do with her death. It was assumed that he needed Consuela out of the way because he did not want it to become too widely known that he was in any way connected with a Jew; this might have impeded his rise within the ranks of the Gestapo. Consuela's death resulted in Udo being completely shut out of Breslau society.

Some ten years had passed. Udo could force himself upon people but he could not fail to be aware that he would never be received with a welcome. So Friedrich Schaffgotsch's „Komm, setz dich zu uns," had stirred in him a wave of gratitude.

In 1942, Maisie travelled to Vienna to plead with the Gestapo for Ernst. Yet again she came away feeling despondent and defeated. She had spent every penny she had in her efforts to win Ernst's freedom and now she did not know where to turn. Because money was so short she threw herself, together with her son, upon the hospitality of the Schaffgotsch family at Schloß Koppitz in Silesia. Perhaps Sophie had suggested this move.

The local authorities viewed the presence of Maisie in their midst with disapproval – she was the wife of a concentration camp prisoner. Maisie sought work but the only work she could find was as a gardener. Day by day she tended tomatoes and courgettes and beans. It was exhausting work, the hours were long, and she earned little. Night after night she returned crushed. But her efforts did something to lift the opprobrium of her situation as a concentration camp prisoner's wife and Schaffgotsch was willing to do what he could to ease her situation.

As the local saying goes, Friedrich Schaffgotsch had not hung that promise of help from Udo von Woyrsch on the big bell. On the contrary, he had pushed it aside and done all he could to forget about it. But now his other daughter, Sophie, was on to him to do something for their 'Hohenberg cousin'. So Friedrich Schaffgotsch girded his loins and set off for Dresden where Woyrsch now served as Chief of Police. Woyrsch was delighted to see the old man again. He would see to the matter. It would be sorted in the twinkling of an eye.

It proved to be rather more difficult than that. The problem was that Hitler himself had indicated his wish to see the Hohenberg boys rot in hell and nobody wished to be the one to over-ride that. But Woyrsch invited the Countess Sophie Schaffgotsch and Maisie Hohenberg to take tea with him. He wished to understand more about the situation.

That meeting was not an easy one. Maisie could not have been more uncomfortable and it didn't help that her growing deafness was making it increasingly difficult for her to enter into any kind of conversation. But before they left Woyrsch had a suggestion: Maisie should write directly to Himmler and he would pass the letter on to the right person.

Nobody knows whether Hitler himself was ever aware of the move to release Ernst Hohenberg. Did anyone tell him? or was it a matter, as Friedrich Schaffgotsch always believed, that the papers were hidden in a pile of other papers and Hitler signed them without being aware of what he had done? Against that Hitler was known for his pedantic going through everything with a fine-tooth comb. No, despite this, Schaffgotsch remained convinced that for once Hitler slipped up - luck was on their side.

A few weeks later the Schaffgotsch family were informed that a favourable decision might be forthcoming. And then Maisie got a letter confirming this. On 11th April 1943 Maisie was on the platform of the Westbahnhof in Vienna to greet her husband as he got off the train. "I hardly recognised him, he looked so thin and starved!" But he was there and Maisie's heart was overflowing!

Like Max, Ernst's freedom was constrained by regular reporting to the Gestapo at the Hotel Metropol in the Morzinplatz in Vienna. He also found that getting work of any kind was particularly difficult. Ernst desperately sought work on the land, perhaps as a forester, or something of that nature. But when he did get a positive reply to his applications the Gestapo found reasons why he could not accept. Ernst's spirits sank. In August he wrote to Stéphanie's husband, Elemér Lónyay, to ask him to give his son, Ferdinand, a home in Hungary. It was not obvious but Ernst was beginning to tidy up his affairs and prepare for some very hard decisions. Ensuring future support for Ferdinand was a part of this.

You wonder whether perhaps Ernst was considering committing suicide at this point.

Elemér did not receive Ernst's letter until October. But when he did get it his reaction was immediate. He wrote back warmly, clearly so glad that Ernst had been released – though he made no mention of the camp or of the release in the letter. He wished Ernst all the best for his health and a quick recovery and this was as far as he dared go in referring to where Ernst had spent the last six years. And yes, he and Stéphanie would be more than delighted to welcome Ferdinand to Oroszvár where they would do all they could to care for the lad.

But then unexpectedly there was something to live for – Maisie was expecting her second child. "Thank God! The future lies in God's hands and is often, if not almost always, different from what we had imagined it would be!" Maisie's pregnancy had given Ernst renewed hopefulness. He started to refer to 'the second life', not making it clear whether he meant the unborn child or his prospects, but that 'second life' had given him a will to tackle what had to be tackled.

Ernst no longer wanted to send Ferdinand off to Oroszvár. The family had to stick together. Ernst only had to look at Maisie's face which seemed to beam with a gentle contentment that had not been there on the face of the stranger standing on the platform of the Westbahnhof Station.

Ernst had not wanted to take in that it was not just he who had changed but so had Maisie, too. She had changed and grown into someone new, someone he almost felt in awe of. But that contentment on her face gave him back the old Maisie and did so much to restore their old closeness. It allowed him a curious freedom: this was a kind of permission to remember the early years, their getting to know each other, their falling in love and their bonding in the early years of their marriage. Waves of emotion breaking through the rigid control he had imposed upon himself. Ernst could look at Maisie's face and feel hope.

On 1st March 1944 little Ernst was born.

But the war was coming closer and closer with air raids every day. In the autumn of 1944 a bomb hit their tiny flat in the Schweighofergasse, forcing the family to find other accommodation.

Finally, Ernst and Maisie felt compelled to send the two boys somewhere where they hoped they would be in greater safety. There is sad resignation in Maisie's words: "It was terrible for me to part with them but they were in God's hands and He would hold them safe." News of how the children were doing came rarely and now, in spite of his weakened health, Ernst was engaged in civil defence work which meant that Maisie once again spent long hours alone and very lonely.

Ernst and Maisie's marriage was a strong one. Their nephew Max's youngest son, Gerhard, spoke of them with deep affection. They were, he reminisced, honestly fond of each other but then theirs was a generation that did not complain. And after the war they were conscious that they had survived and they still had each other. Gerhard remembered that they never looked back to what they had lost with any anger or bitterness.

But they did bring up old memories full of fun and humour. They always could poke fun at themselves or at their compatriots. There was one particular topic they enjoyed. They liked to recall how after the war suddenly no Austrian had ever been present to welcome Hitler's triumphant entry into Vienna. No one had heard Hitler's rousing speech. No one knew what had occurred that day. And then either Ernst or Max would suggest, "It must have been a city of phantoms."

Gerhard's older brother, Georg, used to say, "They laughed. Their children laughed. Laughter was the best medicine." Laughter sustained Ernst for the years that remained to him, even though his health was broken by his time in Dachau and the hardships he had experienced when he returned to Vienna.

In March 1954 there was a reunion in Graz for the survivors of Dachau. Ernst travelled to Graz but he was not present at the reunion. Having settled into the Steinhofer Hotel in Graz in high spirits, Ernst did not live through the night. He died of a massive heart attack. Ernst was buried alongside his parents at Artstetten.

That same year Franz Janaczek also died.

It was fortunate that young Ferdinand did not go to live with Elemér and Stéphanie. Stéphanie had reached her eightieth birthday in May 1944. Her determined spirit was unchanged and throughout the war she had held her head high and refused to seek greater safety. But physically she was beginning to struggle. She was now old and frail and very thin after the privations of the war years. Bringing a small child into the house would have been a great strain upon her. Getting about was becoming increasingly difficult so that more and more she found herself confined to her room and her bed.

By 1945 the big issue had become the question of who would arrive first:

the Russians or the Americans? Younger people were leaving while they still could but for the Lónyays it was too late. Back in 1919 they had fled to safety in Switzerland and it had been Elemér's nephew, Carl, who had remained to look after the castle at Oroszvár. In 1945 they could do nothing other than await their fate.

"The Russians are also human beings," said Stéphanie.

Did she really believe that? The moment she feared came on 2nd April 1945. Stéphanie was unable to leave her bed but with a spine as straight as a poker she was sitting up in bed watching the door intently. In her old, twisted hands she held her crucifix tightly. Elemér was sitting on a chair nearby and in the background stood their religious chaplain, a young man named Father Andreas Szennay. And they waited. Before long there were sounds below, orders barked, sudden laughter, sounds of banging and doors slammed. There were heavy feet on the stairs. Then suddenly the door burst open. Faced with the three figures in the room the soldiers stopped in their tracks. Stéphanie raised the crucifix. It was not clear whether the gesture was defiant or imploring.

The foremost soldier stared at the scene before him. Something wasn't quite right. He stepped up to the bed and lifted the coverings. There, trembling, crouched two peasant girls from the village. They had fled to the castle in the hope of escaping from the soldiers. In their search for a hiding place they had burst into Stéphanie's bedroom where Stéphanie, now bedbound, lay.

Shocked at finding themselves face-to-face with the lady of the castle, the two girls froze on the spot. It is likely that they had never seen the Princess before and here they were standing ashamed in front of her. It was Stéphanie, in all her imperious dignity, who gestured to the two girls to hide under her bedclothes. In her croaking voice she insisted that the Russians wouldn't dare pull the bedclothes off an old and sick woman. And perhaps they would not have done so – except the bulge in the bed was so very much larger than Stéphanie's pencil-thin legs might explain.

But the old lady, helpless and bedridden, with her crucifix and her untroubled dignity, somehow impressed the Russian. He let the covers fall back and left the room. The other soldiers behind him turned too and left the room. Finally, the two girls burst out their stammered thanks. And Stéphanie smiled.

But the incident had shown Elemér, at least, that they could not stay there. By July Elemér had succeeded in finding an old cart pulled by oxen and on to this Stéphanie was placed. By then the Russians had indeed been back to the castle and plundered it until there was little left to steal. It was noted that when Stéphanie left her home for the last time she did not have a single shoe to put on her feet, but she could not have stood in them even if she had had shoes.

The cart rattled south towards the old town of Raab and then on a further fifteen kilometres into the Bakony Forest. Their destination: the thousand-year-old Abbey at Pannonhalma. Here the International Red Cross had set up a station of succour for those in need. Here Stéphanie and Elemér found protection.

On 23rd August 1945 Stéphanie left this earth to go to her maker. And forty-five years of marriage with Elemér came to an end. They had been good years. She had loved Elemér, she had esteemed him and found contentment with him. They had created a marriage so very, very different from Stéphanie's first marriage. The world had forgotten Stéphanie. Few were even aware that she was still alive.

She was buried in the crypt of the abbey. Few were there to say goodbye to a great lady. Rudolf and Stéphanie's only daughter, Erzsi, was not there, nor were any of Erzsi's four children. By then the rift between Stéphanie and Erzsi was too deep and too bitter. For years Stéphanie had not even mentioned Erzsi's name, nor would she allow anyone to speak of Erzsi in her presence. In return Erzsi wanted no part in her mother's last years. Long since, Erzsi had wished her mother's soul in hell, and Erzsi was never one to give way.

Elemér outlived his wife by only a year. During that time he saw to it that all the books, letters, papers and all those other things that were full of Stéphanie's memory were brought from Oroszvár to Pannonhalma for safe keeping. They are still there.

On 29th July 1946 Elemér died. He was eighty-three.

Chapter 117

Erzsi grew up into a very spoilt young woman. She had her mother's looks, turning into an unusually tall, slender girl with very blonde hair. She inherited her grandmother's forceful determination and, like her grandmother, she was for most of her life intensely self-centred. Like her father she possessed great charm and in her youth she swam in the warm waters of adulation. But like her father, too, the picture she left behind is one of someone who was ever deeply lonely and empty at the core of her being. Only she didn't know it.

When Stéphanie married her second husband and left her daughter behind at the imperial court in Vienna, she must have done so believing that Erzsi's future would be both secure and comfortable. In 1900 there was no reason to think differently. Come September Erzsi would celebrate her seventeenth birthday and there was every reason to think that marriage and a settled life lay not far off after that.

Stéphanie would have been aware that her daughter was utterly determined to marry a man she adored and respected and she must have hoped that in Prince Otto von Windischgrätz Erzsi had found that man. However, Stéphanie may well have wondered whether the Emperor would ever allow Erzsi to marry someone who was not her equal by birth. If Franz Joseph did refuse to give his permission for their marriage, sooner or later some other more suitable figure would be certain to appear. Did Stéphanie ever suspect that Erzsi was nearly as ignorant of what sort of man she had chosen as Stéphanie herself had been when she had accepted Crown Prince Rudolf?

However, Stéphanie may well have wondered whether the Emperor would ever allow Erzsi to marry someone who was not her equal by birth. If Franz Joseph did refuse to give his permission for their marriage, sooner or later some other more suitable figure would be certain to appear. And Erzsi would in the end get married.

Stéphanie would have assumed that Erzsi would accept what she found in marriage and adapt to it just as she herself had. Stéphanie might have remembered her sister, Louise's, refusal to accept Prince Philipp von Coburg and thought back to Louise's ultimate fate with a shudder. She would have hoped that Erzsi would have the sense to face up to the demands of marriage and its compromises.

Unfortunately, uncompromising obstinacy was Erzsi's key feature. Erzsi was the most self-willed, intransigent, determined and ruthless of beings. She could be so delightful; she had great personality and a fascinating character, but let anyone cross the Emperor's granddaughter and they would discover a force not to be resisted. She believed that the world revolved round her and that she could have and always would have what she wanted. She could not even imagine not getting what she wanted. At the smallest hint of opposition and all Erzsi's determination kicked into play. Her ruthless energy took over. Nobody could gainsay Erzsi once on her high horse.

Certainly not Prince Otto von Windischgrätz.

After Stéphanie had left for Hungary Erzsi had her own household and started to be seen more in public life and at court functions. As mistress of this small circle she was largely free to organise her activities to please herself and this included tennis parties – she had inherited her mother's love of tennis – garden parties to which young aristocrats and senior army officers were invited, and days out riding. Otto von Windischgrätz appeared at a number of these parties and the two began to know something about each other.

The day came when Franz Joseph told her that as a Habsburg Princess she had an important place in the public eye which would involve many duties, sacrifices and a great deal of responsibility. He told her that her demeanour would need to be demure and obedient. He also told her that she should be prepared for marriage and that he, the Emperor, would choose her husband. Erzsi's reaction was neither demure nor obedient. She immediately became excitable and wound up.

"I would rather enter a convent than enter a marriage without love!"

Franz Joseph shook his head. "You will learn from life that happiness is more often to be found in accepting one's duties. Love is a fleeting illness that too often only leads to depths of sorrow."

Desperately upset, Erzsi withdrew to her own rooms. There, one of her ladies-in-waiting, thinking that the cause of her upset had to do with her mother, tried to find words of comfort. But Erzsi wasn't listening. And deep down she did not really believe that it would ever come to her having to accept a man she did not love. Her grandfather had always given in to her pleas. She had always been able to wind him round her little finger. For her, his words were just conventional words, words he had to say but they did not mean anything and he would not hold out against her when she found true love. True love was more powerful than anything on earth. Erzsi never doubted that she would find true love and it would lead her to a life on an exalted plain of intense, ecstatic emotion against which nothing could hold out. Her whole being would be fired by a force she could not resist and could not be expected to resist. Love could never falter, never fail. Love was the meaning of life.

Love walked into her life one brilliant June day.

A day at the races. An international event where the finest riders from all over Europe were competing and where all who belonged to elegant society would be there in all their finery to watch the races. Of course, the Emperor was there; the finest riders in the Imperial Army would be among the competitors. Should any one of the Austrian riders carry off the prize he would bring honour to his whole regiment and would be seen from that moment on as a national hero to be adulated and fêted.

A few minutes after the entrance of the Emperor Erzsi appeared with her suite and made her way up to the imperial box. Her appearance was described in the fashion journals in detail. She was wearing a long dress, pale gold in colour with a broad belt heavily decorated with tiny golden discs and from which hung a bouquet of lily of the valley like a tiny waterfall. The way the folds of the skirt spread outwards from her delicate, tiny waist and swirled around her graceful body lent grace to her movements. Reporters waxed lyrical about her charm. They described her as a figure out of a fairytale, just as her father had once been seen as a fairytale Prince. They gushed over her modesty, her delicacy and the sweetness of her expression.

Erzsi was not a shy person; she loved it that all eyes followed her every move, she loved being the centre of attention. She was aglow with pride. Ever since she had separated from her mother she had grown to enjoy being admired and fêted. She held herself as though poised to float away into the blue sky above. If Stéphanie had seen her at that moment she would have wished her daughter possessed a little more humility. Erzsi was glad that her mother was no longer there to reprove her and she enjoyed the total absence of all restraint.

The main race of the day which carried an international prize was the second race to be run. For this the jumps were higher, the ditches deeper and wider and the dangers greater. Waves of excited anticipation ran through the crowds as the finest horses in Europe, burnished to perfection, danced restlessly on the spot, waiting for the off.

A ripple ran through the spectators as a whisper spread that the course was too difficult. But the horses were off and now all anyone could do was watch heart in mouth as these animals faced their challenges. One rider seemed to separate himself from the crowd, seemed to float over the jumps effortlessly, almost seemed to be lit with an unreal brilliance as he covered the ground making not a single error and winning with flawless ease. And this rider was none other than the handsome Uhlan officer Erzsi had danced so many dances with at her first ball – Prince Otto von Windischgrätz.

At that ball Erzsi's very obvious admiration for this particular officer had provoked many mutterings of disapproval because her attention had been so pointed. But time had gone by and it had all been excused and explained away because of her immaturity. But Erzsi had not forgotten. And here in the summer sunshine was her Prince Charming, tall, handsome and outstanding in all he did. Astride his chestnut thoroughbred stallion, Metallist, he was even more handsome to her eyes than he had been on the dance floor. At the ball her feelings had been lit by candles; here they were set aflame by the sun.

His talent for sport, his vigour and his energy whether on the tennis court or in the saddle or when he was fencing fired her excitement. The way he moved sent shivers through her. She could not turn her eyes away from him. Erzsi had found true love. She was now driven by a desperation for it all to be brought out into the open for all to see. That desperation was so urgent she could not wait.

In the autumn of 1900 Erzsi travelled to Gries to spend some time with her mother. Erzsi wanted one thing only: her mother's approval and support, particularly since Prince Otto von Windischgrätz was most certainly not of equal birth. Erzsi knew that she would not be allowed to marry without the consent of the Emperor but her mother had won consent to marry a man who was not her equal by birth and surely her mother would understand and be behind her?

Her mother did not seem to understand; on the contrary, she seemed to be completely immersed in her own contentment. Erzsi found this enraging. It was not long before Erzsi burst out, "You keep on about your happiness and not even given a thought to whether I am happy!"

Stéphanie told her to enjoy her youth, assuring her that happiness would find her one day. This enraged Erzsi all the more. She may well have, at that moment, drawn herself up to her full height. Coldly she stated that she stood before the door to happiness – and her mother had to open that door for her! Stéphanie listened. Erzsi poured forth her story at great length; one thing only she held back – the name of her heart's desire.

Stéphanie did not ask who this man might be – she went on listening. Doubt and disquiet went through her. She probably hoped that the whole thing would burn itself out.

It was not until the evening before Erzsi was due to return to Vienna that she revealed who had won her heart. Stéphanie may well have been even more concerned about the likely outcome of this first love but with her usual quietness she let Erzsi depart confident of her mother's understanding and support.

By the time Erzsi reached her seventeenth birthday a number of possible marriages hung in the air. Her other grandfather, King Leopold of Belgium wanted to see a marriage between Leo's nephew, Albert, who would one day be King of Belgium, and Erzsi. Leo had never forgiven Stéphanie for marrying Elemér Lónyay; he had never spoken to her again; he had barred Stéphanie from ever seeing her own mother again and prevented Stéphanie from attending her mother's funeral. Had Erzsi ever married Albert she would have gone to live in Belgium and Leo would have prevented Stéphanie from ever seeing her daughter again.

The other contender for Erzsi's hand in marriage was no more acceptable to Franz Joseph than Prince Albert. Kaiser Wilhelm was keen to welcome Erzsi to Berlin as his daughter-in-law and the future Empress of Germany. Franz Joseph brushed all possibility of that aside. It would seem that Franz Joseph quite simply was not ready to see his beloved granddaughter marry and leave his side – not yet.

Towards the end of the year Erzsi set about making her wishes clear to the old man. With some uncertainty and apprehension – an uncertainty she refused to admit even to herself – Ezsi held her head high and in a firm voice she put to him her request. She was totally unaware that she had raised her voice and adopted an almost aggressive stance.

Franz Joseph allowed her to speak. He waited until she had finished. There was a moment's pause and then he spoke slowly and gently, "Listen, Ezsi, you are still so young. Bear that in mind before you make up your mind. In any case, an official announcement before your eighteenth birthday is wholly out of the question," and with that she had to be content. Erzsi was stunned.

When the door was closed behind her it is likely that Franz Joseph shrank a little. It upset him to refuse her anything. That Christmas he gave her a pearl necklace of enormous value. It was an attempt on his part to soften her. To distract her from brooding over Otto, Franz Joseph sent her to Miramare and then to Abbazia for the winter. She then spent the summer of 1901 in Traunkirchen and here, away from the court and its gossip, she enjoyed the attentions of the Duke of Württemberg. These attentions were intense enough to spark off speculation that Ezsi had switched her feelings and become interested in the Duke.

Nothing could have been further from the truth and as her eighteenth birthday drew near Erzsi made that quite clear.

Franz Joseph did not have the energy to go on refusing her. However, his consent came at a price. Because she would be marrying a man not of equal birth, Erzsi would have to renounce her rights within the Habsburg family. Just as Franz Ferdinand had had to renounce all rights his wife and his future children would normally have been entitled to, so Erzsi, too, would have to formally appear before the Emperor and formally swear that she renounced all her rights. Erzsi did so without giving much thought to what she was renouncing; she had little understanding just how much was at stake here – that she would find out later. One right only she retained: she continued to enjoy the title of „kaiserliche und königliche Hoheit".

Years later she became very angry that her mother had allowed her to make that oath. This was unreasonable. Stéphanie had no authority to control her daughter or what became of her. Even though she was Erzsi's mother Stéphanie did not have any guardianship rights over her daughter. There was only one person who could have stood in her way and prevented her making that oath and that person was Franz Joseph himself. But he was the one insisting that if she intended to marry Otto von Windischgrätz then, to obtain his consent, she had to renounce her rights.

Surprisingly little was known about the man Erzsi had set her heart on. His family was a junior branch of the Windischgrätz family. They were aristocrats but not of the highest rank. Otto had a particularly strict upbringing where religion played an important part. Like his father, Otto became an army officer. By all accounts he was a fairly indifferent officer – he was too inclined to waver uncertainly, too unsure of what action it might be best to take, to be a good leader. He was a man who always sought to fit in with others. All his instincts were to please others.

He could smile and charm and fit in and he was a superlative sportsman, the one area where he stood out and excelled. He could ride as though there was no divide between his flesh and that of the horse. He had a natural sense of balance and his movements were deft and assured. He could dance the waltz, gracefully taking the lead and swirling a girl round and round with a sense of rhythm so confident that she could not help but be stirred by it. He was tall and elegant, blond-haired and blue-eyed. This was as much as most people knew about him.

It was about as much as Erzsi knew about him, too. Except that she would never, ever have recognised or admitted that the man who had captured her heart might be a ditherer. She was so sure that any man who could take the lead in a dance the way Otto could had to be strong and clear-sighted. He had to be in perfect command of the moment and everyone around, just as he was in command of her as she melted into his arms and swayed to the rhythm of the music.

But the man she had fallen in love with was a creation of her imagination. She believed him to be her Prince Charming, the perfect cavalier. Someone so elegant, so handsome, so virile and energetic had to be perfection in every way. And to her mind it was not possible to love someone as much as she did without his loving her with equal force and intensity.

Ever since she was small Erzsi had nourished fervent feelings. She felt that this was her father's gift to her. She felt that Rudolf was within her, understanding and encouraging her. Endlessly she replayed in her imagination Rudolf's battle against the bitterness of life. She had long since come to understand that love and death might go hand in hand, weaving themselves into a single flawless emotion. Secretly she admired Mary Vetsera and sometimes almost wished that it could have been she herself who had died alongside her father. She was now sure that she had found such a love with Otto.

She never doubted that he loved her. It never crossed her mind that he might not love her as much as she loved him. She should have doubted it. There is a story that Otto von Windischgrätz had to be ordered to marry her by the Emperor himself.[66] Rumour had it that Otto was commanded to appear before Franz Joseph at Schönbrunn. When Otto realised what was at stake he protested that he was unable to accept so great an honour and furthermore he had already promised himself to another. He could not honourably break his word.

Franz Joseph called his granddaughter to him and explained the situation to her. Erzsi broke down dramatically, she collapsed screaming that she had to marry Otto. Erzsi's outburst was of shocking, unbridled, desperate intensity and Franz Joseph was stunned and bewildered by the force of it.

"My father chose death rather than give up love! I am like my father; I do not fear death either!"[67] and Erzsi went on to insist that only Otto could quench the passion within her, a passion so great that she was willing, if need be, to sacrifice her life for him! And Franz Joseph must have thought, with terrible weight, "not another Mayerling."

The next time Otto appeared before the Emperor Franz Joseph is supposed to have said that he had agreed to Erzsi's marrying Otto and then when that failed to move Otto, Franz Joseph hinted that his army career might be blighted if Otto continued to oppose him. And Otto promised his obedience. For Otto life was all about giving in to what others wanted and bending to the orders of those who really did command.

Otto must have viewed marrying Erzsi with very ambivalent feelings. He was far too much of a gentleman to reveal what his true feelings were. Nothing in his manner had ever at any time hinted at anything more than that he felt the most profound respect. And that was how Erzsi saw it; as honourable a man as Otto would never for one second overstep the line that divided him from her. But did not his eyes glow when he looked her way? Did he not lean towards her ever so slightly more than the strict 'Haltung' of an officer allowed? Of course, she, as a woman, sensed the depth of his love for her. His respect and his holding back only proved that she was right.

---

[66] There are various versions of this story and there is no hard evidence that there is any truth in it, but the fact that it exists at all suggests that there were many who seriously questioned this marriage.

[67] Erzsi's words are quoted in *Kaiseradler und rote Nelke* by Ghislaine Windischgrätz, who was Erzsi's daughter-in-law.

When Otto had retired from the presence of the Emperor for the second time, he sought out Baron Max Venninger, a German officer in the Prussian Guard stationed in Vienna. Long afterwards Max Venninger would look back and remember their meeting; all he would ever say about it was that Otto was confused and desperate.

Max Venninger was eight years older than Otto. He seems to have been the man Otto found most easy to be with and to talk to. Both men were utterly committed to military life and its values and both men were passionately involved with horses. Otto had never had a good relationship with his own father and he found in Max the support his own father could never give him.

That day Max was shocked by the grey expression on Otto's face. The two men withdrew to the smoking room where Max pressed a strong cigar upon Otto. Max then ordered cognac and hung back, waiting for Otto to open up about whatever might be the problem. But Otto could not speak. He smoked heavily, filling the room with the acrid smell of tobacco and several glasses had been emptied before Otto began to get any words out at all. The thing that seemed to be going round and round in Otto's mind was his disbelief that he could be asked – no, pressured – into going back on his word to another woman. Where in all of this lay his honour? Was not the word of an officer his deepest commitment?

Max Venninger was older and a good deal more worldly-wise. This would not be the first time that a man did not quite live up to the image of the fine nobility imbued in every army officer. Late into the night the two men sat and smoked and emptied bottle after bottle of cognac until their befuddled brains were no longer thinking straight. Max grew certain that Otto could and would find an honourable way out. Otto slowly became fired with exalted feelings, a strange recipe of the need for an officer in all honour to embrace unwelcome duties, all mixed up with an instinctive distancing himself from Erzsi and everything to do with her. Nothing made much sense. He came to feel that he had to face the obligation imposed upon him and that his integrity could only be upheld by lifelong repenting for it.

He may even have swung between optimism and pessimism about the whole matter. He had seen enough of her to be aware that she was a handful. She was self-centred, wilful, and domineering. Erzsi on her high horse could be a nightmare. She was also very conscious of her superior position as a member of the Imperial Family and she vaunted her importance. Otto was not the man to stand up to Erzsi.

Once the news was out that he was to marry the Emperor's granddaughter, Otto was lost. He could read the fulsome newspaper reports and wonder whether they were really about him or some other mythical being. The *Pester Lloyd* wrote, "All the conditions essential to a perfect meeting of hearts lie here, sending out waves of warmth and love so that all hearts can share in this blessed bond."

The article went on to speak of the Emperor's delight in this happy outcome. It is very unlikely that Franz Joseph viewed what was happening in such a light. He did, however, provide Erzsi with a generous income 'for the duration of the marriage' to ensure that she would never lack for anything and he bestowed upon Otto a higher title.

On 23rd January 1902 they were married in the Josephi Chapel in the Hofburg. Stéphanie, watching her daughter get married to the man of her choice, may have found her thoughts turning to her own wedding to Rudolf all those years before. Into her mind's eye came a picture of the large, gloomy, echoing Augustinerkirche. The Josephi Chapel was altogether different, smaller and more intimate and Stéphanie would have been conscious of the difference between her own formal, state-imposed ceremony and this more charming and happier event.

In the months leading up to Erzsi's wedding Stéphanie had been around and seen more of her daughter than had been possible since they had been separated by her marriage to Elemér. She offered an overload of advice that Erzsi did not want to listen to. But Stéphanie would have been conscious that in the years to come she would see less and less of Erzsi. So Stéphanie needed to speak now.

From the little she had seen of Otto Stéphanie had formed a very good opinion of him. Many, many years later Erzsi would insist to her own daughter, Stephanie (Fee), that she only married Otto because her mother did not like him and by marrying him Erzsi could spite her mother. But that was when the marriage had irretrievably broken down. If Erzsi seriously believed this story, then she must have done a great deal of re-writing her memories.

At the time of her marriage to Otto nobody had a bad word to say of him. Everywhere Otto gave the impression of great charm and courtesy and an enormous willingness to fit in and be agreeable. Stéphanie would have been delighted for her daughter's sake and possibly she felt that a man so accepting of everything would be less likely to provoke Erzsi into one of her rages.

Did she in her mind secretly whisper a little message to Rudolf that their daughter had every prospect of a happy life ahead of her? Mentally, she might have told Rudolf that he did not need to worry about her. But Stéphanie could not know what life was going to throw at Erzsi and perhaps that was just as well.

When Erzsi and Otto arrived at the station to board the special train which would carry them away on their honeymoon,[68] other memories would have sprung into Stéphanie's mind as she watched Erzsi bid goodbye to her grandfather. Erzsi bent her head and kissed his hands tenderly, visibly moved and with tears in her eyes. Surely Stéphanie could not help remembering how the old man had come to the station to bid her goodbye when she had left Vienna to go to her second marriage to Elemér? And she would remember how she, too, at that moment had been touched with a stab of great affection for Franz Joseph. Now, with Erzsi reaching out to her own married independence, Stéphanie would have even less reason to come to Vienna.

Through February, March and April the newly-married couple enjoyed a honeymoon journey that took them south through Italy, visiting Florence, Rome, Naples and on to Sicily and Malta before arriving in Egypt. They returned via Athens and from there they sailed back to Trieste, arriving back in Vienna on 13th May 1902.

Otto's thoughts now turned to his military duties. These required him to spend some time in Prague. Just as early on in their marriage Rudolf and Stéphanie had lived in Prague, Otto and Erzsi did the same. They made their home in the Villa Groebe. But in those early months, military matters do not seem to have taken up much of Otto's time and their married life was a round of visits, sports events and special receptions in honour of the young couple.

That first year, to all outward appearances, flowed on a wave of untroubled married bliss and Otto succeeded in giving Erzsi the kind of life she had dreamed of, full of luxury and pleasure but spiced with adventure, too.

Come the autumn Erzsi was delighted to find that she was expecting her first child. Things did not run smoothly. Erzsi had chosen to travel to Nice for the last two months of her pregnancy. Climbing into the train Erzsi slipped on the step and fell. Everyone rushed over to help her up and when she felt steady again she climbed into the train and joined Otto in their carriage. She seemed to be fine and never once complained of any pain but the next day she suffered a miscarriage. Erzsi's tears and grief were extreme.

Then complications set in which required an operation. And on the day before the operation Otto asked his wife to make a will, leaving him her

---

[68]   Note 17 in the Notes Section.

wealth. This request shocked Erzsi who could not believe that in the hours before her operation her husband could be thinking of his future income. Was he more taken up by her wealth than her health?

Erzsi was the sort of person who never forgot or forgave and this remained with her, souring her mind and causing resentment that lingered on and on, festering. At the same time Otto's attention was increasingly turning towards his military duties. He had begun to feel that he had absented himself enough from his regiment. He needed to take part more in regimental activities; his duty to the army demanded it.

Erzsi's reaction was one of outrage. She wanted him at her side, bending to her will. Nothing could be allowed to prevent that. Otto began to get a taste of how highhanded and how strong-willed she could be. It was not in Otto's character to stand up to difficult people. He had given way to her in everything since the day he had found himself engaged to her. Which made it all the harder to stand up to her now. Was there ever a time when he could have done so? Once again Otto gave in. He withdrew from active service. Erzsi calmed down a bit, convinced that he had made the right decision and she looked forward to greater harmony between them and untroubled enjoyment of each other's company.

Erzsi did not make a will until 22nd March 1904 and three days later she gave birth to a boy, Franz Joseph (Franzi). Throughout her pregnancy Otto had bent to her slightest demand. He was tender towards her and concerned for her well-being and Erzsi basked in his unwavering attention. And the baby when he arrived was strong and vigorous. When Erzsi cradled her son in her arms and looked down into his round little face she felt aglow with the feeling that nobody else had ever done anything as wonderful as this or produced anything as exceptional as this baby. Many a new mother might feel like this, but Erzsi could never have admitted that her feelings were not unique. It was Marie-Valérie who was the first person to hurry to Erzsi's side after she had given birth to wish her well and to greet the newborn child.

From that moment on, the force of Erzsi's mother-love was fierce. In a way that smacks somewhat of Elisabeth's smothering of Marie-Valérie, Erzsi would love and smother her own three sons. With her one and only daughter, Stephanie (who was known in the family as Fee), her relationship was always a difficult one, just as Erzsi's relationship with her own mother was a difficult one.

By then there were real and deep rifts in the marriage. The loss of his active military career gnawed away at Otto. He now stonewalled Erzsi, keeping her at arm's length, and all the while his spirits sank lower and lower. Because he buried deep his personal thoughts and feelings, people around him came to regard him as superficial and easy-going. Erzsi was the exact opposite. The more she felt that she could not touch him or even get a reaction from him, the more violent and explosive her behaviour.

Otto might bend to her every demand when he was with Erzsi but increasingly he was trying to get away from her to somewhere where he could breathe more freely. In some ways this was getting easier. As a mother Erzsi found it harder to go out and leave her children behind so Otto would go on his own. He kept up his sports activities. He was building up a social circle into which she did not come.

And because she was increasingly being left alone Erzsi escaped back to Vienna whenever she could. She was happier in Vienna. Little by little they were beginning to see less and less of each other. To Otto this was a relief but Erzsi was increasingly angry that he was not permanently at her side. She felt unloved, abandoned, jittery, frustrated, eaten up with an anguish she could not calm as if she had insects walking all over her skin and no one to caress them away and ease her tension.

She set about having Otto followed to find out what he did do when she wasn't with him.

Nothing in her life up until that moment had ever prepared Erzsi for not getting her own way. She had no resources for dealing with such a situation. Over and over she read the report that in due course was put into her hands. She paced up and down, unable to believe the dry, prosaic words. Her throat had gone dry and she could not breathe.

Marie Ziegler. She was a member of the Prague Opera Company, a singer.

Prince Otto von Windischgrätz had become a frequent, regular visitor to the Prague Opera. And Marie Ziegler had been seen with him driving in the park. Marie Ziegler had been to the Villa Groebe and stayed the night. Perhaps she had even been in Erzsi's own boudoir, perhaps even in her bed. Erzsi was so shocked she could not even summon up anger. Whilst she was here in Vienna, Marie Ziegler was free to go in and out of her home in Prague!

The report ended with the information that on the following day Marie Ziegler had been invited for four o'clock at the Villa Groebe.

With the first grey light of dawn the following morning Erzsi was up. She had not slept and she was exhausted. She had told nobody what had happened, explained to nobody the changes in her arrangements. Accompanied only by her lady's maid, she set off for the station.

Rudolf, in the last years of his life, had insisted upon Loschek placing a pair of loaded pistols under his pillow. Whether Erzsi knew this or not is not known, but for some time she, too, had slept with a loaded pistol under her pillow. She had that pistol with her when she climbed into the Prague train that morning. Throughout the journey she said nothing. One look at her face would have been all it needed to discourage her companion from any attempt at conversation. By the middle of the afternoon they arrived in Prague. They reached the Villa Groebe at very nearly exactly the time when the young singer was expected. By this time Erzsi felt icy with tension.

She did not greet the butler who opened the front door to her. She surged through the hallway towards the salon from where she could hear the sound of voices. She pushed aside anyone who attempted to speak to her, throwing open the door of the salon. And before anybody could even grasp what was happening a shot had rung out, there was a piercing cry of terror, and on the ground lay Marie Ziegler with a thin stream of blood coming from her throat.

The whole affair was hushed up. Erzsi had to be protected from publicity or criticism. She could not be held accountable for her actions.

Fortunately, Marie Ziegler recovered and she now became an embarrassment to the Imperial Family. She was invited to leave the country and never return. Marie Ziegler disappeared as if she had never existed.

She went to America where she was able to pick up her career, singing with American opera houses and making a name for herself. Her story of how she came to leave Austria did her no harm. On the contrary it lent her a romantic aura which she promoted to the fullest possible extent.

She spoke to a journalist which resulted in her dramatic story being blazened across America. In Austria the press did not dare make any mention of her or the reason for her disappearance. But once the American press had made a big thing of the story one hardy Austrian newspaper got round the censors by reporting that there were inflammatory reports circulating in the US press of something shocking that had happened in Prague and in the process revealing the stories themselves.

Chapter 118

Otto never did get his relationship with Erzsi on to an even keel. He was not the powerful, gentle cavalier she could swamp in exalted love and into whose sublime adoration she could sink. And yet he sought to please her, to reassure her, to placate her, he sought to reason with her, he was conciliatory with her, he promised to change his behaviour, to hold back when there were ladies around – everything, except one thing: he refused to concede that he was to blame. But in Erzsi's eyes he was to blame. Apologies were called for – more than apologies, some kind of abasement that acknowledged just how much he had hurt and upset her. Nothing less would wipe away Erzsi's upset feelings. The caress she craved that would smooth her ruffled fur never came, insects walked up and down her skin and her jitters and tension just intensified.

Otto had no idea how to handle her. She was too temperamental. One moment she was so sweet, so emotionally warm and outgoing, the next she was a tiny bundle of fury, her eyes shrunk into pinpricks of exploding sparks, her voice sharp like a blade on metal. His heart would sink – not just because he was the brunt of all this anger, and usually he had no idea why, but because he had come to know that it would take her hours to come down from this peak of emotional fury.

More and more Otto tried to fend off the next outrage. More and more he did everything he could to avoid provoking her. He refused to react, he refused to respond to her accusations, he stonewalled. And in doing so he enraged her. Erzsi could not calm down until she had succeeded in provoking him into a reaction. He was doing everything he could to avoid reacting to her outbursts. She was losing her hold over him.

Otto, for his part, buried himself in his horses. Only when he was around horses did he find satisfaction and escape from the perpetual battle. He spent a small fortune on horses. And more than once the Emperor had to fend off creditors by paying off Otto's debts. Not just Otto's debts. Erzsi, too, spent money as though acquiring clothes, furs, luxuries would assuage her inner emptiness.

There was one occasion when Erzsi had ordered the couturier who made her fur coats to come up to the palace. A massive selection of the finest minks and other furs were laid out and displayed before her. Models sashayed up and down showing off these luxurious garments. Erzsi was so excited by all that was glowingly displayed before her. She was unable to chose. This one? No? Maybe that one? Or the other one? With a flounce and a flourish she bought almost all of them. They remained spread out across the salon in all their glory.

Then in rushed Erzsi's four small French bulldogs and set to playing and gambolling in amongst the furs. Now that they were hers Erzsi no longer found them so magnificent and she brushed aside the damage her dogs had done. Otto, when he got back, could not believe his eyes. He was also horrified by the bill. It must have crossed his mind that she had the gall to complain about his spending on horses!

After the birth of her second son, Ernst Weriand (always known as Erni), Erzsi was slow to recover her strength and her doctors suggested recuperating somewhere warm. For Erzsi this meant Italy. Erzsi loved Italy. Otto was completely indifferent to all things Italian; lounging about in the sun bored him silly. Erzsi loved the sun, the warmth, the bright colours, the whole atmosphere. She also loved being constantly on the move from one place to the next; Otto found her restlessness exasperating. Otto's greatest pleasure came when the land was hidden beneath a white, untouched blanket of snow and he could race his horse-drawn sleigh over its crisp, cold whiteness. In this as in everything else they had little in common and their differences only exacerbated their frustrations. Erzsi had dreamed of a passionate love that could only grow and grow; instead her marriage had turned into bitter disappointment.

For the sake of appearances Otto never failed to accompany his wife to the round of balls, soirées and social events that Vienna offered, but when the doors closed behind them at the end of the evening the masks fell away. Like a wild cat Erzsi would turn upon him and Otto's visor would come down blanking her out. One night, Erzsi's state was so overheated that Otto withdrew to the safety of his own room, leaving her floundering. She struggled to go to sleep herself but her nerves were too taut. Pistol in hand she went over to his room. A servant barred her way, murmuring that His Highness was asleep and could not be disturbed. Blazing with cold rage, Erzsi fired at the door, missing the frightened servant by only inches. The bullet penetrated the door and ended up buried in the parquet floor.

And if she had managed to enter the room and actually shot her husband? What might have been the outcome then? Erzsi herself would have taken it for granted that she, a Habsburg, was above the law and the matter would have been hushed up just as the shooting of Marie Ziegler had been hushed up. She would also have felt utterly justified in her actions.

She had been let down as a wife. A woman had to have love and she had been denied love. Her great, overwhelming love had been trampled under foot. No feeling woman, in Erzsi's eyes, could have withstood the hurt and provocation she had endured. And with all the protection she could count upon from the Emperor she would have got away with it.

But that was the moment when Otto knew that there was no saving their marriage.

Not only was it beyond his power to resolve their differences, he no longer had the smallest wish to do so. There was an exchange of accusatory letters, mostly passing through either lawyers' or doctors' hands, rather than directly between the two of them. In these letters Erzsi was a great deal more explicit than women of her time would normally have been. She bluntly accused Otto of being unable to satisfy her sexual needs and failing her as a woman.

"He had undoubtedly," she wrote, "so weakened his health in youthful excesses that he came to our marriage as less than a full man." She saw him and his failure to be a man as the root cause of her nerves and unhappiness. She called him frigid.

Otto replied that it was her frigidity that drained the ardour from him. We can imagine Erzsi laughing a raucous, sarcastic laugh at this. She, who was so passionate, frigid? And coming from a man who was cold through and through! What had he ever done to show he cared for her? All those years they had lived in Prague, a city she now disliked intensely. He had never learned how to understand her and offer her what she needed. For ten years they had been married and now Erzsi came to think that Otto had stolen those ten years from her.

During those last two years before the outbreak of the First World War they lived apart. Much of that time she chose to live somewhere along the Adriatic coast, sometimes on the island of Brioni which lay just off the port of Pola, sometimes at Miramare, and occasionally she returned to Vienna where she would find her old apartments in the Hofburg or at Schönbrunn awaiting her. As a result the young men whose company she sought were, for the most part, young officers in the Marines. They came to accompany her on rides on horseback into the wonderful countryside; they came to play tennis with her; they came to soirées and evening meals that lingered late into the night.

With these Marines she often behaved with a total lack of decorum. On one occasion she laced their meals with a strong laxative, causing the unfortunate young men considerable anguish. The laxative was potent enough and took effect fast enough that the Marines desperately had to find a way of escaping the dinner hall – but the conventions of the time demanded that guests could not rise from the table until the hostess herself rose. In the end, in desperation they had to flee. Did they come back and feel they had to apologise for their lack of manners in not waiting until she had risen from the table? How did Erzsi behave? Did she find it all funny?

Was she giggling? History does not relate. Did she not realise that such a thing was tasteless in the extreme?

The separation between Erzsi and Otto was not complete, for Otto regularly visited his wife. This did much to keep up appearances. He also did his best to fend off and contradict the growing gossip that swirled around Erzsi. Otto was far more concerned about the effect the gossip might have upon his children. Otto adored his children and his visits were really to see them. The elder two boys, particularly, were aware of what was going on between their parents. The eldest, Franzi went through a period when he was particularly critical of his mother.

It was during the second half of 1913 that Erzsi came to know Lieutenant Egon Lerch, a young naval officer. Egon Lerch was to be the second great love of her life. Just as thirteen years earlier she had lost her heart to Otto von Windischgrätz, so she now lost her heart to Egon Lerch. From the first moment she saw him her heart flipped. Just as she had once gone after Otto single-mindedly, so she now went after Egon and pursued him with every bit as much determination as she had pursued Otto. And the two men were certainly cut from the same cloth. Egon, like Otto, was tall, blond and blue-eyed. Like Otto, he had an oval face with strong masculine features. He was a fine sportsman and a military man to the core, subscribing very much to the same pride and principles as Otto. He was very much a ladies' man who enjoyed the attentions of a large number of attractive women and had no wish to tie himself down with any of them. At the core of his being was a love of adventure and taking risks. He was hotheaded and high-spirited, everything that Erzsi admired. He was never one to conform.

Up until the moment Erzsi met Egon she had shown just enough discretion for gossip about her not to explode into scandal. Now she threw discretion to the wind. Love was a woman's destiny and for true love no price was too high to pay. Conventions were artificial constraints that should not be allowed to impede great love. And Erzsi was caught in the grip of a great love. She was powerless to resist. She was fired by great new strength to go after it.

One cold, gloomy winter's evening in December stood the express train to Trieste in Vienna's Südbahnhof waiting the guard's whistle to signal its departure. Otto guided his wife down the platform while on her other side was Erzsi's personal doctor. Erzsi herself was wrapped almost to her eyeballs against the bitter cold in a thick, envelopping fur coat. The two men helped her climb into the carriage which had been reserved for her. She had lost weight and was as thin as a lamppost which only emphasised Erzsi's unusual height. She was pale and looked more fragile than ever. Erzsi had been in a clinic for observation and now she was heading off to warmer climes for recuperation.

Then, leaning through the window of the carriage door Erzsi smiled one of her warmest smiles at Otto. She had not smiled at him like that in a long time and that smile must have twisted Otto's heart. He had collected her from the clinic, brought her to the station and was seeing her off, knowing that she was going straight to join Egon Lerch. That smile was the smile of anticipation and joy at the thought of what lay before her.

Otto would return home and tell anyone that she needed to recuperate, knowing how far from the truth that was. He would speak of how pale she had become and how much she needed to build up her strength. And across his mind would flash the picture of her face looking unusually vulnerable. Yet no one knew better than Otto how strong she was, how forceful her determination to get what she wanted.

It was not the loss of Erzsi that was upsetting Otto so much – he had lost her years ago. He was not even sure whether he had ever had her or even whether he had ever wanted her.

No, it was what impact what she was doing was having upon his children that gnawed away at Otto. Unlike so many aristocratic mothers, Erzsi had always insisted upon taking her children with her everywhere. She was intensely maternal, clinging to her children and smothering them with her overpowering love. As a mother she was as impulsive and as extreme as she was in everything else. She had taken them where Otto would have preferred they did not go. What had they seen and learned that might harm them? How were they coping with a mother like Erzsi? Otto later found a photograph of his daughter, Fee, sitting on Egon's knees which he found deeply troubling. And Otto didn't know what he should do about it.

When the train reached Graz there was Egon waiting for her. He climbed into the train and joined Erzsi in her sleeper carriage. Erzsi fell into his arms.

Erzsi's great love affair with Egon did not last long. He never had the chance to rub her up the wrong way; she never did uncover his little flaws. The outbreak of war took him away from her. On 21st August 1914 he was promoted to commander of the submarine U12. To begin with the sorties of the U12 were neither risky nor heroic. This chafed Egon Lerch. He yearned for exciting action. But the submarine was not called upon to go far from its base on the Adriatic coast of Dalmatia, its main function being to patrol the coast for enemy ships.

On 7th December the U_{12} torpedoed a French ship, the *Jean Bart*, and sank it, but it was not until May 1915 when Italy entered the war on the side of the French that defending the Dalmatian coast became more critical. On 28th May the U_{12} crossed the Gulf of Trieste when Egon Lerch noticed an unidentifiable ship. The U_{12} followed it for some three hours until midnight when Egon Lerch gave the order to fire and sink the ship.

It turned out to be a Greek ship, the *Virginia*, at a time when Greece was neutral. The Austrian authorities sought to play down the matter, insisting that the ship had been sunk by a mine, but at the same time they offered to recompense Greece for its loss. Egon Lerch received a mild reproof and he seems to have come away from the matter all the more fired up to get involved in the action.

On 7th August 1915 the U_{12} was lost at sea. First reports were that the U_{12} had been torpedoed; later it was established that U_{12} had hit an enemy ship, the *Brandolo*, and then followed the ship to finish it off. The *Brandolo* had suffered only minor damage. Its commander, who knew those waters well and knew also that his ship had been designed for sailing in the relatively shallow waters of the Venice lagoon, then ordered it to sail across a part of the ocean known to be mined. The *Brandolo* sailed unscathed over the danger zone but the submarine was too close to the mines and one exploded. A second mine exploded ten minutes later but it has never been established whether the U_{12} had by then been fatally sunk. The U_{12} should not have been following the ship – Egon Lerch's orders were to observe the *Brandolo* and when he sailed after it he received orders to withdraw, orders he ignored. He and his crew never returned to shore.

When Erzsi first learned that her lover was missing she hurried to Trieste, still clinging to hope that he might yet be found alive. But it was not long before all hope was gone. She returned to Vienna, taking with her Egon's Alsatian bitch, Lona. In her bag she had a small paper packet with Egon's uniform buttons and a pair of engraved cufflinks and the band from his officer's cap, embroidered with the letters U_{12}.

In 1917 the Italians set about bringing back to land the sunken Italian submarine, the *Medusa*, and in the process they raised the U_{12} from the seabed as well. The explosion had cut the U_{12} in half. Seventeen bodies were found inside but these could not be identified. The bodies were then taken to the island of St. Michele to be buried.

Otto's war was fought on the Russian front. He sought to share his men's hardships with them and he endured with them the worst of the

Russian's campaign. He was a crushed and exhausted man when he returned to Vienna on his first leave from the front in 1915. There he learned that Egon Lerch had been a frequent visitor to his home. In fact, his arrival interrupted Erzsi's happiness and she turned upon him, spitting hatred and resentment at him.

On the next occasion he came home on leave it was to find Erzsi in the depths of grief for Egon. Otto became the brunt of all her anger and desperation. She felt that he was – somehow – to blame for Egon's death. She could not bear Otto even being in the same building. Erzsi now knew that the only way forward was a complete break with him. She never wanted to see him again. She never wanted him in her house again. And she did not want her children to have any further connection with him. But she also did not want the separation to turn into a legal divorce. If it came to that Otto, according to Austrian law and tradition, would get custody of the four children.

Throughout their marriage Erzsi had remained unshaken in her conviction that all the problems that existed between them were entirely the fault of Otto. She still believed that the whole matter of Marie Ziegler had come about because of Otto's unreasonable behaviour and in no way could any fault be attributed to her. On a number of occasions she had insisted that he had to change his attitude. Now she wrote to Otto proposing another attempt at reconciliation, again demanding that he change his behaviour towards her.

But Otto too had changed. For the first time he was not willing to give in to her demands. Otto replied that without a change in her attitude he was not prepared to go along with her proposed reconciliation. But the attempt to rebuild their relationship was scarcely put to the test. Otto was away at the front fighting. Erzsi's grief over Egon's death had begun to sink into a dull ache and she had begun to live her life through her children.

Her two older sons, Franzi and Erni, had need of her attention. Neither boy had ever been particularly strong and that winter of 1916 both were seriously unwell. Professor Pirquet, a specialist in tuberculosis, believed that they were suffering from consumption which would explain why they were so very weak. Professor Pirquet's treatment involved a restrictive diet and he pressed Erzsi to get the boys away and into the mountains where the cold, clean air would be good for their lungs. Erzsi hated the mountains and the snow but for her children she would do anything. She nursed the boys herself and barely left their sides.

She did, however, leave them when the news reached her that her grandfather's health had taken a turn for the worse. The days passed as the old man sank. Erzsi sought out the company of Marie-Valérie, the one person who was allowed in to see her father more often than anyone else during those last long hours. Erzsi stayed in Vienna just long enough to play her part in the final ceremonies in honour of Franz Joseph, and then she collected up her boys and hurried them away to the Tirol for the rest of the winter.

From the moment that Franz Joseph died that November 1916 Otto was aware that the most powerful man in the country, whom Erzsi could twist round her little finger and from whom she had always got what she wanted, was now no longer there to take her side.

In this new situation Otto knew what he wanted. He wanted a much greater say in how his children were being brought up. In a letter of 18th January 1919 he wrote, "In particular it is unacceptable that my children in future continue to remain in the care of my completely deranged wife. It seems to me in these circumstances that it is my duty as a father to take over the care and the upbringing of my children."

Chapter 119

Emperor Karl soon proved to have little sympathy for Erzsi. She had expected that Karl could be persuaded to influence the course of the divorce so that, firstly, matters did not come to court and, secondly, that she, and she alone, had care of the children and that she, and she alone, took all decisions concerning their welfare.

Karl was formal and unforthcoming. He told her that she was no longer a member of the Habsburg family, reminding her of the oath she made renouncing her rights before she married Otto. It was at this point that Erzsi's fury turned upon Stéphanie for letting her sign away her rights so as to be allowed to marry Otto.

Karl went on to tell her that he could have no part in the divorce process. And then he dismissed her with cool assurances of both his sympathy and Zita's for her. To Erzsi's ears these words sounded like a mockery. What enraged her even more was the fact that any divorce petition had to come from Otto and that the courts would regard her behaviour as having been unreasonable. It would be her unfaithfulness that would be dragged through the courts. She chose to ignore the fact that she was currently having a fling with one of her sons' tutors. Franzi was well aware of what was going on and she knew it, which should have been a cause for shame, but that did not ruffle Erzsi in the least.

Early in 1913 Erzsi wrote Franzi a letter which was to be given to him on his eighteenth birthday. Erzsi wrote that he should listen to his mother who loved him so very, very deeply. She then went on to write about duty. He should choose a career and then stick to it no matter how demanding or difficult that might be. Never forget that life means work. Titles and rank mean nothing, at best are a burden and that it is only inner worth emanating from what one is and what one has achieved that has any real meaning. He should turn his back on the so-called pleasures of the world.

How Franzi felt about that letter when he finally got it is not known but you might wonder whether it did not turn the knife in the wound. Franzi was fond of his father and he enjoyed it whenever he could spend time with his father. How much did these words push Franzi into thinking about his father? Franzi must have considered how much his father had lived just the kind of life Erzsi was describing. Franzi must have felt all the more drawn into supporting his father's side of the story. In the battle that was about to be fought between Erzsi and Otto, Franzi clearly was not wholeheartedly on his mother's side in the way she assumed.

One card, at least, she did have up her sleeve. The children were not strong and robust and she could argue that they needed a mother's care and nursing capabilities. Tuberculosis threatened them; both boys were anaemic and suffered from relentless vomiting. None of the four children could be described as really well.

Their divorce was very public. It was also very bitter and acrimonious, a wildcat fight fought in full view of all. Erzsi must have drawn herself up to her full, imposing height. It was beneath her dignity to even consider Otto's accusations against her. The only one she replied to was the accusation that she had had a passionate affair with Egon Lerch. Here it was beneath her dignity to deny something so fine and wonderful as the great love that had existed between her and Egon. But the fault for it lay with Otto. It was he whose neglect of her had forced her into the arms of a great man and a great hero.

She tore into Otto's character with every insult she could think of, ending up that he had always treated her and her children heartlessly and when enraged he would not hold back from any brutality.

Amongst all the other shafts she launched at him was the accusation that he had given up his active military career to live idly off her wealth. What seems to have obsessed Erzsi the most was Otto's weakness of character and his superficiality. He was only interested in appearances, in being seen at the most prestigious occasions, and in clothes that revealed his status and prestige – badly pressed trouser creases could send him into a rage. His vanity and his greed knew no limits.

Erzsi also got a string of doctors, tutors, pedagogues, servants and observers to stress to the court that she was a totally devoted mother while Otto had only a cool and distant relationship with the children. He had seen little of them and taken little interest in them.

There was some truth here – Otto had seen little of the children, partly because of his military career and partly because Erszi did all she could to prevent the children ever seeing their father. Again and again Erzsi had moved the children around to make it difficult for their father to see them. And no one could doubt Erzsi's close, almost overpowering, attachment to them.

It took the court weeks and months to divide up property and capital and it was not until the spring of 1920 that the issue of the custody of the children really came to the fore. In the end the court decided that it fell to the father to have the care of the children. However, in this case, because the two older boys were seriously unwell the court felt that Franzi and Erni should remain with their mother. Thus Rudolf, their youngest son, and Fee should be handed over to Otto. Both parents should have access to all four children.

On 15th July 1920 Otto arrived at the palace at Schönau to collect Rudolf and Fee. They were twelve and eleven years old. He did not, of course, go alone but brought with him a number of his companions from his war days. He needed their presence to bolster his position. Otto expected trouble and he had told his men that his ex-wife was capable of using violence against them but above all they were not to use any force at all. He was aware that this bunch of soldiers would be intimidating and he wanted to minimise that. If the children refused to go with Otto then they would not be made to go with him.

As might have been expected the two children shrank back and refused to go with him. Nobody knows what they had been told to expect. They had shared their mother's ups and downs throughout the proceedings and she had drawn them into her emotions as things progressed. They would have been very familiar with her angers and fears. Their lives had been lived within the compass of Erzsi's emotional extremes. And they probably feared them. But this was all they had ever known and what might lie ahead must have felt strange and frightening. They clung to their mother. It didn't help that their older brothers would be staying with their mother. And Erzsi had trained them well.

The next day Otto was back. This time Erzsi created an emotional scene – her children had been so frightened and now they were seriously ill with high temperatures. The court ordered that a police doctor of their chosing should go to Schönau and check just what state the children were in. Dr. Stoiber reported back that the children were in no state to travel. They were suffering from nervous exhaustion. They must be protected from all excitement.

So Otto ordered an independent medical examination. Erzsi refused to let the children be further disturbed. To find out what really was happening the Court Judge himself went out to Schönau. There he found two children, very weak, both in tears begging him not to force them away, and insisting that if they were taken against their will they would run away from their father's house.

Otto then applied to the court for the two older boys, Franzi and Erni, to come and spend the remainder of the school holidays with him while Erzsi nursed her two sick younger children. The court learned that Franzi and Erni were desperately against going with their father and it then conceded that perhaps it was too early to make changes in the children's lives.

The summer came to an end and Otto had got nowhere. The matter was then handed over into the jurisdiction of the Baden Court and it fell to a senior lawyer, Dr. Lamel, to sort it all out. Before Dr. Lamel had had the time to read through the court papers a petition from Erzsi fell upon his desk. When it came to defending her own interests Erzsi suffered from a form of verbal explosion. It must have seemed to Dr. Lamel that the equivalent of *War and Peace* had landed in his hands.

This first volley from Erzsi recounted an incident that took place in January 1921. The children were due to visit their father. Their tutor, Tibor Kerekes, had accompanied them there. Once face to face with Otto they insisted that they would not stay with him. Standing in the hallway they refused to take their outdoor clothes off. They refused to listen to their father. According to Erzsi, Otto lost his temper and slapped Ernst Weriand on the ear. In a terrible emotional state the children fled their father's house.

It is not clear whether Tibor Kerekes was the tutor whose favours Erzsi was enjoying at that time. It was certainly in Tibor's interests to remain on the right side of Erzsi, his job depended upon it. Erzsi treated her servants badly – even her own daughter-in-law, Ghislaine, admitted that. Erzsi was imperious, high-handed, demanding and often unreasonable with them. So it seems pretty certain that Erzsi had pressed Tibor into supporting her stories and he would have done so. The children could never, ever have formed an understanding of their father that was not highly coloured by Erzsi's attitude towards him.

Dr. Lamel proceeded with caution. His first move was to send a doctor, Dr. Raab, and two female officers from the court's childcare department over to Schönau. They came back to report that the children's health made it impossible for them to leave their mother. Dr. Lamel called Otto in for a two-hour meeting where he was impressed by Otto's warmth and affection for his children. Once again the law gave Otto rights that clearly Erzsi was not going to concede.

The first day of spring that year of 1921 was overcast and gloomy – appropriate, given what was to take place that day. One Johann Zach headed up a bunch of officials along with a number of armed soldiers and went over to Schönau. They met a small army of bystanders curious to watch the dénoument of this drama. In the car with them were Alexandrine Windischgrätz and Gabriele Rechberg who were there to take care of the children and comfort them. The time was a quarter to eight in the morning. All the doors and windows of the palace were locked. Outside the front door stood a bunch of estate workers headed by one Georg Geissler who stepped forward as Johann Zach and his men approached. No one, thundered Geissler, was to be allowed into the palace.

But one door round the back was not locked and an entrance was gained. (You might wonder whether somebody from inside the castle had found a way of letting sombody in Zach's party know that they could gain entry through this particular door.)

Zach's group of men soon found themselves faced with Tibor Kerekes. The house was filled with screams. And none was making more noise than Erzsi.

In the car Alexandrine Windischgrätz and Gabriele Rechberg sat frightened as the surrounding crowd pressed up to the car windows hurling insults and shouting abuse at them. In amongst all this abuse was a lot of stuff about Otto von Windischgrätz having stolen money that was now in Yugoslavia which Erzsi had promised to them, the workers, and they, the workers, were not going to let the children go.

It started to rain.

Johann Zach came back to the car and climbed in. He had called the whole thing off. He was not going to drag terrified, weeping children away from their mother.

A few days later Erzsi gave some journalists an interview. She was a spitting fury who could not find enough insults to launch at her ex-husband. Otto had taken Yugoslav nationality, inspired by the treacherous instinct of the Serbs against the House of Habsburg, in order to rob her of her wealth. Otto had given his support to the Serb government and accused her of conspiring with Admiral Horthy (the Hungarian leader). Otto's family castle was now in Yugoslavia and he had been offered a Yugoslav passport. In fact, Erzsi herself and her children also had Yugoslav passports, but she did not mention that. Nor did she mention that she had written to her mother begging Stéphanie to go urgently to the Yugoslav Consulate to obtain her papers;[69] Erzsi did not obtain Austrian nationality until some time later.

"He represents," she finished, "the kind of aristocrat who in literature and on the stage is scorned as an unworthy, morally weak, cowardly 'Geck'..."[70] She described Johann Zach as a man with a horsewhip prepared to thrash the children into submission. But the wonder was, she went on, that the people had turned out to defend the great-grandchildren of their beloved Emperor. What she did not say was that she might have had a hand

---

[69] The reason for all this was to protect Stéphanie. There was a fear that Elemér's and Stéphanie's home at Oroszvár might be confiscated by the state on the grounds that they were members of the Habsburg family. The papers were to be sent to Paris and Erzsi believed that from there she could do much to get her mother's property back. But these nationality complications lingered on. In 1922 Franzi, Erzsi's eldest son, was called up for military service by the Yugoslav authorities. Erni was called up a year later. Both of them ignored the call to military service and they were declared deserters. For the rest of their lives they never put foot on Yugoslav soil.

[70] 'Geck' = fop, dandy, crook.

in their turning out and throwing insults around. What she did not say was that she had become a paid-up member of the Social Democrat Party and could call upon the support of a small army of workers.

The matter now became an issue to be debated in parliament. The accusations that Otto was now a Yugoslav had clearly caught some people by surprise and that too needed to be investigated. The President of the Austrian Republic, Michael Hainisch, also got involved as he later mentioned in his memoirs. Things had swung round to the view that the four children should be kept together and stay with their mother.

Elisabeth Windischgrätz in all her dignity presented herself personally to the President to offer him her profoundest thanks. She walked away from it all, her head high. She had won – her children remained in her care.

But some of the servants had always been aware that the younger children especially had been afraid of their mother. Franzi certainly had begun to show signs of mental health issues. He was to become someone who was always unsure of himself in social situations. And all four of the children pulled away from her as soon as they were old enough to do so. All of them eventually became estranged from their mother.

Chapter 120

Erzsi had always placed her father on a pedestal. In her mind Rudolf had not a flaw in any way and Stéphanie was the cause of his final descent into despair. She collected up everything she could lay her hands on that related to him: weapons, garments, uniforms, furniture, newspaper articles and documents. She needed to obtain everything that might relate to him, however remotely. Anything that did not fit her picture of him she refused to consider at all.

The more intensely Erzsi came to revere her father the worse her relationship with her mother became. As a result she had less and less contact with Stéphanie. Stéphanie went on trying to maintain a close relationship with Erzsi. Her letters to her daughter are effusive in tone; she poured out words of fondness and signed herself affectionately '*deine innigst liebende Mamminkerl*' ("your deeply loving Mummy"). But Erzsi remained cold to all this. In the end the rift between mother and daughter reached a pitch where neither was speaking to the other and Stéphanie ended up cutting Erzsi out of her will.

Erzsi also saw herself as Rudolf's reincarnation, in female form. She saw herself as being imbued with his force of character. She believed in his capacity to uphold fine principles and, if need be, to take whatever came his way in defence of those principles.

But Erzsi was unaware of how much Rudolf was a wavering character, always unsure of himself deep down, or how much he craved support and approval. And for all her forcefulness, she, too, had something of these characteristics in her. Father and daughter were alike in that they were both lonely people through most of their lives. Would Rudolf have liked the person his daughter had turned out to be? You suspect that he probably would not have liked her very much. Rudolf had never liked it when people surprised him or caught him out on the hop, as it were. It is even possible that Rudolf would have found her somewhat unfeminine. Rudolf needed his women to be pliable. He did not care much for dominant women.

At the end of the war Erzsi needed all her ability to stand up to whatever life threw at her. Austria, like so much of Europe, was a crushed country where real hunger reigned. Rationing had been brought in fairly early on during the war. Revolution was simmering. The old Austro-Hungarian Empire had been torn apart. For centuries the Austrian economy had depended upon raw materials and food coming from the regions that had now split away and become new nations, independent of the old Empire. These new nations, Hungary, Poland, Czechoslovakia, Yugoslavia, ringed a crippled country, like wolves waiting to fall upon its dying body. Italy took the Sudtirol, region of fruit and wine. No longer did corn and coal come from Hungary. Returning fighters found in Vienna a ghost of a city. There was no work and scarcely any food or fuel. Spanish flu and tuberculosis were rife. In a total population of seven million people, two million of whom were crowded into Vienna, around a million were suffering from TB, which came to be known as the 'Viennese disease'. It must have seemed that those who were not dying of TB or starvation were committing suicide.

Erzsi up until that point had never given much thought to politics. Now she could not ignore it. She became a socialist. And Erzsi was the sort of person who never did anything by halves. She became a fully paid-up member of the Austrian Social Democratic Party thanks to one Leopold Petznek. It was sometime during 1919 that she got to know Petznek, one of the senior officers in the party. It is not known whether she met Petznek and then, persuaded by him, she chose to join the party, or whether she presented herself to the party and later came into contact with Petznek.

Erzsi, like her grandmother before her, was an all or nothing person. She expected those around her to support her point of view totally and without reserve or hesitation. She tolerated no criticism or contradiction. She resented the gossip that spread about her various activities and relationships. She dealt with gossip and disapproval in fighting spirit, fired up with hatred for those behind it. But the aristocracy had begun to retreat from her and to avoid her and this only provoked even more intense resentment. She saw no reason not to come out with cutting, cruel comments about people she saw as being against her and to do so in their presence.

It could hardly have been a bigger U-turn. It certainly did not entirely spring from a political conscience. In many ways her turning to the socialists was her way of dealing with her growing isolation.

One hot day at the end of June 1881 Frau Maria Mackmayer, a farmer's wife married to Franz Petznek, gave birth to her only child, a son. Franz and Maria were simple peasant farmers, living hand to mouth. Before little Leopold had reached his ninth birthday his parents had lost their farm and everything they had. They died of starvation.

Leopold was taken to the Hyrtlschen Orphanage in Mödling. He was an intelligent little boy. He did well at school and ended up with qualifications for teaching. He then returned to the same orphanage at Mödling at the age of nineteen as a teacher. There he taught German, history and geography. He married Emilie Bärnat and they had a son, Otto. During the war he fought on the Russian front and later in Italy. He rose from the ranks to become a lieutenant. On 16th December 1918 he returned to Mödling to his position as a teacher there.

He was serious, hard-working and conscientious. He was a self-effacing man leading a life almost beyond reproach. There seem to be no pictures of Leopold Petznek as a young man. All the photographs of him show a shiny bald dome and an intense, dark gaze. Behind that mask it is impossible to see what kind of personality, what thoughts and feelings formed Leopold Petznek.

On the face of it it is hard to see what it was that drew Erzsi to him. He could not have been more different to Otto von Windischgrätz or Egon Lerch. Perhaps she recognised his profound sincerity. She was beginning to be aware of political factors and almost nobody could have been better placed than Petznek when it came to opening her eyes to the ways in which people lived and worked and their desperation in the aftermath of a terrible war. Erzsi also found that being drawn into political activities not only gave her a sense of purpose in life, but also brought with it friendship and camaraderie, and that, too, was something she had never had.

She also found that she was gaining a new sense of importance with her new activities. The socialist newspaper, *Die Arbeiter Zeitung*, wrote articles making special mention of Erzsi and her war. Erzsi felt a glow each time she read one of these articles and she liked to cut them out and kept them tucked away in a drawer.

So she turned to Petznek and from him she learned how the consequences of political measures determined the lives of ordinary people. Her knowledge and understanding of economics and politics came from him. She hung on his every word and came to revere him. Clearly all this was taking place right in the middle of her divorce battle and Erzsi had the sense to keep her political activities very much under wraps. But once again she was falling in love. Once again she was ready to give herself up, heart, mind and soul, to this man.

Erzsi, when she was falling in love, must have been a delightful person. She was open and warm-hearted. She was unstinting in her affection. She had a powerful sexual attraction and she was not afraid to show that she loved the physical side of loving. She had charm, wit and warmth. But she had something else – that special aura that people confer on royalty, that special glow that hangs around someone with the unique significance of birth and position. You could argue that none of that counted for anything in post-war Austria where all titles had been banned but it is not lost that easily.

Erzsi did not, of course, completely change her spots.

Just as her grandmother, the Empress Elisabeth, had adored large hounds, so did Erzsi. She was good with animals and could handle creatures that others would not go near. In 1921 she took to developing a new breed by mating Alsatian hounds with wild wolves which had been trapped in Poland. The most notable result of this breeding were four half-wolves called Rolf, Prinz, Satan and Caesar.

These animals were near impossible to train and could only be handled by certain people. Erzsi could handle them; so could Franzi and it was upon him that Erzsi conferred most of the responsibility of looking after these half-wolves. Franzi was the one who would be with the Alsatian bitch when she gave birth; no one else was allowed near. Only Franzi and Erzsi would care for, and handle the puppies, caressing them and taming them. As they grew Franzi took on the job of exercising them in the grounds around the castle at Schönau.

There came a day in spring when the lightest of breezes caused the leaves on the trees to barely tremble. Rolf, Prinz, Satan and Caesar were out on their walk when suddenly one of them heard or scented something and the four of them were off, crashing through the undergrowth, utterly impervious to all shouts and whistles calling them back. The hounds plunged into a field of sheep and within minutes some eighteen sheep lay on the ground bleeding or dead. Franzi finally succeeded in rounding up the hounds but the sight that met his eyes when he had done so was horrifying. The farmer whose herd of sheep had been decimated was furious.

Erzsi, when she learned what had happened, was unmoved. She adored her hounds and would do anything for them. She was not interested in sheep in any way. The protesting farmer was a nuisance. As far as she was concerned he could be paid off and she wanted to hear nothing more from him.

But this was only one of many incidents. There were to be too many instances of local people being bitten or damage done to flocks. In due course, the police started becoming involved. They began to threaten Erzsi with removing the hounds and destroying them. Erzsi ended up paying out large sums of money to quieten people down. The cost of feeding the animals was also horrendous and in a country where human beings were starving this provoked even more bitterness.

Erzsi, however, saw herself as above their concerns. She kept up her breeding until 1927 but in the end she stopped mating Alsatians with wolves and stuck to the dogs. Throughout the rest of her life she was never to be without these dogs. Even when she was bedridden at the end of her life her dogs slept on her bed with her.

Erzsi still considered that the law did not apply to her. She believed passionately in the equality of people but she drew the line at changing the way she lived. She considered that she shared the hardships of those around her. She had no intention of giving up the castle at Schönau but in 1923 she began to rent a fourteen-room apartment in Vienna which she then proceeded to furnish and decorate to her taste.

To satisfy the authorities she had to sublet a part of this. Erzsi and her tenant then had to share a single telephone line which led to arguments – Erzsi was heard shouting, *„Der Saujud soll später telefonieren!"* ("That Jew should make his phone calls later!") This apartment was for Petznek's use when he was in Vienna, somewhere where they could be together, and no doubt she hoped that he would spend more time there. It was situated in the Marxergasse, not a particularly attractive street but perhaps Petznek appreciated the name.[71]

A year later in 1924 the court finally ruled that the marriage between Otto von Windischgrätz and Erzsi was finished.[72] There was no further need to keep Erzsi's relationship with Petznek a secret and the first thing she wanted to do was take him on a journey to Italy. Petznek had never been outside Austria and Erzsi was eager to show him the country she loved so much.

That same year, too, Marie-Valérie died of cancer of the throat. There had always been a close understanding between Erzsi and her aunt. Marie-Valérie had often taken Erzsi's side and defended her. When she died Erzsi felt once again, just as she had when Franz Joseph died, that she had lost an important support in her life and she felt, too, that she was drawing further and further away from her Habsburg roots. In a way that left her freer than ever to build her life in future with Petznek.

By 1930 Erzsi had sold the castle in Schönau and she and Leopold Petznek had given up the apartment in the Marxergasse. Franzi and Erni had left home to build their own lives; only Rudolf and Fee remained with Erzsi. The family, including Petznek, had moved to a smaller villa further out from the centre of Vienna in Hütteldorf. Their relationship had gelled. They would remain together right up until Petznek's death.

Outside reigned political chaos. On every side there was poverty, distress and insecurity. There must have been a sense of not knowing where things were going or even where you might fit into what was happening around you. They, like so many others, needed the support that the other offered. Already the rise of Nazism was looming and everything that the Nazi movement stood for was anathema to Petznek and Erzsi. Slowly,

---

[71] Marxergasse was not named after Karl Marx but after the Bishop Anton Marxer.

[72] The court did not have the power to give them a final divorce because Austria was still under foreign occupation and it would have required the occupying authorities to make such a ruling.

Petznek's political activities became more muted until by the time the Nazis marched into Austria Petznek was doing all he could to avoid drawing attention to himself.

Yet nevertheless on 22nd August 1944 he was arrested by the Gestapo in the street and on 20th September that year he was taken to the concentration camp at Dachau.

Once again Erzsi was on her own. When Russian soldiers entered Austria Petznek's son, Otto, drove out to Hüttelsdorf to persuade the woman he had come to regard as his stepmother to come back with him to Mödling where he felt she would be safer. To begin with Erzsi agreed and she set about packing a suitcase. But suddenly she changed her mind.

An Archduchess of Austria, the granddaughter of the Emperor Franz Joseph, does not capitulate. When the Russians finally arrived at her doorstep she stood boldly before them and with her right hand she tapped her breast and shouted at them, "Shoot here, shoot here!" They did not shoot her but she was turned out of her house.

She ended up in a convent, the Congregation of the Servants of Jesus' Heart. Sister Dorwina remembered how she arrived at the gates with nothing but the clothes on her back and her hounds. Soon a servant arrived at the convent to cook for her. And other members of her entourage later appeared to continue in their service of her. She did not make a good impression; she tended to treat both the sisters and those who served her as underlings to be ordered about.

Erzsi kept herself apart from the sisters of the convent, having as little to do with them as she could. Sister Dorwina also remembered with sorrow that she took no part in any of the convent's religious services.

Eventually Leopold Petznek was released from Dachau and able to return to Vienna. With his arrival everyone was struck by the contrast in manners. Petzneks's enormous thoughtfulness for the comfort of others and his warm humanity delighted everyone in the convent all the more because Erzsi's manner had been so highhanded.

Virtually nothing is known of Petznek's time at Dachau. He never wanted to speak of it. He was, however, on the so-called „*Todesmarsch der Dachauer*" ("Death march of Dachau prisoners"). The guards received orders on 26th April 1945 to round up the prisoners and to be ready to march within the hour. Jews, Russians and Austrians were to be marched away from the camp and then liquidated. In spite of the large number of guards guarding the prisoners, orders were no longer being obeyed blindly and some of the prisoners escaped. These escapees, who were almost all Austrian, sought protection from local peasant farmers who hid them in their barns. They were found on 2nd May by American soldiers who put them on a train for Austria.

The train was held up at Bischofshofen, partly because there were Russian soldiers nearby who did wish to let the train through and partly because the Lueg Pass was still unpassable. But in Bischofshofen the Assistant of the Mayor was one Maria Emhart. Some twelve years before Petznek and Erzsi had helped Maria Emhart out of prison and across the border into Switzerland where they had recommended her to a socialist doctor who worked in a TB sanatorium in Davos. Petznek and Erzsi had also provided Maria Emhart with the funds she needed to stay in Davos long enough to be cured.

And here was Maria Emhart in Bischofshofen and she recognised Petznek among the prisoners on the train. She it was who saw to it that the carriage holding the Dachau escapees was heated so that they survived the bitter cold night. Petznek almost certainly owed his life to her that night, as did many of the others.

It was a very sick man who returned to Vienna.

On 13th February 1948 Erzsi finally got her official divorce from Otto von Windischgrätz. Otto was not there; he was living in Switzerland.

Then on 4th May 1948 Leopold Petznek and Erzsi got married. It was a quiet, unobtrusive event without ceremony. Erzsi was sixty-four years old, Leopold two years older. Both of them were sick beings. Erzsi was crippled with arthritis. Leopold had been suffering from heart disease since before he was arrested and taken to Dachau.

Compared to the life Erzsi had known before the war, she and Petznek now found themselves living in miserable circumstances and many of Erzsi's letters reveal how hard done-by she felt herself to be. She had cause for she now found herself living in rooms that were ill-heated and often damp and with each year her arthritis became more painful.

Erzsi was still waiting to re-possess her house in Hütteldorf. The Russians had long gone, having caused enormous damage to the house and to its contents and taken what they could as well. But after the Russians left the house had become the official residence of the French occupational authority and they seemed, in spite of assurances to the contrary, to have little intention of ever releasing the house. It was not until April 1955 and the end of foreign occupation in Austria that the French went and by late autumn Erzsi had got her house back.

But Petznek had less than a year more in which to enjoy their old home. On 30th June 1956 he celebrated his seventy-fifth birthday and an article in the socialist newspaper, *Die Arbeiter Zeitung*, wished him many more years there enjoying good health and good spirits. Four weeks later he was dead. In the eight years of life left to Erzsi, she would go out little, becoming ever more of an invalid and more and more housebound. Right at the end of her life Erzsi was alone, having lost her second husband and become totally estranged from all her children. Her only companions were two old retainers, Pepi Steghofer and Paul Mesli, who remained devoted to her until the end.

Erzsi's children had all escaped from her control. In later life Franzi spent a great deal of his time in Africa. Looking after those four half-wolves had given him a taste for large wild animals and large, wild spaces. Franzi sought escape from Europe in Kenya where he felt at home in the open spaces and a landscape so much less altered by man than was so in Europe. Nevertheless, for a long time Franzi returned from Kenya from time to time to see his mother, duty visits that offered little warmth or affection to either party.

Erzsi demanded that he arrive at the appointed time. On one occasion his appointment was for three o'clock in the afternoon. Franzi went to see Paul Mesli at the porter's lodge, knowing that he was a moment or two late, and asked, "Would you find out, please, whether I might still go in?" Erzsi's reply was a blunt, "Three minutes too late!" She did accord him permission to enter the grounds and look round. Three quarters of an hour later he departed without having seen his mother.

Fee's visits were equally infrequent although she did not have the excuse that she had to come from Kenya. Fee by this time was living in Belgium with her second husband, the Swedish businessman, Carl Axel Björklund. Erzsi disliked Fee's husband and refused to allow him to enter the house. Erzsi had also disliked Fee's first husband but then Fee was to insist that she only married him because her mother had taken against him.

By the time she reached middle-age Fee had in her own mind gone over the events of her growing-up years and also the many possible interpretations of her parents' difficult relationship. Finally, she ended up with her own personal view of it all. No doubt Fee nursed memories of how delightful Erzsi could be when she was relaxed, but that picture was totally overshadowed by all the occasions when Erzsi's treatment of Fee had been so hurtful.

Those meetings between Erzsi and Fee were never very relaxed. Fee was critical of her mother's treatment of her father, and for Erzsi that would have been intolerable. Erzsi did not care that at the end of his life Otto's financial situation was so bad that he had come to depend upon his daughter just to stay alive. It had been Fee who had during the last years of Otto's life done all she could to care for and support her father.

On Christmas Day in 1952 Otto Windischgrätz died in Lugano, only two days after the death of his son, Erni. Otto's youngest son, Rudolf, had died in 1939, so now only Franzi and Fee were still alive.

The only other person who regularly visited Erzsi during those last years of her life was Petznek's son, Otto. Erzsi held Otto in great affection and he never ceased to be concerned about her. The only other beings that Erzsi gave her love to were her Alsatian dogs. One, named Lido, would keep away from his mistress any human being he did not trust. Anyone wishing to see Erzsi had to get past Lido.

By the beginning of March 1963 it was clear that Erzsi's health was going downhill. By 15th March Paul Mesli was aware that her end was not far off. Paul Mesli and Pepi Steghofer had stuck with Erzsi longer and more loyally than anyone else; they had been with her through the war and they had nursed and cared for her in the last years of her life. The following day Erzsi fell into a coma. At midday Pepi Steghofer called Paul Mesli to Erzsi's side and the two of them were with her when she breathed her last. After her death Pepi was heard to say, „*Hoheit is nicht mehr da!*" ("Her Majesty isn't there any more!") as if she could not believe it. The Red Archduchess had gone.

Chapter 121

For many Austrians it must have seemed that the end of an era came with the death of the Emperor in November 1916. Franz Joseph had outlived his son by twenty-seven years; and his Empress, the exquisite Empress Elisabeth, had died eighteen years earlier. He had been left an isolated figure whose only support and understanding came from Kathi Schratt. And he had outlived his ability to manage all the complex demands that went with ruling over the Empire.

He knew it. The last years of Franz Joseph's life were spent at Schönbrunn which made running the war machine particularly difficult. With Karl away at the front busy with his military duties, Zita brought her two small children to live at Schönbrunn as well. Franz Joseph took to visiting Zita regularly every day in her apartments in the east wing of that enormous palace. Zita soon proved that she was the perfect companion for him. Alone together in those grand, imposing rooms Franz Joseph liked to reminisce. To Zita he confessed that for him, ever since he was crowned Emperor in 1848, it had seemed that the Empire was like a volcano sleeping uneasily. She came to sense that deep-down he was aware that the war they had unleashed would strike the death-knell of his Empire.

"My wars have always begun with victories," he told her, "but they finish in defeat." He added, "...and they will say 'He is old and cannot rule any more;' then revolutions will break out and the end will come." Revolution had brought him to the throne and given him the task of holding the Empire together and now he saw that the Empire would finally be torn apart by revolution.

This was right at the beginning of the war when things were going well, and to Zita his pessimism was just the tiredness of an old man. Later she would remember.

In many ways it feels as though Franz Joseph was the last Emperor. Few remember that the last Emperor was Emperor Karl and Empress Zita the last Empress. Their reign lasted only two years from 1916 to 1918. In many ways it felt during those two years as though Germany was ruling Austria.

From the moment he became Emperor, Karl worked ferociously to end Austria's part in the war. Had Franz Joseph died a year earlier he might have succeeded. Had Franz Joseph died two years earlier there might well not have been a war. Franz Ferdinand fended off the warmongers with every fibre of his being and the young man he was grooming to succeed him was as much an opponent of war as Franz Ferdinand had been.

In his first words to the nation as the new Emperor, Karl said, "I will do everything to banish, in the shortest time possible, the horrors and sacrifices of war and to win back for my peoples the blessings of peace that they miss so much." Both in public and secretly he sought to sound out the possibility of Austria's concluding an independent peace with the allies. He used in a last-ditch desperate attempt to get a message to the decision-makers on the other side the fact that his wife's brothers were actively fighting with the French against Germany and Austria.

Karl, the forgotten Emperor, spared no effort either in making the first moves towards a fairer, more democratic society. On 12th January 1917 Karl faced his first cabinet meeting and the theme he wanted to press forward with was a total reconstruction of the way the Empire was ruled so as to conciliate the many nationalist issues that had so long been trodden underfoot. There never was any chance of his succeeding. It would have been difficult enough in a time of peace; in wartime it was impossible.

Karl's new government was about as different to Franz Joseph's as it was possible to be. Karl's thinking had been developed in long conversations with Franz Ferdinand and it seems plausible to suggest that Karl's aims and intentions reflected his uncle's. Protocol went out of the window. The first seeds were being sown for a new way of governing which no longer consisted of one man deciding and thereby imposing rigid inflexibility.

Karl and Zita also began to show enormous concern over the social welfare of their country. There were long discussions with Joseph Baernreither, who was becoming Karl's chief adviser, and within six months the new ministry was set up to deal with health, housing, care of invalids, the weak and the elderly.

Zita could not help pressurising him. She was eager for success. She was eager to serve, to play her part. And since Karl had his hands full with military matters much of the social issues fell to her to organise and promote. For ordinary people the first obvious signs of these changes came when – for example – they saw coal carts in the streets taking fuel to Viennese households and learned that the horses pulling those carts were the horses of the royal household taken from the royal stables. And there were so many other signs. Zita insisted that the new Imperial Family pulled in their belts as much as anyone else and their meals became spartan in the extreme. In her endless visits to military hospitals Zita felt she should share and understand others' privations.

In January 1917 came the blow that would end up with the Empire broken into pieces and Karl and Zita exiled from their homeland. Germany gave the order to operate unrestricted warfare. German U-boats (submarines) would sink ships in open waters, whether military or otherwise, whether enemy ships or the ships of neutral countries. Innocent civilians from neutral countries would become the victims of German torpedoes. And countries that up until that moment had remained outside the conflict would now be drawn in, and in their outrage they would be drawn in against Germany – and Austria.

The plan to introduce unrestricted submarine warfare was published in a memo in December 1916 and presented to Kaiser Wilhelm II in January 1917. This proposal was the work of Admiral Henning von Holtzendorff, the Chief of Staff to the Head of the German Navy, Admiral Alfred von Tirpitz. Von Holtzendorff predicted that unrestricted submarine warfare would starve Britain and bring her to her knees. He was convinced that the United Kingdom would be forced to sue for peace within six months.

There had been a time when von Holtzendorff had strongly opposed the huge drive to expand the German Navy so that it could equal the British Royal Navy in strength and military capacity on the high seas. In 1913 he was forced into retirement due to his opposition and his bitterness had festered. But in 1915 he was recalled to duty to serve as Head of the German Imperial Admiralty Staff and within a year his views had completely turned around. Nobody was more committed to the new policy than he was.

Karl was appalled. Zita was enraged. She was not afraid to let anyone know what she thought. She was not afraid of von Holtzendorff. There was a dinner at Pless on 27th January at which she made her views perfectly clear. Von Holtzendorff turned his guns upon Zita.

"I know you are against the U-boat war, just as you are against war in general!"

Zita had the grit to respond coolly. She told him that she was against war. She told him that any woman who would rather see people happy than suffering had to be against war. Never had her head been higher. Never had her gaze been more direct. Her voice was icy and steady.

Von Holtzendorff was here at Pless to inform the Austrians of the course that Germany had adopted. Their agreement or otherwise was irrelevant. But across the table he was faced with a slender, wiry young woman with flashing dark eyes whose cool manner somehow got under his skin and wound him up the wrong way.

Von Holtzendorff spluttered.

"Suffering – what does it matter? I work my best on an empty stomach; it is a case of tightening your belt and holding out!"

Zita's eyes ran down his corpulent form and she said nothing. Then after a pause she spoke. "I do not like hearing talk of 'holding out' when one is sitting at a fully-laden table." And her thoughts probably turned to the picture of her small children back in Vienna being told that they could not have a piece of cake when there were so many who did not have enough to eat.

On 6th April 1917 America declared war on Germany. None of von Holtzendorff's predictions were working out in the way that he had insisted they would.

Karl admired Zita. Her fervour, her conviction, her determination all impressed him. But behind that there was her intelligence. As a man of that time it would not have been easy for him to acknowledge it but with her clear-sighted understanding of everything that was going on she gave him support. There was nobody he felt more able to discuss things with. Before the outbreak of war Karl found that he could enjoy long discussions and interesting debates with Zita's two brothers, Sixtus and Xavier. This had been new to Karl and he came to love it.

Duke Roberto's large clan of children had always been embroiled in arguments, opposing points of view, trumping each other's assertions and marshalling opposing ideas and counter-arguments. They had no idea how much this had sharpened their intelligence and their understanding of the world. They had learned how to think quickly on their feet. They had learned how to hone in on the weak point in the other's assertions. They were sharp as weasels and fun with it. This must have been a big part of their attraction for Karl who had never experienced anything like this. To begin with he had felt somewhat out of his depth. They went too fast, their ideas turned corners leaving him behind, they switched subjects on a single word and went off at a tangent. But the more Karl tuned into this the more he found it exciting and thought-provoking.

After the wedding in 1911 there were so many long evening talks with Sixtus and Xavier after which Karl came away feeling alert, aglow and wildly stimulated. In his world there had never been anyone to play devil's advocate. Here the total absence of sycophantism made Karl feel more alive. The most fascinating topic of all was what would the future bring in this exciting new century. There was a certain gung-ho thread running through the ideas of the young men.

Zita found it hard to be quite so optimistic. She was proud. Proud to be called upon to serve. Proud to be royal which should give her the opportunity for service she so craved. Far more than her brothers or her fiancé she could not push away thoughts of the dangers of nationalism or of republicanism – and then where would they be?

In 1914 when war was declared Zita's family were divided. She as the new bride of the heir to the throne was, of course, on the side of the Austro-Hungarian and German Axis. Two of her younger brothers, Felix and René also joined the Austrian Army. But back in 1883 when Henri Chambord, the pretender to the French throne, died he left his entire estate to Duke Roberto. Sixtus and Xavier had settled in France and built their lives there. They regarded the Château de Chambord as their home, not Schwarzau in Austria.

They were in London when Franz Ferdinand was assassinated in Sarajevo. Initially they were confident that the coming war would be confined to hostilities between Serbia and Austria and their feelings were that they should join up in the Austrian Army. Xavier wrote, "I think our place is in Vienna. We shall probably join up to help out against Serbia." When he wrote those words war had not yet been declared. But when the brothers learned that France was mobilising then Xavier wrote, "It is high time we returned to France. Our country is in danger."

They never did fight in the French Army. They were blocked by the law which banned all members of the former royal family from taking part in any French organisation, just as Ferdinand, the duc d'Alençon, Sophie-Charlotte's husband, was. Sixtus and Xavier then sought to join up with the British Army, volunteering to work as interpreters – but without success. They ended up serving in the Belgian Army.

From London Sixtus and Xavier travelled to Munich to visit an aunt and now found themselves declared enemy aliens. They were refused travels papers. Karl approached Franz Joseph on their behalf who agreed to sign special permits for them to leave the country. Finally came the day when Zita had to say goodbye to her brothers. "But Zita is very, very brave and she hid her feelings," said Xavier.

Karl told the pair that just as it was his own duty to serve his country so it was their duty to serve France. They knew what that meant but none of them yet knew how big the divide between them would become. They had little idea how long it would be before they saw each other again. "Where now are the days of Frohsdorf and Schwarzau?" thought Xavier.

Sixtus and Xavier were able to pay their mother one last visit in Schwarzau. Xavier could not help thinking of Karl and Zita's wedding and the huge happy wedding party on the terrace wishing the young couple every happiness. Xavier on this occasion remembered how at that wedding party they had felt that they all belonged together, "bound to each other by indestructible ties". He described how his mother also tried to conceal her feelings, how she told them that she would set up a hospital while the war was on, and then suddenly as they moved to leave she burst painfully into tears.

It was two years on before they would meet up again. By this time Germany's new policy of unrestricted warfare and U-boats attacking any ship on the open waters around Europe had jolted Karl. He was convinced that this represented a dangerous escalation. He wanted to bring the war to an end before things got too bad, and he ordered his military attaché in Berne, Colonel von Einem, to find a way of making contact with Sixtus and Xavier to sound out whether there was any readiness for peace on the other side. What followed was an exchange of secret meetings and letters all aimed at ending the war with as much dignity on all sides as could be achieved.

This came to be known as the Sixtus Affair.[73] Initially there were seeds of real interest from the French. Sixtus had about a year earlier been approached by a member of the French government, M. de Freycinet on behalf of M. Briand, the head of the French government. For Sixtus a rapprochement between France and Austria might mean a drive to reinstate a Bourbon King in Paris and this would have made the French wary if they suspected his thinking. When Karl's letter reached Sixtus in 1917 there were feelings of renewed optimism on both sides. Nobody was more eager than Zita to see this succeed.

Yet it became a muddled matter of wrangling over who should cede what and which conditions were the sine-qua-non of the whole business. For Austria one of the biggest difficulties was that Germany was far from ready to end the fighting.

Karl and Zita's positions as Emperor and Empress were severely damaged because the whole attempt failed. Right at the beginning of his reign Karl had been known as 'the People's Emperor' or 'the Peace Emperor' but now they became encompassed in a relentless campaign of vilification. Nor were the attacks on the Emperor and his Empress merely words. The young couple did not just feel isolated and beleaguered but also threatened by conspiracies. For some time Karl had been fearful that it was Germany's intention to annex the whole Austro-Hungarian Empire. Karl and Zita were aware of Operation O, the German plans to invade Austria if Austria ceased to be a totally loyal and subservient ally. In fact, towards the end of the war some military units did enter the Tyrol illegally.

On top of this was their fear that their Foreign Minister, Count Ottokar von Czernin, was acting treacherously against them and conspiring with the German military and passing on information to various German generals.

Czernin was a highly independent and forceful character, a loose cannon, who flaunted his ideas and aims flamboyantly without regard for his duties towards his sovereign. One of the problems with Czernin was that he had been in on the negotiations of the Sixtus Affair, as well as an attempt by Karl to broker peace with Woodrow Wilson using King Alfonso of Spain as intermediary. Czernin knew just too much. Czernin was the kind of man who, as he shifted his connections and friendships for his own benefit, left

---

[73] *Die Mission Sixtus*, by Tamara Griesser Pečar, 1988

in his wake a slipstream of distrust and insecurity. He wove a devious path using lies and blackmail to escape first one confrontation and exposure and then the next. There ended up being so many in whom Czernin had spiked feelings of being betrayed and manipulated, and their reactions spread to include the Emperor.

It is a measure of the man that, when everything was completely falling apart, he suggested that Karl, Zita and he himself should commit suicide together. At his last meeting with Karl and Zita, Czernin was doing everything he could to get Karl to abdicate and when that failed he exploded in nervous agitation, weeping and then suddenly offering his resignation.

Karl accepted it.

The Sixtus Affair ended up being a massive international scandal. A bigger débâcle would have been hard to engineer. For the Germans it proved that her ally in the war was a potential deserter.

Karl, perhaps, was the only person involved in the Sixtus Affair whose part in it was not dishonourable but the world did not see it that way. True or not true, Karl was now seen as a man capable of double-dealing, a weak figure struggling to escape from the net of lies which it was believed he had woven for himself.

During those last two years of the war Karl's right to rule was being undermined by another, rather surprising, source.

As the war rumbled on and on, Zita came to be regarded in Vienna with growing mistrust. She was referred to as the 'Italian woman' and her loyalty to Austria was viewed with suspicion. The German Ambassador in Vienna wrote to Berlin, "Even though the Empress is both charming and friendly at all times her popularity is on the wane. People do not entirely trust the Italian and her large clan of relatives." She was accused of betraying war plans to the French, suspected of interfering in the military strategy on the Italian front and criticised, when visiting the war-wounded at a military hospital, for talking more to the Italian wounded than to the Austrians.

This undercurrent of ill-feeling seemed to offer an opportunity to depose both Karl and Zita and to place on the throne the Archduke Albrecht, the only son of Archduke Friedrich and his wife, Isabella.

Karl, soon after coming to the throne, removed Friedrich from his position as Commander-in-Chief in the Austrian Army and this inflamed Isabella's fury. The woman who had once done all she could to engineer a marriage between Franz Ferdinand and her eldest daughter, Maria Christina, had later turned her attention to Karl in the days when he was still a bachelor. Isabella had lost none of her drive and ambition. But Karl was no more keen to have her as a mother-in-law than Franz Ferdinand had been. Isabella was not going to forgive Zita for winning his heart and hand. Her voice became one of the loudest against the 'Italian woman'. Isabella was one of the most vigorously keen to see Karl and Zita removed. She also wanted her one and only son, Albrecht, to ascend their throne.

When the news broke that 'Foxy Ferdinand' had fled his country and was now suing for unilateral peace it came as a shock. The Axis had consisted of four major powers: Germany, Austria-Hungary, Turkey and Bulgaria. Now one of them had pulled out. On 4th October 1918 'Foxy Ferdinand' crossed the border into Austria-Hungary. He was looking for a retreat and he owned properties in both Austria and Hungary. 'Foxy Ferdinand's' train stopped at Marchegg but Karl had sent Count Berthold to board the train and order Ferdinand to remain on it and continue his journey. There was a heated exchange late into the night before Ferdinand was obliged to give in.

Karl had long believed that when the collapse came it would come suddenly. When he learned of Ferdinand's move he was not surprised. Karl knew that everything had fallen apart. By the last days of September the German generals had finally bitten the bullet and told Wilhelm that the German Army faced outright defeat. The generals then packed Wilhelm off to Holland like some kind of embarrassing encumbrance. It galled Karl that now Germany was moving to seek the kind of peace settlement that he had been struggling to achieve for most of the last two years.

In Vienna Karl kept going, trying to rule his country as though it had a future and he a future as its Emperor. But the country was ungovernable. The Czechs had broken off all ties with Austria. Revolution broke out in Hungary at the end of October 1918. And in the mountains between northern Italy and Austria the last battles were being fought with a forlorn and desperate ferocity. What defeated the Austrians here was not so much the terrible hunger that soldiers were enduring, nor the tactics of the enemy but simply mass desertions. The time had come for *sauve-qui-peût*.

Vienna crumbled. There was no real revolution. There were no mobs surging into the courtyards of palaces. The Emperor was no longer needed in the new republic.

On 11th November Emperor Karl relinquished his involvement in public life (he did not formally abdicate, imagining that popular demand would see him eventually restored).

On the morning of 11th November the huge wrought-iron gates of Schönbrunn swung open for a car carrying two members of the government. They brought the document creating the republic and they required the Emperor's signature. Without the Emperor's signature the republic would not be legal. Karl was in no mood to sign it.

He walked out of the room. His heart was thumping but no one must suspect that. He had dreaded this moment. He had known it was coming. But he had not known exactly how the blow would fall. There was something cruelly wrong about this businesslike demand for his signature. Things didn't feel real. He almost felt like laughing, ridiculous as that was. In what capacity would he sign such a document? If he was not the Emperor then his signature was not appropriate. And if he was not the Emperor then who or what was he? Thinking about such things in so momentous a moment also felt unreal. All around him he was looking at things so very, very familiar and yet it felt as though he had never seen them before.

His ministers chased after him, protesting loudly. Finally, Karl with a dry throat pointed out that he could hardly be expected to sign something that he had not even been allowed to read.

Zita was aghast! "A sovereign can never abdicate! He can be deposed... But abdicate – never, never, never! I would rather fall here at your side." Karl could hear her, he could see her but it seemed as though she was an ocean away. Everything was different now. She didn't understand; Karl had no choice. He 'relinquished' his state functions.[74] Later that day he received a visit from the socialist leader, Karl Renner. As he departed Karl Renner bade Karl farewell with the words: "Herr Habsburg, the taxi is waiting." A few hours earlier he had been the Emperor and entitled to all the deference due to an Emperor. Now to be addressed as 'Herr Habsburg' – that must have hit him hard. Karl left the palace for the last time. He hoped that there would be a return one day.

There never was. And there would have been no Empire to come back to, even if it had been possible. From then on any member of the Habsburg family was barred from the country unless they swore an oath renouncing all claims to the throne. Karl and Zita refused to swear. They went into exile for the rest of their lives.

Karl died in 1922 on the island of Madeira. Whatever the doctors may have had to say about his death, it must have seemed that he had really died of a broken heart.

Madeira was far from ideal for the family but Karl and his family had little choice. There had been two attempts to win back the throne in Hungary, both of which came close to succeeding and yet failed. And then

---

[74] The form of words meant that Karl had renounced his right to rule (for the time being) but not his throne or his crown.

they had hung on, never knowing quite what form their lives would now take.

Their fate was batted back and forth among the various European governments who were now trying to re-establish some sort of order in Europe. There seemed to be no country willing to take them in and accept their presence on its soil. The British government feared becoming responsible for housing and supporting them in perpetuity. The French government feared the trouble that Zita's Bourbon relatives (and especially Prince Sixtus) might be capable to stirring up. And the Italians did not want to know. All of Europe feared that Karl, and more particularly Zita, would not give up the struggle to regain his throne. As a result, all the discussions focussed upon some island – Malta, the West Indies, the Canary Islands or the Balearic Islands.

In the end the Portuguese government agreed that they could stay on the island of Madeira but the Portuguese nation would not support them financially. The Imperial Family finally arrived at Funchal on 19th November 1921 with no money and no idea what they should be doing, or where they would in future live or what kind of lives they would have henceforth. Initially they were sent to an annexe attached to Reid's Palace Hotel. But they could not afford the bills[75] and soon had to find somewhere else.

Whatever Karl and Zita attempted to do was viewed with suspicion. Even if they were not suspected of nefarious plots it was feared that any support given to them might provoke others elsewhere to attempt to seize power, ostensibly on their behalf. So the Habsburg family had to be restrained. Out on the island of Madeira they were safely away from things. And they could be forgotten.

When Karl and Zita went to Hungary on their second attempt to win back their throne, their children had been left behind once again with old Archduchess Maria Theresia at Wartegg Castle in Austria. Zita knew that the children would be loved and cared for by the woman who had loved and cared for everybody and anybody who ever needed it, but she longed to have her children with her and until Karl's fate was decided there was nothing she could do except wait. She was barred from entering Austria.

However, when news reached Zita that one of her younger sons, six-year-old Robert, had to have an operation urgently to remove his appendix, Zita immediately set about travelling to Zurich to be near him. There were so many suspicions that this was not the only reason why she was going to

---

75 They were not completely penniless. They had some funds in Switzerland but over time various frauds prevented them from ever getting back what they did have. Almost all governments in Europe refused to consider what should be done. The British Foreign Secretary, Lord Curzon, eventually brought enough pressure to bear on Britain, France, Italy and even Japan to provide some funding which was wholly inadequate.

Zurich. In fact, Zita's efforts to find their money and her jewels failed completely. But by the second week of February she was back with Karl and their children were united with them. The need to move somewhere cheaper and more spacious became urgent. They ended up moving to the Quinto do Monte, a villa owned by a Portuguese banker which he was willing to allow them to live in rent-free.

Zita knew when they arrived on Madeira that Karl was a very, very sick man. The move to Quinto do Monte made things worse because the mists and damp, rain and fog never seemed to lift. In the house there was no electric light and running water only on the first floor of the building. Fuel for the fires was green wood which smoked horrendously. The house was damp through and through and there was not enough food for those living there that winter. It was the worst possible place for someone who did not have a strong heart[76] and suffering from a weak chest.

In early March Karl caught a cold. Within days he was suffering from a high temperature and bronchitis and before long pneumonia had developed. The children too went down one after the other with various infections and bronchial conditions. Only Zita, in spite of being eight months pregnant with her eighth and last child, kept going from one sickroom to the next.

Karl lingered on, sinking slowly. He became delirious. At one point he believed that a group of Austrians had come to swear allegiance to him. In his delirium he thought of the green fields and the water meadows around the castle at Persenberg where he had been born and mumbled on about going back there. The days went by as his hold on life ebbed away and Zita could do nothing but sit by his bedside and promise him that they would do all that he asked for.

„Ich hab' dich so lieb!" ("I love you so much!") – she could barely distinguish the words. He was floating in and out of consciousness, his breathing becoming ever more difficult and irregular.

It was the first of April, April Fool's Day. Karl was only thirty-five years old, a broken man. He was not at fault but he left a broken Empire and a broken world. Karl, the forgotten Emperor, was laid to rest in the graveyard of the Church of Nossa Senhora de Monte. Zita turned to her eldest son, Otto, and told him, "Now the responsibility is yours. You must live up to it."

After Karl's death Zita and her family were eager to move away from Madeira as soon as they feasibly could once Karl's body had been buried. They needed to get away from the place that was full of ghosts and a sense of loss, particularly Zita. Knowing that most European governments wanted Zita and her family to spend the rest of their days on an island by which they meant Madeira, Zita approached King Alfonso of Spain for help. The only ally that Alfonso thought would lend a sympathetic ear was King George V

---

[76] Karl had already had more than one heart attack.

of England and by the middle of May agreement had been reached that Zita and her children could go and live in Spain. And then, on 31st May 1922, Zita gave birth to her last child, Elisabeth.

They were offered somewhere to live in Lequietio, a small fishing village on the northern coast of Spain. The Palacio Uribarren overlooked the Bay of Biscay but it lacked many comforts. But the best thing was that the people of Lequieto fell in love with the newcomers and for the next six years Lequieto was home. For most of the children it was the first real home they had ever known.

A small income began to trickle in, some from properties in Hungary and in Austria that Zita could no longer go to, some from private collections on their behalf and some from political supporters. There continued to be efforts to restore Otto to his throne. There was a strong movement to bring this about in Hungary but the news Zita received from Hungary seemed to be full of hope and wild professions of love and loyalty but little more. Two humiliating attempts to regain the throne of Hungary that had failed ignominiously had made her wary.

Yet she was determined to ensure that Otto got an education that would prepare him to be an Emperor one day, and she did not doubt that this would happen. And two of Otto's most ardent supporters turned out to be Max and Ernst Hohenberg.

Max, Ernst and Otto first met each other in Lequietio in 1923, a year after the death of ex-Emperor Karl on the Island of Madeira. The meeting between the cousins led to a wonderful friendship which would last right up until the deaths of Max (1962) and Ernst (1954). Otto was a number of years younger than the Hohenberg boys and he outlived Max Hohenberg by almost half a century, living well into the twenty-first century.

In 1926 for his honeymoon Maximilian chose to take his new bride to meet the exiled Imperial Family in Lequietio. And this gave Maximilian another opportunity to exchange ideas with Otto.

It was Maria Theresia who had played a big part in engineering all this. She had supported Franz Ferdinand throughout his life and after his death she set about supporting his children. One of Franz Ferdinand's grandsons, Albrecht, would later recall how close had been the relationship between his father, Max, and Maria Theresia. He would also remember how Maria Theresia set about bringing together Max and Ernst and the sons of Karl and Zita, especially their eldest son, Otto.

During the 1930s there were strong moves to restore the monarchy which focussed upon Otto, now head of the Habsburg family, and involved Max who had a unique role as Otto's greatest supporter in all the political moves that went on to re-establish the throne of Austria. Max's legal training proved useful.

Just as his father had looked up to Franz Ferdinand so Otto would look up to Franz Ferdinand's sons. However, Sophie, Max and Ernst never forgot the difference that lay between them and the legitimate Habsburgs; they considered Otto the rightful Emperor and always addressed him as "Your Majesty". In all the correspondence between Max and Otto there is not the smallest hint that Max ever considered that he should have been the pretender to the throne of Austria.

In the end Otto chose to accept the fact that there was no chance of his ever ascending the throne of Austria or Hungary. He decided to take the oath renouncing all claim to the throne and after that he was able to return to Austria. As a little boy of six he had left behind the Austro-Hungarian Empire. Ninety-two years later he died in 2011.

After Karl's death Zita lived on for another sixty-seven years, an Empress in exile whose job was to prepare her family for the day when they would return to their homeland and their throne. During those years she would spend time in Spain, in Belgium and then in 1940 flee from the Nazis with her family through France to reach Portugal and from there to America. Her older children were by now independent adults but Zita sought refuge with the younger ones in Canada. Some of Zita's younger daughters later chose to make the New World their permanent home.

But Zita always wanted to return to Europe and since she could not go back to Austria without taking that hated oath of renunciation she finally returned to Switzerland. She lived out her last years in Zizers in Switzerland.

As a very old woman she was allowed to visit Vienna one last time. The Austrians went wild about that visit, overwhelming her with their gestures of warmth and affection. As a little old lady she charmed them with her dignity and the aura of another long-lost world she brought with her. How much did she feel at home there after so long a time away? It must have seemed like a strange world in which she no longer belonged. Her eldest son, Otto, had become a politician and worked many years for the EU Commision in Brussels. Some of her children and grandchildren had built their lives on the other side of the Atlantic. Her family with its many branches was scattered.

During the summer of 1988 she caught pneumonia and was confined to her bed through the autumn. For Zita the sands of time were running out and in the very early hours of 14th March 1989 she died.

Her funeral took place in Vienna with all the pomp and ceremony due to an Empress and she was buried there. The reason why she was buried in Austria was because the Spanish King, Juan Carlos,[77] intervened on her behalf, but in 1989 a large part of the population of Vienna were only too glad to offer her this last gesture recognising who she had been and what she had once represented. She was buried in the Imperial Crypt under the Capuchin Church in Vienna where for so long all the members of the Imperial Family had been laid to rest.

It was the first of April.

THE END

---

[77] Zita and Otto had looked very much to Spain to support their cause. They had been at one time very cosy with General Franco who even offered Otto the Spanish throne. But the only throne Otto ever yearned for was the throne of his father and his forebears.

Notes Section

1   Princess Clémentine of Saxe-Coburg-Koháry, one of the daughters of France's last King, King Louis-Philippe, decided that she wanted her youngest son, Ferdinand, to become King of Bulgaria. Her eldest son, Philipp, was married to Stéphanie's sister, Louise of Belgium; but Ferdinand had neither a wife nor an occupation.

Ferdinand entered Bulgaria in August 1887 to mount his new throne. He was a successful King who ruled right up until the outbreak of the First World War. Once King he resisted attempts by all the great powers to pull the strings from behind the scenes. He refused to have further dealings with Archduke Johann Salvator once he had become King.

Franz Joseph never liked Ferdinand and hated the fact that Kathi Schratt was great friends with him. However, Franz Joseph used Kathi as a source of information about what Ferdinand was thinking.

2   The Imperial Family had at all costs to be protected from anything that remotely smacked of scurrilous fault-finding. This was necessary to protect the system. Blame could never be attached to a member of the Imperial Family and invariably a scapegoat would be found. Undoubtedly throughout all the institutions that served the Imperial Family and the government it was understood that sometimes a scapegoat might be needed and someone was going to have to fall on their sword. But since it is not in human nature to want to be that person, those who served the Imperial Family always sought to play safe and to protect their own backs and this resulted in an obsequious system where no one dared stick his neck out. For this reason it is probable that a man like Major Menrad Laaba von Rosenfeld had been leant on by someone else.

3   Since 1870 France had been a republic. In the background hovered two pretendants to the throne should the French ever choose to return to the rule of a royal or imperial dynasty. The royal line based its claim through its connection with the last kings of France. The descendants of Napoleon Bonaparte upheld an alternative claim to the throne.

That France intended to remain a republic was confirmed in 1886 when the republican government in Paris felt that growing pressure within the country to restore either a King or an Emperor demanded a strong response. The Law of Exile was passed on 22nd June to prevent those who believed they had a claim to the French throne from stirring up a following against the Republic and its government.

According to the Law of Exile the heads of those families that had once reigned in France and their direct heirs were barred from living in France. This was the law that prevented Clémentine's fiancé, Victor Napoleon, and Henri Chambord from returning to live in France.

4 The rules as to who was a member of the Arch-house, as well as who could be accepted into the Arch-house, were laid out in the Family Statute. Many people who were related to the Habsburg family were not, in fact, members of the family in accordance with the code.

5 Bertha von Suttner was born Bertha Kinsky and she grew up in Bohemia not far from the area where the Battle of Königgrätz was fought. The whole family were shocked and horrified by the loss of life of Austrian soldiers at that battle and by their suffering. Bertha could never quite get over it. In later years she wrote a novel that shocked Europe – *Die Waffen Nieder* ('Put down your weapons'). This book had a strong impact upon the weapons manufacturer, Alfred Nobel. It was one of the triggers that led Nobel to give his wealth in order to found the famous Nobel Peace Prize. *Die Waffen Nieder* was the first work of literature to win the Nobel Peace Prize. Brigitte Hamann wrote a biography of Bertha Kinsky entitled *Bertha von Suttner – Ein Leben für den Frieden* (1991). Herta Pauli wrote a novel about Bertha Kinsky and her relationship with Alfred Nobel, entitled *Cry of the Heart* (translated by Richard and Clara Winston).

6 Bohuslav's full title in Czech was Bohuslav hrabě Chotek z Chotkova Vojína. His wife's name was Vilemína in Czech and Wilhelmine in German. Choteks had been Bohemian Barons since 1556, Counts of Bohemia since 1723 and Counts of the Empire since 1745. In the fourteenth century, there is mention of Otto Chotek of Chotkow und Liblin. The Chotek von Chotkowa und Wognin branch of the family was first honoured with the title Count in 1732.

7 The Kinsky horse was a recognised breed of horse known for its stamina and athleticism. The Kinsky family had been ordered by the Emperor to breed the horses to provide mounts for the army. Kinsky horses were ideal not just for military uses but also for steeplechasing and they became known as the original sport horse in continental Europe. They had the perfect temperament for endurance sports because of their unflappable natures.

8 Albrecht (1897-1955) was named after the Archduke Albrecht who had adopted the Archduke Friedrich when his own only son had died in childhood. This would have been a diplomatic gesture to ensure that Archduke Albrecht did bequeath his wealth to his nephew. Young Albrecht married three times and divorced his first two wives. He had two daughters by his second wife.

9 Because Margutti knew both Franz Joseph and Franz Ferdinand well and a great deal about what went on at court, Margutti's comments are an important source of first-hand information. Margutti's comments about both Franz Ferdinand and Sophie Chotek are frequently quoted by historians.

Baron von Margutti was appointed General Staff Officer of the 38th Infantry Brigade in Budweis in Bohemia under the command of Archduke Franz Ferdinand. This was when Margutti first met Franz Ferdinand and up until Franz Ferdinand was diagnosed with tuberculosis Margutti saw a good deal of him. It is usually noted that Margutti strongly supported and admired Franz Ferdinand. There is no doubt that this is true particularly during the period he was in Budweis.

Margutti first met the Emperor face-to-face in September 1900 when he accompanied Count del Mayno to an audience with Franz Joseph. In the interim Margutti's career had taken him to Berlin on a military mission. On his return from Berlin he was appointed to the Imperial Aide-de-Camp Department, then under Count Paar. Margutti became personal Aide-de-Camp to the Emperor in 1906. He remained in the service of the Emperor until Franz Joseph's death in 1916. In 1921 Baron von Margutti wrote his memoirs under the title *The Emperor Francis Joseph and His Times*.

Margutti was initially so strongly for Franz Ferdinand but later when Margutti was working for Franz Joseph his views began to switch over and become aligned with Franz Joseph's views. Margutti clearly admired and venerated the Emperor whole-heartedly. He approved of all Franz Joseph's actions and decisions. He clearly did not like Sophie Chotek. It is not clear how well he knew her or whether he really knew her at all. But Margutti went along with the opinions of Gottfried Marschall and Count Paar, neither of whom had a good word to say for Sophie. Once Franz Ferdinand had married Sophie Margutti's view of the Archduke grew increasingly critical. He continued to admire Franz Ferdinand's drive to learn all he could about governing Austria, as well as Franz Ferdinand's intelligence and his decisiveness.

10 Paul Nikitsch-Boulles was Franz Ferdinand's private secretary. In 1925 he published his memories of the Archduke and his family in a book entitled *Vor dem Sturm* ('Before the Storm'). His very real attachment and admiration for Franz Ferdinand slowly become increasingly obvious. Unlike Margutti, it would seem that Paul Nikitsch-Boulles had little contact with the Emperor although he was present on a number of occasions when Franz Ferdinand had an audience with Franz Joseph. As a result Paul Nikitsch-Boulles took on his master's point of view. The extent to which he did this is made very clear in his opinion of Prince Montenuovo. He took a very embittered view of Montenuovo's treatment of Franz Ferdinand and Sophie, particularly in the handling of their funeral arrangements. As a result almost all the biographies of Franz Ferdinand take from Paul Nikitsch-Boulles' writings extensive descriptions of the army's role at Franz Ferdinand's funeral service in Vienna.

11 The Hohenlohe family were one of the most distinguished and high-placed within the aristocracy. Rosa von Hohenlohe's middle daughter, Nora, grew up very much at the centre of court life. After the First World War, Nora wrote her memoirs of life in Vienna during the 1880s and 1890s, *Im Glanz der Kaiserzeit*. In January 1887 Nora married Count Carl Függer. Nora Függer was a close friend of Franz Ferdinand. Virtually no biography of Franz Ferdinand does not contain quotes from Nora's writings about him.

12 Hungary is still to this day famous for its beautiful, brightly-coloured traditional embroidery. Every region of Hungary has its own particular style and tradition, but the best known is the 'Matyó' embroideries of Mezőkövesd. Isabella took many photographs of the local people wearing their age-old costumes, richly embroidered in this traditional style. In *Photo Habsburg – Frederick Habsburg and his Family* on page 16 there is a photograph of Isabella with six of her daughters and two ladies-in-waiting wearing folk costumes embroidered with 'Matyó' embroideries.

13 The cymbalom or dulcimer was a very popular instrument throughout the Austro-Hungarian Empire and Eastern Europe. It consists of a trapezoidal box with metal strings stretched across the top and it is played with two hammers. There are certain similarities with the zither which is also an instrument with metal strings stretched over a wooden box. But the zither is plucked either with a plectrum or fingers whilst the cymbalom is played with hammers known as beaters. The cymbalom was a folk instrument that originally came from Asia and was brought to Europe by wandering gypsies, hence, it is associated particularly with gypsy music. In the 1870s Josef Schunda, a Hungarian piano-maker, first produced a concert cymbalom which included pedals. This instrument caught on and became very popular among the different nationalities of the Austro-Hungarian Empire. It was possibly this instrument that Sophie Chotek played.

14 Alfred Montenuovo was married to the Countess Franziska Kinsky, daughter of Ferdinand Bonaventura, 7th Prince Kinsky von Wchinitz und Tettau, and his wife, Princess Maria Josepha of Liechtenstein. The Kinskys were a very old and aristocratic family in Bohemia, proud of its standing. Sophie's mother, Mintzy, had been a Kinsky, and it had been thought that she lowered herself when she married Count Bohuslav Chotek.

Karel Kinsky had had an affair with Lady Randolph Churchill, the American-born Jennie Jerome. Jennie was one of the most fascinating women of that time and Karl was completely infatuated with her. The Kinsky family did not care for Karel's obsession but for as long as Lady Randolph Churchill was married their dislike of Karel's behaviour remained muted. When Randolph Churchill died things changed.

15 The Catholic Church also recognised a '*matrimonium conscientiae*' (in German *Gewissensehe*). This marriage of conscience would be celebrated in church in secret. However, it was legally binding. There would be no witnesses to the marriage and all evidence that it existed at all would be kept secret. There would be no documentation and the only reference to prove that it had ever occurred would be an entry in a book that itself was kept secret. After the war, for a marriage to be legal in Austria required not just a church ceremony but also a civil ceremony and this could not be kept secret.

The story of a marriage between Franz Joseph and Katharina Schratt is related in Georg Marcus' book *Katharina Schratt – die heimliche Frau des Kaisers*, 1982.

16 In Greek mythology Cerberus was a many-headed dog with the claws of a lion, a mane of snakes and a serpent for a tail. Cerberus guarded the entrance to Hades, the underworld, and it was his job to ensure that the living could never enter the underworld and the dead could never leave it. One of the labours of Hercules was to kill Cerberus. Echidna, Cerberus' mother was a gigantic creature, half woman, half snake. As well as Cerberus her offspring included Hydra, Orthrus (a hellhound) and Chimera (a three-headed monster). To compare Montenuovo to Cerberus who was fearsome seems appropriate. In Montenuovo's case his difficult legacy came from his grandmother rather than his mother.

17 In 1902 when Otto Windischgrätz and Erzsi embarked upon their honeymoon, their first port of call was Cairo where they received the most effusive welcome from Khedive Abbas Hilmi. Erzsi had a particular and intense interest in Egypt because she knew that her father had been greatly attracted to the country and that Rudolf had written a book about his oriental travels. Before the young couple left Egypt Erzsi asked whether she might be allowed to meet Princess Djavidan.

Erzsi's daughter-in-law, Ghislaine Windisch-Graetz, in her biography of Erzsi described this meeting in great detail. Ghislaine Windisch-Graetz stressed how the two young women had much in common, both having given up much for passionate love and accepted a loss of freedom for their great love.

Princess Djavidan was born an Austrian citizen. She was related to Count Nikolaus Török de Szendrö who was the husband of Johanna Buska, Rudolf's first mistress. Another member of the Török family, Count Josef Török de Szendrö, and his wife had a daughter who was born in Philadelphia while her parents were visiting the United States.

It seems that the Count and his wife were much impressed by America and in particular the freedom of spirit and thought they experienced there. Countess Török decided as a result to bring up her daughter in a much more free and open manner than was usual in Europe at that time. Their daughter received no religious teaching at all and was never baptised into the Catholic Church. When she reached adulthood her hand in marriage was sought by the Egyptian Khedive Abbas Hilmi II who was in Vienna studying at the university. This unlikely pair got married and Khedive Abbas Hilmi's new wife was given the name Zobeida when she went to live in Cairo. After having studied the Koran and become a Muslim she then took the name Djavidan.

PRINTED AND BOUND BY:
Copytech (UK) Limited trading as Printondemand-worldwide,
9 Culley Court, Bakewell Road, Orton Southgate.
Peterborough, PE2 6XD, United Kingdom.

ND - #0037 - 120623 - C0 - 228/152/22 [24] - CB - 9781739162160 - Matt Lamination